Building States and Markets

Building States and Markets

Enterprise Development in Central Asia

Gül Berna Özcan
Royal Holloway, University of London, UK

First published 2010 by
PALGRAVE MACMILLAN

Palgrave Macmillan in the UK is an imprint of Macmillan Publishers Limited, registered in England, company number 785998, of Houndmills, Basingstoke, Hampshire RG21 6XS.

Palgrave Macmillan in the US is a division of St Martin's Press LLC, 175 Fifth Avenue, New York, NY 10010.

Palgrave Macmillan is the global academic imprint of the above companies and has companies and representatives throughout the world.

Palgrave® and Macmillan® are registered trademarks in the United States, the United Kingdom, Europe and other countries.

ISBN 978–1–4039–9161–4   hardback

This book is printed on paper suitable for recycling and made from fully managed and sustained forest sources. Logging, pulping and manufacturing processes are expected to conform to the environmental regulations of the country of origin.

A catalogue record for this book is available from the British Library.

A catalog record for this book is available from the Library of Congress.

10 9 8 7 6 5 4 3 2 1
19 18 17 16 15 14 13 12 11 10

Printed and bound in Great Britain by
CPI Antony Rowe, Chippenham and Eastbourne

*To my parents, Nedret and Yusuf, with love
and gratitude for the seeds of life and learning*

Contents

List of Tables		viii
Preface		ix
Acknowledgements		xxiii
Map		xxvi
1	Introduction: Building States and Markets in Central Asia	1
2	Market Building and Social Stratification	30
3	Entrepreneurs and their Perceptions	59
4	The Political Economy of Bazaars	96
5	The Gendered Economy	122
6	Business Interest Representation	146
7	International Assistance and Enterprise Development	169
8	Entrepreneurs as Moral Men	191
9	Conclusion	220
Appendix		237
Notes		239
References		268
Index		286

List of Tables

1.1	Population growth in Soviet Central Asia between 1926 and 1959	10
1.2	Demographic, economic and market transition indictors of selected post-Soviet countries in 2006	21
3.1	Personal attributes of the surveyed entrepreneurs	69
3.2	The size of businesses according to employee numbers	73
3.3	Establishment year of business	74
3.4	How often entrepreneurs consult state institutions to obtain information	79
3.5	Advertisement about the business through newspapers and street billboards	81
3.6	Opinions on how the judiciary and courts work	84
3.7	How customs work	85
3.8	Opinions on how the national assembly work	86
4.1	The characteristics of the three selected bazaars	101
4.2	How often entrepreneurs consult other businessmen in the same locality	118
5.1	Educational attainments of entrepreneurs	134
5.2	The age distribution of entrepreneurs	135
6.1	The effects of bureaucracy and bribery on businesses	149
6.2	Addressing business problems or issues through business associations	150
7.1	Tourism indicators in the Kyrgyz Republic between 2002 and 2005	180
7.2	The growth of tourism in the Kyrgyz Republic	180
8.1	A typology of entrepreneurs' moral dispositions	199
A.1	Number of enterprise surveys by town	237
A.2	Sectoral composition of the sample	238

Preface

I had no connections with Central Asia until 2002 and first visited the region in 2004. However, over the years I rediscovered an awkward personal history that connected me to this region. As a Turk who grew up in a small eastern Anatolian town, raised by staunchly secular and socialist parents, my early upbringing strangely gave me a taste of left-ist ideology and communism. My father was a leftist leader in the local youth movement of the social democratic Republican People's Party (CHP). In our apartment, where we lived a life of modernity that was not available to many in our town until the mid-1980s, my father tried to convince our relatives of the virtues of social democracy, equality and leftist ideology. He was, in fact deep down, a communist sympa-thiser and a student of Marxism. However, 'communism' was a taboo word in our town during those cold war years when Turkey defended one of NATO's most important borders against the Soviet Union. Local connotations of communism stretched as far as believing that under communist order one couldn't have a proper moral life and family vir-tue; shady moral ethics impelled comrades to share their wives as well as everything else. I was not much concerned if this was the case, but I remember vividly how common this prejudice was and how horrifying it sounded to the ears of our devout Muslim relatives; my mother tried to calm and reason with them, though unsuccessfully. However, we lived in a land of ignorance and naivety that also nourished prejudices about religious and ethnic differences among the locals.

My father read *The Communist Manifesto* and *Das Kapital* aloud with young sympathisers whenever he could find an eager soul; not many had the patience or interest except my cousins who sometimes visited us during their short holiday breaks and sparked some moments of joy. Our several cousins in Ankara were among the leaders of the underground communist world and at the forefront of the so-called extreme left in Turkey under state repression during those years. This generated a sense of secrecy in talking about politics but also pride at home. However, there were important ideological differences between them, and my father chose not to join the *Revolutionary Workers and Peasants Party* of Turkey, established and long-led by one of his cousins.

Russian literature was introduced to us very early on and my younger sister and I hungrily read the classics along with many other books. They took us to unknown places and new journeys away from our isolated and sleepy town. Among all those books I read, Mikhail Aleksandrovich Sholokhov's great epic, *And Quiet Flows the Don*, gained a special place in my mind and the alien, almost unworldly, visual memory I crafted out of this long masterpiece stayed with me for many years.

I had a pen pal from a small town in Slovenia, Alenka. We exchanged goodwill and described the routines of our distant lives, content to know we were both part of a larger world. We never missed a play when it visited our town's theatre on tour from Ankara and enjoyed the company of our friends and went to see films during long winter nights in the elegant movie hall. In breezy summer nights the town's social life centred on the teagarden. The movie hall and teagarden occasions quickly faded as televisions took over the chatty warm living rooms. Along with other families of civil servants, we would go to organised campsites at the nearby lake to enjoy the novelty of swimming and sunbathing. Until television broadcasting began, initially only for a few hours a day, the whole town was living with the excitement that the Turkish movies of the early 1970s brought. Many were clumsily drama-tised love stories that made women weep and sigh. Later they felt good about narrating these tales and chatting about the handsome stars at frequent house visits and tea parties. Women lived vicariously through these movies and their excitement was a cure to endless family routines, disputes and household chores.

I noticed that my little hometown had many visual similarities to the landscape in Central Asia. I also often thought that Turkey's elite bureaucracy of those years had some strange resemblance to the life and spirit of the old Soviet nomenclature. Both were isolated in their own truth and idealism. Those were years of naivety and innocence for Turkish middle-class intellectuals, nourished by the nation's heavy external borrowing and overspending. Life was simple and good but a deep-seated instability was building up that we children were not aware of at all. Turkey's state-controlled economy was running out of steam and losing its ability to provide goods and services to its growing urban population. The economy was skewed towards state-run enterprises and a handful of family-run conglomerates. The deepening economic crisis of the oil shocks combined with ideological confrontations paralysed the whole country. There were many battles between right and left wing groups which were aggravated by economic inequalities and high unemployment.

During the mid- to late1970s, the CHP and the underground political left were divided into many factions. As a teenager, I listened to endless discussions about how the virtues of economic and social development would come with Marxism or Maoism and witnessed deepening indoctrination, conflict and violent ideological confrontations at my high school and its surroundings. This political divide formed even deeper fault lines among ethnic and religious groups, secularists and traditional nationalists. Our small town with its calm and modern outlook turned into a battleground. Even secondary school children got politicised over the merits of socialism or nationalism. A strange breed of Turkish nationalism popularised by the Nationalist Movement Party took root among many teachers and students of my secondary school that we at home feared and deeply resented. Political fanaticism disrupted our city. When the town became unsafe and my father, as a known leftist, began receiving hate messages, we moved to western Turkey and to a new life, and bid goodbye to our seemingly small and secure cocoon forever.

My attitude to leftist politics and to communism in particular has always been ambivalent despite my parents' strong convictions and beliefs in its virtues. Its slogans did not appeal to me; unlike many of my peers I found it uninspiring and tautological and resented its 'one size fits all' collective and conformist pressures. I always believed in social democracy and justice but felt that the imminent success of a proletariat dictatorship of toilers and peasants that my classmates pledged allegiance to was alien to me and the society I knew. The left began to fragment into many factions ranging from 'True Leninist-Marxist' to 'Trotskyites' and 'Maoists'. A different revolutionary youth culture was emerging with solemn looks, uniform dress styles and slogans.

Girls were divided into two camps: those who were considered to be stupid and feminine and those who were brave and revolutionary. The first group would dress and act like silly girls. They ignored politics and nobody cared about them. The second group merged with the boys. Those who managed to look and act like their male counterparts were the most respected and popular and were even happy to get involved in fist fighting. It was a hopeless situation for the rest of us who got stuck in between. Once, I was forced to attend a canteen pledge for the Marxist-Leninist group in my high school and was terribly embarrassed for having faked it. In the late 1970s, one had to choose one side or the other, the peer pressure at schools as well as work places was suppressive, intimidating and it never allowed any room for individualism or the right to remain silent or indifferent. We were forced to take sides in our looks, gestures and rhetoric. The symbolism grew deeper and deeper; revolutionaries used the Soviet sickle for the Turkish letter 'sh' (Ş), and they improvised other symbols to portray their allegiance.

A pathetic language emerged, filled with accusations of reductionism and counter-revolutionary thinking along with a confusing politicised vocabulary. Our schools and streets were alive with the parroting of such jargon. The punishment awaiting us for acting out this naïve and dim-witted entertainment was quick, brutal and unforgiving.

In the western city where we moved, my mother, a staunch atheist as well as a leftist, got involved in the union of revolutionary teachers. One year we spent a fortnight in the summer camp of the union. It was a miserable holiday full of colourful slogans but physically quite uncom-fortable; it lacked basic services, sanitation and even simple aesthetics. I remember watching the idealised and didactic revolutionary play one evening presented by enthusiastic union members. I tried to make sense of its weird artistic message. Only after travelling in Central Asia and watching early Russian movies was I able to understand how well they depicted Soviet iconography with slogans, stylised body movements, exposed arms and desexualised protagonists! Above all how awkward it was, as an adolescent, to sense the masculinity in which men and women converged into a single gender. That summer camp was an important turning point for our slowly disintegrating family.

Later that year, my mother was taken to court and suspended from her teaching position by the 1980 military coup government for tak-ing part in 'illegal' leftist and communist activities including an anti-government teachers' strike. She was later punished further by being appointed to teach at a distant village school far from the city. This ruthless treatment caused deep resentment and hardship for us all. The books my father collected over the years became a liability and one day we packed them all, along with Marxist-Leninist propaganda leaflets, and hid them away. Many young and bright people, among them my father's cousins, were imprisoned and tortured by the right wing rulers. Many fled abroad or perished in prisons for advocating Marxism or its derivations during the 1980s, but we narrowly escaped.

In the following years, I remained in the dark about the massive developments taking place in the USSR and Central Asia and had no contact with the region. I often wondered what was achieved by com-munism such that millions around the world, including my parents and friends, supported it so passionately. Retrospectively, compared to what we had in our small town, the societal and economic developments that took place in the USSR were enormous in scale and scope. However, the Soviets had no regard for economic sustainability beyond a technocratic and party command structure which itself was quickly corrupted by per-sonal as well as collective manipulation. More importantly, the Soviet system misjudged and misused the abundance of nature and labour in its vast territory. Environmental and material resources were overlooked and economic units were badly managed within a regime overwhelmed by free riders. In the name of creating a classless society, the Soviet Union eventually brought about material inequalities and environmental injustices among its regions and populations.

Those who thought that capitalism was the ultimate winner in the race between the communist and capitalist ideologies were mistaken, too. As the depth of another cycle of fraud, abuse and lax foresight began unravelling with the financial crisis of 2008, we have been forced to reflect on the future of unfettered capitalism and its global implications.

Carrying out research in Central Asia

My interest in enterprise development in Central Asia began when I heard about the oddities of entrepreneurship in societies that had remained ignorant of market economy and were cut off from the rest of the world for many decades. During the early 1990s, all of Central Asia suffered from the economic shocks of the dissolution of the USSR. In addition to macroeconomic turmoil and high inflation, there were almost no well-functioning businesses. The cities lacked decent hotels, restaurants and shops. Many foreigners visiting the region were perplexed by its isolation and the apparent lack of business development. In response to economic meltdown, thousands lined up on pavements to barter and sell small items to survive. With the opening of external flights and international connections, many travelled abroad to see the other side of the fence and began shuttle trade. The lack of financial concepts, simple routines of accounting and marketing, intrigued many observers. Over the years, the situation has changed and the growing number of indigenously owned enterprises has proved that the region's people are willing to take risks and learn to operate with a sort of market economy. The dissolution of the Soviet state assets and the diffusion of entrepreneurship brought about new social classes with property ownership. However, the nature of the post-Soviet market and private enterprise development has largely been seen as an undifferentiated whole because of limited empirical research.

Despite growing market developments and entrepreneurship, there has been very little scholarly effort to analyse Central Asia's changing economic landscape, the nature of new enterprises and the character of its entrepreneurs. The lack of scholarly interest in social differentiation in transition from Soviet structures to capitalist markets is especially surprising.

The evolving social stratification in relation to property ownership, the distribution of economic and political resources and changing value systems clearly deserve much more attention from scholars and policymakers alike. Yet to date we know very little about the emerging entrepreneurial class and the nature of small- and medium-sized enterprises beyond large scale, aggregated opinion surveys carried out by international aid agencies.[1] Entrepreneurs have contributed to the pace of transition as market builders and also, de facto, reformers.[2] However, the transition literature is mute about who these new property holders are, what kind of social and economic role they play, how they interact with the new authoritarian state structures and other capitalists, to what extent they form a cohesive group and if they indeed have a future in these economies. In this book, I address the diverse realities of this region's emerging entrepreneurial class and its position in the state-market axis.

I will use the terms 'entrepreneur' and 'business owner' or 'businessman/woman' interchangeably throughout the book. A separation of terminology implying a sharp differentiation between routine simple business undertakings carried out by the self-employed or owner-managers versus innovative ones performed by entrepreneurs does not hold much validity. Rather than confining the concept of entrepreneur only to those who are assumed to have innovative capabilities and special traits, I regard entrepreneurs to be all those who run businesses and endure risks and uncertainty in the market, irrespective of their enterprise size.[3] These men and women pursue market opportunities and family survival at once. Such risk-taking initiatives extend both the scope of economic freedoms and individual creativity.

I began my fieldwork in Bishkek in 2004 after several months of preparation in New York and London. After my first month in Bishkek, I went back to the region many times between 2004 and 2007, each time visiting a different region to carry out interviews and to collect data.[4] Straightforward access to business information, statistics and locational details on firms is almost impossible in Central Asia. In post-Soviet cities where business can be found everywhere from apartment blocks to warehouses and to locations with no obvious markings or street signs, an office or production facility requires detailed personal networking. Institutions often lag behind societal changes taking place and there are hardly any credible business statistics, no reliable official information and no up-to-date business directory. Existing data are geographically uneven and often scattered among various ministries, organisations and donor-funded projects.

Face-to-face business surveys are also difficult to carry out for several reasons. Time and budget constraints hinder the scope. Many businesses function without routines or even administrative staff. Entrepreneurs of small businesses personally carry out essential business tasks themselves, move around and often have limited time to spare. Entrepreneurs everywhere tend to shy away from sharing sensitive business and personal information. In Central Asia, this attitude is often combined with a general suspicion of empirical research and wariness about whether it could help their business and improve market conditions. Officialdom tends to have low expectations generally and no understanding of the utility of research for policymaking. Furthermore, there is a longstanding suspicion of the relationship between the state and businesses. Entrepreneurs often feel threatened by being questioned about their business ventures and fear possible consequences. Widespread inspection practices, tax investigations and formal and informal extortion make businesses balk at strangers and surveys.[5] Initially, I targeted the businesses which were using micro and small credit schemes launched by the European Bank for Reconstruction and Development (EBRD) for the survey. Several specialists at the London headquarters of the EBRD helped me to gain access to local banks and their business clients in the cities I selected. This allowed me to have credible access to firms and helped me to limit my sample to the emerging entrepreneurial middle stratum with reliable records. The EBRD has been providing short- and long-term loans to the post-communist states of Eastern Europe and the former Soviet Union since 1992. The micro and small finance programme was introduced by a consortium of national and international banks in the region. The EBRD is the largest investor in the non-oil private sector in Central Asia; its cumulative financial commitment was 1.8 billion Euros by 2004. Apart from project-based loans, these mostly aimed to improve infrastructure. The bank has also developed extensive business lending to enhance small and medium-sized enterprise growth.[6] Kazakhstan, Kyrgyzstan and Uzbekistan became part of the EBRD's 'Early Transition Countries Initiative' in 2004. In that year a multidonor fund was established to provide further credit lines to medium-sized businesses and the bank invested more than 316 million Euros. Kazakhstan was the largest recipient (246 million Euros) followed by Uzbekistan (34 million Euros) and Kyrgyzstan (30 million Euros). The bank increased its financial commitment to the region significantly in 2007 by offering 531.6 million Euros to Kazakhstan, 14.7 million Euros to Uzbekistan and 11.7 million Euros to Kyrgyzstan.[7] These included project-based finance, investments in sectoral transformations and loans to the banking sector.

The range of micro and small credits used by businesses showed sharp differences among regions, countries and sectors. Between 2004 and

2006, I investigated very small loans (between 100 and 500 USD) in poor areas of Kyrgyzstan and significantly higher ones in major urban areas (mostly between 1,000 and 10,000 USD). Those in Kazakhstan were significantly larger (between 10 and 50,000 USD). These loans, mostly on a short-term basis, required collateral, a formal procedure and a thorough inspection by loan officers. Although microfinancing has been criticised for having high interest rates and limited penetration into some societal segments, the EBRD programmes were among the best managed ones that I have observed. Other microfinance programmes such as the ones provided by the World Bank, the European Union (TACIS), USAID and many others have had extensive operations in urban and rural areas of Kyrgyzstan, mostly being used for poverty alleviation.[8] External finance played a crucial role for all entrepreneurs in the region. However, legal and institutional uncertainties and high transaction costs inhibited borrowing. During the survey the annual interest rates on loans were between 30 and 60 per cent, well above inflation rates in each country. Overall, the impact of external finance has been positive for business survival but it has had a rather limited impact on the growth of medium-sized enterprises. Most of the businesses I observed used their line of credit to deal with cash flow problems, to meet family needs and to build secure investments through property development.

I carried out interviews in person with my fieldwork assistants who were fluent in several languages. This has been a multilingual research in many respects. Frequently, the medium of our dialogues swung between Russian and Turkic dialects. The language of interviews was Russian in most cases in Kazakhstan and Kyrgyzstan. Mostly Uzbek was used during interviews in Uzbekistan. Altogether about 15 per cent of enterprise interviews were carried out in modern Turkish, as the dialects of Khorezm, Meshketian, Azeri and Uyghur are close to Anatolian Turkish. Interviews with foreign experts and some locals were carried out in English.

Personal interaction gave me a tactile sense of the business environment, its size and nature. In some cases interviews took place at homes, socialising with families and accompanied by wide-ranging conversations, often with food and tea. These visits provided a deeper sense of engagement with real life in the region and were the most enjoyable and memorable part of my survey. Building my sampling of business interviews among small and microcredit loan clients allowed me to select fairly well-established middle-class entrepreneurs. After initial introductory meetings and discussions with the local bank consultants, I selected a number of enterprises from different sectors and geographical areas. Entrepreneurs were assured about the academic nature of my work prior to being interviewed and I visited them after arranging a suitable time and confirming their address on the phone whenever possible. Except in a small number of cases, my sample entrepreneurs run established businesses. However, I came across some who were simply trying to survive on loans, too. Once, in the outskirts of Bishkek, I visited a business address which was the home of a young couple with an infant. There was an unbearably heavy smell inside their two-room house. I soon noticed animal parts scattered around. This couple had used a loan to buy and slaughter animals and sell the meat in the market to make a living. On another occasion, I met a perfume seller who borrowed over 1,000 USD, more than the annual salary of a civil servant then, but he only had a tiny stall with a few products in the provincial city of Osh and did not seem to be engaged in any other venture. Such cases are not uncommon and there are many people who simply try to get by through marginal trade and exchanges.

The Bishkek office of the EBRD was my initial contact point and their support led to the successful implementation of my first survey questionnaires. In Kazakhstan, the KSBP (Kazakhstan Small Business Programme) ran the EBRD-lending operations along with local banks. However, due to uncertainties involved in the process of handing over to local banks, there were long delays in getting access to firms. In Uzbekistan, my contact was the J-USBP (the Japan-Uzbekistan Small Business Programme) which coordinated small business lending across the country. All bank consultants were cooperative, yet I still encountered significant problems in Kazakhstan and Uzbekistan.[9] In Kazakhstan, I completed 58 surveys. Gaining the trust of the microfinance bureaucracy was much harder than what I had experienced in Uzbekistan or Kyrgyzstan and this caused long delays. In the meantime, there were also administrative changes in the EBRD and all my initial contacts left the bank during my period of research. In Uzbekistan, after my first fruitful research trips to Tashkent, Bukhara and Samarkand with 49 surveys, anti-government protests took place in Andijan in May 2005. These protests were silenced militarily and were followed by a clampdown on NGOs and international assistance. I was only able to visit the Fergana Valley and Khorezm in autumn 2006 in order to carry out my planned fieldwork. Along with the major changes that took place in the microfinance programme, I found the general climate of fear and suspicion too constraining to carry out any written survey. The long-standing suspicion of foreigners and the post-massacre trauma of ordinary people inhibited my efforts to carry out a structured questionnaire. Instead, I carried out over 30 semi-structured interviews and developed case studies among numerous artisans and businessmen and women.

The second major source of primary evidence came from semi-structured interviews and focus group discussions with journalists, politicians, NGO groups and experts in all three countries. I also carried out interviews among artisans in several towns of the Fergana Valley and enjoyed long social interactions with them in their homes. I employed eclectic routes in order to expand my information base in the survey cities. Some of these connections came from journalists, international experts, local students and others in London, and some others from business and the financial community in Istanbul and New York City. Most of these individuals either travelled to the region for work or lived there for a certain period. Many new contacts emerged during the fieldwork through social networks. Thus, I employed a snowballing technique to extend my survey links through multiple contacts and their networks. Yet in dealing with all local and international institutions and individuals I strictly maintained my financial and intellectual independence. This may have been difficult for some to come to terms with, but in the end everybody respected my efforts to establish research integrity.

Getting around in the post-Soviet geography

New enterprises are not only situated in commercial zones and urban residential neighbourhoods but often in old Soviet factories. Thus, throughout the fieldwork I had to move in and around cities and experienced different geographical settings and circumstances. Intercity travel was in particular difficult and required careful planning due to poor transportation connections and long distances. I travelled by air and train in northern Kazakh regions. The railway has long been the symbol of power and authority of the state in the steppe and it remains the main connection to the outside world for many small towns and hamlets. Railways also sustain the networked economy as the main means of long distance transportation for raw materials, finished goods and common folk. At other times, I rented a car and a driver as this provided maximum flexibility. The intercity road system had long been neglected and is still rather poor. Bad road signs and the difficulty of getting precise directions make site searching especially difficult.

The main metropolises, Almaty, Bishkek and Tashkent, all have a peculiar urban fabric with a strong Soviet character. The layout of these cities looks alike. In the middle there is a grid plan for the city centre with public buildings, museums, an opera house, science academies and monumental parks. The major streets and avenues are often named after Slavic revolutionaries, poets and writers (Lenin, Pushkin and Gorky are essential) along with 'secondary indigenous figures' (like Abdurrahmanov, Toktagul and others of national significance). However, there has been a process of indigenisation of street names and squares replacing Slavic idols and heroes with local ones. Built as symbols of the modernity of autonomous states, the institutions of research, art and bureaucracy have long been meant to signify the distinctiveness of national cultures from one another while being part of the Soviet unity. However, these institutions ceased to produce any worthwhile work long ago. Their publications were small in number and poor in quality. Many that I visited, like the archaeological and film institute of Kazakhstan, became part of a myriad of sleepy Soviet institutions. Others, such as the opera houses and music academies continued to produce talent, but the best usually left for Moscow or points West.

Public buildings with Russian and Soviet architecture still today symbolise power and order. The residential areas of the elite expand from this sedate power grid and urban sprawl stretches to large concrete blocks and later more disorderly neighborhoods. A dark dominant figure, a massive coal-fired urban heating plant, invariably looms above the lesser neighborhoods. It puffs a dark plume that pollutes the air and clouds the cities. The whole city is firmly shackled together with patched heating and utility pipes crossing over roads and running along pavements. These cities have many pleasant sights as well; many examples of early Russian architecture are interesting and highly decorated, such as the public library in Almaty. Some Soviet art deco buildings can be surprisingly delightful, too; the post office building in Bishkek has considerable artistic merit. Canals built to irrigate parks and roadside trees bring a nice cool feeling during the spring and summer. On sunny and warm days people line up along verdant boulevards, sell bric-a-brac or play chess in parks. Old Russian women might be singing and dancing. One can have long walks without being disturbed by cars or intruders. Yet behind this tranquillity there are the rather ugly truths of Soviet planning as well.

More than its modest urban projects, industrial structures remind us of the Soviet order and power that once spread its concrete and iron across an immense geography. Soviet economic policies and planning targets inflicted irreversible damage on nature over large parts of the land mass stretching from China to the Caspian Sea. Land, air and water pollution caused by mining, industrial waste, nuclear tests and waste deposits and excessive use of fertilisers and water are among the major environmental problems that Central Asia inherited from the USSR.

Depleted natural resources lead to another set of economic, social and environmental distortions that will be a continuing economic burden and humanitarian challenge for the new states.

Massive single factory towns and industrial complexes such as Temirtau in Kazakhstan and Navoi in Uzbekistan look horrifying. These ghastly complexes were designed to meet all worldly needs of the proletariat but instead they stand senseless and de-humanising. New social stratification leads to differentiated tastes, consumer attitudes and varied architecture. Shopping malls and gardened villas spring up in neighbourhoods of the rich and the middle classes. Astana's highly eclectic range of experimental architecture reflects the grandeur of oil wealth and ambitions for a new urban destiny, one that denies the massive steppe and long cold winters.

A sketch of the book

The following nine chapters examine different dimensions of the state-market relationship through the experiences of the entrepreneurial middle stratum in all major cities of Kazakhstan, Kyrgyzstan and Uzbekistan. These chapters examine the social characteristics of entrepreneurs and their collective identity; the degree of social and moral harmony that they portray; the influence of gender divisions in shaping entrepreneurship; and the impact of external actors and aid organisations in entrepreneurship and business formation.

Chapter 1 introduces the nature of state formation and economic development in Central Asia along with a concise historical and geographical analysis. I argue that the post-Soviet evolution of Kazakhstan, Kyrgyzstan and Uzbekistan resulted in diverging forms of personal and authoritarian states along with deepening resource-dependent economic structures. Since they rely heavily on oil, gold, cotton and other commodity exports, they are increasingly exposed to international price fluctuations and heavily dependent on global economic cycles. By exporting their young labour force, both Uzbekistan and Kyrgyzstan try to accommodate their economic distortions with workers' remittances. These state and market structures in essence define the contours of entrepreneurial opportunities in these countries.

Chapter 2 extends the central theme of the book: the new social differentiation and the origins of the entrepreneurial middle class. I first examine the origins of stratification in relation to the nature of Soviet markets and elite control in the distribution and reallocation of economic opportunities and later explain why this can best be understood in relation to a game of reallocation rounds, for which I use the metaphor of a Mikado game, also known as 'pick-up sticks'. I examine how diverging patterns and discontinuities affect stratification and the position of middle-stratum entrepreneurs.

In Chapter 3 I assess the characteristics of entrepreneurs and business sectors based on survey evidence. The personal attributes of entrepreneurs in terms of age, gender and ethnicity will be presented. Entrepreneurs' perceptions about business and markets, and about institutions and governance, are elaborated pointing out in what way this emerging class has increasing expectations and demands from the ruling groups and the state.

Chapter 4 emphasises the growing importance of bazaars in the new commercial landscape and points out the crucial role played by entrepreneurs in building solidarity networks, negotiating with authorities and mediating conflicts. I illustrate how new interests in the Mikado game are articulated in bazaars with three exemplary cases.

Chapter 5 focuses on the gendered economy and provides a discussion of the changing roles of women in relation to state and market building, providing an analysis of female entrepreneurship starting with the shuttle trade and the formation of bazaars. The empirical evidence on the qualities and skills of female entrepreneurs demonstrates new forms of business diversification.

Chapter 6 examines collective identity and representation in terms of business groups and associational affiliations. My analysis shows that, paradoxically, the state does not have a monopoly over the use of coercion and indeed it does not fully control state institutions, yet, at the same time, interest groups' representation through associational structures is very rare. The weaknesses and arbitrariness of state coercion and of law enforcement create opportunities for alternative institutions of governance, in particular as eclectic self-governing syndicates. This is most common in Kyrgyzstan and Kazakhstan.

In Chapter 7, I explain the role of international actors in enterprise creation with a focus on Kyrgyzstan. Despite a decade and a half of involvement by international finance and aid institutions, enterprise development in Kyrgyzstan has been limited. For the most part, poverty alleviation policies preoccupied aid strategists at the expense of capacity building and enterprise development. However, small but important initiatives such as the community based tourism allow us to understand how this vicious circle can be broken and wider business opportunities can be generated in the market.

Chapter 8 examines the moral world of entrepreneurs in the fluid ideological setting of the post-Soviet societies. By using a combined method of empirical observation and secondary literature review, that is, relevant scholarly work as well as literature, poetry and dictums, I examine the moral positioning among entrepreneurs in three analytical categories: the core morality of doing business, the virtue of duty, and the greater good. This analysis shows how studying the moral dimension in entrepreneurial activities within the context of faith and ideology can broaden our understanding of the relationship between markets and morality, and also in relation to the pursuit of self-interest and wealth in market building. The concluding chapter expresses the theoretical implications of this work and its contributions to policy design in the fields of enterprise development and market building.

Acknowledgements

For the past six years, Central Asia has become part of my personal as well as academic life. When I decided to study enterprise development in Kazakhstan, Kyrgyzstan and Uzbekistan in 2002, I could not have anticipated how fulfilling a project it would be. Retrospectively, it has been an exciting endeavour and a worthy enterprise. This enriching journey took me into the lives of hundreds of ordinary Central Asians as I travelled across massive steppes, mountains and towns interviewing fascinating people and gathering data. After completing many travels and compiling a large data set on emerging entrepreneurs in the region, conceiving a concise set of arguments into a book has been another challenge. I am indebted to many people without whose help and support this book could have never seen daylight.

My friend and colleague Murat Çokgezen, of Marmara University in Istanbul, first opened the gates of Central Asia for me in 2001, when he took a year off and taught economics in Bishkek. My early hesitation towards these far lands turned first into a deep curiosity and later into a passion. Another friend, Firdevs Robinson of the BBC Central Asia section, offered encouragement, many exciting contacts and support throughout the years. I am grateful to the help of Laurent Guye, Ayşe Dönmezer and Elvira Lefting, all formerly with the London office of the European Bank for Reconstruction and Development (EBRD) for offering instrumental help to get access to the microfinance programme managers and consultants in Kyrgyzstan, Kazakhstan and Uzbekistan. I would like to acknowledge in particular the help of EBRD consultants, among them Heike Nonnenberg and Margarita Cherikbaeva in Kyrgyzstan, Timur Bekpaev in Kazakhstan and Dan Balke in Uzbekistan. The Kyrgyz-Turkish Manas University in Bishkek and the Kazakhstan Institute of Management, Economics and Strategic Research (KIMEP) in Almaty offered valuable logistical support. Eamon Doren of the United States Agency for International Development (USAID) generously helped me to get access to local projects and offered me the benefit of his hard-earned experience in Kyrgyzstan.

I am grateful to my Central Asian assistants for their patient, kind and good hearted support throughout the long travels we shared together during the fieldwork research. Koblan Yassenbatev and Nur Mirzamurat in Kazakhstan, Aybek Aytbayev in Kyrgyzstan and Sergei Shirov and

Shavkat Yaqubov in Uzbekistan were my companions, translators and compasses through many weeks. Erkin Adylov and Aziza Zahkidova from the London School of Economics (LSE) helped a great deal with the literature survey and made many useful suggestions on early drafts of some chapters. Another graduate student from the LSE, Funda Bilgiç, heroically tamed the massive amount of questionnaire data, anecdotal evidence and many semi-structured interviews. Funda has been magnificent in her dedication and skill. An old friend and colleague, Mina Moshkeri Upton, at the LSE Design Unit, has kindly produced the map at short notice.

With his insightful knowledge of the region, Ian MacWilliam, the former Central Asia correspondent of the BBC, offered clear analyses and improved greatly my understanding of political and social realities of the region. Ulugbek Hojiahmedov, Tohkir Sultanbayev and Murad Megalli not only became great friends but were indispensable for my research in Uzbekistan. Without Mohirbek Zohidov, I would have spent days of anxiety to sort out logistics in Almaty, and without Kürşat Çetin, Aziz Murtaza and Deniz Tura, I would not have even dreamt of being able to talk to as many people as I did in Tashkent and in the Fergana Valley. I met many resourceful people through spontaneous contacts. Among such people Fatih Malcı in Atyrau, Nikolai Pakosh in Karaganda and Natalia Bragina in Bishkek offered insightful remarks, cheerful moments and fabulous conversations. I am deeply grateful and feel very fortunate to have the intellectual wisdom and friendship of all these people.

I would also like to pay my dues to many others who were directly or indirectly involved in my research. As formal respondents or casual companions, people in Kazakhstan, Kyrgyzstan and Uzbekistan offered kind friendship and opened their hearts and thoughts to me. Without their cooperation and hospitality I would not have had access to information and could never have been able to see how life worked for them. But, more importantly, they made my research endeavour worthwhile and enjoyable. I have deep empathy for the people of this region and hope that this book would make at least a small contribution to foster economic development and build a brighter future for them.

I am grateful to the Nuffield Foundation Social Science Grant (2004–5) and the Leverhulme Trust Research Fellowship (2005–7) which provided generous financial support for the fieldwork research. I finished the last stages of the book when I was a Wilson Fellow at the Woodrow Wilson International Center for Scholars in Washington DC. The Center's outstanding facilities and supportive staff provided an excellent environment for the completion of the manuscript. Last but not least, I am deeply indebted to Jonathan Liebenau, my husband, for his emotional support and tolerance of my physical and mental absence through many months that I spent travelling, moaning and writing the manuscript. His editing guidance greatly helped to improve the final text. All these people and institutions, however, bear no responsibility for the opinions expressed in this book. Those who helped with the fieldwork survey and offered their analyses did not have prior knowledge of the style or content of this book. Therefore, I am solely responsible for the general theoretical framework, empirical arguments and opinions expressed here.

Map of Modern Central Asia

Credit: M Moshkeri Upton, Design Unit, LSE

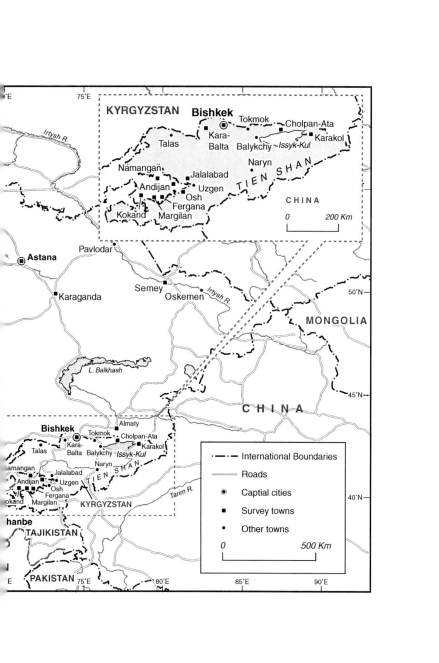

1
Introduction: Building States and Markets in Central Asia

> I wonder who, amongst the Kazakhs of today, I could possibly love or respect.
>
> I would have respected a bey but there are no true beys any more; even if there is one, he is not the master of his will and his wealth...
>
> I would have respected a myrza, but now you cannot find a truly generous one;
>
> as to those who give out their livestock to the right and left,
>
> there are as many of these as stray dogs.
>
> I would have respected a volost chief and a biy,
>
> but on our steppe there is neither divine nor human justice.
>
> *Abay [Qunanbayuli], Kazakh poet and essayist, 1995*[1]

Introduction

At the dawn of the nineteenth century, the Kazakh poet and essayist Abay saw his steppe society in decay, besieged on the one side by the victorious Russian Empire with its modernising tools of railways, telegrams and science in education, and on the other side by the dissolution of moral values and cultural integrity. His long lament became famous as a telling example of how the societal structure, shaped by shared responsibilities and the values of each stratum, was under threat. Abay expressed how the interests of rulers and leaders were captured by outside forces and how this delegitimised their societal role. He knew that his society was being transformed towards some kind of an aimless future without legitimate governance. Today Central Asia is going through a similarly profound change and moral dislocation in the protracted aftermath of the dissolution of the Soviet Union in 1991. Former Communist Party leaders remain at the forefront of property ownership and wealth accumulation. The region's intelligentsia remains confused and disenchanted. One-time managers of collective enterprises and leaders of youth and party organisations are involved in an all-out campaign to accumulate wealth. Thus, dissolution of the state's property through privatisation and the reallocation of assets has not only changed the economic fundamentals but also led to social disarray with increasing differentiation among social groups in access to political power and economic wealth. The most striking result of this massive transformation is the emergence of a capitalist class.

Along with the concentration of economic and political power, the key phenomenon is the creation of the new forms of businesses, markets and entrepreneurs that constitute the focus of this book. The development of an entrepreneurial middle class along with market expansion signifies a remarkable turn in Central Asia's history. For the first time since its merchant and artisanal classes were severely weakened by the eighteenth-century colonial Russian advances and later dissipated by the Soviets, Central Asia is witnessing the growth of indigenous businesses owned and operated by its own entrepreneurs. This transformation is slowly reversing the trend of almost 150 years during which the role of Central Asians in the economy declined. From becoming mere recipients of state provisions and labourers in Soviet farms and enterprises, indigenous Central Asians today run their own businesses and accumulate wealth. Nevertheless the move towards market economy carries numerous new problems. Although the region's leaders have attempted to de-Sovietise the state apparatus through the rhetoric of national awakening and authentication, their parliaments are now controlled by single-party structures dictated by national presidents. In less than two decades the presidential families and their associates have internalised authoritarian political structures to their own advantage. The weak rule of law and the arbitrary workings of institutions facilitate the absorption of economic opportunities by a tiny elite. This transformation led to new societal dependencies and just the sort of injustice that Abay abhorred.

Business owners form a heterogeneous group with diverse regional, ethnic and social allegiances. Nevertheless, they provide the single most important source of social cohesion in the newly independent states, often filling the vacuum left by depleted public provisions.

The dissolution of the Soviet economic command structures and its mass provisions of goods and services through central planning has been partly compensated for in the growth of market-based enterprises owned and managed by individuals. However, the expansion of capitalist markets through privately owned businesses has not entirely been disenfranchised from the Soviet market structures and social norms the region formerly possessed. Partial or full privatisation of land and state enterprises, and deregulation, brought about a transition to markets in a way that was influenced by the prevailing social stratification. The eventual growth of the new entrepreneurial stratum is, hence, a by-product of the Soviet legacy. At the same time, the deepening of the markets has also instigated a disintegration of Soviet institutions, paving the way to new social structures. This is still an evolving phenomenon, and in this book I provide evidence of the early stages of this emerging social diversification and its relationship to the penetration of capitalist markets. We will also see the sources of conflicts and the spread of enterprising culture among the middle stratum of this region. Kazakhstan, Kyrgyzstan and Uzbekistan illustrate well how their specific historical legacies, Soviet-era standing and the choices made by their ruling elites led to consequent diverging paths in state formation and market building since their independence.[2]

The entrepreneurial class occupies a central position between the growing poor and disfranchised population and the increasingly unaccountable bureaucratic regime entangled with oligarchic business groups. Yet we know too little about entrepreneurship in relation to oligarchic control built into states and markets in this region. Who are these new entrepreneurs? What social roles do they play and how do they operate in these peculiar markets? How do they align their business interests with the autocracies? What effects have aid, trade and other international connections with Western organisations had over entrepreneurship and enterprise development? How do these entrepreneurs accommodate the ideological dislocation that they have experienced?

It is necessary that we analyse economic and political transformation in relation to the new interest-group dynamics of this middle stratum. Such an approach is also timely since most scholarly work dealing with transition to democracy and market economy has failed to provide the explanations and future predictions they claim. The transition debate, which offered useful avenues for early researchers, is increasingly becoming irrelevant to the realities of post-Soviet societies. Similarly, two decades of Western advice aimed to provide the ideas and know-how necessary to introduce new institutional designs and the legal structures for capitalism and democracy have reached a dead end. There are many reasons for this stalemate but the prime cause stems from a general lack of understanding of societal and economic changes taking place in post-Soviet societies and the short-sightedness of simplistic transition assumptions guiding these Western efforts.

There is a general absence of conceptual and theoretical understanding of social stratification and economic differentiation in scholarly works and policy studies. Transition literature has rarely gone beyond assertions about the influence of the ruling elite. However, by positioning the emerging entrepreneurial class in a state-market relationship we can extend the reach of scholarship to account for a dynamic understanding of business interests and wealth accumulation among different social groups. It is particularly encouraging to note that social differentiation and class-based analyses beyond rigid Marxist assumptions have recently emerged in the economics literature. In their seminal work, *Economic Origins of Dictatorship and Democracy*, Daron Acemoglu and James Robinson developed an economic-based approach to explain democratic and non-democratic political choices made by a society.[3] They emphasise the fundamental importance of conflict among different groups and social classes and illustrate how opposing interests of different segments of society translate themselves into political institutions. They explore how outcomes emerge through a process of bargaining, negotiation and sometimes coups. This work is important in many ways for scholars who are interested in the origins of democracy and democratic consolidation, and it offers a fresh perspective using game theory. Seeing political institutions within the sphere of the economic interests of social groups and linking political outcomes to underlying economic structures in different societies form the essence of their work. In this economic theory of democratisation, political institutions are partially historically determined and partially consciously chosen. Social conflict is not narrowly defined along class lines but more importantly it is an outcome of multiple factors affecting group behaviour such as race, ethnicity and ideology. Thus, Acemoglu and Robinson's analysis offers a useful perspective in seeing economic and political institutions in dynamic relationship with each other and with conflicting social group interests. Such an analysis that is sensitive to social stratification and dynamic interaction among groups allows us to see enterprise development and entrepreneurship through the prism of social consolidation and conflict in relation to property and wealth accumulation.

The nature of social stratification in post-Soviet Central Asia and its power and interest-based dynamics are subject to a complex interplay among the presidents, government officials and business groups. In almost two decades, the families and associates of presidents have now entered into the markets through ownership stakes and managerial control of sectors such as mineral and gold mining, oil and gas extraction, cotton farming, banking and the media. Their style of management and degree of flexibility define the level of redistribution of strategic resources and governance of the markets. This takes place through a dynamic reallocation and positioning which I characterise as a Mikado game. This game puts players in a position to deconstruct a jumble or tower of numerous parts without disrupting or toppling the whole. Through the Mikado game, different parties periodically accumulate wealth and business advantages at the expense of others. The entrepreneurial middle class plays a critical role by generating new goods, services and market opportunities for new allocation rounds. Their economic role now replaces the Soviet economic system. Thus, new enterprises serve both the needs of the growing domestic demand for goods and the interests of the ruling elite. By holding a critical middle ground between the impoverished majority and large business interests, entrepreneurs and small businesses expand their opportunities in relation to the state and the market. The thousands of business ventures created by individuals also form the backbone of local economies and communities. They deliver goods and services, create jobs and incomes and they reproduce to provide stimulus for further market deepening. These enterprises not only constitute the building blocks of the market but also act as a buffer between concentrated economic power and the dispossessed masses. Yet the benign role of the entrepreneurial middle class as economic and social facilitators should not be taken for granted. The middle stratum entrepreneurs are also likely to be the source of social upheavals and big ruptures in the state-market fabric due to their fragile relationships with all other market players and political power. Indeed, as events in recent years both in Kyrgyzstan and Uzbekistan illustrate, the social motivations for anti-government protests originate from a general discontent but tend to be sponsored by middle stratum entrepreneurs.

The region's political and economic elites followed different paths towards market transition. The position of new entrepreneurs in the state-market relationship is also precarious, shifting between conflictual and subservient positions vis-à-vis the state and dominant business groups. While the region shows a growing divergence in business development and market building practices, the opportunity structures for entrepreneurs and their enterprises depend on the context of market reforms and the nature of governance in each country. Kyrgyzstan implemented 'big bang' shock therapies most enthusiastically. Throughout the 1990s, Uzbekistan promoted a policy of 'gradual developmentalism' which was a clear euphemism for minimum reform. Kazakhstan followed hybrid policies and, in the long run, its ruling elite demonstrated greater ability in managing their rich oil and mineral resources than their neighbouring states.

Central Asia: geography, history and demography

Modern Central Asia covers five landlocked former Autonomous Republics of the Soviet Union, namely, Kazakhstan, the Kyrgyz Republic, Tajikistan, Turkmenistan and Uzbekistan. It is often constructed also to include the Xinjiang Uyghur Autonomous Region of China, and sometimes Mongolia, Afghanistan and some districts of Siberia.[4] In total area, the five post-Soviet states occupy a land mass larger than India with only five per cent of its population. The largest country, Kazakhstan, has a land area equivalent to almost one third of the total area of the United States. However, much of the western part of this region, extending to the Caspian Sea, is composed of two deserts, the Kara Kum (Black Sand) and Kyzyl Kum (Red Sand). To the north, immense steppes extend to Siberia. The mountain ranges of the Kopetdag and Pamirs separate the region from Iran and Afghanistan in the south. The eastern part, rough and hilly, rises to include the mountains of Alatau and the Tian Shan range. In the north there is no geographical boundary between the Kazakh and Siberian steppe. Central Asia, a term originating in Russian, does not carry any particular cultural or historical meaning for the people in the region apart from reminding them of a sense of being in-between. Nevertheless, it has entered into common usage both in geographical and political contexts. All the countries in the narrow designation except Persian-speaking Tajikistan are mainly populated by Turkic-speaking peoples predominantly adhering to the Sunni form of Islam (Turkic-speaking people also occupy some of southern Siberia, Xinjiang and parts of northern regions of Afghanistan and Iran). There are many other ethnic groups living in the region. The largest ethnic minority is Russians who settled in the region mainly over the past century.

Central Asia has been at the crossroads of civilisations and cultural spheres for more than two millennia. Trade flourished and intellectual exchange was long established in lands between China and Europe. All major religions and faiths found adherents in the region.

Buddhism, Taoism, Zoroastrianism, Hellenistic faiths, Judaism, Nestorian Christianity and Manichaeism were widely practiced even after the early spread of Islam from the Arab raids of the seventh and eighth centuries. Early Persian Kingdoms periodically established strongholds in this region. In relation to its ethno-linguistic and dynastic traditions it was known as Sogdia and Bactria during the age of Alexander the Great of Macedonia in the fourth century. Transoxania formed the core of Central Asia with the earliest settlements of sophisticated civilisations dating back to the 6th century BC. The region of Transoxania (today divided between Kazakhstan and Uzbekistan) lies between the two rivers; the Amu Darya which springs from the Pamir Mountains and the Syr Darya which rises in two headstreams in the Tian Shan Mountains in Kyrgyzstan and eastern Uzbekistan (the Naryn and Kara Su Rivers). The Amu Darya and Syr Darya flow towards the Aral Sea; the Amu Darya passes through parts of Turkmenistan and Uzbekistan while the Syr Darya flows through Kyrgyzstan and Kazakhstan. Transoxania was the most northeastern extension of Hellenic influence where it mixed with Persian and Buddhist cultures.[5] Attila the Hun established another Eurasian Empire originating from the east and extending its influence from the Central Asian steppes to modern Germany during the 5th century. In Iranian folklore, Transoxania came to symbolise one of the earliest divisions between the worlds of Iran and Turan, the Amu Darya (Oxus River) being the border between Iran and Turkestan.

With the large exodus of Turkic tribes from the Altay Mountains westwards, the region's Indo-European and Persian-speaking peoples increasingly took on a Turkic character. These initially formed a tribal confederation under the Kök Türk Empire (552–744 AD) in a territory stretched along a narrow latitudinal steppe fringed by mountain chains dominated by the Altay and Tian Shan ranges into the Fergana Valley on the western edge.[6] This empire was later split into the eastern and western kingdoms between the Orkhun Valley of northwest Mongolia and the western Tian Shan and Semireche (Jetysuu). Several centuries after the Arab conquest, Genghis Khan unified the whole of Asia, stretching its frontiers from Mongolia to Eastern Europe and fundamentally altering the political and demographic character of this vast territory. The succeeding rulers of his contiguous Mongolian Empire spread Turkic-speaking dynasties across Central Asia, Iran, the Caspian region and Crimea. A new fusion between the Turco-Mongolian and Persian worlds empowered by Islam and Arab influences emerged triumphant in administration, art and literature. By the fourteenth century, most of inner Asia stretching from western China to the Volga River was ruled by fluid

confederations of Turkic speaking dynasties with vibrant multiethnic
and religious identities. However, Turkic population movements did not
take place in a single cultural domain or a territorial continuity. While
retaining certain common characteristics, the territorial meaning and
belonging was foremost associated with family dynasties and tribal confederations in fluctuating ways. Until the late nineteenth century when
reformers initiated national independence movements, the connection
between land and nation remained vague and contested among tribes
and dynasties.[7]

The Turkic people are classified into three major Turkic language
groupings which only roughly correspond to today's political borders:
the Oguz to the south and west of the Aral Sea, the Qipchaks to the north
and east and the Turki of the settled populations of Central Asia (mainly
the present-day Uzbeks and Uyghurs). The Oguz moved towards Iran
and Anatolia, leaving Central Asia with what in modern times has come
to be known as Turkmens. The second group remained between the
Volga River and the Kazakh steppes, and this language group contains
the Volga Tatars, the Kazakhs, the Kyrgyz, the Karakalpaks and other
tribal confederations. The third group became ethnically Uzbekised.
These major groups were also divided by tribal lines and periodically
contested their territorial rights. The Mogul and Uzbek Emirates fought
to control the heartland and urban centres of Central Asia, while Kyrgyz
and Kazakh tribes sought to control pastoral lands and the steppe.[8] The
influence of Islam has been diverse and was historically most strong
in the Fergana Valley and was far less systematically absorbed by the
nomads.[9] Bukhara, Samarkand, Kokand and Khojand became centres
of learning and science linked to the wider sphere of Islamic civilisa-
tion starting from the eighth century. In the northern steppe, however,
indigenous nomadic and pastoral traditions remained less affected by
the spread of Islam's theology and political power. All these factors of
ethnicity, regionalism, tribalism and life style (especially nomadic versus
urban, agricultural and artisanal heritages) have continuing influence
on the political economy of the region.

By the nineteenth century, tribal and dynastic rivalries succumbed to
a much larger game among the major powers as the territorial expansion
of the Russian and Chinese Empires clashed with British colonial interests. The British Empire extended its control from India to Afghanistan
and Iran while Russians took control of the northern steppes in today's
Kazakhstan and continued to expand their military and economic
control southwards. China extended its grip on Xinjiang. The Russian
Empire won the final bid for most of Central Asia. In 1865 they captured

the city of Tashkent, thus laying the foundations of Russian rule over a Muslim population. Subsequently, the 'Governorate-general of Turkestan' emerged as a Russian administrative unit along with three suzerain khanates (Bukhara, Khiva and Kokand; all in Uzbekistan today).[10] The name 'Turkestan' was erased from the maps and it ceased to exist in Soviet parlance. Due to the fear of nationalist independence movements among indigenous people, the Soviet Union encouraged competition among different ethnic and tribal groups and designated new national borders, assigned national languages and modified ethnic identities for the people of Central Asia. The Turkestan Autonomous Soviet Republic, created in 1918 along with the Khorezm and Bukhara Soviet Republics in 1920, was divided into autonomous Republics; the Uzbek SSR, the Turkmen SSR, the Kyrgyz SSR (first autonomous and in 1936 a Union Republic) and the Kazakh SSR. There is now only a small town, formerly Yesi, in southern Kazakhstan, that bears the name of 'Turkestan'. However, the Uyghurs of Xinjiang still retain their dream of independence for the Eastern Turkestan Republic that they briefly enjoyed during 1930–45.

Central Asia became a new melting pot as well as a dumping ground during the past century. The influx of Russians, Europeans and other Slavic people altered the region's demography and ethnic composition. Initial waves of resettlement aimed to create a long-term power base for Russian imperial administration in the region and later formed the essence of Soviet power consolidation. With the penetration of Tsarist and later Bolshevik order, the region suffered one of its most catastrophic episodes in modern history. The disruption of livestock-herding nomads was devastating for the Kazakhs and Kyrgyz. Uprisings were defeated and tribes destroyed. The biggest blow came during the consolidation of Soviet power with collectivisation. Hundreds of thousands of people perished during the armed uprisings by indigenous people against the Soviet regime in the 1920s. Many fled, creating new Central Asian communities in Mongolia, China and Afghanistan, and stretching as far as to Turkey and the United States.[11] Soviet grain policies and collectivisation of livestock resulted in a great famine in the Kazakh steppe during which one in every four Kazakh perished.[12] The Soviet census shows this devastating decline of population in relative terms between 1926 and 1939 (see Table 1.1). During the Second World War thousands of Central Asians were mobilised to the western front. Almost all outspoken, independent-minded Central Asian intellectuals and nascent entrepreneurs were murdered, sent to labour camps or fled the region.[13] Hundreds of thousands of people were displaced mostly from the Caucasus, Crimea and eastern Siberia and deported

Table 1.1   Population growth in Soviet Central Asia between 1926 and 1959

Central Asians residing in Soviet Union*	1926 census	1939 census	1959 census
Kazakhs	3,968,000	3,099,000	3,581,000
Uzbeks	3,905,000	4,844,000	6,004,000
Tajiks	979,000	1,229,000	1,397,000
Turkmens	764,000	812,000	1,004,000
Kyrgyz	763,000	884,000	974,000
Karakalpaks	146,000	186,000	173,000
Taranchis	53,000	n.a.	n.a.
Uyghurs	56,000	n.a.	95,000
Total Central Asians	**10,634,000**	**11,054,000**	**13,228,000**
Others residing in Central Asia **			
Russians and Ukrainians	2,726,000	n.a.	7,300,000
Tatars	119,000	n.a.	786,000
Germans	61,000	n.a.	791,000
Koreans	n.a.	73,000	213,000
Total others	**2,906,000**	**n.a.**	**9,090,000**

Source: Matley (1994: 106).
n.a.: Not applicable.
(*) These are various branches of Turkic-speaking people and Persian-speaking Tajiks.
(**) Another Turkic diaspora, the Crimean Tatars, dates back to the annexation of the Crimea by Russia in 1783, after which the Crimean Tatars were forced to emigrate in a series of waves between 1783 and 1917. Some others came to Central Asia as part of Russian administration. During the Stalin era, Tatars were once again deported, mostly to Central Asia and Siberia en mass.

to far-flung lands. As a result, Central Asia became home to Chechens, Koreans, Kurds, Meshketian Turks, Tatars, Volga Germans and others who were forcibly relocated and aimlessly scattered across Central Asia during this brutal era. The region also became a refuge for many Soviet intellectuals and others. Labour camp survivors and outcasts, along with many Uyghurs and Muslim Han Chinese, locally known as Dungans, made Central Asia their home.

The scale of demographic engineering that took place in Central Asia under Stalin surpassed other Soviet lands. The Russian Federation appears to be least affected by grand-scale population movements and demographic engineering as the Federation maintained its ethnic homogeneity by accommodating a range of scattered ethnic groups in relatively small numbers. The 1989 census of ethnic groups in the Russian Federation showed that Russians formed 81.5 per cent (almost 120 million) of the total population.[14] By comparison, the scale of change imposed on

Central Asia by the Soviets was massive. The so-called Virgin Lands policy of the Khrushchev era expanded the irrigated land and brought an influx of Slavic people to the northern Kazakh steppe. In 1959, there were 3.5 million Kazakhs, 6 million Uzbeks, 1.4 million Tajiks, about 1 million Turkmens and fewer than 1 million Kyrgyz and others as opposed to over 7 million Russians and Slavs in Central Asia (see Table 1.1). Russians and non-indigenous people formed the majority in urban areas and occupied most of the professional and managerial positions.[15] However, from the 1960s onwards, benefiting from improved sanitation, living conditions and food production, the indigenous ethnic population began growing faster than the Slav and European population. The most significant population growth took place between 1959 and 1970 with annual average growth exceeding 3 per cent while the average growth across the USSR was barely 1.3 per cent and only 0.9 per cent in the Russian Republic. This growth slowed down in the period between 1970 and 1979 to 2.8 per cent on average in Central Asia (except in Kazakhstan with a lower rate of 1.8 per cent) but it was still one of the highest growth rates in the USSR, where the Russian and the Ukrainian Republics grew only 0.6 per cent each.[16]

This change shifted the centre of gravity southwards. The northern regions containing the historical core area of the Soviet states witnessed a significant decline in their share of the USSR population, from 40 per cent in 1959 to 35.9 per cent in 1979.[17] A steady growth of the urban population also occurred across Central Asia throughout the 1970s and 1980s. In the 1960s and 1970s, the number of Russians coming to Central Asia continued to decrease each year, except in Kazakhstan and Kyrgyzstan, where the Russian population remained large. According to the 1979 census, there were 9.5 million Russians in Central Asia.[18]

With the disintegration of the USSR, there has been another wave of emigration to the West and back to Russia, once again changing the ethnic and democratic composition of the newly independent states. Many Russians and Europeans began leaving the region as a result of high unemployment, deteriorating national economies and the fear of nationalist backlash in the 1990s. Between 1989 and 1999 around 1.5 million Russians and 500,000 ethnic Germans left Kazakhstan alone.[19] Their major migration destinations were Russia and Germany. A new pattern of labour migration from China to Central Asia as well as from Uzbekistan and Kyrgyzstan to Russia and Kazakhstan is introducing new demographic dynamics and influencing national economies and regional politics.

Personal and authoritarian states

I characterise Central Asian states as oligarchic and personal in their power legitimisation and management of economic assets. The foundations of these states rest on the shifting sands of weak legitimacy.[20] After almost two decades of privatisation and market transition they are still as resource dependent as they were during the Soviet era. In governance, one-party domination and rule by presidential decree became the norm. Although the region's leaders and political elite have attempted to de-Sovietise the state apparatus from its Moscow-centred orientation, their efforts fell short of a genuine reform agenda. Instead they tried to vitalise the state through a discourse of authentication calling on nationalism and traditionalism. Consequently, without major reform efforts, the Soviet era institutions are now blended with inconsistent legislative and financial reforms leading to severely distorted legal structures.[21]

Conventional economic theory assumes that the state has a monopoly over the use of coercion, and that the state designs and enforces laws with the objective of maximising social welfare. Yet, as Avinash Dixit shows, building a functioning state apparatus is highly costly and difficult to run.[22] Only advanced countries in modern times came close to this ideal definition in which governments supply complete legal institutions and guard them. Economically and politically viable states are far less numerous than failed states. Therefore, taking the state as a historical construct shaped by a set of competing actors and institutions helps us to see Central Asian states from a much more realistic angle.[23] As in many post-colonial states in Africa and Asia, Central Asian states today function without cohesive economic structures and socially and ecologically meaningful boundaries. Such unconsolidated states fail to advocate their citizens' well-being; they tend to limit personal freedoms and are weak on guaranteeing law and order. Post-Soviet states are not unique in their weak legal and institutional capacity but are special due to the peculiarities of their recent historical experience. Rather than similarities in the legacies of colonial states, their distinctive patterns in historical trajectories make broad generalisations difficult. The hybridisation between Soviet state legacies and patrimonial traditions makes Central Asian states uncertain but also seemingly durable authoritarian regimes as opposed to states in flux, such as many in Africa.[24]

The cliché 'Potemkin institutions' was frequently applied to the post-Soviet states. The emptiness of institutions in Central Asia stems from the legacy of the Soviet state structures that bifurcated economic goals and the actual low-level achievements.[25] Similarly, as the discrepancy between daily experiences with state institutions and the corpus of laws grew wider, it led to a state of widespread disbelief and dissemblance. This phenomenon is explained by Timur Kuran in a book about the political and economic consequences of 'preference falsification'. In *Private Truths, Public Lies* Kuran shows how the gap between personal beliefs and public discourse and institutions grew wide in the communist regimes.[26] Upon independence the post-Soviet states found themselves to be in a double bind of weak institutions and enforcement without the Soviet machine to wield power and to arbitrate. The second legacy comes from the imperial and colonial origins of very early state formation in Central Asia which sets the region apart from Eastern Europe and Russia. The state, as a modern administrative body with a supposed rational bureaucratic machine, emerged as a construct that had mostly been shaped by outsiders without a sufficient assertion of national will, cultural identity or indigenous economic interests.

At present there is a competitive arena for economic reallocation. These regimes are not only imbued with amorphous and fluid personal ties, networks of interests and private groups but they also show considerable diversity. Some scholars, such as Kathleen Collins, link this character of the state to the clan-based social structures with informal patronage relations dating back to the Soviet period.[27] Others see the problem of state formation in Central Asia in its colonial origins. They emphasise weak legitimacy as holding back these societies from forming accountable and representative states. In opposition to this view, Russian ethnographers asserted that the political backwardness of Central Asia was due to its own cultural deficiency that led to poor penetration of modernisation in the region.[28] Others argued that the Soviet Union was the first affirmative action empire with a modernising, anti-colonial and anti-imperial self-identification that changed the fate of all nations within its reach.[29]

Although the diversity of authoritarian regimes is a function of multiple historical, structural and agency factors, the economic logic of such regimes plays a critical role in their character of governance. The state-market relationship, social stratification and group interests influence the ways in which personal and authoritarian states function. Thus, in state-market relations the depth and breadth of economic fortunes for different groups within and outside of the state materialise under a competitive regime. State-market relations are more diverse and complex than clan-based dealings even if these are largely fictitious identities.[30] Multiple large clans, subgroups and interest politics compete for new roles and larger shares in the market but these cannot be understood through a clan-based analysis. Surprisingly, studies of state formation in general and post-Soviet transition in particular have rarely dealt with market conditions and the position of privately owned businesses in the economy. Therefore, it is paramount to analyse the state not only in relation to political power but also to ownership and control mechanisms within the economy. We also need another set of explanations and tools in analysing social diversification and its implications for the entrepreneurial class in different stages of state building. Present-day state formation in Central Asia is in its third cycle. Thus, we can see state formation as influenced by three key phases during the past two centuries: colonisation by the imperial Russian administration; incorporation of Soviet peripheral statehood; and accidental independence leading to today's authoritarian states.

Cycles of state building in Central Asia

The first phase of state building was exclusively colonial and it infiltrated existing power bases and expanded through the resettlement of Slavic people, through military occupation, railway construction and telegraph lines. Prior to the advance of territorially contiguous Russian rule to the south, nomadic and steppe people (mostly Kazakhs and Kyrgyz) were ruled by rival khanates. The khans derived their power base from nomadic pastoral groups and clan alliances and gained their legitimacy through the sanctity of lineage. Settled and agrarian people (mostly Uzbeks and Tajiks), in contrast, were ruled by emirs whose powers rested on family dynasties, ritualising traditions and Islamic law. These different polities had different allocation and redistribution mechanisms. The economy of the former was based on animal husbandry, the fur trade and raw materials extraction as tribes exchanged meat, pelts and minerals with sedentary people. Nomadic social formations relied on flexible governance structures with an emphasis on redistribution and sharing rather than accumulation.[31] The settled people formed city economies that afforded accumulation of wealth by rulers, merchants and aristocrats under a rigid societal hierarchy.

The region lacked social differentiation and stratification associated with industrialisation, but it had vibrant city economies along the Silk Road. Some twentieth-century Western travellers provided the view that Central Asian society was long cut off from the rest of the world, ignorant about advances in science, and its cities were in a dismal state.[32] However, despite the gradual decline of east-west trade, the region remained an important conduit between rising Russia and prosperous China and India until around 1900.[33] By the early twentieth century the economic and social status of indigenous traders, merchants and artisan classes were threatened by Russian manufactured goods and direct competition from Russian businessmen operating in the region. The growth of the colonial economy increased cotton cultivation and mining in the region to feed Russian industrial demand while it increasingly undermined the steppe nobility and urban aristocracy.

The spread of the Tsarist Empire brought the first glimpses of modernity that Russians transmitted from Europe. However, education and social changes introduced through Russian schools, hospitals and other institutions were self-serving in nourishing the interests of the empire and in cultivating allegiance from a minority of the indigenous people.[34] While the region retained its cultural autonomy increasingly in isolation, the colonial regime incorporated and consolidated Islam to strengthen the stability of the empire and to solidify loyalty and social discipline among its Muslim subjects. However, an indigenous aspiration for modern nationhood evolved during the nineteenth and twentieth centuries concomitantly, partly in response to Russian advance and partly in conjunction to other modernist movements in the region. Jadidism, an indigenous modernist movement led by the region's intellectuals, emerged as a new method of education and as an intellectual path in Muslim Turkestan.[35] Coming in contact with the modernists of the Ottoman Empire and the Tatar diaspora significantly influenced the indigenous reform movements. With its schools, books and plays, this movement symbolised an indigenous reawakening and national consciousness.[36]

The second phase of state building, again imposed externally by the Soviet Union, fundamentally changed the societal fabric, its power base and the composition of different ethnic groups. Soviet power consolidation increased Russian influence through the expansion of mass education and promotion of Russian culture and a total elimination of the Jadid movement. A Soviet policy of indigenisation and authentication through nationalities policies introduced folkloric symbolism, national languages and borders that aimed fundamentally to differentiate the people of the region. This form of satellite statehood did not rest on an armed struggle, national consensus or a contract-based negotiation; it was designed and forged from an external political and military power. Despite early communist propaganda, Central Asians were not mobilised to bring communism, and their representation in the party organs was marginal until the 1950s. Communism was imposed on them by social engineering that also brought war, famine and political purges.[37] The first act of the Soviet regime during the Lenin and Stalin eras was to eliminate independent minds, nationalists and entrepreneurial spirit across Central Asia as elsewhere in Russia and the Ukraine. Many Central Asians and Jadids were regarded as bourgeoisie class enemies or kulaks and either sent to labour camps or systematically murdered. The armed resistance was finally crushed in the early 1930s.[38] Central Asians' influence in Moscow remained minimal and served only their fragmented regional interests.[39]

The autonomous republics allowed only an insignificant level of interstate mobility and the state elites interacted through the intermediation of Moscow. The region remained rural providing agricultural and mineral resources for industry mostly located in Russia and the Ukraine. Central Asia's industrial establishments were constrained to mining and resource extraction sectors with a growing cotton monoculture. Institutions, including the army, higher education bodies and the party bureaucracy, provided physical and social mobility and constructed the image of Union and Soviet middle stratum identity. In foreign affairs, Central Asian states were occasionally used as showcases to the third world and Islamic countries. For the most part, however, the autonomous republics played almost no role in critical decision making, either in Soviet planning or international affairs. It was not surprising then that the Soviet invasion of Afghanistan, launched from Uzbekistan, was exclusively planned in Moscow and executed mainly by Russian officers.[40]

From 1920 to 1952 major leadership positions in the Communist Party locally were controlled by non-titular groups. Indeed, until the vast majority of the indigenous population submitted to its will and joined the rank and file of the Communist Party, loyal Bolsheviks, mainly from western reaches of the Soviet Union, were trusted to bring order and socialism to the 'uncivilised and ignorant masses'. These often-violent military men who emerged from the chaotic Bolshevik Revolution repeatedly used brutal tactics to eliminate societal resistance.[41] Bishkek (formerly Frunze), Almaty (formerly Verniy) and Tashkent were strategic military garrisons of the colonial past and facilitated the rise of military leaders. Mikhail Frunze, a Russian born in the town of Pishpek and whose name 'Frunze' replaced it, was a military terrorist who captured Khiva and Bukhara and waged war against civilians in the Fergana Valley.[42] In Kazakhstan, the first party secretary, Filipp Goloshchekin (1925–33) was a Ukrainian Jew who was the military commissar of the Urals region and spearheaded the devastating collectivisation policies in Kazakhstan.[43] He was succeeded in that post by an Armenian, Levon Mirzoian (1933–7) who was followed by a Georgian and a Belarusian. Between 1945 and 1954 a Kazakh, Zhumabai Shaiakhmetov, was the first secretary of the Communist Party, paving the way for ethnic Central Asians to take leadership roles. Even so, it took another 16 years for a Kyrgyz to ascend to the position of first secretary.[44]

With the elimination of opposition groups, the belief in the Soviet Union as a benign anti-colonial power took roots at home and abroad. Modernisation and urbanisation combined with demographic trends promoted indigenisation. With rapid population growth among indigenous people, along with some ideological softening of the Communist Party, political decolonisation began in the 1960s accompanied by the economic decentralisation and political regionalisation of the Khrushchev era. Literacy became widespread and public health and food provisions improved. Universal education and health provisions as well as employment and housing nourished a loyal indigenous elite. The role of titular nomenclature and party bosses in economic and social affairs grew steadily during the reign of Leonid Brezhnev, who was General Secretary of the Communist Party from 1964 to 1982. SSR first secretaries, Sharof Rashidov (1959–83) in Uzbekistan, Dinmukhamed Kunaev (1964–86) in Kazakhstan and Turdakun Usubaliev (1961–85) in Kyrgyzstan, enjoyed the favour of Brezhnev. Russians and other Europeans continued to hold deputy positions next to titular appointments. The stability of long tenures fostered consolidation of power for local elites with the party leadership and administration.[45]

This stability and longevity of leadership also deepened patron-client relations between Moscow and the Central Asian republics, leading to further regionalisation and deepening corruption. The critical implication of these developments, however, was that they led to the emergence of state autonomy in local politics and enterprise management. This transformation brought about a significant devolution of power to titular groups and their networks while Communist Party organisations and state enterprises grew increasingly insulated from Moscow.[46]

The third and current cycle of state formation began with the unexpected independence gained when, on 8 December 1991, the presidents of Russia, Ukraine and Belarus signed the Belavezha Accords which declared the dissolution of the Soviet Union and established the Commonwealth of Independent States (CIS).[47] Nine months earlier, on 17 March 1991, in a referendum, Central Asians had voted overwhelmingly in favour of remaining within the Union.[48] The region's political leaders were unsure about how to steer their country to independence and gave confusing signals to their people for a while. As the former Communist Party leaders remained in charge, independence brought about a deep legitimacy problem for the ruling elite. The new independence meant statehood without a binding core ideology, no centre of gravity and being cut off from the power of Moscow. Both Islam Karimov of Uzbekistan and Nursultan Nazarbayev of Kazakhstan who initially advocated that their nation would fare better within the Union, had to appeal to ethnic nationalism and Islam to fill the vacuum left by the Soviet regime. However, the leaders as well as the ruling cadres were cautious not to generate a major disruption in the societal balance through indigenous mass movements. Therefore, their first objective quickly became to avoid regime change as they tried to steer their societies towards continuity and stability under authoritarianism. Decades of social engineering, political purges and economic isolation left the region with weak civic capabilities and almost none of the entrepreneurial stock that was needed for market transition. The leadership that was in place at the time of independence retained its position by default. Their first task was to construct the base for a new legitimacy and later solidify their grip in the economy. Since they lacked any of the prerequisite conditions for state-building such as a well-articulated national identity, historically accepted borders or legitimate local institutions, they embarked on the task of constructing personal states.

Subsequently, the personal state and regime stability both became associated with the ruler, who took responsibility to create an aura of confidence. This is a form of the patrimonialism described by Max Weber. In ascribing the right to rule to the person at the expense of the office, Central Asian states created their own form of neo-patrimonialism where personal loyalty and dependence permeate all political structures.[49] Central Asian neo-patrimonialism assumes an administration based on hierarchical bureaucratic order and an economy structured around oligarchic markets. This turns out to be a remarkably resilient structure because it is able to cater for multiple group interests.

In this Mikado game, three distinctive features modify state structures: fragmented power bases, extra-legal coordinating mechanisms and fluid multiple moralities. The fragmented power bases of Central Asia are characterised by regionalism and clan relations reconfigured by Soviet institutions. In contrast to other weak states in developing countries, Central Asian leaders were better placed to co-opt the functionaries of defunct Soviet institutions.

First, the modern roots of neo-patrimonialism and its association with multiple power centres historically evolved in the political culture since the Khrushchev-era decentralisation policies.[50] Kathleen Collins points out that the complex clan relations in Central Asian society have long shaped state institutions.[51] While weak states in the developing world struggle to eliminate or co-opt local strongman and/or tribal leadership, Central Asian leaders benefited from already muted traditionalism while alternative intellectual bases were long co-opted by the Soviet system.[52] Thus, they had every incentive not to overhaul the already consolidated state apparatus. These consolidations were amenable to the extra-legal coordinating mechanisms that worked through self-governing syndicates and provided the coercive powers necessary to serve the leadership cadres. Although in some instances military and police powers are used in a manner typical of authoritarian regimes, powerful groups more often further their interests through solidarity networks utilising techniques of cooption, extortion and violent coercion, as we shall see in some case studies.

Secondly, new state formation proceeded based on power structures built into the state and society but not secured through military strength.[53] The political culture and leadership cadres stemmed from Soviet bureaucratic elites. The political leadership and their market extensions allowed the modification of Soviet political cultures and reproduced Soviet behavioural norms and regional structures in arbitrating competing interests and group advancement strategies. This evolved in a competitive arena with major swings of tension between solidarity and conflict. However, with the exception of Uzbekistan, these states have weak internal security systems and almost no military power. As I will explore in later parts of this book, these three Central Asian countries diverge in their procedures to construct personal authoritarian state structures. These divergences defined their market outcomes despite having inherited similar political institutions from the Soviet Union.

Finally, the ideals of 'Soviet man' have been displaced by fluid multiple moralities. The resultant slippery moral compass points alternatively towards ethnic nationalism, pious Islam, capitalist individualism or Soviet nostalgia. However, this ideological dislocation has no mission, or spiritual depth. Neither Islam nor ethnic nationalism, nor democratisation defines the mission of the state and its ruling elite. The Communist Party ideology that was paramount for justifying cadre positions had long ceased to hold moral sway and so the dislocation caused by the collapse of the Soviet regime decoupled personal ethics from state legitimacy.

In practice, it is the marketplace which has taken over the function of the state. The emergent personal state then provides some new freedoms and opportunities for self-advancement through accumulation. There are many new norms of these oligarchic markets. Competition among groups is dynamic and leads to occasional dissolution and regrouping. However, these new norms fall short of a rule-based system wherein the state protects its citizens and provides fair access to justice. This soul-lessness of Central Asian states and their elite today has resonances with Abay lament.[54]

Resource-dependent economies

Kazakhstan, Kyrgyzstan and Uzbekistan all inherited resource-driven economies from the USSR. Although industrial assets in mining, arma-ments and mechanical engineering were built during the Soviet era, they were functionally dependent on far-flung regions and rapidly obsolete. The command economy reallocated and managed resources and input and output quotas centrally. Interregional divisions imposed by Moscow promoted Central Asia as a source of raw materials while placing it in a dependent position upon Russia and the western SSRs for many essential goods, subsidies and international security. The lack of interconnected networks further disadvantaged Central Asia while obscuring deep regional asymmetries. Isolated industrial complexes, commonly known as 'kombinats', determined the labour market and controlled the economies of many industrial and mining towns, further deepening the economic isolation.

One of the major limitations of this landlocked region has been its dependence on international transit routes. Their geographic isolation has aggravated economic integration and market penetration. Expanding energy resources based primarily on oil and gas are difficult to export without using Russian infrastructure. The political and economic closure of Iran makes it difficult to reach the Persian Gulf while the Caspian Sea creates another geographical barrier to the west. The legacy of Soviet borders fosters natural resource conflicts and further limits economic growth potential.

Following the first flush of liberalisation in the early 1990s, economic divergence was accentuated among the CIS countries.[55] The differences can be seen not only in the extreme variation in population and area but also in divergent economic indicators (see Table 1.2). The dominance of Russia in territory, politics, and economics is rather obvious. However, the trend of private sector growth indicates that greater expansion has been occurring in Kazakhstan, Kyrgyzstan and the Ukraine while

Table 1.2 Demographic, economic and market transition indictors of selected post-Soviet countries in 2006

Country	Population (in millions)	Area ('000 sqm)	GDP (in billion US, 2006)	GDP per capita in 2006	Private sector share in employment	Share of industry in GDP (%) in 2006	Private sector share in GDP (%) in 2006	EBRD index of enterprise reform
Kazakhstan	15.4	2,728.0	80.4	5,221.5	77.0	23.4	65.0	2.0
Kyrgyz Republic	5.1	200.0	2.8	549.0	81.2*	17.6	75.0	2.0
Russia	142.2	17,075.0	977	3,834.7	n.a.	24.6*	55.0	2.3
Tajikistan	6.6	143.1	2.8	426.5	51.9	28.0	55.0	1.7
Turkmenistan	6.5	488.0	10.2	1,564.2	n.a.	n.a.	25.0	1.0
Ukraine	47.1	603.7	106.4	2,258.6	n.a.	25.6*	65.0	2.0
Uzbekistan	26.0	448.9	17.0	655.0	n.a.	22.1	45.0	1.7

Source: Adapted from European Bank for Reconstruction and Development (EBRD), *Transition Report 2007*. The EBRD index of enterprise reform shows the scale of low achievers such as Turkmenistan (1.7) in relation to better reformers such as Kazakhstan (2.0) and Russia (2.3).
n.a.: Not applicable.
(*) Available data in 2005.

private sector growth has stagnated in Tajikistan, Turkmenistan and Uzbekistan, and even in Russia.

Kazakhstan is territorially the largest and economically most advanced country in the region after Russia. Kazakhstan managed to achieve a degree of macroeconomic stability from the late 1990s and retained much of its industrial strength. Kazakh's per capita income grew fourfold in recent years (from 1,491 USD in 2001 to 5,221 USD in 2006), faster than Russia, which only doubled its GDP per capita during the same period. The Kyrgyz Republic, in contrast, is small and resource poor. It fares better than its civil war-torn neighbour of similar size, Tajikistan, and has been a forerunner of economic reforms. Yet, its GDP per capita growth has been dismal, from 309 USD in 2001 to only 549 USD in 2006. Like Russia, Uzbekistan has only doubled its GDP per capita, and private sector growth trailed behind its neighbours', bar Turkmenistan. The European Bank for Reconstruction and Development (EBRD) data show that the private sector share of GDP remained at the same level since 2001 at 45 per cent. With high tariffs and import substitution policies, the Uzbek government has diverted resources to an uncompetitive and obsolete industrial sector.[56]

The national economies and their labour markets have been affected by the unprecedented mobility of people across the CIS since the dissolution of the USSR. The increasing seasonal migration has affected local and national economies as Russia emerged as a new source of jobs and income for all CIS jobseekers. Russian capital outflow through remittances to the CIS increased by a factor of ten between 2001 and 2006; from 836 million USD to 8,868 million USD.[57] Russia received almost half of the CIS migration despite overt discrimination against Central Asians while being the source of half of the outgoing migration. The number of both emigrants and immigrants exceeded 11 million. Although there are many complex issues in relation to source and definition of this population movement, these data provide some clues about mobility. Kazakhstan received almost 4 million people, a quarter of its total population and as such is a major migrant receiving country along with Russia and the Ukraine. Kazakhstan is attractive to Kyrgyz and Uzbeks because of the ease they have with regards to geography, culture and language.

The Kazakh economy

Soviet collectivisation left a big scar on Kazakh culture and society, which had long suffered from Russian territorial expansion.[58] As seen in

Table 1.1, the Kazakh population declined by almost a million from 1926 to 1939; the total loss is greatly under-counted in that census data. Stalin-era collectivisation began to dismantle clan structure by classifying owners of herds and employers of labour as 'kulaks' and then continued to prosecute owners of ever-smaller assets. According to the memoir of Mukhamed Shayakhmetov, around 5 per cent of the population was small property owners (kulaks), but the regime stretched its punishment to more than 15 per cent of the population and sent thousands to labour camps.[59] The bigger disaster was the subsequent great famine, during which between 1.5 and 2 million people, one in every three or four Kazakhs, died of hunger. This was similar in scale to the catastrophic suffering of the Ukrainians during the same period.

Kazakhstan is a world leader in minerals and mining, having about one-third of world's chromium and manganese deposits as well as substantial reserves of tungsten, lead, zinc, copper, bauxite, silver and phosphorus. The major iron mines are located in the north of the country. Large coal reserves are found in central and northern parts. Ispat-Karmet, a subsidiary of Netherlands-based Mittal Steel, is the largest steel producer and is located in the northern town Karaganda. Kazakhmys was formerly owned by Samsung and is now a UK-registered copper mine business in Dzhezkazgan province.[60] Increased oil prices generated massive earnings, fuelled foreign direct investment (FDI) and in 2007 it accounted for almost one-third of GDP and half of exports.[61] Kazakhstan attracted about ten per cent of FDI into the former communist bloc and over 80 per cent of all FDI into Central Asia.[62] With new pipelines reaching eastwards into China and westwards into Russia and the Mediterranean, Kazakhstan is increasingly playing a crucial role in Eurasian energy supply.[63]

Starting from 1999, Kazakhstan's economic outlook improved significantly; the pattern of steady growth between 2000 and 2006 averaged above 9 per cent of GDP and replaced the negative growth rates of the early 1990s. After securing his third presidential term in 2005, Nursultan Nazarbayev increased the influence of state leadership in economic development and industrial policy by announcing a few key measures. The government set up the Kazyna Joint Stock Company and the Kazyna Fund for Sustained Development in order to coordinate development initiatives and enhance the governance of key institutions.[64] With an agenda of corporate modernisation and reform, the Samruk Holding Company was set up in 2006 to preside over several large state companies including the state-owned oil company, KazMunaiGas. This reform process is intended to move the resource-dependent country into a more diverse and self-confident economy. In consequence, it reduced the country's dependence on Russia for the first time since the nineteenth century.

With its wide range of extractive industries and growing oil fields, environmental issues, work safety and pollution are becoming widespread problems.[65] One such concern is the shrinkage of the Aral Sea, once the world's fourth largest lake, now 30 per cent of its former surface area. Along with toxic waste, nuclear remains and air pollution, Kazakhstan as well as Uzbekistan face severe public health and economic burdens.[66]

The Kyrgyz economy

The Kyrgyz Republic is the smallest Central Asian state with 5.1 million inhabitants and second smallest in its land area after Tajikistan. It is surrounded by Kazakhstan, Tajikistan, Uzbekistan and China. The titular group, the Kyrgyz, constituted less than half of the country's population until the 1980s and only recently became the dominant ethnic group because of the out-migration of Slavs and Europeans. The country still has a large ethnic mix consisting of 69.5 per cent Kyrgyz, 14 per cent Uzbek, 9 per cent Russian, 1.9 per cent Tatars, 1.1 per cent Uyghurs, 1.1 per cent Tajiks, 0.7 per cent Kazakhs and others. Overall, perhaps around 100 different ethnic groups can be found, including Azeris, Armenians, Germans, Meshkhetian Turks, Koreans and Ukrainians. The terrain of Kyrgyzstan is dominated by the Tian Shan and the Pamir mountain ranges, which together occupy over 80 per cent of the national territory.

The republic is divided into seven oblasts (provinces) and two additional administrative regions (Bishkek and Osh). These are Batken, Chuy, Jalalabad, Naryn, Osh, Talas and Issyk-Kul. A regional division between north and south that is marked by economic, cultural and tribal characteristic remains fragile. During the Soviet era, Bishkek and the region of Issyk-Kul, the world's second largest alpine lake (at 1,608-metre high), in the north were mostly dominated by ethnic Kyrgyz and Russians. This region had some Soviet industries and tourism investments and had considerable political influence. The less developed southern regions remained more agrarian and its population is more dominated by Kyrgyz and Uzbeks. After independence, tribal divisions deepened and the economic resources were contested between north and south as well as among the local clans. This tension has been further exacerbated by the large Uzbek minority in the south, concentrated around the city of Osh where ethnic Uzbeks inhabit the eastern edge of the Fergana Valley.

Kyrgyzstan has made significant macroeconomic progress since the comprehensive and rapid reform movement was initiated in 1993. It joined the World Trade Organisation (WTO) in December 1998. Since 1996 the economy has begun to recover with up-and-down swings in its expansion of GDP, and its growth remained positive even during the regional financial crisis of 1998. Kyrgyzstan was the first Central Asian country which had a peaceful leadership change when a popular uprising forced President Askar Akayev from office in 2005. This event, popularly known as the Tulip Revolution, seemed akin to similar events in Georgia and the Ukraine. However, it proved to be less a revolution then a popular putsch. An alliance of mostly southern-based groups under the leadership of Kurmanbek Bakiyev and Felix Kulov formed the new government. President Bakiyev and Prime Minister Kulov later had major disagreements and Kulov resigned from the government. There were more demonstrations in 2006 against Bakiyev indicating further turbulence within the opposition.

In addition to having substantial gold deposits, the Kyrgyz Republic is rich with some rare minerals, such as tungsten and molybdenum. The government has tried to revive its uranium-processing capacity which once was part of the Soviet Union's nuclear industry and included a large complex at Kara-Balta (near Bishkek) for mining and to mill both local and Kazakh uranium. Another uranium mining complex was developed at Maili-Suu in the south in the 1960s. Since 1992, the Canadian-run Kumtor gold mine has provided a significant share of GDP but an accident in these mines and subsequent poor industrial production negatively affected industrial growth and demonstrated the vulnerability of a resource-driven economy.

While living standards have recently been improving in Bishkek and Osh, unemployment and rural poverty is rampant in many oblasts, aggravated by poor public services. The provision of health and education has severely deteriorated since independence and according to a recent report by the Asian Development Bank (ADB) 40 per cent of the total population is living below the national poverty line.[67] The Economist Intelligence Unit (EIU) estimated that real unemployment was around 14 per cent in 2006.[68] There is a large unregistered economy which many believe to be around 50–70 per cent of total economic activity. Growing unemployment and deteriorating local economies have resulted in an upsurge of labour migration while periodic labour shortages in Russia and Kazakhstan provided pull factors.

A World Bank report on migration and remittances shows the dependence on remittance earnings in national economies. According to that study, migrant workers' remittances provided 27.4 per cent of the GDP in Kyrgyzstan in 2006 with a flow of 739 million USD. This reflected an almost quadrupling of remittances for Kyrgyzstan from 189 million USD only two years earlier which then constituted just over 8.5 per cent of GDP. The other two small CIS states, Tajikistan (36.2 per cent) and Moldova (36.2 per cent), have the highest dependence in the world followed by Tonga and Kyrgyzstan.[69]

In addition to maintaining one of the strategic US airbases near Bishkek, the Kyrgyz governments have in recent years begun appeasing Chinese and Russian interests in the region. Russia is renewing its strategic ties with Kyrgyzstan as with some other post-Soviet states. During the Soviet period, the Navy operated an extensive facility at the eastern end of Issyk-Kul where submarine and torpedo technology was tested. A recent agreement provides for a renewed base for the Russian defence industry. It is reported that Russia will receive 3.5 square miles of territory for a naval centre, located in the Jeti-Oguz district on the northeastern shore of Issyk-Kul for an indefinite period. The region also has high radioactivity that most assume is due to military testing activities during the Soviet era.

There are growing numbers of Kazakh investments in banking, tourism and services while Russia's influence in the economy has also been growing.[70] There has been continuing disagreement between Uzbekistan and Kyrgyzstan leading to gas shortages and price increases. Russia's corporate expansion through its state-controlled firms has emerged as a new broker in recent years. Gazprom Neft Asia, an oil products and liquefied gas subsidiary of Russia's Gazprom Neft, is based in Bishkek and has began operating regionally.

Kyrgyzstan's open-door policy has allowed the country to become a more liberal society and an emerging hub of regional trade. A number of huge wholesale and retail markets, the Dordoi, Karasuu and Osh bazaars, provide jobs and income to local economies while hundreds of wholesalers and retailers from Russia, Uzbekistan, Tajikistan and Kazakhstan travel to these centres. Goods mainly from China, Russia and Turkey and to a lesser extent from Kazakhstan and Uzbekistan are brought to and traded in Kyrgyzstan. Growing tourism in particular provides new business opportunities. Almost a million tourists, mostly from Kazakhstan and Russia, visited the Issyk-Kul resorts in 2006, the highest figure since 1991.

The Uzbek economy

Most of Uzbekistan is sandwiched between Kazakhstan in the north and Turkmenistan in the south and it has borders with Kyrgyzstan and Tajikistan, and a short boundary with Afghanistan in the south that constitutes an ancient north-south trading route. With its population of 26 million spanning the renowned cultural and historic heartland of Asia, Uzbekistan was expected to play an important role in the region. Throughout the early 1990s, there was hope that the country would provide a new model of economic growth, political stability and regional leadership. However, the past decade and a half proved otherwise. Democratic and economic reforms seem halted and the authoritarian tendencies of the former communist leadership further expanded. Uzbekistan's average GDP per capita is 655 USD and there are pockets of deep poverty and isolation. With its poor industrial base and slow private sector growth, the Uzbek economy is heavily dependent on agriculture, natural resources and, increasingly, worker's remittances.[71]

Less than 10 per cent of Uzbek territory is intensively cultivated with irrigated land. In the east, the Fergana Valley is the most populous fertile agricultural region while a vast desert, the Kyzyl Kum, covers most of western Uzbekistan creating a massive economic and geographical barrier in the country between the fertile eastern lands and the arid western regions. Uzbekistan is divided into 12 provinces (*viloyat*): Andijan, Bukhara, Fergana, Jizzak, Namangan, Navoiy, Kashkadarya, Samarkand, Sirdarya, Surhandarya, Tashkent and Khorazm; and one autonomous republic, Karakalpakistan; and the independent city of Tashkent. There are about 60 different ethnic groups in Uzbekistan. However, compared to its neighbours, the country has a large titular population ratio as ethnic Uzbeks comprise roughly three quarters of the population and entirely dominate rural areas. Although the national statistics are not reliable, the largest ethnic group after Uzbeks are Tajiks (thought to be around 15 per cent) and a declining Russian population (believed to be less than 5 per cent), Kazakhs (3 per cent), with Tatars (2 per cent) and dozens of other smaller ethnic groups.

Uzbekistan initially looked less affected then its neighbours by the dissolution of the USSR and showed a degree of resilience with better economic performance up until 1995. While Kazakhstan and Kyrgyzstan were suffering from the ills of Soviet economic dissolution, Uzbekistan looked relatively prosperous and insulated throughout the early 1990s. Its apparent choice to maintain a slow pace of reform stood in contrast to the rapid big bang policies which at a time were followed by many transition economies including Russia and Kyrgyzstan. However, over the years the country lost its regional advantage and became a laggard and insular economy. Its import substitution policies, continuing state domination over the economy and the skewed financing of its inefficient agricultural sector soon showed the weaknesses of the supposed Uzbek model of developmentalism.[72]

According to the World Bank, agriculture generated one-third of GDP in 2003, mostly from cotton. The London-based Environmental Justice Foundation claims that only 10–15 per cent of the income generated by the sale of cotton goes back into agriculture.[73] In 2005, with revenue of 1 billion USD, cotton exports constituted 60 per cent of Uzbekistan's hard currency export earnings, making the country the world's second largest exporter of cotton.[74] According to UN data, as much as 60 per cent of the population relies on cotton for their income.[75] Only about 30 per cent of the total output of cotton fibre is processed locally into textiles (up from only 13 per cent in 1996). The conditions for cotton production and farming in general face massive problems. Large areas are negatively affected by high levels of salinity and rising water tables. Salinisation affects 63 per cent of irrigated land and leads to crop yield losses exceeding 30 per cent. The outdated and poorly managed and maintained irrigation canal system, mostly built in the 1970s, is the main source of salinisation along with poor farming technologies and know-how. To overcome this, 20–25 per cent of annual available water is used for leaching, causing further reduction of water flow to the Aral Sea.[76]

Throughout the Soviet period, cotton was used to appease Moscow and to advance local clan interests. This abuse got out of proportions under President Sharof Rashidov during the Brezhnev era. The Uzbek leadership exaggerated figures of cotton yield to transfer substantial amounts of Soviet funds into Uzbekistan for their personal interests. Moscow considered Rashidov as a loyal communist and he gained the support of the party leadership and regional elites by allowing them to exploit resources within their jurisdiction.[77] In one of the biggest frauds uncovered during the final years of the USSR, not only the Uzbek leadership but also Brezhnev's son-in-law, Yuri Churbanov, was implicated in a scandal of embezzled receipts from cotton exports.

Gold is another major source of income. It was the second largest export earner after cotton, at around 13 per cent of the total export revenue in 2006.[78] The country's main gold mine, at Muruntau in Navoi province, is operated by a Soviet-built complex still owned by the state.[79] Heavy dependency on fluctuating commodity prices introduces considerable economic risks. However, Uzbekistan is also self-sufficient in oil and natural gas. Oil production increased from 2.8 million tonnes in the early 1990s to a peak of 8.1 million tonnes in 1999, but since then the depletion of oil fields has resulted in a fall in annual output, down to 5.4 million tonnes in 2005.[80] FDI has been very low and many foreign joint venture and business deals are subject to the ruling family's opportunistic interests and erratic political behaviour. One major investor, the American Newmont Mining Corporation, had been working in gold mining until it was forced into bankruptcy in 2006.[81] Another joint venture, UzDaewoo Auto, with Daewoo of South Korea, began car production 1996; but when Daewoo went bankrupt in 2000, the government bought the company and monopolised the domestic market with high tariffs and little competition.

According to a recent report by the Asian Development Bank, 26 per cent of the total population was living below the national poverty line in 2003.[82] However, the large population of the country indicates a much larger problem of poverty than its neighbours in absolute numbers. Up to 3 million Uzbek citizens reportedly leave the country every year to work in seasonal jobs, mostly in Russia and Kazakhstan. Labour migration helps ease the pressure generated by severe unemployment inside Uzbekistan, a condition that many officials see as perhaps the most serious threat to internal security.

In order to maintain its political leverage at home, the Karimov regime made a fundamental shift away from the West in order to deepen ties with Russia and to a lesser extend with China. Increasing economic and, in particular, energy ties with Russia and China through new oil and gas deals also provided a renewed leverage to Moscow and Beijing in the region.[83]

In 2007 Uzbekistan announced an extensive privatisation of more than 1,400 enterprises in most sectors over the following four years. However, the state will retain major control of strategic economic sectors such as telecommunications, media, energy, oil, gas and mining. A partial privatisation, between 25 and 50 per cent, of banking, textile and automotive sectors was recently planned. Full privatisation is only envisaged in tourism, light industries and for small businesses. Agro-processing industries, including cotton processing, Uzbek Airlines and UzMetkombinat (the only steel producer in the country) are all excluded from this privatisation programme.

It is against this background of political and economic history that the region's markets and entrepreneurs are emerging. In the following chapters, I will address in what way this change is taking place and how the post-Soviet dynamics and its corresponding economic, moral and social characteristics shift Central Asia towards a new regime.

2
Market Building and Social Stratification

> During the Soviet era we were a tiny gadget of a massive machine.
> The Soviets were like a big computer that knew everything and exploited our resources.
> We should now develop our own capitalists but these people should not only think about themselves, they must be patriotic, too.
>
> *From a discussion with a group of businessmen*
> *and civil servants, Astana, Kazakhstan*

Introduction

A new entrepreneurial class emerged as a consequence of capitalist market building and political patronage across the whole of post-Soviet Central Asia. This class rested on access obtained and opportunities generated by the political elite. Overall the relationship between this emerging entrepreneurial class and the political elite defines the character of the regime and the nature of market development in this region. Entrepreneurs provide social stability that balances powerful elites and impoverished masses. At the same time, they are obliged to negotiate their positions using propriety rights under the hegemony of the ruling elites. The behaviour of these elites during regime change has been commonly addressed by scholars in connection to state formation and political institutions but their relationship with social differentiation and the emerging entrepreneurial class has been overlooked. Similarly, very little attention has been paid to the dissolution of Soviet-era social and professional structures and the emergence of new property owners.

Today, a highly heterogeneous group of business owners, along with marginal salaried public service employees, form the emerging middle class. The economic entrepreneurship and leadership exercised by the ruling elites and their associates provides selective incentives for enterprise development and the growth of entrepreneurial classes. Social differentiation breeds opportunistic capitalists and these men and women increasingly feel free from moral and ideological inhibitions. They operate within an institutional setting characterised by corruption and the weak rule of law. The quote above, yearning for a new patriotic capitalist class, echoes a feeling that I often came across in Central Asia. Most people in the region realise that they are facing a historic turning point and see that nourishing an indigenous capitalist class is imperative for their society's future well-being. However, these feelings are also mixed with a deep concern about the economic exploitation by zealous profit-seeking and self-serving entrepreneurs and oligarchs, especially because everyday experience is riddled with uncertainty and corruption. The absence of fair allocation regimes and opportunity structures undermines public trust in governments, businesses and institutions. Even many opportunist entrepreneurs would ague that capitalism should be moderated with a sense of patriotism and social responsibility.

In this chapter I introduce my main arguments about post-Soviet social stratification and the status of new entrepreneurs in a competitive reallocation regime. Modern scholarship on social stratification and class formation has rested on two schools of thought: Weberian and Marxist. Yet these have limited applicability to this region due to the fluidity of class identity and ambiguous implications of social status, class saturation and enclosure. The concept of status defined by Max Weber is a dimension of stratification and is a function of market dynamics. Where class is a mere economic situation, status becomes a function of society.[1] Distributional and relational theories form the broad frameworks in which social differentiation have been analysed within societal categories. The former divides people into groups based on divisions such as education, income and profession. The latter regards classes as part of social formations based on mutual interdependence. The emphasis on distributional attributes in scholarship obscured the relational and dynamic elements of social stratification in sociological class analysis. This, along with a general lack of interest, contributed to the decline of class analysis in contemporary sociology.

However, it is precisely these relational and dynamic elements that help us explain the social changes we see in Central Asia. In his pioneering work, Anthony Giddens suggested that a theory of class must show the influence of the institutional order upon the formation of collectivities.[2] His theory of structuration connects class, as an institutional form, with an account of how class relations are expressed through group formation and consciousness. Differing layers of relations of autonomy and dependence can be observed without assuming an immediate move from a part to the whole of society. Hence, any conception of class needs to explain both mobility and its constraints.[3]

Individual and collective differentiation, which is an essential part of our societies, is shaped by multiple factors, most notably in relation to property ownership, political influence and power. Other factors include cultural, racial and ideological assumptions about social status and identity. Social stratification in economic terms emerges from competition for limited resources and assets (for example, natural, economic, bureaucratic, etc.) as well as uneven access to power, status and opportunities. This uneven access leads to varying social endowments through which individuals and groups take positions and learn to identify themselves with certain collectivities. It is this economic aspect of social differentiation and its corresponding political power that I will primarily be addressing here.

We will consider the implications of social stratification and markets during the Soviet-era and thereafter. The literature of market transition portrays this as a flawed effort to emulate Western capitalism. I will show, on the contrary, that market building redefines political and economic power, and the emergence of an entrepreneurial middle stratum should rather be seen as a unique attempt to navigate among changing social structures. We conclude this chapter with a description of the role of elites in markets and a sketch of post-Soviet stratification. We will see how social stratification has created five groups based on the reallocation of opportunities: the ruling families, oligarchs and courtiers, protégés and apparatchiks, the middle class and the underprivileged. These groups are engaged in a dynamic reallocation regime, our Mikado game.

Social stratification in the USSR

The concept of totalitarian dictatorship became an early prevailing explanation for the communist political system. This simplistically depicted the USSR merely as a state with an official ideology and a single party controlling the military and communication, and with a terrorising police force. Later, in an era of rapid industrialisation, Western scholars sought similarities in class stratification between the USSR and the United States. Full speed industrialisation brought similar social outcomes on both camps in the 1960s. The division between mass labour and managerial groups seemed to look alike. The growth of salaried industrial workers in both camps indicated a converging social trend under mass production and industrialisation through scale and scope economies. Managers in capitalist countries had their counterparts in the communist world, too, and both served the interests of bosses.[4] Thus, it appeared that mass production would lead to similar class systems in socialist and capitalist economies alike.[5] Further research on social differentiation pointed out the rise of white-collar positions under rapid industrialisation. Socialist regimes sought deliberately to depress the social and economic position of the white-collar stratum while coming increasingly to rely on the type of expertise and knowledge they possessed. The emphasis on economic rationality and the allocation of men to elite positions on the basis of meritocratic criteria led to the erosion of traditional socialist ideology and paved the way to a form of class stratification that was much more in common with Western capitalism.[6]

Milovan Djilas, the widely cited Yugoslav intellectual, sparked an unexpected self-criticism among Marxists by describing class conflicts in communist regimes. Djilas formulated his 'new class theory' on the basis of antagonism between the working class and the communist bureaucracy.[7] The fundamental character of the communist regimes rested on party control within which political power became a form of property itself; so, political power could be exchanged and used to control productive resources. Indeed, the propriety character of political control in communist regimes continued to play a critical role in influencing the direction of transition to capitalist markets.

However, with social stratification new interest groups mediated between working classes and the communist party bureaucracy. Forming a middle ground, white-collar positions facilitated dynamic interaction and mobility between the top and bottom layers.[8] Party apparatchiks, the security police, industrial managers, economists, writers and jurists were among the most prominent of these.[9] Various organisations in addition to the Communist Party gained influence in co-opting social groups into power politics; including trade unions, youth leagues, women's committees, unions of writers and journalists. Nevertheless, the influence of modernisation, urbanisation and the mass elite assertion changed the configuration and articulation of group identities and motivations.[10] Some interest groups grew powerful in voicing dissent and opposition and gaining the support of the workers (these eventually confronted the communist regimes in Eastern Europe) while others remained marginal and fractured (such as the ones in most CIS countries). In Central Asia, deepening patronage relations between local and national groups effectively co-opted organised interests in party politics and undercut their political leverage over the masses and threatened their legitimacy.[11]

Soviet society was transformed through three phases of social stratification that came to characterise the Stalin, Khrushchev and Brezhnev eras. The first was societal levelling that came about during the early years through the elimination of formerly powerful economic and political groups such as the landed aristocracy, artisans and the bourgeoisie. Apparatchiks, recruited from lower social classes, were rewarded for their coercive actions which consolidated the new party powers. Social alliances between party cadres and new beneficiaries effectively resisted opposition by other groups. Thus, the Stalin-era purges fundamentally altered social stratification by suppressing those who remained from the upper levels of the pre-socialist establishment. Secondly, during Khrushchev's thaw, the Party expanded its political base among peasants and labourers. This new party base was rewarded through the upward mobility of their children in education and party positions. Flexing the muscles of state coercion helped to widen the new occupational opportunities, along with improvements in social provisions. Finally, throughout the Brezhnev era, a gradual bifurcation occurred between the party and administrative cadres; upward mobility slowed down and productivity growth was slashed. Well-positioned bureaucratic and managerial elites created a dual power base upon the Soviet state and the market. This duality perpetuated institutional malaise as cadres began to stagnate and that later led to a deepening clash between the two dominant groups.[12]

This simplified trajectory points out that revolutionary changes and turmoil under Stalin were followed by, first, an opening in cadre positions and rapid mobility and, then, a deepening enclosure. With intensified efforts to industrialise, socialist stratification was strained because of the need for more qualified personnel. While the system increasingly relied on the type of expertise and knowledge of white-collar professionals, party language deliberately diminished their critical social and economic position vis-à-vis workers. The emergent emphasis on economic rationality and the allocation of men to elite positions on the basis of meritocratic criteria led to the further erosion of traditional socialist ideology and paved the way to a form of class stratification in favour of upper party cadres and professionals. Economic and industrial reforms in Eastern

Europe, and to a lesser extent in the USSR, granted industrial enterprises more local autonomy and flexibility in measuring profitability. As a result, wage differentials between individual factories increased and the gap between qualified and unqualified workers grew.[13] Thus, the need for a more rational and efficient organisation of industry in socialist societies shifted the balance of material and social advantages steadily away from the low-skilled working class towards professional middle classes. The Communist Party structures were affected by this transformation as the representative power of peasants and workers began to weaken.[14]

A slowing down of vertical mobility in the Soviet Union was already noted in the 1960s. Professionals came from white-collar and party-linked families and their children were on the same trajectory; cadre children benefited from early closure.[15] Lenin observed that 'classes are groups [that exist] such that some can appropriate the labour of others' and indeed Soviet white-collar workers and professionals controlled the resources and substituted labour for capital and technology.[16] Marxist sociology diminished the significance of this differentiation in earning and status and argued that this was a result of functional division.[17] The availability of middle-class positions allowed a degree of upward mobility for minority children of working-class background. This expansion, however, almost came to halt in the 1970s despite rising urbanisation and an increasing number of higher education graduates. Slow productivity growth across the USSR resulted in stiffer competition for resources and outputs leading to rising intra and interregional tensions, diminishing upward mobility and decreasing living standards. This situation also had an ethnic character as indigenous Central Asians had to share economic and political fortunes with increasing numbers of Slavs and Europeans. Therefore, ethnic heterogeneity further limited class mobility for titular groups in the autonomous republics, especially in urban areas.[18] Instead, Central Asia's titular groups broadened their participation into party politics and, along with deepening patronage relations, they created stable recruitment regimes through regional and tribal alliances.[19]

In sum, behind the façade of monolithic party and regime stability, the USSR experienced continuous struggle among rival social classes and factions. The conflicts in the USSR were not merely personal struggles as was commonly depicted. They did occur as centre versus periphery disputes and among apparatchiks and bureaucrats, as well as between the members of the intelligentsia. These struggles were a deeper and more profound expression of interest politics that rested on allocation conflicts among social groups, enterprises, regions and republics. Theoretically, this allocation was done by planners and technocrats according to a Soviet economic rationale. In practice, however, different groups followed their self-serving aims in bending the rules and diverting resources to themselves in a way that led to common patterns of falsification.[20] The social and material privileges of the middle classes rested almost wholly upon two advancement paths: first educational and occupational achievements and second political party positions and patronage. Thus, rather than having inherited property, individuals increased their share through collective bargaining. In later decades interest politics took on increasingly ethnic and national character as well.[21]

Consequently, institutional continuity and regime stability were met through favouring cadre maintenance and reproduction leading to a form of class enclosure.[22] This form of group consolidation in politics and economy often generates insular regimes with small middle classes and limited upper-level social mobility. While the economic malfunctioning, slowing productivity and shortages deepened social discontent, the reform agenda of the 1980s failed to ameliorate the situation. It rather deepened continuing class conflict for better occupational positioning and higher returns. Four popular explanations of the collapse of the USSR dominate: economic crisis, loss of political legitimacy, nationalist disintegration and elite defection. However, we can see that the secession of reproductive social mobility and the power loss through the bifurcation of the dominant classes led to the collapse of the regime.[23] The two dominant classes, namely the party bureaucracy and administrative cadres, experienced an extreme loss of power during the reform stages of the Gorbachov era. Thus, their ability to restore the regime was weakened in comparison to the emerging capitalist classes and the masses. This, coupled with a deepening crisis of their political legitimacy, led to their loss of authority and credibility.

Market transition and social change

The post-Soviet societal shift towards property ownership and wealth accumulation has received scanty attention in transition theory. Although the term 'transition' was used in different contexts prior to the collapse of communist regimes for developing countries and authoritarian regimes alike, it came into common parlance associated with the fate of the post-communist states during the past two decades and has become a dominant discourse.[24] The value of these theories was weakened by the simple assumption that democracy and capitalism would eventually emerge through a transition stage.[25] Overall its neoclassical economic assumptions and linear logic contained a teleological perspective. After twenty years of efforts to apply transition theories to economic policy, it is evident that any progression from market inhibiting structures to a well-functioning capitalist system is much more difficult then was initially expected. However, earlier studies by economists analysing Chinese economic reforms and other market transitions revealed important dynamics between expanding market opportunities and social change. They better took into account local factors, stratification dynamics and the effects of deepening control by the ruling elites. These studies should have been more influential in assessing CIS transitions but have not been followed up by economists and were largely ignored by political scientists.

The early studies of market transition assumed that economic reforms would restructure communist social stratification by expanding opportunities to private individuals, privatising state assets and deregulating the economy. Social transformations would follow market changes with far-reaching institutional effects. The expectation was that these countries would inevitably move closer to the model of Western regulatory states. It was this approach that led to the shock-therapy policies of the World Bank, the International Monetary Fund and other international players in the post-1990 era. Even the gradual reformists were influenced by the idea of a market-driven social and political transformation in post-communist states. However, a range of evidence from China to Eastern Europe indicated that market transition and its impact on social stratification was very much more complicated.

Perhaps the most useful theories of market transition were those focused on labour markets and those focused on small capitalists in relation to bureaucratic elites. The Hungarian economist Iván Szelényi addressed the problem of labour mobility in the late 1970s. In state socialist economies, the price of labour was set administratively and distributed according to centrally defined plans and goals.[26] Szelényi saw that transition from central distribution to labour markets was based on three kinds of economic effects. First, as markets replace the centralised redistributive mechanisms in the allocation and distribution of goods, there will be a shift of power to the marketplace. Second, the market would provide more incentives to enterprising individuals than do central planning institutions. Finally, the shift to markets would give rise to new opportunities and thus change social stratification.

Others argued that loosening state control would change social stratification in favour of producers and small capitalists and reduce the power of bureaucratic elites. Based on data about Chinese agricultural reforms in the late 1970s, Victor Nee pointed out that the transition from redistributive to market coordination shifts sources of power and privilege in favour of direct producers relative to redistributors. The emergence of markets would create new growth opportunities as well as better allocation of resources. Subsequently, this would also reduce social inequality.[27] A significant change in social stratification implicitly meant a regime change towards a more amenable market economy. However, Nee's subsequent work contradicted his earlier convictions when he saw that some administrative cadres retained their privileges despite market reforms.[28] More importantly, this work and others pointed out a positive link between cadre position and high incomes while indicating that the markets failed to weaken the political and economic position of incumbent elite cadres.[29] Thus, expectations of some far-reaching effects of market transition on bringing deep societal and political change proved to be wrong.

By the mid-1980s it became apparent that partial economic reforms could exacerbate inequalities and deepen market distortions. The results of economic reform efforts in Eastern Europe and the Soviet Union were far less encouraging than China's gradual shift to capitalist market relations.

Partial economic reform in the state sector brought out its worst aspects, exacerbating the problems of shortage economies.[30] Subsequent studies questioned the notion of transition in generating new market conditions and argued that post-socialist societies would go through a path-dependent transformation of social change and corresponding social stratification.[31] As illustrated in the case of Eastern Europe, rather than convergence, power was retained by different factions of the elite in market transition.[32] Thus, overall findings indicated that economic actors improved their positions through connections to institutions and Communist Party power along with the expansion of markets. The institutional legacy of communist political order, thus, many researchers concluded, gave rise to the persistence of the pre-existing stratification order.[33] More discontinuous but still path dependent change was also evident in regions and sectors characterised by mixed economies in which market institutions and private property forms were most advanced.

Market transition and its corresponding impact on social stratification followed three different cycles with varying impacts.[34] First, market reforms begin with petty commodity markets as occurred in urban areas of Hungary and Poland between 1968 and 1980, and through agricultural reforms in China (1977–85). The result of these early market reforms led to the increased power of producers and social inequality showed some decline. While peasants and workers made gains, redistributors were losers. The second phase emerged through labour markets when actors became free to sell their labour power and small businesses increased. This took place in Eastern Europe between 1980 and 1989 and in China since 1986. The effects of this socialist mixed economy brought about increased social inequality in Eastern Europe but an even larger increase of inequality occurred in China. In the third cycle, when market relations deepened, the winners in both Eastern Europe and China included the petty bourgeoisie, technocrats and cadre children. The losers were the old bureaucrats and no-hopers who were excluded from emerging market opportunities.[35]

These results are highly simplified and have limited utility for post-Soviet market building and associated social change in Central Asia. However, there is sufficient evidence to argue that market transition in former communist regimes everywhere took place under a competitive struggle among upper layers of the respective societies. Party hierarchy and professional administrative cadres played a defining role in market transition and regime change. However, the ability and cohesion of these groups showed stark differences among the countries.

Markets, states and elites

The relationship between elites and the rest of society differed markedly among communist countries.[36] The pre-regime change elites in some countries protected their powers by assisting democratisation and fostering links with the European Union and other multilateral organisations. In some Eastern European countries the shock of foreign policies altered reallocation regimes and widened political participation.[37] However, in many cases the old ruling elites became depoliticised and gradually lost moral standing.[38] In Central and Eastern Europe the winners were better-educated middle-aged men, especially those with training in economics and engineering. Of these, the biggest winners were the members of technocratic groups, especially those who were promoted during the 1980s, when technical competence took precedence over party loyalty. The biggest losers were those who didn't develop marketable skills; people who lived by exploiting loopholes in soft state budgets. Their bureaucratic patrons were also among the losers. Old political capital frequently found it difficult to transform itself into new.[39] These twists and turns point out that although the transition to capitalist markets and democratic institutions require the incumbent elite's activism and benefit them most, they are not yet mature nor are they likely to remain stable.[40]

In the former USSR, elite competition in state-market relationships produced an overall stalemate in some countries (such as in Georgia, Kyrgyzstan and Armenia) and deepening authoritarianism in others (such as Azerbaijan, Uzbekistan, Turkmenistan and Kazakhstan). This occurred irrespective of the degree of their market liberalisation. In Russia, under the leadership of Vladimir Putin, the old elite who were in favour of authoritarian and centralist powers took the reigns of the markets and institutions by purging oligarchs. They were broadly supported by people who feared anarchy and who had nostalgia for their stable lives under the USSR. An assertive segment of the old communist elite, linked to the KGB, sought greater control in the economy and in governance; aiming to insulate their governance regimes and personal political interests from western economic and political influences. Consequently, competition between different cycles of economic and political elites changed character in Russia from 2000 towards more insular authoritarian structures. In contrast, elite reshuffling has been a permanent feature of the seemingly more stable authoritarianism in Central Asia.[41] Indeed, further consolidation under single leader authoritarianism looked more stable and safer than disputed electoral regimes. Authoritarianism, along with clanism and regionalism, constitute the three defining control mechanisms that elites use to shape markets.

These control mechanisms constitute structures that elites utilise to further their interests and they evolve through an interplay between structure and agency. Central Asian elites maintained continuity through clan alliances; utilising elimination strategies and political pacts.[42] Kathleen Collins showed how further deepening of clan relations in the aftermath of the dissolution of the USSR undermined reforms and worked towards deinstitutionalisation and weakened the state. The informal decentralisation of power and economic assets among clan elites had multiple effects upon cultural identity, economic allocation and political bargaining. The inter-group conflicts of interest made the clan based governance susceptible to clashes while the hegemony of presidential clans created a fragile system of power in the region. These clan-based autocracies, Collins argues, are unlikely to provide long-term stable political regimes or stable transition alternatives for the region.

The other cultural mechanism, regionalism, is most apparent in the electoral systems of Kazakhstan, Kyrgyzstan and Uzbekistan. Pauline Jones Luong showed the persistence of old formulas in resolving political conflicts. Regionalism allowed for new institutional arrangements to emerge while it maintained the vested interests of central and local elites and continued to avoid widening participation in decision making.[43] Institutional legacies and power asymmetries showed certain patterns of continuity and change in three ways that enhanced the significance of regionalism. First, despite the fact that the political and economic elites were one and the same, new market forces led to power asymmetries. Second, intra-elite bargaining played a crucial role in shaping the institutional and regime change. Regionalism in politics and resource allocation provided a foundation for the legitimacy of both local and national elites. Finally, the regime change preceded in Central Asia without the mass mobilisations that drove change in Eastern Europe. Thus, rather than large-scale social mobilisations a muted social reaction accompanied regime transition.[44]

Authoritarianism is apparent in institution building and elite recruitment. These authoritarian regimes rely upon strong control of institutions by ruling elites and they systematically eliminate opposition movements. Focusing on power elites in Kazakhstan, Sally Cummings showed that continuity and change can be observed in three spheres of elite systems: institution building, recruitment and legitimation. A high degree of elite reshuffling prevents security of tenure of executive leaders while at the same time elite consensus becomes the norm and works in favour of top-down central control. This nature of elite recruitment follows a strategy of compartmentalisation for incremental reforms. A high degree of negotiation and co-option by the incumbent elite diffuses opposition and mediates discontent.[45] Cummings also pointed out the fluidity, unpredictability and ambiguous identity of power elites. Neither the institutional position nor demographic and career background or attitudinal variations can predict how an individual member of the elite would categorise himself or herself vis-à-vis the state, nation and region. However, 'Kazakhisation' emerged as a powerful force binding national elites towards a shared goal of overcoming the historical marginalisation of Kazakhs in administrative and economic positions.

Thus, agency theory and structural approaches explain many aspects of the character of regime transition and the behaviour of the ruling elite. However, the missing link in these analyses is the lack of foresight on the nature of the layering among elite positions and its relationship to social stratification. Additionally, we need to explain the ways in which economic assets and opportunities are allocated and internally used to cement political power and patronage. To do this we turn our attention to the critical layer between the elites and the masses: the middle class entrepreneurs.

Post-Soviet stratification and reallocation

The first stage of the new stratification occurred during the early period of mass privatisation when small property owners began to emerge and major assets ended up in the hands of ruling families and their courtiers. The dissolution of less successful state enterprises, small-scale enterprise privatisation schemes and land privatisation benefited early disguised entrepreneurs and administrative cadres, among them komsomol and kolkhoz chiefs, and professionals. The second stage emerged with the fight for control of assets among state elites, oligarchs, courtiers and protégés while technocrats diffused their control in the economy through elaborate corruption. Enterprises and assets began to change hands and competition among different business groups, typically oligarchs in major sectors, intensified. This affected foreign owners and their local partners, too. The ethnic and regional implications of these first two stages of reallocation were reflected in the increasing dominance of urban, university educated, indigenous groups as opposed to their Slavic counterparts. It also marginalised the rural and semi-skilled indigenous population. Most dramatically in Kazakhstan, young ethnic Kazakhs, trained in the West, began to play leading roles along with the Soviet-trained old guard. However, political purges periodically eliminated the rising economic powers of oligarchs and courtiers who had opposing political ambitions in Kazakhstan and Uzbekistan. In the mid-2000s, Central Asia approached its third stage with the prospect of change of leadership and a major reconsideration of the distribution of economic assets through consolidation. This process has been influenced by Russia's new regime and the ambitions to regain control of major economic assets by the state elites.

While there is a degree of continuity of the Soviet elite in power and wealth positions, a diverging pattern of oligarchic and chaotic reallocation regimes began to shape new wealth and opportunity distribution in society. During the past two decades, former Soviet bureaucrats and their counterparts benefited most from privatisation and enterprise development. But, many others lost their former status and emerged as losers. Soviet professionals, writers, managers and workers have shrunk in prestige as their political influence and economic status diminished. Thus, in a decade and a half, a new more differentiated and more polarised social strata emerged under a sort of capitalist regime of accumulation and control by old party bosses and new economic elites.[46] The emergence of an entrepreneurial middle class is the most distinct outcome of this stratification.

What defines the entrepreneurial middle class is its relative access to opportunities and resources and the ability of its members to utilise them. Their market opportunities are mostly determined and shaped by the three layers above them: the presidential family, oligarchs and courtiers, and apparatchiks and protégés. This is a dynamic and relational stratification and its workings are entirely different from deterministic Marxist views on class separation, identity and struggle. Power struggle and conflict exist not only among strata but also within each stratum. This stratification does not rest on consciously formed cultural entities, pure wage or income levels, or ethnic homogeneity or identity. It is fluid, slippery and non-ideological. Thus, unpredictability and ambiguous identity are not unique to the privileged classes. Indeed, this opportunistic fluidity characterises the essence of allocation regimes and capitalist relations.[47]

(i) *The presidents and their families*: The president is the ultimate arbiter, the symbol of stability, and the power that stands above the hierarchy of business fortunes in all three countries. The presidents are not only sources of legitimacy and symbols of the state, they are also involved directly or indirectly in all major business transactions and decisions. Their families and close allies control all major economic assets and direct the flow of foreign investment. Their close relatives extend their influence through business ventures as managers of state assets usually through disguised ownership and always with minimum accountability. More distant relatives and close friends and allies use their access to the presidents to acquire big stakes in secondary markets and enterprises. Ruling families and their close allies are frequently accused of holding bank accounts and investments abroad. Along with Swiss banks and Dubai based ventures, Moscow and London are two metropols where corporate and banking transactions go through and international deals take shape.

The mechanism of ownership and management of major enterprises are opaque across the region. The major holders would be unknown to the media and the public. Many assets are registered in the name of relatives, associates or friends. The limited company structures and institutional ownerships can hide the real owners. The president's authority is feared and often respected by all parties but he is also restricted by his role.

Presidents are also often captured by powerful interests. Internal coups and power wrestling among family members and courtiers generate a slippery and deceitful game. The ruling families often act to protect their power and prevent social upheavals through different legitimisation strategies by distributing favours and economic assets to competing groups, building loyalties by promoting allegiance to clan and blood ties, and evoking fear of uncertainty among the public. The president frequently shifts the power balance within and among groups through new distribution regimes. Periodic purges of rival family members, ministers and governors eliminate alternative power basis and change the inner circle of the ruling cadres.

Case 2.1 – The presidential families' penetration into the markets

The most well-known mechanism for market control and personal enrichment is through direct business involvement of the family members. The elder daughter of Uzbek President Karimov is probably the real owner or beneficial partner of many key businesses in the country. Gulnara Karimov directly manages many firms including Oxus Gold, where she is believed to be a major shareholder. She has accumulated massive wealth, mostly banked in Moscow and plays a key role in business dealings between Russia and Uzbekistan. One such deal resulted in the bulk of Uzbekistan's natural gas reserves being allocated to Gazprom, the Russian state energy company. This deal was negotiated with Alisher Usmanov, an Uzbek-Russian oligarch with businesses interests in metallurgy, energy, and in London's famous Arsenal Football Club.

Ms Kerimov uses her political power to deepen her business interests. She also chooses businesses which benefit her political and social position such as night clubs and restaurants where major political as well as business deals are sealed. Through charities and voluntary associations she channels philanthropic activities that extend her political influence even further than her father is able to do through mainstream state services. She is believed to be the most ambitious and strongest person in the family and she would remain in power even if the president is succeeded by a close ally.

Case 2.2 – An example of the sources of instability

Presidential families are vulnerable to the greed and ambitions of relatives. Rakhat Aliyev, one of Nazarbayev's sons-in-law, exploited his position not only to enrich himself but also to destabilise the regime. The son of a former Kazakhstan SSR Health Minister, he was not content to pursue a medical career after having being trained as a surgeon. During the 1990s he held a series of high-level positions in law enforcement, financial police and tax collection agencies, rising to first deputy head of the KNB, the Kazakh security service. He and his wife, Dariga, acquired substantial assets in the newly privatised sugar, media and banking sectors.

Since the 1990s, Aliyev has had strained relations with President Nazarbayev and his circle. In 2001 Aliyev was suddenly removed from all of his public positions and sent into virtual diplomatic exile as Kazkah ambassador to Austria. However, in a few years Aliyev returned to Astana as deputy foreign minister after the family reconciled. Soon after, new controversies emerged about Aliyev's conduct as he was accused of being involved in the killing of Altynbek Sarsenbayev, a leading opposition politician, in 2006. In 2008, the Kazakh National Security Committee accused Rakhat Aliyev of an attempted coup along with Alnur Musaev, the former head of the National Security Committee. While Aliyev denies these charges and remains in exile, he has clearly lost this round of a game to increase his political power, probably to President Nazarbayev's other son-in-law, Timur Kulibayev who has been playing a key role in the Kazakh oil and gas sector's development.[48]

(ii) *The oligarchs and courtiers*: The thin layer beneath the president and his family associates often provides close allies in economic management as well as in politics. Thus, they offer the deep pockets that finance the regime. Courtiers generally emerge from the administrative and bureaucratic elite and they are not only functionaries and deal setters but often shadow owners in business partnerships. This includes a heterodox group of the president's associates, former party colleagues and friends, and current parliamentarians and ministers. This top stratum directly or indirectly controls all major sectors in the economy with some specialised in banking and insurance, media and telecommunications, oil and gas, mineral resources and heavy industries, construction and real estate. Since most of the actors come from the Soviet nomenclature and had their formative education and professional development under the previous regime, they still carry a residue of the Soviet norms and mentality.[49] Senior administrators and managers have maintained their positions and converted their skills to play new roles in emerging enterprises, partnerships and allocation mechanisms. Their official assurance and protection is often necessary for any large business deal. In a fashion similar to large holding companies in emerging economies, these groups build their own power base with business diversification aimed to reduce their exposure to risks and secure their financial capital.

Oligarchs, more numerous among ethnic and religious minorities, are shrewd entrepreneurs and manipulators often with good international links, access to financial markets and political connections. As seen in Case 2.4, Kazakhstan's wealthiest oligarchs are not even Kazakh born. Yet, despite their economic power, the oligarchs' political influence has been purged and strictly controlled. Thus, oligarchs need the courtiers for the smooth functioning of their business operations. Their large shares in heavy industries, finance and energy are often coupled with state partnerships and the presidents' inner circle. Many oligarchs emerged during the early phase of privatisation in extractive industries, metallurgy and energy, most clearly apparent in Russia and Kazakhstan. In a highly controversial scheme described as 'the sale of the century', Yeltsin's administration agreed to exchange some of the state's largest properties in return for cash and political support. The wealth accumulated by a handful of men with humble backgrounds has been labelled as 'the biggest robbery' of this century.[50] During the first phase of power building these men extended their political tentacles into the regime. However, under Vladimir Putin, this came to an end and they lost their political influence and shed considerable wealth. Under Putin, Russia's major resources were renationalised, rebellious oligarchs were disciplined, and major energy and metallurgy companies were nationalised. In recent years, they were recruited to serve the geopolitical interests of the Kremlin.[51] In Central Asia, Russian oligarchs play a critical functional role in serving the geopolitical and market interests of the Kremlin (see also Case 2.1).

Case 2.3 – A privatisation tale and the power of courtiers
Byelkamit, once a Soviet torpedo factory in Kazakhstan, was successfully converted to civilian production under a US defense conversion programme. This took place through a US-Italian-Kazakh joint venture that developed pressure vessels for the oil industry in Almaty. The joint venture was 37.24 per cent owned by Supco Due (Italy), the managing partner, and 30.24 per cent by Byelocorp Scientific (US). The Kazakh government owned 22.84 per cent, while the remainder belonged to FBM-Hudson Italiana (Italy) (7 per cent) and employees of the old Soviet factory (2.68 per cent). However, the company changed hands under political pressure. In 2004, the Kazakh government sold its shares to a Kazakh company reportedly owned by a former transport minister. Later the US and Italian partners were asked to sell some of their shares because the new owner

wanted to increase its stake to become a majority shareholder. However, the buyers listed were three little-known Kazakh companies. Conflict and financial claims deepened between foreign and local interests. The company has since come face-to-face with the opaqueness of the Kazakh court system and the foreign partners felt that the diplomatic pressure on the Kazakh government was their only remaining card.[52]

Case 2.4 – Swift growth from zilch to millions: mining oligarchs
Alexander Mashkevich, Patokh Chodiev and Alijan Ibragimov have appeared in Forbes' list of the 500 richest men in the world in recent years. Mashkevich, a Jewish academic born in Kyrgyzstan, along with Chodiev and Ibragimov, both Kyrgyz-Uzbeks, founded the Eurasian National Resources Corporation (ENRC). Their company became one of the world's largest mining firms and by 2006 employed 62,000 people and contributed 4 per cent of Kazakhstan's GDP.[53] Their speedy ascent to the heights of the corporate world looks familiar as a story of Russian oligarchs.[54] They used a web of offshore companies and Swiss bank accounts and with the public support of President Nursultan Nazarbayev, gained control of the privatised chromium, aluminum, and gas operations in the country. Mashkevich enjoys close ties with Nazarbayev and almost certainly contributes generously to the president's family fortune. They were able to gain massive wealth and transferred billions of dollars out of Kazakhstan into Switzerland in the late 1990s.

Since the early 2000s, along with other oligarchs, the ENRC has run a publicity campaign to flatter its image and secure a position in the western corporate landscape. As part of this effort, they turned to Ispat-Karmet to recruit their new CEO. Ispat-Karmet, now a part of the gigantic AccelorMittal, had been the Soviet Union's major iron and steel complex. Although these three men stayed away from Kazakh politics, Mashkevich, as the president of the Euro-Asian Jewish Congress, built a global public profile with philanthropic activities and influence around the world. ENRC was listed on the London Stock Exchange in 2007 with a market capitalisation of roughly 15 billion USD. Some investors were unhappy about the founders sitting on the board of ENRC due to an alleged fraud in the 1990s and they were each subsequently represented by other members of the board. In 2007, while the three men held 15 per cent each, the largest single share was the Kazakh government's 20 per cent. Kazakhmys, the London-listed Kazakh government copper mining company, owned another 15 per cent and has threatened to move to take over ENRC.[55] This is consistent with the government's recent focus on tightening control over its major economic assets.[56]

(iii) *Protégés and apparatchiks*: Considerably more numerous than oligarchs and courtiers but still far fewer than middle stratum entrepreneurs, the protégés and apparatchiks include powerful regional governors, chief financial, tax and customs officials, secret service and police bosses, and others who occupy high positions in local governments, ministerial and state departments. In this group there are numerous Soviet era managers and administrators who utilise their knowledge of sectors and take advantage of information asymmetries. As in Russia, these people have become key players in enterprise restructuring and management.[57] Their bureaucratic assets, personal ties, critical information and manipulative skills merged with new economic opportunities leading to unaccountable wealth accumulation. The communist bureaucratic structures, especially those of the party and komsomol, were mainly involved with the distribution of goods provided, and that allowed them critical positions in the new allocation and appropriation regimes. Nevertheless, the protégés serve above all the interests of courtiers while building their own brigade of apparatchiks who are financial and business collaborators, task managers, and petty officials. They get involved in large business deals, land speculation, privatisation and foreign investments in regional governments on behalf of courtiers or share the proceeds among themselves (see Case 2.5). The titles and positions of civil servants do not automatically make them protégés but it is their individual loyalties, reciprocal ties and clan relations that provide them diverse privileges. The regional governors preside over allocation regimes and mediate among interests of competing groups. They tend to be both shrewd businessmen and politicians with extensive loyalties and mutual reciprocity relations. The presidents expect regional governors to arbitrate reallocation according to the hierarchy of economic interests and their importance.

Case 2.5 – A monster protégé positioned by courtiers

Courtiers use public office to deepen their economic controls and favour protégés to carry out management tasks. They do this by controlling appointments, insider information, and rules and access to markets. A case from Karaganda illuminates the intricacies of these processes. A courtier who was a relative of President Nazarbayev used a close ally as a protégé to run the city tax office in the Karaganda region (oblast). This office presided over a range of revenues and rents from all businesses and 15 bazaars in the city. Within six months the protégé was promoted to the management committee of the entire province responsible for all assets of the provincial administration. From this position he became familiar with details about regional business development, spread of assets and the scale of commercial sites. Then, he was able to make judgements about how the market operated in the region.

All strategic sections in the regional finance department were amalgamated under the Department of State Procurement in the following months. After this administrative reorganisation, he was promoted to head the regional finance department and presided over all tax and revenue related sections, including procurement. His powers, according to a distinguished lawyer familiar with this case, exceed the province governor's and he was the so-called real owner of the province. This centralisation helped him to serve the vested interests and pay back his dues to associated businesses and to the courtier who placed him there.[58]

(iv) *The middle class*: This stratum consists of the emerging entrepreneurial class and the shrinking number of salaried professionals. The rapid growth of the indigenous middle class took place during the later stages of the Soviet Union. Most of the urban middle classes were formed by Slavs and Europeans and with their departure, professional and administrative positions were depleted.[59]

The private sector is not extensive enough to provide middle class life styles for most who aspire to it. The former intelligentsia has disintegrated and the character of professional life has changed dramatically. In Uzbekistan the most numerous middle class wage earners are those in the security forces and army officers, along with civil servants in the bloated bureaucracy of the Karimov regime.[60] In Kazakhstan the police and the army are almost insignificant, although there have been attempts at institutional modernisation. The most significant growth among wage earners has been in banking, financial services, and the private sector. Professionals and senior civil servants are also being nurtured through scholarships to study abroad. Since 1994, more than 3000 students benefitted from study abroad programmes, known as the Boloshak scholarships. The most serious depletion in civil service and professional positions took place in Kyrgyzstan as the economy shrank.

Entrepreneurs form the most numerous and important group in the new middle class. Although they are not the direct beneficiaries of major privatisation programmes, entrepreneurs are residual beneficiaries of the dissolution of Soviet enterprises and land privatisation. They constantly negotiate to solidify their domain and expand market opportunities. Many professionals and civil servants are also engaged in entrepreneurial activities in a fashion similar to households during the Soviet era. They utilise their positions to gain access to information that benefits their business interests. Although these are not typically entrepreneurial individuals, the needs they have to supplement their meagre salaries and the opportunities they are presented with allow them to benefit from off the record business activities.

Unofficial business comes in many forms. In addition to outright graft, many officials as well as shady entrepreneurs run protection rackets. These fill the gap left by the retreat of the state in the provision of public goods and the protection of property. These become self-governing groups that help to facilitate business transactions, including contract enforcement. Various forms of self-governing syndicates flourished across the region.[61] These syndicates are amorphous groups often run by a charismatic leader with significant economic and political assets and commonly call upon the persuasive powers of armed men. They were initially regularly employed by the oligarchs for business protection. However, over the years they have expanded their influence and function as versatile facilitators and power brokers. As is common in weak states, big and small gangs vie for influence and spread illicit activities, especially with regard to cross-border trade. Some of these are merely youth gangs, some specialise in the intimidation that body builders and martial arts aficionados provide, while others employ somewhat more sophisticated former KGB operatives and security servicemen. Many of these groups provide social externalities by reducing the propensity for anarchy. This can be seen as one of the public goods along with the employment they provide to otherwise unemployable youths and occasional philanthropic activities. In Kyrgyzstan, they enjoy public recognition and sympathy as moderators of wealth and justice and we might even regard their political influence as having been earned.

(v) *The underprivileged*: The most populous group is the marginalised and dispossessed. The majority of pensioners, agricultural labourers, unskilled workers, seasonal migrants, unemployed youth and the elderly are underprivileged. There are also those who fell from grace and ended up as prostitutes, drug addicts and alcoholics. Most of the underprivileged live on marginal earnings and are entirely cut off from opportunity structures of the new stratification. A few enterprising people survive on small street trade and casual market exchanges on the margins of growing urban wealth. The deterioration in public transportation, health and education disproportionally affected the underprivileged and the rural population fared even worse. Peasants in Uzbekistan live on subsistence farming; they are the majority of the population and are totally dependent on farm subsidies, especially in the form of irrigation services. Many small towns and communities in far-flung regions of Kazakhstan and Kyrgyzstan have high unemployment and little or no economic activity. The quality of education, health and other public services has deteriorated sharply over the years; only a small minority is able to afford these provisions from the private sector. Central Asia now has dramatic social and geographical imbalances; neither the market nor the state, nor any other overarching institution has emerged to compensate for the loss of the welfare provisions of the Communist Party.

The consequences of social stratification

The impact of this emerging stratification on both markets and states will have long-term implications. First, upper strata interests penetrate the bureaucracy and undermine its neutrality and law enforcement capacity. A myriad of unaccountable relationships among the ruling elite, their associates and self-governing syndicates bend the state institutions and divert resources away from social provisions. Second, this stratification is a function of deepening market control by the upper strata. Both the spread of wealth and market opportunities for new entrepreneurs are dependent on this top-down allocation regime. Finally, the hierarchical distribution of authority and its narrow power base limits not only market growth and business creation but perpetuates societal exclusion.

The character of this social stratification shows differences among the countries. It has been diversifying and expanding in Kazakhstan while it is monolithic and very narrow in Uzbekistan, and highly chaotic in Kyrgyzstan. In all these cases, the power base of each stratum originates in Soviet social structures. Those structures assisted the diffusion of oligarchic control during the period of early market transition.[62] However, the new social stratification has also been diverging without an ideological base or moral standing. There are no clear corresponding cultural attributes or identity structures, either. Instead, a common pattern of political apathy shapes day-to-day actions of individuals and groups within each stratum. Traditional family and friendship ties, spatial proximity relations in small communities and clan relations play important roles in providing stability, continuity and opportunities. Another important characteristic of this stratification is its multiethnic character, especially in major urban centres. Balance and control also change periodically through defectors and new entrants. Oligarchs and courtiers periodically bring new players, partners and foreign investors into the game. Political purges of the ruling family periodically shift group alliances and change opportunity structures in the market. Due to these factors, this emerging social stratification is relatively flexible and open to new participants. This elasticity provides a degree of structural durability, societal dynamism and mobility.

Rounds of allocation through the Mikado game

The success of the entrepreneurial middle stratum depends on the mobility and steady expansion of opportunities in a dynamic relationship with the other social strata. However, there is a fine balance: the system depends on the maintenance of rules of behaviour and a sequence of moves. As in the Mikado game, the players need to ensure that stability is preserved as they reallocate resources. The traditional Mikado game can be played by five players ordered hierarchically from emperor and courtier down to worker, symbolised by blue, yellow, orange, green, and red sticks.[63] In the Mikado game, players have hopeful expectations from each round and in Central Asian hierarchies a similar dynamic mollifies potential discontent. While pressure groups, civil society organisations and multiparty politics articulate group interests in most democracies, such channels, which are either blocked or non-existent in post-Soviet societies, are accommodated within the Mikado game. Thus, in the real world of Central Asian markets and politics, diverse interests find channels to penetrate into reallocation regimes without formal political representation.

Social stratification rests on expanding opportunities through the repositioning of courtiers, protégés, and others. One mechanism is to reshuffle the upper tiers who guard the redistribution mechanisms and extract most benefits (economic as well as political) from the game. The reshuffling often limits the power of established groups, widens the scope of opportunities to new contenders and changes the direction of reallocation regimes to new loyal cadres. President Nazarbayev and his courtiers have been the most entrepreneurial and imaginative in employing reshuffling techniques without hampering the growth of opportunities in other strata. Their major advantage over neighbouring countries is their rich resource base. The Kazakh upper strata are comprised of both old and new cadres including a growing number of young professionals and foreign educated experts. Because the Kazakh economy has been growing, each upper stratum is expanding and there are new opportunities for vertical movement.[64] In the much smaller economy of Kyrgyzstan political contesting generates some mobility and opportunities.

The Mikado game is played somewhat differently in Uzbekistan. The loyal cadres of the Karimov regime restrict mobility and purposely retain a large gap between higher and lower strata. Security forces and state employees enforce the rules of a rigid game. Market relations are controlled by the Karimov's courtiers as well as hidden protégés and he and his family control the economy with a few oligarchs. This structure rests on interdependency among oligarchs to ensure economic stability in the nation as a whole while extracting monopoly rents. The oligarchs need the state's protection to continue their domination in specific sectors with no external competition. Thus, the two parties hold each other hostages. In this structure, the protégés and courtiers are highly dependent on the entrepreneurial middle class for social stability and income generation. So, for example, a provincial governor knows that the state budget is insufficient to provide basic necessities and must rely directly on entrepreneurs' efforts that he can manipulate. Otherwise, his position as well as social stability are threatened. In some ways Uzbekistan's Mikado game is true to the rules of the game; it is an almost entirely closed system where the state acts as a rentier at the expense of economic benefits that would otherwise enrich the country.

In the normal functioning of a Mikado game, players extract and accumulate their sticks until the system is disturbed where upon the opportunity moves to another player. When the pile becomes too unstable and collapses a new round is forced. Such a collapse occurred in Kyrgyzstan in 2005. Players failed to agree how to generate new opportunities and the structure of allocation regimes became unstable. These events, widely known as the 'Tulip Revolution', unseated President Akayev who probably underestimated his need to use coercive power. Several years after his overthrow, the upper echelons of Kyrgyzstan's strata have yet to establish the next round of their Mikado game and until they do the country will lack the legitimacy and stability that the rules of the game provide.

Case 2.6 – International implications of reshuffling assets

Former President Askar Akayev, his family and courtiers controlled major economic assets including the Kant Slate and Cement Plant, the largest grocery chain, gold mines, the largest mobile phone operator, and a fuel company. Akayev's son, Aydar, controlled the telephone industry and partly owned the company that provided fuel and other services to the American military base that opened in 2001.[65] During the Akayev era, Manas International Airport was an 87 per cent government owned joint-stock company and collected 2 million USD annually in lease payments plus landing fees. All related businesses were controlled by Akayev's allies. The most lucrative source of income came from fuel contracts with Aalam Services, owned by Adil Toiganbayev, the president's son-in-law.[66]

After the March 2005 uprising, Akayev's successor President Kurmanbek Bakiyev began renegotiating a contract for the American military base and demanded a large increase, to 200 million USD. After long negotiations a total of 150 million USD in assistance and compensation was settled upon in 2006 and Bakiyev allegedly redistributed the proceeds among his supporters through his own allocation mechanism.[67] Within two years the priorities of the Bakiyev regime shifted again, Russian military contracts seemed more lucrative, and the status of the American military base became a pawn in a larger geo-political game.

As we have seen in all three countries, the stability of social stratification and the rules of its Mikado game rest on three critical mechanisms: competition and compromise, coalition and cadre retention, and repression and exile. First, both within each stratum and among them there are constant negotiations to shape competition and to reach compromise. For example, oligarchs and courtiers often compete against one another and set their boundaries in the market according to each other and the ruling family but engage in complex negotiations at the same time. Similarly, middle class entrepreneurs defend their positions through negotiated competition. Solidarity networks and clans facilitate bargaining and bring new opportunities. Patronage networks and clans also offer protection for smaller players. Local resources, such as housing and services, as well as new market opportunities are distributed within social networks through the mechanisms of negotiated competition.[68]

The second critical component of durability is coalition and cadre retention. Many of the core cadres in Uzbek and Kazakh state administration had either worked closely with Presidents Nazarbayev and Karimov in the pre-1991 period or have extended loyal clan and family relations. Others seem to have been chosen because of the networks, knowledge and experience they amassed or opportunities they brought. Other critical qualities include the specialised knowledge and international contacts. Cadre retention and political coalitions rest on personal and networked trust and mutual loyalty; these are shared among individuals rather than institutions. Trust emerges through reciprocal beneficial relations and enhances the ability of networks to forge new transactions leading to enduring personal relationships.

Finally, repression and exile protect the interests of the players against deviators and the growth of alternative power bases. This allocation mechanism is exclusively controlled by the two upper strata. This appears in three forms depending on the scale of vested interests in all three Central Asian states. First, the major problems are addressed through cabinet reshuffles and changes of prime ministers. This aims to disrupt the establishment of any opposition base by alternative groups. The second method is to destabilise political opponents and oligarchs, including foreign investors, through changing business laws, political pressures, or most frequently and easily through accusations of tax evasion and embezzlement. Periodically dismissing and publicly embarrassing governors, chief officials and other protégés is also a frequently used reshuffling technique. These manoeuvres are often displayed to the public as a fight against corruption and bad management. The third method is total elimination through political conspiracy charges, imprisonment, exile or even murder. These three forms of political retunings exist in all countries to varying degrees. The following two cases illustrate different techniques of repression and attrition.

Case 2.7 – Suppressing alternative economic interests

In Uzbekistan almost all alternative political activities and opposition groups are either in exile or silenced. The first opposition movement, Birlik (Unity), was formed in 1988 by members of the Uzbek Soviet elite, a year later the movement split and the Erk Democratic Party was formed. The leaders of these two groups, Muhammad Salih and Erkin Vahidov, were both eventually banned from politics and their parties were eliminated. Salih was forced to leave Uzbekistan in 1992 and has lived in several European countries ever since. During an interview in London, Salih described the Uzbek political regime as a dictatorship and denied accusations that he is a radical Islamist, stressing simply that 'Uzbekistan should follow a peaceful democratic path'.[69] Another opposition group, the Sunshine Uzbekistan Coalition, was led by Sanjar Umarov, a powerful businessman. Their stated aim is a just society, a fair economic order, and an end to the tyranny of the Karimov family. Umarov's business interests in cotton and telecommunications were probably closely allied to the Kerimov family initially. After moving his family to the United States, he became an outspoken critic of the regime.[70] A courageous but foolish act that led to his arrest on charges of embezzlement and money laundering and a 14-year jail sentence.

Other members of the opposition are routinely harassed by the secret police.[71] Nadira Khidoyatova, a business woman and leading member of the Sunshine Uzbekistan Coalition, lost her husband to what was probably a political assassination. Khidoyatova and other members of the coalition insist that all they want are political and economic freedoms. These instances of repression are part of a pattern to intimidate business interests that might form into successful political opposition movements. Khidoyatova is one of many secular minded and educated intellectuals who are systematically accused of offences such as Pan-Turkism or radical Islam. The Karimov regime uses these sorts of accusations to justify acts of oppression, legitimate state violence to the international community and first and foremost to protect their economic and political positions.

Case 2.8 – Co-option and annihilation

In November 2001 a group of political activists founded the Democratic Choice Party of Kazakhstan, a moderate opposition movement that advocated social reform and economic liberalism. In subsequent years the Democratic Choice Party was divided and reconstituted in various forms driven by conflicting personalities and business interests.[72] In the spring of 2002, the first split resulted in the formation of Ak Zhol (Bright Path) by Oraz Zhandasov, Bulat Abylov and Alikhan Baimenov, and soon after an ex-government minister, Altynbek Sarsenbaev joined the party. This formation lasted only three years until Sarsenbaev, Abylov and Zhandasov formed a dissident faction named True Ak Zhol. Abylov and the others have been systematically harassed since 2001 but the viciousness of those who worked to counter the anti-Nazarbayev opposition of True Ak Zhol was most apparent with the killing of Altynbek Sarsenbaev in February 2006.

Bulat Abylov has faced various charges of corruption, embezzlement and illegalities surrounding the sale of land in 1999. The embezzlement charge stems from his position as the technocrat who presided over the biggest privatisation fund, Butya-Capital. In the years following independence, Nazarbayev privatised many state assets through voucher schemes. Some of the most lucrative assets, however, he appropriated for his family and close associates. When the government accused Abylov of cheating his 2.2 million depositors through the embezzlement of 2.4 million USD, Abylov denied these charges and countered with many examples of the Nazarbayev family's immunity from massive fraud accusations. He cites examples of land speculation through new urban development in Almaty and capital accumulation through appropriated state property by oligarchs and their technocratic cadres. As a result of his confrontational stance, Abylov remains entangled in interminable legal disputes.

Politics and business are also mixed in the case of Alikhan Baimenov who, however, has acted more cautiously. He recognises corruption as a big problem and emphasises the importance of the rule of law in his political activities, but he also cautioned that Kazakhstan will not be ready for democracy until it has a well-established middle class, civil society and a mixed economy with independent enterprises and healthy small businesses. This incremental and sly stance has earned him the reputation of a Trojan horse of Kazakh politics.

These methods are also employed laterally within the upper strata by protégés and courtiers against their own rivals using their influence in the judiciary, security services and elsewhere in the bureaucracy. Infighting takes place in many forms but the main prize is to gain favour with the president, his allies and relatives. The president's authority and the cohesion among his courtiers reduce the chances of all out wars and this cohesion limits the frictions among competing courtiers and protégés. Although business interest allocation tends to be volatile and unpredictable, any large-scale battle requires the permission of the top stratum. Family infighting, conflicts of interests among oligarchs, and power building mechanisms carry constant tension as seen in the case of daughters and sons-in-law of the Kazakh and Uzbek presidents.[73]

In order to preserve business stability the ruling elite has recognised that they must be increasingly cautious. They have to accommodate the growing influence of young technocrats and managers by giving them responsible positions and allow more societal expression. They cautiously allow donor sponsored democratisation projects, foreign media and tolerate the influence of western NGOs but ensure that all internal and external threats remain under control.

Conclusion

Soviet social stratification evolved from the Bolshevik revolution through the Gorbachev reforms but eventually reached a dead end with low mobility and bad economic performance. We have seen in this chapter how a new form of social stratification emerges along with market change and the new allocation regimes. This occurred through the diffusion of the Soviet elite into the new markets, through the application of Soviet norms, and through the new reallocation mechanism that I described as a Mikado game.

Control of the ruling elites in the economy sometimes inhibit and at other times facilitate market opportunities depending on the type of allocation regimes they foster. The difference can be seen in the manner in which the Soviet elite diffused into the market and the extent to which a new generation of capitalists emerged in the three countries. This perspective extends market transition theories and the elite power thesis by showing how social stratification and internal conflicts and negotiations among groups have shaped economic empowerment as well as social relations.

The dissolution of economic assets and privatisation took place according to Soviet norms and cadre positions. We have seen how the norms associated with five hierarchical groups shaped the reallocation of wealth and created opportunities. Continuity rather than interruption characterised these Soviet cadres and allowed their legitimacy to remain unchallenged as their former positions became translated into the new ownership structures. I have described the dynamics of this process by analogy to the Mikado game. The new reallocation processes and its various cycles follow rules that respect the opportunity structures within and among social strata. They operate through three mechanisms: negotiated competition and compromise, coalition and cadre retention, and repression and exile. Therefore, enterprise formation and business growth emerge strategically linked to the nature of market control exercised by power bases within and among strata and the dynamics of the Mikado game. In the next chapter we will see the middle strata players of this game in order to understand who is using these reallocation mechanisms to shape market expansion and how they generate income and job opportunities in post-Soviet markets.

3
Entrepreneurs and their Perceptions

The state is doing business; our job.
We do the state's job by acting as social providers.
This should be reversed.

An entrepreneur, Karaganda, Kazakhstan

Here there is no business group but the state.

An entrepreneur, Tashkent, Uzbekistan

Introduction

The entrepreneurial middle stratum plays a key role in income distribution, social cohesion and economic sustainability. Their position is intricately linked to the dynamics of the Mikado game and its reallocation rounds, but small business entrepreneurs operate in an increasingly autonomous market domain. Compared to the oligarchs and courtiers or apparatchiks their business structures are detached from the major sources of economic fortune: oil, mining and cotton. In many cases they barely know anything about the business deals of these major sectors, beyond rumours. Instead, they aim to insulate their market positions through closely interlinked business operations. Nevertheless, they also function as subordinates and functionaries of the upper layers of stratification in both social and economic senses. As illustrated in the quotes above, many entrepreneurs have deep contempt for those in the upper strata and disdain their subservient role in the market.

The new middle stratum entrepreneurs emerged from the rubble of Soviet era markets. Although privatisation and new enterprise formations took place in an anarchic manner, the Soviet bureaucratic elite retained economic control. Rather than dismantling Soviet institutions, they

opted for gradual modifications. This proved to be essential for mini-
mising social dissent and securing political power. The priority given to
continuity stifled much potential economic activity while political insiders and oligarchs set about accumulating massive wealth. This strategy
was mostly successful since none of the Central Asian states experienced
major social upheavals despite their massive economic shocks, high
inflation and severe shortages during the first decade of independence.

The position of small and medium-sized enterprises (SME) in capitalist
markets and the societal and political role of their owners have long been
subject to polarised ideological debates. For Marxist scholars small property
holders had no future. They were merely a dumping ground to receive the
refuse from large capitalists and the state and also a convenient cushion
to ease the impact of capitalist economic fluctuations. They had to be
eliminated to make way for the triumph of the proletariat revolution. Even
non-Marxist scholars did not have much sympathy for this in-between
class who were regarded as holding opportunistic attitudes and often-
conservative political tendencies. In the developing world, however, the
inadequacy of modern industries was often associated with the shortage of
'innovative entrepreneurs'. Small producers and traditional forms of entrepreneurship held back industrial development.[1] Throughout the 1970s and
1980s, a new spotlight shone on to small businesses and local economies
with intermittent economic crisis of mass production in advanced capitalist systems. Small and medium-sized enterprises gained recognition in academic and policy circles as a panacea for the industrial world's economic
troubles in an era of industrial restructuring.[2] A range of new scholarship
pointed out the diversity and endurance of SMEs and their economic
advantages and competitive strength in different economic structures.

Here we will see how the position of the entrepreneurial middle
class has been subject to fluctuating ideological and economic cycles
in recent decades. This will be followed by an analysis of Soviet market
conditions and their implications for new enterprise creation. I will
then present survey evidence on general characteristics of the entrepreneurial middle class and their standing in relation to markets, institutions and governance. The material provides a first hand account of
the characteristics of entrepreneurs, their views on governance and the
ways in which they handle capitalist markets.

Perspectives on the entrepreneurial middle class

After decades of purges of landed gentry, artisans and merchants, a new
property-owning entrepreneurial class is emerging. These new property

owners are largely disconnected from the property owners of the past, with the exception of some merchant families (most common among Uyghurs, Tajiks and Uzbek artisanal families of the Fergana Valley). Thus, they developed their social consciousness about capitalism recently, while engaged in business. The process of new accumulation began with no industrial class, corporate structure or capacity to run policymaking institutions to guide economic restructuring. Therefore, in many ways this is a hectic and contested market building process with no clear templates to emulate. The process they went through seems to reverse the order that Marxists and Weberians would have predicted.

The fate of small property holders was supposed to be predictable for both Weberian and Marxist sociologists. In theory, independent producers who own and operate their own means of production would fight a losing battle in the conditions of an industrial economy. Marx used the term 'petite bourgeoisie' to describe the heterogeneous stratum of small-scale producers who earned their livelihood from the ownership of income-producing property by using their skills without employing a significant workforce. Marx claimed that in the long run, the development of capitalism would lead to the dissolution of the entrepreneurial middle class along with the rest of the bourgeoisie; it was a phenomenon of the past, not the future.[3]

Alternative approaches demonstrated convincingly that small scale businesses had a more functional and integrated relationship with large businesses than assumed under orthodox Marxist conceptualisations and their fate was not predictably dismal. Small enterprises filled the gap in the modern economy by operating in high risk sectors servicing large corporations, sustaining local economies and allowing larger profit margins for large capitalists because of their cheaper production costs.[4] In developing countries the modern capitalist sector is too weak to absorb the unskilled labour stock, thus self-employment, the informal sector and very small businesses serve as a labour sump and are direct consequences of underdeveloped capitalism and a historical outcome of colonialism.[5]

Salaried workers and small business owners together form the middle stratum.[6] This middle class plays a critical role in ameliorating economic upheavals as they absorb the shocks better and adjust to new circumstances faster in both advanced economies and developing ones. Like an accordion's bellows, they respond to market opportunities and pressures by expanding and diversifying or by shrinking. When mass production and heavy industries began to tremble and collapse in the aftermath of the first and second oil shocks in the UK, the United States and other major industrialised countries, flexible small and medium-sized enterprises emerged as a solution for the necessary structural transformation of capitalism.[7]

A group of the newly industrialising economies, benefiting from the favourable global economic climate, export-led growth and global outsourcing, upgraded their industrial base and enjoyed the steady growth of a modern SME sector. Along with rapid urbanisation, the growth of new middle classes in conjunction with small business ownership have had significant political and social impacts in these countries.[8]

In Central Asia the transition to entrepreneurship and business ownership emerged out of necessity, as in developing countries. At least half of the working population is one way or another self-employed in the region. This high figure is an indication of the lack of alternative job opportunities rather than entrepreneurial choice.[9] Entrepreneurial traits such as motivation, alertness and innovative thinking develop while entrepreneurs learn to cope with market conditions.[10] Despite its involuntary origins, small business entrepreneurship emerges as a critical source of change in transition to markets with a wide range of business forms. However, the Soviet political and market conditions make this entrepreneurial class unique. The USSR had a remarkable networked economy that integrated disparate resources and formed them into a functioning production and distribution system. While developing countries never had such a networked economy, Central Asian businesses inherited this legacy. Unfortunately, the networked economy did not survive the dissolution of Soviet markets and Central Asian entrepreneurs had to cope in unique ways to compensate for this failed legacy. As state employment has been declining and privatised industrial enterprises have shed their bloated workforces, private businesses became the sole source of employment for families and the backbone of many local economies. Thus, all forms of entrepreneurial activity increase the density and scope of markets, sustain populations and provide essential goods and services.

Different exchange regimes in Soviet markets provided early incentives for entrepreneurship. Many disguised forms of entrepreneurial activities existed and rapidly grew during the final years of communism.[11] Cooperative formations and reform cycles towards small ownership in the 1960s and 1970s in Eastern Europe and later during the 1980s in the Soviet Union allowed privately operated businesses to grow and take advantage of endemic shortages of consumer goods and raw materials. In Western regions of the Soviet Union, these spurred workers' cooperatives and other entrepreneurial forms while in other regions it failed to penetrate into society. The case of Estonia and three Central Asian republics illustrate these points well. With a historical legacy of international trade and manufacturing prior to them being part of the Soviet Union, entrepreneurial activates remained alive in Estonia and quickly grew along with the economic reforms of the 1980s. In Central Asia, however, private and disguised entrepreneurship remained small in subsidy dependent regions. Not only was the number of cooperative formations much smaller in comparison but new enterprises also faced societal and official resistance. Both in Kazakhstan and Uzbekistan violent riots broke out against cooperatives, along with bouts of ethnic strife. These had political undercurrents as incumbents imposed restrictions on economic activities and the transactions of new cooperatives in favour of preserving their stakes in Soviet markets.[12]

Soviet markets and enterprise development

Soviet market structures have long inhibited the growth of entrepreneurial activities and business diversification. Even many years after the dissolution of the USSR, this continues to be a major impediment to enterprise growth. The Soviet system under its planned and command economic order had both spontaneous and induced market relations. Horizontal and vertical interactions among different units forming Soviet official markets evolved as did the behaviour of individual units. In vertical interactions, each unit in the hierarchy possessed administrative authority over the units below. Horizontal interactions were characterised by direct interrelations between units, in which neither unit had administrative authority over the other. Legal markets, semi-legal markets and illegal markets formed an array of exchange regimes.[13] In the post-1965 period, there had been various attempts to increase participant discretion in enterprise transactions and this led to deepening layers of transactions of goods and services beyond state control. A range of entrepreneurial activities by institutional players, households and individuals steadily grew.[14] Submerged entrepreneurial exchange regimes first and foremost flourished out of distortions and endemic shortages for input materials and consumer goods. They benefited from information asymmetries and logistical problems for enterprises in far-flung regions.

Households got engaged in exchange activities within a range of markets with each other as well as with state enterprises and collectives. Households had a substantial proportion of the sales of certain food items, sharing the total market with collective farms. A broad array of goods and services were sold in interhousehold transactions. These included summer homes (dachas), the servicing and construction of these houses, plumbing, electricity as well as private tutoring and private doctors. The household-to-household black market formed a second economy and was quite widespread. It was composed of individuals who confiscated or stole state property and sold it for private profit, and those who illegally produced consumer goods, usually with state property as inputs, using state machinery and equipment. In these submarkets there were also goods produced by state enterprises but which were kept in short supply. The demand and supply mismatch led to speculative activities by individuals who accumulated scarce goods and traded them on the black market.

Despite the unofficial accommodation of individual entrepreneurial activities, businesses were long suppressed leading to distortions that still impinge on Central Asian markets.[15] The sources of these distortions include (i) an inflexible industrial structure; (ii) a contrived regional specialisation; (iii) an illusion of full employment; (iv) an obscure pricing policy; and (v) profound information asymmetries.

Manufacturing, especially in defence and heavy industries, and in construction were advanced and developed mostly in Russia and the Ukraine. In contrast, many service sector activities such as trade, catering services and finance were underdeveloped due to the priorities central planning gave to manufacturing. Central Asia as well as the Caucuses had a resource-driven economic structure and regional specialisation which limited the growth of a diversified industrial base. Private firms were virtually non-existent outside of a few cooperatives. Despite the widespread practice of bartering and other exchanges by households, clandestine small markets and kolkhozes, entrepreneurial activities remained tiny.

The faith planners placed in economies of scale and vertical integration led to massive industrial complexes utilising the subsidised transportation of railroads for bulk distribution. Large industrial complexes (such as massive metallurgical industrial compounds commonly referred to as kombinat) led to rigidities in economic restructuring.[16] They often faced input shortages and distribution problems in meeting their planned targets. It became increasingly very expensive and operationally difficult to upgrade their technological base or to break them into manageable units. This form of resource driven large industrial structure made market transition to smaller and more functional enterprises much harder. Specialisation and regionalism created further distortions as far-flung regions developed into mono economies according to the priorities of the command system with poor coordination and inadequate transportation infrastructure. Therefore, regional exchange regimes created long-term dependence on subsidies. Cotton monoculture in Uzbekistan, hydroelectric power and animal husbandry in Kyrgyzstan and the metallurgy industry in Kazakhstan are examples of such regional specialisation. Networked economies and input-output relations among industrial units collapsed with the dissolution of the USSR. As countries diverged in their pace of economic reform, enterprise restructuring and customs policies, it become impossible to run many economic units with neighbouring country's inputs.

Although full employment was a basic provision of the Soviet state, the mismatch between the needs and skills in the economy deepened over the years. Enterprises faced labour shortages for a range of reasons: short budget constraints, low technological innovation, frequent supply interruption and idiosyncratic managerial styles. Although workers were free to change jobs if they wished, patronage relations, geographical isolation and institutional structures promoted lifelong employment within a single organisation and location. In Central Asia this meant low skill development and poor work discipline for most of the indigenous people who occupied mainly manual industrial jobs or worked in rural kolkhozes. The Soviet regime systematically used slave and forced labour until the death of Stalin. During the Second World War, a large number of war prisoners were employed in infrastructure, urban development and social projects as well as in auxiliary units in front lines. Millions of workers concentrated in massive farms, in single company complexes and satellite industrial and mining towns formed the essence of today's trapped labour markets.[17]

Along with different levels and types of Soviet markets, the pricing of raw materials, goods and services varied a great deal in sub markets and in the regions. Bartering and periodic shortages distorted pricing leading to multiple variable effects on the price of final goods as black markets for raw materials grew over the years. The surge of black markets in consumer goods led to higher shadow market prices and encouraged smuggling while the price of goods sold or traded by state enterprises was suppressed through indirect and direct subsidies. The real costs of utilising human capital and resources in unit production remained obscure. This lack of appreciation of input costs in the long-term not only distorted the efficiency of production techniques and enterprises but also led to wasteful management habits. This legacy of obscure pricing is still a continuing problem for Central Asian businesses due to inherited Soviet structures in the management and ownership of energy and infrastructure. For example, the use of gas, electricity, water and transport services have not been fully accounted and priced for domestic users as well as enterprises, leading to obscure cost calculations. At the same time, these public services are not reliable or standardised, either.

The party bureaucracy, state-controlled printing and media as well as the education system formed an integrated machine which monopolised information in favour of insiders and shrewd manipulators. As in similar regimes, the real advantage rested on the ability to control key information in order to retain power and privilege. Local party leaders, the heads of youth organisations (komosmol), kolkhoz managers and enterprise chiefs all had specialised knowledge and local inside information at their disposal. Those who had commanded strategic knowledge and political connections had stronger economic advantages. Such individuals traded specific information and favours through patronage networks. Disguised entrepreneurs, who identified and exploited information gaps, emerged as intermediary functionaries in running state enterprises. Their business was to fix the needs of Soviet markets and open blockages in the system. The party nomenclature needed both technical managers in enterprises and disguised entrepreneurs in the market to meet their targets. Thus, entrepreneurs today function in the debris of this Soviet market and find intricate ways to cope with new challenges stemming from authoritarian state structures and the haphazard growth of the markets.

Entrepreneurs and their businesses

I have complied a profile of entrepreneurs through an extensive survey of personal attributes, business paths, political opinions and market perceptions (see the Appendix). Most businesses emerged in the retail and distribution sectors through the early years of the dissolution of Soviet markets. In the early 1990s, only very small shuttle traders, street sellers and 'Perestroika entrepreneurs' were involved in trade. Later trade in both retail and wholesale sectors grew into large markets, trade centres and even shopping malls. Businesses diversified and moved into many new fields including entertainment, tourism, construction, real estate and manufacturing. This expansion brought the growth of professional and business services in accounting and finance, legal advice and information technology services. Another recent development began to take place with the growth of foreign franchises and their marketing and distribution agencies; mainly in luxury goods, detergents, body care and cosmetic products. These developments not only fuelled more entrepreneurial activities but also intensified competition, raised customer expectations and changed demand conditions, especially in urban areas.

Central Asian entrepreneurship arose in three waves, the first occurred before independence, the second was led by early movers and the third is characterised by the younger generation, professionals and late comers. In the first group, there are those who deployed their entrepreneurship talent and strategies during the Soviet period. These include small traders, craftsmen and peasants whose entrepreneurial activities expanded in the 1980s. Some of these activities were allowed in the kolkhoz markets but many were carried out discreetly. Another group of entrepreneurial activities took place in distribution and wholesale markets. However, since 1991, intensified competition, changing political priorities and coalitions resulted in a new economic ordering of wealth and power. Consequently, assets and enterprises changed hands as the rules of our Mikado game were being contrived.

The second wave consisted of pioneering capitalists and comprised two social groups, professionals and former members of the nomenclature who became new market opportunists. The professionals felt forced into entrepreneurial activities due to low salaries, the collapse of industrial establishments and the lack of options that were as attractive as those of the market. Many such entrepreneurs initially began trading consumer goods and a significant number of them got involved in shuttle trade with foreign countries. Within this group a growing number of entrepreneurs managed to survive and successfully penetrate into new markets. The other early movers were typically those who utilised direct links with Soviet era enterprises. They used their party positions to exploit access to newly privatised assets and emerging market opportunities.

Young entrepreneurs and other late comers emerged quickly. While some utilised well the rules of the Mikado game and made quick success, a great majority occupied lower echelons of the market. Among them there are many struggling business owners in small trade and services. An increasing number of young professionals with entrepreneurial ambitions, some with Western education, and often good political connections, have been establishing new businesses in emerging sectors such as media and marketing, information technology, mobile telecoms and advertising. These young entrepreneurs have bigger opportunities in Kazakhstan than in Kyrgyzstan, while Uzbekistan's closed and regimented economy undermines the efforts of even the most willing young entrepreneurs.

Business owners differ in respect to their personal attributes across the three countries. The analysis below shows the nature of this diversity in ethnic origin, religion, education, age and gender (see Table 3.1).

Ethnicity

Entrepreneurs somewhat reflect ethnic varieties found in each country. In my survey, the majority of entrepreneurs (60 per cent) are ethnic Uzbeks within Uzbekistan, reflecting their majority status within the country. Other ethnic groups include Tajiks, Koreans, Crimean Tatars, Uyghurs and Meshketian Turks. Russians constitute only 4 per cent of the entrepreneurs I surveyed. This contrasts with Kazakhstan where almost one third of entrepreneurs are Russians (31 per cent). Kazakhs are the largest single group but make up far less than half (38 per cent). A wide range of other ethnicities, many from diaspora communities from throughout Eurasia participate in entrepreneurial activity including Armenians, Azeris, Greeks, Germans, Koreans, Kurds, Turks, and Uyghurs. In Kyrgyzstan, ethnic Kyrgyz entrepreneurs occupy half of the sample (49 per cent) and Uzbeks constitute a fifth. Ethnic Russians account for a little less than ten per cent (8 per cent). The rest came from a variety of communities (24 per cent). These include Dungans (Han Chinese Muslims), Koreans, Germans, Meshketian Turks, Tajiks, Uyghurs and a set of other ethnic groups from the Caucasus (Chechens and Avars in particular).

Kazakhs and Kyrgyz are underrepresented in the entrepreneurial stock. In addition to ethnic diversity caused by Soviet resettlement policies and deportations, new migrants seek opportunities as Central Asian economies begin to show positive growth. There are a few attractions for such groups: market opportunities are not fully explored; the heterogeneity of cities makes it easy to blend in; local business know-how and competition is limited in the production and trade of many goods and services. The most populous recent trans-national entrepreneurs include Chinese, Koreans, Turks and Uyghurs. The first three benefited from recent liberalisation in trade regimes. Uyghurs, however, are following a long tradition of intercultural trade. The recent influx of this leading merchant group is also a response to the fierce suppression of Uyghurs in Xinjiang, the Uyghur Autonomous Region in western China.

Along with ethnic variety comes religious diversity and entrepreneurs from old sedentary cultures such as Dungans, Meshketian Turks, Uzbeks and Uyghurs are more visibly religious and traditional in following Islamic rituals of fasting, daily prayer and dress code. However, their adherence to Islam shows variety and is often shaped within the customs

Table 3.1 Personal attributes of the surveyed entrepreneurs

		Kyrgyzstan	% of Country	Uzbekistan	% of Country	Kazakhstan	% of Country
Gender	*Male* % of Total	34 (36.6%)	45%	34 (36.6%)	71%	25 (26.9%)	43% (100)
	Female % of Total	42 (47.2%)	55%	14 (15.7%)	29%	33 (37.1%)	57% (100)
	Total Cases	**76**	**100**	**48**	**100**	**58**	
Ethnic Origin	*Kyrgyz* % of Total	37 (100%)	48.7%	–	0%	–	0% (100)
	Russian % of Total	6 (23.1%)	8%	2 (7.7%)	4%	18 (69.2%)	31% (100)
	Uzbek % of Total	15 (34.1%)	19.7%	29 (65.9%)	59.2%	–	0% (100)
	Kazakh % of Total	–	0%	–	0%	22	38%
	Other % of Total	18 (33.3%)	23.7%	18 (33.3%)	36.7%	18 (33.3%)	31% (100)
	Total Cases	**76**	**100**	**49**	**100**	**58**	

(Continued)

Table 3.1 Continued

		Kyrgyzstan	% of Country	Uzbekistan	% of Country	Kazakhstan	% of Country
Education	*Middle School*	8	11%	3	6.7%	1	2%
	% of Total	(66.7%)		(25%)		(8.3%)	(100)
	High School or technical lycee	25	33%	19	42.2%	18	31%
	% of Total	(40.3%)		(30.6%)		(29%)	(100)
	University	42	55%	18	40%	36	62%
	% of Total	(43.8%)		(18.8%)		(37.5%)	(100)
	Postgraduate	1	1%	5	11.1%	3	5%
	% of Total	(11.1%)		(55.6%)		(33.3%)	(100)
	Total Cases	**76**	**100%**	**45**	**100%**	**58**	**100%**
Marital Status	*Married*	62	82%	43	88%	47	82.5%
	% of Total	(40.8%)		(28.3%)		(30.9%)	(100)
	Single	7	9%	3	6%	5	8.7%
	% of Total	(46.7%)		(20%)		(33.3%)	(100)
	Divorced	4	5%	3	6%	2	3.5%
	% of Total	(44.4%)		(33%)		(22.2%)	(100)
	Widow	3	4%	–	–	3	5.2%
	% of Total	(50%)		–		(50%)	(100)
	Total Cases	**76**	**100%**	**49**	**100%**	**57**	**100%**

Note: Total number of cases (N) = 183. Missing cases are not included in some categories.

of their own ethnic community. Russians and other Christians such as Ukrainians, Greeks and Armenians in the sample expressed little interest in religion.

As there has been an increasing penetration of faith based groups and initiatives in post-Soviet lands, entrepreneurs feel the influence of both Islamic proselytisers and Christian evangelical groups. There is also some evidence of increasing piety among entrepreneurs. This ethnic and religious variety is often recognised and tolerated well in the cosmopolitan major cities of the region. However, there are also different ethnic and religious undercurrents which breed tension and occasional violence among trading groups and businesses as well.

Education

Almost 60 per cent of all entrepreneurs surveyed have university education. This high educational attainment is associated with the middle class character of the entrepreneurs across Central Asia. It is also related to entrepreneurs' previous social status, which includes many professionals, as well as the fact that the majority are urbanites.

Many of the others are graduates of technical or vocational high schools and most of them come from artisanal backgrounds. Those with lower educational attainments tend to have stronger ties to small towns or rural communities. There are significant differences among the countries in relation to educational attainments. The significance tests show that entrepreneurs are more likely to have higher educational attainments in Kazakhstan than in Uzbekistan. Rural and semi-rural backgrounds are also more likely to be observed in Uzbekistan.

Gender and marital status

Slightly more than half of entrepreneurs interviewed in Kazakhstan and Kyrgyzstan were female. These female entrepreneurs were mostly concentrated in bazaars but they also engaged in professional services such as dentistry, pharmacy and legal consulting. In Uzbekistan patriarchal gender roles have led to a male dominated business life with 71 per cent of all interviewed small businesses owned by men.[18] However, there are also regional variations of this patriarchal character. While women are often confined to their homes with crafts in agrarian communities, especially in the Fergana Valley, more liberal attitudes prevail in Tashkent and Samarkand.

The vast majority of entrepreneurs are married (83 per cent). In Uzbekistan, however, only 12 per cent are single (classified as unmarried, divorced and widow). Traditional attitudes towards the maintenance of marriage as part of the social fabric are more frequently observed in Uzbekistan as marriage defines the social status of both men and women. Entrepreneurs tend to have smaller than the average families, with 65 per cent having two and fewer children. This feature also varies among the countries and Uzbek and Kyrgyz entrepreneurs are likely to have large families while only 16 per cent of Kazakh entrepreneurs have more than two children. These indicators also show the predominantly urban and professional character of entrepreneurs.

Size of the businesses

The size of business is measured according to the number employed at the time of the survey and most are very small. One of the most distinctive characteristics of the Central Asian market is this preponderance of very small businesses and the paucity of medium-sized firms. Only in Kazakhstan is there a significant proportion of somewhat larger firms, with 41 per cent of the sample employing between 11 and 50 workers. This compares with 24 per cent of firms between 11 and 50 employees in Uzbekistan and 27 per cent in Kyrgyzstan. The significance tests also confirm that countries differ with respect to the size of the business.

The fieldwork observations provide three possible explanations. First, positive economic growth in Kazakhstan contributed to business growth while in Kyrgyzstan political insecurity and the small domestic market inhibited business growth. Second, entrepreneurs in Uzbekistan as well as Kyrgyzstan frequently report that inspections and tax pressures constitute a major hurdle to business growth. Third, there are low entry barriers to very small trade and bazaar activities while few people have the capability to overcome impediments to growth (see Table 3.2).

Origins of the business

Overall slightly more than half of entrepreneurs (54 per cent) said that the current business was their first private business enterprise. This rate is slightly higher in Uzbekistan (57 per cent). Although these entrepreneurs experienced changes in location or minor shifts in the business, product or service, they remained within the same sector. Predictably, the majority of such cases occur in retailing and in commercial businesses. Although small in proportion, the first wave of entrepreneurial activities dates back to the mid-1970s and around 5 per cent of the sample established their business activities between 1974 and 1991. Most of these were formed during the Perestroika era after the mid 1980s, as illustrated in cases 3.1 and 3.2 (see Table 3.3).

Table 3.2 The size of businesses according to employee numbers

			Country			Total
			Kyrgyzstan	Uzbekistan	Kazakhstan	
Size of the business	1–5	Count	41	27	17	85
		% size of the business	48.2%	31.8%	20.0%	100.0%
		% within Country	53.9%	55.1%	29.3%	46.4%
	6–10	Count	13	9	13	35
		% size of the business	37.1%	25.7%	37.1%	100.0%
		% within Country	17.1%	18.4%	22.4%	19.1%
	11–50	Count	21	12	24	57
		% size of the business	36.8%	21.1%	42.1%	100.0%
		% within Country	27.6%	24.5%	41.4%	31.1%
	50+	Count	1	1	4	6
		% size of the business	16.7%	16.7%	66.7%	100.0%
		% within Country	1.3%	2.0%	6.9%	3.3%
Total		Count	76	49	58	183
		% size of the business	41.5%	26.8%	31.7%	100.0%
		% within Country	100.0%	100.0%	100.0%	100.0%

Note: Significant tests show no particular association.

Table 3.3 Establishment year of business

			Country			Total
			Kyrgyzstan	Uzbekistan	Kazakhstan	
The year of establishment	1974–1	Count	6	3	0	9
		% establishment year	66.7%	33.3%	0%	100.0%
		% within country	7.9%	6.1%	0%	4.9%
	1992–6	Count	19	15	10	44
		% establishment Year	43.2%	34.1%	22.7%	100.0%
		% within country	25.0%	30.6%	17.2%	24.0%
	1997–2001	Count	30	15	32	77
		% establishment year	39.0%	19.5%	41.6%	100.0%
		% within country	39.5%	30.6%	55.2%	42.1%
	2002–6	Count	21	16	16	53
		% establishment Year	39.6%	30.2%	30.2%	100.0%
		% within country	27.6%	32.7%	27.6%	29.0%
Total		Count	76	49	58	183
		% establishment year	41.5%	26.8%	31.7%	100.0%
		% within country	100.0%	100.0%	100.0%	100.0%

Note: Countries differ with respect to the entrepreneur's start-up period, with 90 per cent confidence. Uzbek and Kyrgyz entrepreneurs had earlier establishments, with Kazakh businesses expanding in the late 1990s.

The most rapid period of business formation was between 1997 and 2001 when 42 per cent of current businesses were established. Once again Kazakhstan stands out in these data and only 25 per cent of Kyrgyz and 30 per cent of Uzbek entrepreneurs started successful businesses in the whole period between 1992 and 2001.

Although comparative firm birth and death statistics are not available, the survey findings and other macroindicators show greater business dynamism in Kazakhstan. The sample shows that from 1992 to 2006, a significant segment of entrepreneurs did stay in the same business in Uzbekistan and Kyrgyzstan for more than a decade but in Kazakhstan more than half of the entrepreneurs (55 per cent) set up their current business from the late 1990s. This has various possible causes. First, the fieldwork observations indicate that business saturation might have occurred in Kyrgyzstan and Uzbekistan. This allowed longer survival times for businesses. Second, the post-independence economic performance of Kazakhstan was wobbly until the rise of oil prices and some economic reforms were introduced at the end of the 1990s. This might have affected the opportunities for enterprise survival and growth. Finally, the poor market reform performance of Uzbekistan and Kyrgyzstan since 2000 might have limited the growth of entrepreneurial activities and new business ventures. The accelerated economic growth of Kazakhstan since the late 1990s has been a major driving force behind new entrepreneurial activities in this country.

Case 3.1 – Early entrepreneurship and Perestroika

Residing in the northern Kazakh city of Semey, Rafail, born in 1956, has always had a strong instinct for survival. Rafail's family was among thousands of Tatars who were deported into Central Asian exile by Stalin; many died on the way. Rafail holds firmly to his Tatar identity and is proud of Kazan: the city's 1000th anniversary celebrations paraphernalia surround his office. He barely remembers his father, who died when he was only 5 years old. His mother was left with 6 children and she had to work hard to survive. Rafail left school at the age of 14 to work in a bakery in the neighbourhood and later did casual jobs. From 1979 until 1984, he worked in construction and traded goods on the black market. Rafail says he was a born entrepreneur: 'doing business has always been in my blood'. He got involved in gold production and marketing for a couple of years. During the early years of Perestroika he set up a cooperative with the encouragement and help of his political connections. He got involved in animal husbandry, construction materials and other small ventures in the meantime. During those years, Rafail recalls, major cooperatives emerged in trading wood products, iron and metals and construction materials. In 1995, his cooperative business began to go downhill and in 2000 it was dissolved. Nevertheless, he managed to gain control of its major assets: land, old equipment and some unfinished apartment blocks.

Case 3.2 – Disguised entrepreneurship and punishment in the USSR
Boris, born in 1959 to Russian parents in Almaty, struggled hard to remain independent during the Soviet period and despite the surveillance of the authorities, he brokered business deals. Boris not only suffered from peer pressures and social stigma but was also officially punished for his unauthorised entrepreneurial activities. For a while, he speculated in raw materials and inputs for state enterprises and was arrested, but later was released without consequences. He continued to pursue business dealings on the black market and in the consumer goods trade in the 1980s. He repaired cars for a while in addition to conducting shuttle trade after the fall of the USSR. However, as such activities began to die out and became less profitable with increasing competition, he began to look for new business ventures. In 1999, through a friend, he got involved in the printing and publishing business and later set up his own firm along with his wife to print posters for private events and public offices, billboards and family occasions. The business began to thrive and he invested in high quality European machinery and gained a good reputation. Orders began to flood in from other major Kazakh cities. However, Boris is deeply concerned about the future of his business since the import of cheap Chinese machinery has intensified competition from his imitators in polygraphic printing.

Perceptions about markets and information

Access to information is an essential component for business survival and growth. The survey data show that information about a range of fundamental areas such as finance, regulation and technology are either not available or only controlled by a small minority. This points out the continuity in Soviet structures but causes market segmentation and asymmetric relationships among businesses and with state institutions. This evidence indicates that along with widespread mistrust among entrepreneurs, market information is geographically and socially constrained and defined mainly by entrepreneurs' personal relationships.

Laws and finance

Countries differ with respect to the regard placed on information about laws and regulations in doing business. The statistical significance test shows that Kazakhstan and Kyrgyzstan display two contrasting cases, with the latter country's entrepreneurs perceiving information about laws and regulations as important. While acknowledging the significant effect of changes in laws about business regulation, taxation and standards, entrepreneurs are wary of arbitrary implementation. They also commonly feel that they are cut off from the consultation process of law making. For many, the laws seem drafted by and for powerful interests. When entrepreneurs were asked about how often they consult state institutions about business information and legal assistance, more than half stated that they never do it. Only 5 per cent of Kazakh entrepreneurs said they consult state institutions very often while this rate is around 10 per cent for both Uzbekistan and Kyrgyzstan.

The majority of entrepreneurs think that information on finance and credit opportunities is much needed. Yet there are differences in attitudes in relation to differing national circumstances. In Uzbekistan entrepreneurs complain about the rigidity of the banking sector as the government strictly controls cash turnover in the economy in a Soviet fashion (see Case 3.3). The recognition of external finance in Kazakhstan is associated with the relative openness of the banking sector to small businesses and the availability of widespread microfinance programmes. There was an increasing perception among Kazakh entrepreneurs that their country was becoming financially sound. Kyrgyzstan and Uzbekistan had poorly functioning banking sectors and weak financial regimes and entrepreneurs limited their use of formal financial institutions.

Case 3.3 – Cash collection in Uzbekistan: *incassatsiya*
The banking sector is highly concentrated and unreformed in Uzbekistan. The two top state banks account for between 60 and 70 per cent of total bank assets. The government uses daily cash collection, known as 'incassatsiya', to reduce the cash supply for exchange rate stabilisation and to control inflation. Bankers and tax inspectors work together to administer the collection of daily excess cash declared by business owners. They also observe businesses and bazaars to assess the daily turnover rates. Collected cash is deposited in entrepreneurs' bank accounts. There is a deep mistrust between the state and the entrepreneurs. The majority of businesses don't declare their real earnings and generally show only around 20 or 30 per cent of it. In principle, the entrepreneur

has access to his/her accounts but in practice the banks might delay or refuse prompt payments due to lack of cash or for other bureaucratic reasons.[19] The fieldwork observations showed that it typically took 15 minutes to half an hour for a business owner to prepare the cash to be dispatched. It was a matter of minutes for officials to collect it in cloth bags and get the necessary papers signed.

Business information and advice

Many entrepreneurs stated that they rely on the help and advice of family members for their day-to-day business management and information gathering. Overall 68 per cent said they ask help and advice of family and friends 'often' and 'very often' (that is, on a daily basis). Countries do not significantly differ in relation to the importance of family and friends in business dealings and market advice. After their families and friends, entrepreneurs obtain information about the market from their customers. Across the board, almost half of the sample entrepreneurs said that on a day-to-day basis they gather information from their customers. There appears to be a sharp difference between ordinary retailing activities and specialist businesses. In the service sector entrepreneurs stated that they seek specialist knowledge.

The third source of market information is from businesses in the same locality. Information transmission of business and political rumours is strongly bounded by physical proximity. The bazaars as entrepreneurial hubs provide this information externality with multiple exchange opportunities. Entrepreneurs in urban or suburban locations often obtain information from their business associates and social networks. Overall over one quarter (28 per cent) of entrepreneurs said that they consult other businesses on a daily basis. The rest of the sample entrepreneurs said often (38 per cent) and rarely (15 per cent) while nearly one-fifth (18 per cent) said they never consult or ask advice from other businesses in their locality. When asked if they consult business associations on business matters, many said they were not interested in doing so. The great majority in all countries said they never consult such organisations.

Television, newspapers and the Internet emerged as peripheral sources of information. The use of media channels is most common in Kazakhstan and this might be related to the fact that Kazakhs enjoy a degree of press freedom, uncensored Internet and other information sources. Overall low usage of media and printed press reflects a range of factors: the lack of trust in media, limited appreciation of its use, difficulties and other costs associated with accessing these mediums (see Table 3.4).

Table 3.4 How often entrepreneurs consult state institutions to obtain information (*)

| | | | Coded country | | | Total |
			Kyrgyzstan	Uzbekistan	Kazakhstan	
State institutions	Never	Count	37	27	27	91
		% state institutions	40.7%	29.7%	29.7%	100.0%
		% within Country	55.2%	57.4%	48.2%	53.5%
	Rarely	Count	12	8	18	38
		% state institutions	31.6%	21.1%	47.4%	100.0%
		% within country	17.9%	17.0%	32.1%	22.4%
	Often	Count	11	7	8	26
		% state institutions	42.3%	26.9%	30.8%	100.0%
		% within country	16.4%	14.9%	14.3%	15.3%
	Very often	Count	7	5	3	15
		% state institutions	46.7%	33.3%	20.0%	100.0%
		% within country	10.4%	10.6%	5.4%	8.8%
Total		Count	67	47	56	170
		% state institutions	39.4%	27.6%	32.9%	100.0%
		% within country	100.0%	100.0%	100.0%	100.0%

Note (*): Missing cases are not included. The association between the frequency of entrepreneurs' consulting with state institutions for advice and the country is not statistically significant.

Marketing and business growth

The great majority of businesses are not looking for new markets and many cannot see export markets as part of their business growth strategy, either. There are many reasons for this. First, many businesses in bazaars cater for local and regional demand only. They may also have international customers who travel across borders to order and buy goods directly. This occurs mostly in the large trading centres and bazaars of Bishkek and Almaty as well as border towns like Karasuu. In such locations there is already a reasonably well-established infrastructure for trading, packaging and shipping for traders from neighbouring countries and the CIS region. Second, international borders with varying customs rules and duties inhibit cross border trade, shipping and exports. This leads to widespread smuggling and illegal trade along the borders, carrying high risks of financial losses, confiscation, and arbitrary customs controls. Third, the nascent entrepreneurial activities of this middle class often lack the capacity to export beyond what is easily accessible. Only a small number of entrepreneurs in the sample were directly involved in exports and many chose unofficial or semi-official means through intermediary groups.

Entrepreneurs do not rely on the media for publicising their business activities and products (see Table 3.5). A significant number of enterprises never use newspapers or street billboards to advertise their business (24 per cent in Kazakhstan, 50 per cent in Kyrgyzstan and 72 per cent in Uzbekistan). In almost two decades of market growth, there is still a remarkable gap in information dissemination in Central Asia. This is most pronounced in Uzbekistan where more than 70 per cent of entrepreneurs said they never used newspapers, billboards, television or radio for advertisements. Kazakh entrepreneurs appeared most progressive in this respect as almost one third stated that they used newspapers and street billboards and one fifth radio and television to advertise their business 'often' or 'very often' (meaning more than one instance within a six-months cycle or monthly).

Three aspects of small businesses in the region negatively affect the use of media or printed press for publicity. The first is accessibility and cost. Information dissemination through the media is also limited due to state control and censorship. This is most noticeable in Uzbekistan but periodic purges also occur in Kazakhstan and Kyrgyzstan. When businesses become more visible and appear prosperous they face new fees and charges. Secondly, many entrepreneurs choose to cultivate business relations with their customers and business linkages through personal contacts rather than open advertisements. Other simpler methods, such

Table 3.5 Advertisement about the business through newspapers and street billboards (*)

			Coded country			Total
			Kyrgyzstan	Uzbekistan	Kazakhstan	
Newspapers and street billboards	Never	Count	34	34	14	82
		% news. billboards	41.5%	41.5%	17.1%	100.0%
		% within country	50.0%	72.3%	24.1%	47.4%
	Rarely	Count	8	6	21	35
		% news. billboards	22.9%	17.1%	60.0%	100.0%
		% within country	11.8%	12.8%	36.2%	20.2%
	Often	Count	16	5	8	29
		% news. billboards	55.2%	17.2%	27.6%	100.0%
		% within country	23.5%	10.6%	13.8%	16.8%
	Very often	Count	10	2	15	27
		% news. billboards	37.0%	7.4%	55.6%	100.0%
		% within country	14.7%	4.3%	25.9%	15.6%
Total		Count	68	47	58	173
		% news. billboards	39.3%	27.2%	33.5%	100.0%
		% within country	100.0%	100.0%	100.0%	100.0%

Notes (*): Missing cases are not included. Countries differ with respect to the frequency of advertising via newspapers and street billboards, at 1 per cent significance levels. While advertising seems limited via these channels in Kyrgyzstan and Uzbekistan, the responses of Kazakh entrepreneurs suggest a frequent use of newspaper and street billboards for advertising purposes.

as individual referrals and network contacts work better for small businesses. Thirdly, the small-scale operations of entrepreneurs could not be scaled up easily under current market conditions; thus wider publicity did not appear to be important or meaningful. However, this general lack of exposure to media and information channels limits the deepening of markets. Consequently, it leads to geographical closure and fragmentation in and around socially embedded relations. In addition, the absence of any free media perpetuates a general sense of ignorance about domestic developments as well as international affairs.

Information technology

Entrepreneurs show limited awareness about new technologies and equipment, especially in Uzbekistan. This is yet another indication of markets being constrained and cut off in this country. In contrast, 60 per cent of entrepreneurs in Kyrgyzstan and Kazakhstan indicated that it was easy to obtain information on new developments and equipment. At least in theory, Kazakh and Kyrgyz entrepreneurs think that they face little difficulty in obtaining such information. As far as information technology is concerned, the use of computers in the workplace is rare among retail businesses but more widespread in service and professional businesses. IT is primarily used for accounting and record keeping purposes. Overall, one in every 5 entrepreneurs has computers but they commonly use them at home and the majority of these do not have regular Internet access; another indication of low engagement with information outlets and broader networks.

Labour market

There are endemic skill shortages, geographical fragmentation and lack of intraregional mobility of labour. Information asymmetries work in favour of the urban elite. There is a statistically significant difference among the countries in obtaining skilled labour. Kazakh entrepreneurs most openly speak about the challenge of obtaining skilled workers. This is in line with macroeconomic indicators according to which the growing Kazakh economy is increasingly facing skilled and semi-skilled labour shortages. In Uzbekistan and Kyrgyzstan, a fifth of entrepreneurs have never hired professional employees for their businesses and the vast majority do not see any labour shortage. Very high unrecorded youth unemployment (thought to be around 30–40 per cent) in Uzbekistan is one reason why these entrepreneurs do not perceive any problem. However, there is a general lack of appreciation of skills and ignorance about their availability. Many entrepreneurs were more conscious of the trustworthiness of employees and of work discipline than concerned about advanced skills. Some argued that young employees often lack interest in hard work in Kazakhstan. These indicators, along with many other observations, show weak labour market formation; businesses mostly relay on relatives and use their social connections as the main source of labour.

Perceptions of institutions and governance

Perceptions on a wide range of governance related issues revealed where entrepreneurs stand in relation to institutions and the state authority. These show significant differences among the countries with no specific difference according to age, ethnicity, or gender (see Tables 3.6–8).

Overall, entrepreneurs see the weaknesses of post-Soviet governance as an important shortcoming in their personal lives, societal relations and day-to-day business dealings. Their concerns with institutions and governance are presented here in four major categories: the legal system and the judiciary, customs and police, the national assembly and the presidencies, and finally municipal and public services. Entrepreneurs place least trust in the judiciary and courts, followed by the customs authorities and the parliaments. Despite their misgivings about the unlimited power of presidents and their families in state affairs, they see the president as the guarantor of a minimal but necessary stability for their societies.

The legal system and the judiciary

Only one out of 183 business owners said that the judiciary in their country is 'very good'. Kyrgyzstan had better satisfaction levels as 30 per cent rated judiciary and courts as 'good'. However, in Kazakhstan and Uzbekistan, there is a deep dissatisfaction; none of the respondents rated their legal system and judiciary as 'very good' and only around one in every ten entrepreneurs said the judiciary was 'good'. Low levels of satisfaction with the judiciary stem from partial and arbitrary law enforcement in each country. Entrepreneurs need to trust the legal system in order to secure contract enforcement and to dissuade abusive behaviour by the parties in their business transactions. Such confidence expands multiple transactions and stimulates market growth. However, the overwhelming majority of entrepreneurs do not trust the justice system and try to avoid courts in addressing their business and personal problems.

Many stated that instead of going to the courts they would seek the help and advice of their influential and powerful relatives and friends. Connections among people provide essential social capital for business

Table 3.6 Opinions on how the judiciary and courts work (*)

Judiciary courts			Kyrgyzstan	Uzbekistan	Kazakhstan	Total
	Don't know	Count	9	18	28	55
		% judiciary & courts	16.4%	32.7%	50.9%	100.0%
		% within country	12.3%	40.0%	48.3%	31.3%
	Bad	Count	22	10	10	42
		% judiciary & courts	52.4%	23.8%	23.8%	100.0%
		% within country	30.1%	22.2%	17.2%	23.9%
	Not Bad	Count	19	11	14	44
		% judiciary & courts	43.2%	25.0%	31.8%	100.0%
		% within country	26.0%	24.4%	24.1%	25.0%
	Good	Count	22	6	6	34
		% judiciary & courts	64.7%	17.6%	17.6%	100.0%
		% Within country	30.1%	13.3%	10.3%	19.3%
	Very good	Count	1	0	0	1
		% judiciary & courts	100.0%	0.0%	0.0%	100.0%
		% within country	1.4%	0.0%	0.0%	0.6%
Total		Count	73	45	58	176
		% judiciary & courts	41.5%	25.6%	33.0%	100.0%
		% within country	100.0%	100.0%	100.0%	100.0%

Note (*): Missing cases are not included. There is a statistically significant relationship between opinions on work of judiciary and courts and the country, with 99% confidence.

Table 3.7 How customs work (*)

Customs			Kyrgyzstan	Uzbekistan	Kazakhstan	Total
Don't know	Count		6	14	22	42
	% within customs		14.3%	33.3%	52.4%	100.0%
	% within country		8.6%	30.4%	37.9%	24.1%
Bad	Count		23	17	8	48
	% within customs		47.9%	35.4%	16.7%	100.0%
	% within country		32.9%	37.0%	13.8%	27.6%
Not bad	Count		22	6	22	50
	% within customs		44.0%	12.0%	44.0%	100.0%
	% within country		31.4%	13.0%	37.9%	28.7%
Good	Count		18	8	5	31
	% within customs		58.1%	25.8%	16.1%	100.0%
	% within country		25.7%	17.4%	8.6%	17.8%
Very good	Count		1	1	1	3
	% within customs		33.3%	33.3%	33.3%	100.0%
	% within country		1.4%	2.2%	1.7%	1.7%
Total		Count	70	46	58	174
		% within customs	40.2%	26.4%	33.3%	100.0%
		% within country	100.0%	100.0%	100.0%	100.0%

Note (*): Missing cases are not included. Countries differ with respect to the perceptions about the functioning of customs at 1 per cent significance levels. On average, dissatisfaction with customs services can be noted in three countries, with negative perceptions among over one third of the respondents in Uzbekistan and Kyrgyzstan.

Table 3.8 Opinions on how the national assembly work (*)

			Kyrgyzstan	Uzbekistan	Kazakhstan	Total
National assembly	Don't know	Count	5	17	26	48
		% assembly	10.4%	35.4%	54.2%	100.0%
		% within country	6.8%	37.0%	44.8%	27.1%
	Bad	Count	24	13	7	44
		% assembly	54.5%	29.5%	15.9%	100.0%
		% within country	32.9%	28.3%	12.1%	24.9%
	Not bad	Count	21	7	15	43
		% assembly	48.8%	16.3%	34.9%	100.0%
		% within country	28.8%	15.2%	25.9%	24.3%
	Good	Count	22	8	9	39
		% assembly	56.4%	20.5%	23.1%	100.0%
		% within country	30.1%	17.4%	15.5%	22.0%
	Very good	Count	1	1	1	3
		% assembly	33.3%	33.3%	33.3%	100.0%
		% within country	1.4%	2.2%	1.7%	1.7%
Total		Count	73	46	58	177
		% assembly	41.2%	26.0%	32.8%	100.0%
		% within country	100.0%	100.0%	100.0%	100.0%

Note (*): Missing cases are not included. There is a statistically significant relationship between the degree of perception of national assembly's functioning and the country, with 99 per cent confidence. Higher dissatisfaction is observed among Uzbek respondents.

survival. Such connections are interim solutions which in general substitute for poor legal and institutional workings but in the long-term they also undermine the development of effective law enforcement. Across Central Asia, there exist many self-help groups consisting of civil servants, police and social network members who solve contractual and business problems on a reciprocal basis. Asil is illustrative of this:

Case 3.4 – Enforcement and law avoidance through self-help networks

A police department employee, Asil, is an old college friend of Erlan and they grew up together in Turkestan, in southeastern Kazakhstan. Both moved to Astana with their families as the new capital city offered growing employment opportunities as well as housing for the expanding middle classes. Asil helped his relatives to buy cheap apartments in the lucrative housing sector of Astana through government quotas allocated to civil servants. Erlan works with his wife in the retail trade and the couple own two small shops. Whenever they face bureaucratic hurdles, unpaid debts and customs problems, they go to Erlan who sorts out problems with his wide network of colleagues in the police department and other governmental institutions; sometimes free of charge, sometimes with a small kickback depending on the scale of the matter. Such help is reciprocated with goods and offers made to Asil and his family as well as others within Asil's social network. The reciprocity and trust built into these relationships form a tight network, and remains above the law and institutions in addressing personal and business matters, big or small.

Customs and police

Customs is the second worst institution according to entrepreneurs. In all countries there is a general level of discontent as only 1 or 2 per cent of entrepreneurs classify their customs as 'very good'. The main problems include colossal bureaucracy and outdated Soviet rules. Businesses suffer from arbitrary treatment and widespread bribery. In Uzbekistan import-substitution policies led to virtually closed borders and encouraged illegal border trade through illicit groups often built into the civil service. During the survey, those who had limited exposure to customs or managed to get by through their special contacts and means, opted out of answering this question by stating 'I don't know'; this was highest in Kazakhstan (38 per cent) and Uzbekistan (30 per cent). While there is a degree of accommodation in Kazakhstan, Kyrgyz entrepreneurs expressed a polarised view; 33 per cent said they had 'bad' experiences and 26 per cent said 'good'. The negative perception was the highest in Uzbekistan (37 per cent) followed by Kyrgyzstan (33 per cent) and it was much lower in Kazakhstan (14 per cent). There emerge three positions. First, dealings with customs officials differ according to the type and size of the business. Many retailers employ intermediary groups and increasingly sort the customs hurdle without personally being involved. Second, in professional businesses and services, often suppliers deal with customs officials. Third, an official cushion or self-governing syndicates are often used as intermediaries.

Overall, only 4 per cent of respondents say the police force in their country works 'very well' and only one in five say it is 'good' across the region. However, significance tests again show a marked difference among countries. Paradoxically, both satisfaction levels are lower and indifference levels are higher in Kazakhstan as 43 per cent say they 'don't know' and almost 14 per cent say 'good'. This indicates a general apathy towards the police in Kazakhstan where there is less police presence in cities compared to Uzbekistan and Kyrgyzstan. In Uzbekistan, which has the most organised and largest police force, 40 per cent of respondents ranked the police as 'bad'. These complained about arbitrary charges, harsh treatment and corruption.

National assembly and the presidency

Surprisingly, a large number of entrepreneurs displayed a clear apathy to their parliaments and a lack of confidence in the electoral system. Many respondents said that they do not have any opinion about how to rank the performance of their national assembly: it is 44.8 per cent in Kazakhstan and 37 per cent in Uzbekistan. This rate is much lower for the more politically active and vociferous Kyrgyz (6.8 per cent), as indicated by several popular political upheavals. There, 29 per cent of respondents said their national assembly does a reasonably good job and 30 per cent stated that it works 'well'. However, almost one in every three respondent still believes that the national assembly is dysfunctional and does not serve the interests of the Kyrgyz people. According to survey results and anecdotal information, Kazakh entrepreneurs were also deeply sceptical about the functions of their representative system. Since the economy was growing and the business climate was becoming stable, many chose to remain apolitical. Statistical significance tests show that the highest degree of dissatisfaction occurs among Uzbek respondents. Uzbeks expressed low levels of trust and respect for their national assembly and complained about its ineffective role in reducing poverty and improving the business climate.

Countries differ with respect to the perceptions about the role of the presidency as well. Among Uzbeks, almost one third of respondents are critical of the Karimov regime and only a small proportion (13 per cent) ranks their presidency as 'good'. There is widespread discontent among entrepreneurs towards illiberal economic management and deep state control in the economy. In Kyrgyzstan and Kazakhstan, the respondents appear to be more cautiously satisfied and acknowledge that their presidency is 'not bad' or indeed 'good'. In Kazakhstan, this is respectively 24 per cent and 29 per cent; and it is 29 per cent and 33 per cent in Kyrgyzstan. Anecdotal evidence shows that until he was ousted, Askar Akayev and Nursultan Nazarbayev both enjoyed widespread popularity and a certain degree of respect among entrepreneurs. However, entrepreneurs were also vocal about the control of economic assets by the presidents and their families; a Kazakh entrepreneur put it:

The laws on paper might be fine. The problem is they don't work because of other factors such as corruption, control of the president and the influence of his family in the economy.

Yet, despite their widespread discontent with laws and institutions, entrepreneurs saw the presidents as guarantors of the stability of the regime in their respective countries. The dissolution of the USSR illustrated well how whole societies came to the brink of total economic collapse. With a fear of future instability and turbulence, many entrepreneurs were willing to compromise and extend their support to the presidents; even in Uzbekistan almost one fifth (19.6 per cent) stated that the current presidency is 'not bad' after all.

Municipal and other public services

Public services are in dire condition in both urban areas and the countryside across Central Asia. Infrastructure built by the Soviets perhaps was better than third world countries at the time but they suffered from poor technical, physical and environmental standards. Water, sewage and heating infrastructures and all other municipal services need upgrading and massive investment. Public transportation is obsolete, making many neighbourhoods and villages cut off, especially during harsh winters. Poor transportation infrastructure further inhibits access to schools, hospitals and workplaces. Simple rail and road connections concentrated around regional capitals of the old economy are no longer sufficient to serve the needs of new economic relations and the delivery of goods and services. First, the national infrastructure grids need to be developed to overcome the interdependence built among the autonomous states by the USSR. Second, priority given to energy exports for revenues limits domestic demand and underdeveloped energy markets lead to periodic shortages and uncertainty, in particular in Uzbekistan and Kyrgyzstan. Third, there are regional imbalances and massive losses due to leakage, wasteful use and sabotage by illegal traders, especially in gas, oil and electricity.

Case 3.5 – The cost of poor energy supply

Poor energy supplies and interruptions negatively affect businesses. Entrepreneurs in Khiva and Andijan complained about gas shortages and cuts suffered throughout the winters. While illegal use was common, there were also wasteful practices such as heating large Soviet industrial blocks with open stoves or common use of inefficient heating units. The lack of gas in winter was blamed on the governments' poor planning and the priority it gave to gas exports at the expense of local demand. An entrepreneur in Andijan, who used electric heaters during the winter of 2004 due to lack of gas supply, was fined 7000 USD for his high usage of electricity. This caused him almost full bankruptcy. The fine was based on a government decree banning the use of electric heaters during that winter. The entrepreneur did not know about this decree and was surprised to find out that there was no legal position to defend himself against a cabinet decree.

However, in the allocation of and access to municipal infrastructure, entrepreneurs have certain advantages. First and foremost, poor pricing and control bring the economic advantages of low charges, abundance of goods, and even graft. I have seen many examples of wasteful use in work places with no regard to insulation or energy preservation. Such behaviour is also linked to Soviet habits of apathy towards government provided infrastructure. Disrespect towards such resources might be seen in relation to corruption. Entrepreneurs see no incentive to preserve, protect or ration public services and energy infrastructure as they claim their taxes were being wasted and local and central government officials deplete their earnings through bribery.

The town centres have better access to infrastructure provision, in particular electricity, gas and water. There is a higher expression of satisfaction among the Kyrgyz respondents as almost half of the sample classifies municipal services as good (46.6 per cent). This rate is 24 per cent in Uzbekistan and 21 per cent in Kazakhstan. The most satisfactory points were recorded for postal and telephone services: in all countries more than half of the entrepreneurs regard them as 'good'.

The countries differ with respect to satisfaction about educational quality. There is a shared perception among respondents that quality of education is not at desirable levels. The strongest dissatisfaction was expressed by Uzbek and Kyrgyz respondents. In education and health, quality of service is dependent upon the connections to get access to good schools or hospitals and more importantly ability to pay. However, widespread corruption in public services limits free access to good quality education and medical services. Many respondents noted that students can bribe teachers to pass or to get good grades even in higher education. Declining quality of educational qualifications in turn generates a huge stock of under-skilled professionals. Deterioration in Russian language education without being replaced by effective titular language teaching mean the youth have poorer literacy skills than the generation of their parents. Anecdotal evidence and casual observations indicate that many entrepreneurs are keen to send their children to the best private schools, or abroad, for better education. In Kazakhstan, state funding allows an increasing number of students study abroad. Both Kyrgyz and Kazakh states encourage foreign investment in education as well. In Uzbekistan, however, the state strictly controls educational institutions and minimises foreign contact.

Entrepreneurs' concerns and demands from the state

Entrepreneurs were asked to list their major concerns and demands from the state. First, almost all entrepreneurs in the sample complained about the lack of clarity in regulation and the legal system. Business owners learn of the implications of legal changes when they need to get paperwork sorted out in government offices or when they see inspectors and tax collectors at their door demanding new charges. In the *Doing Business* ranking of the World Bank, which covers 178 countries, the CIS countries show a widening divergence in their performance. While Eastern European and Baltic states have significantly improved their business laws and institutional workings, the Central Asian states remain at the lower end of this ranking with the exception of Kazakhstan which progressed to the 71st position in 2007. Kyrgyzstan is lower with a ranking of 94th. Uzbekistan, along with Tajikistan, scores significantly worse then its neighbours. It is the 138th country, above only the very worst performing economies, mostly in Africa.[20] Second, taxation and corruption emerged as two other immediate areas where entrepreneurs expected governments to act in order to improve the business climate. The majority of entrepreneurs in Kyrgyzstan (60 per cent) and Uzbekistan (57.5 per cent) see taxation as the main area where governments should change their policies and improve institutions. This demand was somewhat muted in Kazakhstan where government has been decisively reducing the tax burden on small businesses in recent years. Third, an important aspect of business growth and survival is linked to the availability of external finance. More than half of the surveyed entrepreneurs stated that external finance opportunities and the banking system should be reformed by their governments (60 per cent in Kyrgyzstan, 57.5 per cent in Uzbekistan and 48 per cent in Kazakhstan).

Businesses face a constant threat of absorption of their profits from government employees, state institutions and self-regulatory groups. This, combined with the culture of falsification inherited from the Soviet era, leads to widespread cheating by all parties involved, businesses and state institutions alike. State institutions and government employees try to take advantage of this confused state for their own benefit through bribery. Low salaries and deteriorating living standards force government employees and professionals to seek alternative sources of income. Bribing has become not only the easiest but also a socially acceptable form of exchange. Varying forms of extortion and bribery have become routinised. They commonly construct relations between businessmen and civil servants with regard to procedures including taxation, business permits and customs charges.

The legacy of Soviet centralisation emerges as various forms of state capture. In Uzbekistan, it remains highly centralised in a hierarchical manner and applies to all aspects of the bureaucracy. For many years Kyrgyzstan's form of state capture was more decentralised because until recently the central state administration was weak. In all three countries state employees top up their low salaries through illicit fines and charges, the upper echelons of the bureaucracy obtain the lion's share of these transactions.

Entrepreneurs have to cope with the remaining Soviet legal structures and institutional procedures and at the same time follow new laws and regulations introduced for a market economy. Not only does this double track institutional environment creates loopholes, inconsistencies and further confusion, but it also threatens businesses through various forms of arbitrary implementations. A Kyrgyz entrepreneur pointed this out with the following complaint:

> There is too much bureaucracy, both new and old regulation. There are 22 governmental institutions involved in getting a construction and business permit. We would like to build a new business site;

some institutions give permission while others refuse to sign the forms. If we try to satisfy each one of them with a 1000 som fee, this will make in total 22,000 som.

Double cheating and falsification seem most pervasive in Uzbekistan where the state and its insiders constantly introduce new measures to control, streamline and exploit businesses. In response, entrepreneurs develop sophisticated techniques to avoid these measures.

Case 3.6 – Double cheating
Nazira first began sewing at home and selling garments while she was still a full-time school teacher. Later, she started to trade from an open stall at the Hippodrome, Tashkent's large market area. As a parallel business, she also sold fresh flowers. After travelling to Istanbul in the late 1990s, she decided to bring special garments and gowns to expand her business. As the business successfully grew she opened an elegant shop with mechanise from Moscow and Istanbul. She laments:

> Doing business in this country is very hard. Many people take advantage of us. Just recently, I had 280,000 USD worth of goods taken away from my store by people who claimed to be customs and tax officials. Who is thief, who is police and who is customer I hardly know! I hired a lawyer to get my goods back but couldn't get anywhere. I couldn't prove that they were stolen from me.

Since Nazira successfully avoids customs duties she has no clear registration or customs clearance documents to prove that any of the goods are hers. In the meantime, she hides her most expensive garments in secret storage areas at her home.

Since most of the entrepreneurs surveyed were recipients of microcredit, we could see a variety of uses that they made of this source of finance mostly as a strategy to cope with the generally unstable and opaque financial regimes. They used microcredits mainly for three purposes: to satisfy family needs, to address short-term cash flow problems in business, and to lay the foundation for long-term investments, mainly in real estate. The credits sometimes were spent on special occasions such as weddings, funerals and family celebrations. Such spending is not always wasteful because it forms part of the reciprocal relations necessary to maintain the solidarity networks that all entrepreneurs need. The Uzbek system of *incassatsiya* is only the most egregious cause of cash flow problems. These impediments aggravate the already universal cash flow problems that entrepreneurs everywhere commonly face. One Uzbek entrepreneur expressed the general problem in this way:

> The government should let businesses flourish more freely with limited interference. Bribery, taxation and regulations all inhibit cash flow and business growth and it has been increasingly getting worse, not better, since independence. I need to buy stock and need cash, the government collects our excess cash but it is impossible to get this cash back from the state controlled banks.

Conclusion

Despite the pathetic predicament of small capitalists as a class-in-between, there is great potential for entrepreneurship in Central Asia. Albeit strained, this stratum continues to flourish while providing livelihoods and social stability. Some continuity with Soviet social structures is striking: the personal profiles of most entrepreneurs clearly indicate their Soviet era status as middle class urbanites. The entrepreneurial middle stratum today is dominated by middle-aged men and women most likely with higher education while their more provincial, less educated, counterparts survive on the margins of the market. Another Soviet feature is the multiethnic and multifaith character of these mostly urban entrepreneurs. Therefore, we can see that the Soviet era urban professional middle classes and their provincial counterparts became a new entrepreneurial class while the Soviet economic regime and its corresponding occupational and social structures dissolved.

These entrepreneurs function as a cushion to ease the impact of economic fluctuations and meet the societal needs in compensating for weak public services. Their entrepreneurial pathways are intricately linked to market opportunities, regional dynamics and state-market relations. In many cases they suffer from information asymmetries, poor legal provisions and state absorption. In response, they aim to minimise their dealings with institutions and insulate their market positions through socially embedded networks and informal relations.

The survival of the Mikado game necessitates the survival of these entrepreneurs, too. This emerging entrepreneurial stratum is concentrated in sectors such as foodstuffs and consumer goods retailing and services where there are low entry barriers. These businesses form a long tail extending from medium-sized businesses with specialised assets and growing market share to personally managed microbusinesses. While the upper end of this tail is inevitably connected to the ruling elite, the lower-end entrepreneurs survive by scavenging through the rubble at the margins of the market. In between, many businesses manage to prosper, or die according to more recognisable market dynamics. For example, medium-sized manufacturing plants acquired through privatisation are invariably linked to influential cadres within the state bureaucracy. Entrepreneurs acquired these assets either through their direct role as employees within related institutions or because they enjoyed direct access to the administrators of the privatisation schemes through party and/or tribal social networks. Some managed to transform these assets successfully while others failed. Enterprises which emerged autonomously and successfully grew after 1991 came into contact with the upper stratum as they drew their attention through market control mechanisms. I will address these relationships in the following chapters.

Finally, entrepreneurs see taxation, corruption and poor legal protections as crucial issues negatively affecting their business. While the majority of entrepreneurs do not trust state institutions and the parliamentary system, they are concerned about political instability and extend considerable support to authoritarian presidential regimes. Information asymmetries limit business scope and growth. Information is costly, uneven and incomplete due to narrow interest group control, poor linkages among institutions and the lack of a free media. Local and regional economies are cut off from each other because of long distances and poor transportation. The infrastructure built to link such regions among autonomous states is no longer in use and they now face strict customs controls.

4
The Political Economy of Bazaars

> We are land-locked and never had a strong industrial base. Therefore, we must do everything to develop cross-border trade; otherwise we are doomed.
>
> *A Kyrgyz parliamentarian*

Introduction

Bazaars are highly attractive places in most, otherwise indistinguishable, post-Soviet cities. For casual visitors as well as serious customers, they function as avenues for socialisation, entertainment and shopping. The vivid colours of bazaars, the range of sounds and the excitement were often lacking in Soviet urban culture. Much social expression, long disguised in Soviet public life behind a serious and gloomy façade, is unleashed and normalised in bazaars. Stalls display a great variety of goods, retailers anxiously attract the attention of passers by, hawkers chant, porters yell as they push light trolleys through crowded narrow alleys. Ushers try to attract customers, fortune tellers urge shoppers to have their futures read from burning herbs while blind singers and beggars jostle for attention.

Bazaars embody a market, a specific physical place where exchanges occur as opposed to the abstract notion of 'the market'.[1] Throughout my survey, I came across large and small bazaars that contained a wide range of social settings, business activities and entrepreneurs. Most residents of Central Asian cities rely on bazaars for their daily consumption and other general household needs, ranging from food and cleaning materials to electrical appliances and used cars. Some, like the Siyob Bazaar in Samarkand, still operate on the sites where once historic Silk Road bazaars traded spices, crafts and the silks of the Orient. Many such old bazaars lingered on as simple farmers' markets and kolkhoz trading locations during the Soviet Union. Others like the Mal Bazaar, an animal market in Karakol, are places where nomads have congregated for centuries, travelling from their pastoral hamlets to exchange stock for produce and to supply their seasonal needs. Such markets have long been the locales for economic exchange among nomads as well as between them and settled farmers and artisans. Since the collapse of the Soviet economy, new modern mega markets have emerged. The bazaars of Bishkek and Almaty today exemplify the novel phase of capitalism as centres of trade and distribution in regional economies. The physical size, scale and character of these bazaars vary greatly. Yet invariably they stand at the heart of enterprise development, income and wealth generation, and provide goods for millions of people. Central Asia's emerging entrepreneurial spirit and its cultural and ethnic diversity have gained a renewed momentum in the deepening market relations of these bazaars.

Beneath these colourful and vibrant scenes of trade, there is also a continuous battle for control of revenues, taxes and rents. This contested political and economic situation is veiled, just as their chaotic appearance disguises a highly controlled environment. Only when occasional tension erupts in traders' protests and clashes between militia and demonstrators can one really notice the underlying power dynamics and delicate balance between owners and occupiers of these sites. For the most part, the control and reallocation of bazaar revenues remains deeply rooted in the Mikado game of interchange. There is a range of positions leading to cooperation and conflict among self-governing syndicates, business groups and municipal officials. Bazaars serve as the medium in which the business interests of middle stratum entrepreneurs interact with land owners and regulators. Interest groups form, dissolve and re-form alternating between cooperation and opposition in relation to political power as they manoeuvre to gain control. The interplay of these stakeholders constitutes a microcosm of Central Asian market building.

In this chapter, we will see the economic value, significance and functions of bazaars. I will introduce several cases with particular characteristics to illuminate their scale and nature. These cases will include two mega markets, Dordoi in Bishkek and Baraholka in Almaty, and Samarkand's traditional market, Siyob. I will provide a discussion of the economic and political significance of bazaars pointing out the shortcomings of mainstream economic approaches. By examining the contested nature of ownership and co-option mechanism, this chapter will also show how bazaars have an economic logic within a framework of information asymmetries and agglomeration effects that we can see through the character of a layered Mikado game.

Soviet origins of trade

The Soviet regime banned commercial undertakings by individuals and periodically curbed the growth of alternative markets with punitive measures. While small-scale foodstuffs retailing was allowed in kolkhoz markets, sales of consumer goods and industrial input materials took place in unofficial Soviet markets. By the 1980s, there was already a widespread practice of trading smuggled, confiscated or stolen goods from state enterprises. Given the severity of supply shortages and their domino effect on interdependent enterprise networks, unofficial trading mitigated the shortages of input materials. In order to fill their production quota or meet annual targets, managers of state enterprises needed these alternative markets to function. Paradoxically, despite the common knowledge of such widespread underground commercial activity, Soviet authorities had no ideological or practical tools to legitimise them. The common deception led disguised entrepreneurs and state officialdom to pretend that all was in compliance as they reaped the benefits of such markets.

Top party officials were guided by a deep-seated fear of loosing economic and political control to private groups and to local power building in the Autonomous Republics. They understood that the growing economic influence of private interests undermined the state's coercive powers. The Soviet state systematically denied official and legal recognition for such enterprising activities while at the same time, as the Soviet economic system got overstretched, it grew dependent on underground economic activity to ameliorate the endemic supply and demand mismatch. Hypocritically, the state ideology continued to condemn individualist merchants and portrayed private interests as immoral.

Despite several attempts to reform Soviet enterprises from the Khrushchev era, only during Perestroika did the communist leadership seriously attempt to lessen official restrictions on trade while aiming to curb so called 'mafia markets'. With a series of microeconomic reforms in the late 1980s, private interests were allowed to function within new enterprise formations, most notably through cooperatives, joint stock employee ownership structures and through leasing.[2] These changes in enterprise formation created pockets of exchange regimes but overall they failed to produce the expected efficiency outcomes. These enterprises did not rehabilitate the economy, nor did they cure endemic shortages.[3] What the economic reform policies achieved was the creation of new groups of opportunists who emerged from inside the state's control mechanisms with no real competition. This group included the progenitors of today's oligarchs who became insiders as these early market reforms took hold. Many of these were able to take advantage of the meltdown of state enterprises, especially gaining control of extractive industries, banking and heavy manufacturing through voucher privatisation schemes.[4]

In trade, new entrepreneurial opportunities emerged out of the semi-privatisation of kolkhoz bazaars and the establishment of joint stock ownership formations. After the dissolution of the USSR, commercial activities became central to employment and consumption across post-Soviet lands. With the influx of shuttle traders and increased retail activity, demand for new commercial and business sites steadily grew. From the margins of the Soviet economy, trading markets grew to become central to employment and the provision of goods in urban economies. Yet only a few legitimate commercial spaces existed in urban areas during the Soviet times. These included state-owned department stores, kolkhoz bazaars and small neighbourhood markets. Traders and consumers initially filled up these existing markets and spread across pavements and parks. Recognising the need for retail space as an opportunity, local governments and private businesses began building large sites for traders. With no rent control and constantly changing planning decisions, traders faced an opaque and unstable situation. Idiosyncratic land ownership structures introduced by Soviet cooperative experiments and subsequent privatisation schemes gradually led the way to the expansion of old bazaars and the construction of new ones. Bazaars continued to be rebuilt as they became sites of major economic activity. Local authorities and private owners soon diversified their interests by building not only bazaar sites but also shopping arcades and malls to benefit from charges levied on the burgeoning retail and distribution trades. Regional governors and municipal officers play central roles in redistributing lands, allocating building permits, licensing traders and applying myriad of regulatory controls.

Large bazaars have been transformed into main hubs for regional trade. Massive bazaars such as Baraholka and Dodoi led the way. Others have been established along the borders of Uzbekistan in the Fergana Valley such as the ones in Jalalabad (Kyrgyzstan) and in

Khojent (Tajikistan). While the Karasuu Bazaar in the Kyrgyz town of Karasuu is the main centre of Chinese consumer goods in Central Asia, all other bazaars provide new market opportunities for businessmen in the region. Yet there are diverse sources of goods and merchandise from Turkey, Russia, Dubai, Iran and a range of other countries. Dordoi Bazaar in Bishkek caters for Kazakh and Russian markets. Various charter flights and buses run from Dordoi to several major cities in Kazakhstan and Russia. Nevertheless, despite the buoyancy of trade and the willingness of risk-taking traders, incompatible border regimes have negatively affected intra-regional exchanges and the volume of trade. In spite of the range of multilateral and bi-lateral agreements and organisations, such as the CIS agreements and the Shangai Cooperation Organisation, obstruction of trade by customs rules have been detrimental to the region's economy. A UNDP study on regional cooperation, trade and investment illustrates the wider implications of this. The economic costs of the lack of cooperation among Central Asian countries have significant GDP implications and hurt household welfare. Limited transportation options, poor quality roads and closed borders bring higher trade costs and limit the scope of small and medium-sized enterprise development. The same UNDP study calculated that a 50 per cent reduction in trade costs would lead to significant GDP increases in the region (annually 55 per cent in Kyrgyzstan and 20 per cent in Kazakhstan).[5] Border regions suffer most negative effects from limited cross-border transactions with their natural trading regions. For example, towns like Andijan in Uzbekistan and Osh in Kyrgyzstan were close trading partners until Uzbekistan sealed its borders in 2001; after which both sides suffered from the loss of economic exchange.

Three diverse bazaars

The Dordoi, Baraholka and Siyob bazaars illustrate the diversity of origins and ownership structures (see Table 4.1). Although they hold superficial similarities, each of them evolved while being subjected to the contrasting governance regimes of their respective countries and the dynamics of reallocation regimes.

A pioneer bazaar: Dordoi

In the northern outskirts of Bishkek, stretching 2 kilometres along the main road, the Dordoi bazaar covers roughly 1.5 square kilometres within a massive grid comprising mainly standard 60 cubic metre

Table 4.1 The characteristics of the three selected bazaars

Bazaars	Uzbekistan Siyob (Samarkand)	Kyrgyzstan Dordoi (Bishkek)	Kazakhstan Baraholka (Almaty)
Spatial size	7 hectares	150 hectares	650–750 hectares
	257 shops Around 3500 traders in stalls, shops and mostly small hawkers	Around 10,000 traders in dozens of sublocations 20,000 people work in the bazaar and its auxiliary jobs	Over 20,000 retailers and 50,000 people work in trade and auxiliary jobs of 25 submarkets
Origin	Historic Silk Road market rebuilt as a Soviet kolkhoz	Initially a small flea market	Initially a small flea market
	Transferred to the municipality	New commercial site built by private ownership and shipping containers.	Separate bazaars built along the major road
Ownership	Stable	Conditionally stable	Partly stable
	Limited liability company controlled by protégés	Family partnership	Dispersed ownership through limited liability companies and individuals close to the governorate, courtiers and the ruling family.

shipping containers.[6] Dordoi is a pioneer of modern bazaars and is by far the largest one among around 70 markets in Bishkek. Dordoi is a world within a world where multiple layers of trade and human relationships interact.

The bazaar has both retail and wholesale sections. Its narrow alleys are cluttered with foodstuffs in one section, garments in another and consumer goods in yet another. The automobile trade occupies one fringe, and decorative items and school supplies spill out in the other direction. A massive service sector has developed along with trade including banks, brokers and informal currency traders, restaurants, bakeries and snack sellers, packaging services, porters, taxis and hauliers. Colourful marginal activities abound: singers, ushers, beggars and barkers advertising bargains. The bazaar is a mirror of the wider society, gendered and stratified ethnically. Women dominate retailing in garments and small consumer items while mostly men conduct trade in automobiles and large wholesale businesses. Most businesses are shared responsibilities of couples and even extended families. Ethnic groups utilising their own networks have fostered specialised trading such that Uyghurs are prevalent in the textiles section while the Kyrgyz deal in ready-made garments. The greater significance of ethnic ties, however, is in the international links that characterise the market's trading activities. The Dungan and Uyghurs import from China, Uzbeks from Tashkent and the Fergana Valley, Russians from Russia and almost everybody has at some point engaged in shuttle trade with Istanbul or Moscow and Dubai. Dordoi has been a gateway mainly for Chinese products and to a much lesser extent Western merchandise of all kinds. Over half of the goods sold go to neighbouring Central Asian countries and Russia.

Dordoi's economic significance can be seen in a number of indicators. This scale of business keeps around 20,000 people employed, thus making Dordoi one of the most important sources of employment in the country. There are roughly 10,000 trading locations half of which are containers and the rest operate from a variety of stalls, small corner kiosks and shops. Three thousand of the containers are owned by one family, the Salymbekovs, who collect rents and manage the site. Dordoi triggered several imitators in the region including Karasuu Bazaar, near the Uzbek border. By 2004, over 80,000 people were visiting the bazaar daily and generating turnover of many millions of dollars.

The containers on the site can either be rented or purchased. There are daily service charges paid to bazaar administrators and tax authorities irrespective of the container being rented or owned. The container prices indicate the buoyancy of trade as they can vary from 20,000 to 40,000 USD. The daily turnover of the bazaar is probably in the range of 4–7 million USD turnover.[7] Small stall owners have turnover as little as 10 or 20 USD while container owners in lucrative sections can make thousands of US dollars in a day. While the average state employee earned between 20 and 30 USD per month in 2004, retailers with containers in Dordoi reported that they had a turnover of between 400 and 700 USD. Each trader paid a daily fee of roughly one dollar (40–50 Kyrgyz som), and site rents varied between 100 and 2,000 USD per month depending on the location and the type of trade. Additionally, traders paid a security fee and utility costs to the bazaar administration. They also paid a combined tax and licence of 20 USD per month (700–800 som) directly to the tax authorities.[8] In aggregate, these large sums of cash in circulation made bazaars attractive to both the state organs and self-governing syndicates.[9]

Some of the idiosyncrasies of Dordoi are related to the peculiarities of its geography. As Ulugbek Salymbekov, the Western-educated son of the owner, put it:

We are at the dead-end of Central Asia, surrounded by high mountains and isolated from major economic centres and markets. With new international trade connections at Dordoi we can become a hub between China and Kazakhstan. Yet, regional developments are beyond our control as border restrictions hamper trade. Successful businesses are always imitated quickly and that is why we also need to diversify our investments.[10]

A chain of many bazaars: Baraholka

On the northern outskirts of Almaty, a sprawling bazaar, Baraholka, stretches along the main road and extends over an area of ten square kilometres.[11] In the early 1980s, Kazakhstan had 260 bazaars, 8 of them in Almaty. By the year 2000, the city had ten times as many, among 900 bazaars across the country.[12] Baraholka, meaning 'flea market' in Russian, originated as an Uyghur community bazaar. When the border between Xinjiang and Kazakhstan opened in 1985, Uygurs on both sides of the border engaged in cross-border trade at a time when commerce and bazaar trading were not considered to be morally acceptable. Although they are vastly outnumbered, Uyghurs continue to trade and in a few sections constitute one-third of active traders.[13] One ethnographic study showed the multiethnic character of Baraholka, pointing out the large number of Uyghurs, Dungans, Koreans and Russians while ethnic Kazakhs constituted less than half of the traders.[14]

This stretch of land is covered by long concrete blocks, shops, shipping containers and open market places.[15] Like Dordoi but on a larger scale, Baraholka deals with the full range of goods and employs approximately 50,000 people. The rent of stores or containers varies depending on the size, location and type of business between merely a couple of hundred dollars to thousands per month. Also like Dordoi, traders pay fees to bazaar administrators in addition to their rent. The total turnover of trade in Baraholka is roughly eight times more than Dordoi, with a low estimate around 50 million USD per day.[16]

Each bazaar at Baraholka is owned and structured differently. Some are entirely privatised and run by individual owners and others have complex ownership structures that involve several business interests and the local government as partners. The construction of new trade areas and in-town shopping malls has diversified commercial spaces. This generated a new business diversification and social fragmentation; new modern malls and high street shopping areas solely cater to the upper middle classes.

The growth of commerce has made property ownership attractive for business groups and foreign investors. The fragmented ownership structure of many of Baraholka bazaars remains highly obscure as major players are linked to the governor and the mayor's office. Business groups and single landowners often shield themselves behind complex ownership and property rights arrangements. Municipal authorities and private groups increasingly set their eyes on renovating and reconstructing old sections of Baraholka to generate revenue and upgrade the city.[17] One such new market, Adem, has massive long concrete blocks several storeys high. These monstrous buildings are divided into small units comprising dense shopping arcades. This appearance seems to appeal to the modern ambitions of ordinary people as well as the new generation technocrats. They are the result of concerted policies to replace supposedly unhygienic traditional bazaars with buildings deemed more suitable to the self-image of Almaty as the financial capital of a rapidly growing and westernising country. At the same time such modern structures generate new rents and allow owners to control traders more easily in newly designed buildings.

A subdued and aged bazaar: Siyob

Compared to their bustling counterparts, most Uzbek bazaars look impoverished. In Tashkent, the Chorsu bazaar spills out haphazardly from its Soviet-era concrete dome in all directions. Within the dome there is an orderly food market. In the streets and alleys beyond, all manner of stands, carts and traders with goods spread on the ground before them vie for business. Newly built shopping arcades look grim in comparison and traders endlessly complain about the lack of business.

Overall, keeping bazaars physically scattered and relatively small seems to be a municipal and government strategy.[18] Despite its large domestic market and entrepreneurial people, Uzbekistan lagged behind in terms of the economic freedoms it allowed to flourish in trade. The ancient Silk Road city of Samarkand, famous with its roundel bread and pilaf, has long lost its prosperous days in commerce and art. The majority of its 400,000 people live on marginal incomes from small trade and production. Thousands of people try to sell on the streets to get by and survive. Around Bibi Khanum Mosque, one of the most refined Timurid monuments, there is the oldest and largest bazaar of Samarkand, Siyob. This is an ancient trading site and it survived as a small kolkhoz market during the Soviet era. The market grew remarkably since 1991 on 7 hectares (0.07 sq km) of land. Siyob had over 1,900 open or semi-open stalls and 257 shops selling construction materials, foodstuffs, furniture and clothing.[19] But the total number of traders seemed to be around 3,500 as hundreds of hawkers roamed in and around the market, often trying to avoid the security officers and bazaar administrators.

Most goods come from Iran, China and Pakistan through intermediary large wholesalers; others come from Tashkent markets. Cloth sacks of exotic spices sit beside piles of famous Samarkand bread. There are some 20 varieties of Samarkand bread each with a unique pattern and trading on traditional names. Along with ready-made clothes, hand made garments, other craft items abound. Siyob looks more like a traditional market than its Kyrgyz and Kazakh counterparts. But like the others it has an opaque ownership and management structure while the land belongs to the municipality.

The bazaar administrators claimed that store owners paid a land tax annually of around 105 Uzbek som per square metre (roughly 10 cents in USD). They were the privileged group of traders who enjoyed more comfortable work conditions and were able to sell more sought-after merchandise.[20] Hundreds of others had no long-term legal guarantee for their trade. They paid both the daily occupancy fee to trade and also a tax. The daily fee varied according to the type of goods they traded. For spices and dried fruit it was 800 som per day and for fresh fruit sellers it was 200 som. The administrators claimed total net monthly rental income of the bazaar was around 16,000 USD. My observations suggest the real figure could have been twice this amount and this still does not account for numerous additional charges levied on traders. Although prices and salaries have been kept artificially low in Uzbekistan, the shadow market existed in all forms of transactions.

While the land is owned by the municipality, the bazaar was governed by a private joint stock company where 51 per cent was owned by the municipality and the remaining 41 per cent was split among 150 private investors.[21] About 125 people worked in Siyob as cleaners, tax and fee collectors, administrators and security guards. Both traders and administrators commented on the high degree of surveillance in the market. While traders complained about worsening economic conditions, the administrators claim that fees are needed to pay for the peace and security they provide. Salaries were artificially kept low and prices were controlled by municipal administrators. Ordinary Uzbeks were constantly reminded of the chaos in Kyrgyzstan as opposed to the order and authority in Uzbekistan. One bank officer stated,

> Here everything is strictly regulated. Without documents no one can trade in the bazaar. Food prices are also controlled. Thus, turnover is not as high as in poorly regulated Kyrgyz bazaars.

The range of goods, sold in small quantities on tiny stalls is one indication of the impoverishment of small traders. For capital-rich merchant families the situation is different. However, they still lack confidence in the security of their property. One woman explained,

> There are a lot of goods illegally imported from neighbouring countries in Uzbekistan but people are afraid to show it in large quantities as officials or private groups can find reasons to confiscate them.

Later I learnt from long established Tajik trading families in Samarkand and Bukhara that many prefer to keep the excess variety of their merchandise, especially valuable textiles, jewellery and other craft items, in their homes. My observation is that through strict regulation, price caps and municipal control, the Uzbek bazaar regime hinders entrepreneurial initiative, limits the choices of consumers and perpetuates scarcity.

Bazaar economy as market economy

Bazaars are often regarded as peripheral to the market economy. Some see them as backward forms of exchange peculiar to Middle Eastern Islamic institutions and subject to a pre-modern economic rationale.[22] Such approaches ascribe social relations a more important role than economic ones in bazaars. In this view, customers do not necessarily seek the lowest price or best quality. An individual buys from a friend, sometimes to help and sometimes to ensure that the friend will reciprocate. Another assumption is that bazaar firms are not necessarily rivals to each other since the bazaar is a social and cultural system. Competition, for example, is understood to be different with the focus on buyer-seller relations. Prices are determined by negotiation and most transactions lack a formal framework.[23]

Relegating bazaars to a merely socially embedded form of exchange sets them apart from mainstream economic analysis and undermines their real contemporary economic role. Traditionalist and orientalist interpretations that regard bazaars as products of cultural and economic backwardness grossly misinterpret their economic and political role.[24] In classical Greek cities, an agora, a central market place, occupied a pivotal location in the physical and social urban fabric. On the Silk Road, bazaars evolved as major commercial centres where goods transported from far lands were organised and exchanged.[25] Local producers and artisans displayed their craft and production skills and competed against one another on price and quality. Many eighteenth- and nineteenth-century travellers recounted the diversity and vivacity of bazaars in Central Asia. Curiosity about Eastern exoticism even led to innovative business ideas based on copying the concept of the bazaar and influenced the early formation of department stores along the lines of oriental bazaars in nineteenth-century England. This experiment illustrated the transportability of the idea of spatial concentration of variety and the social experience of shopping. The first London bazaar opened in Soho in 1815. Within months, other bazaars emerged in Leicester Square, Newman Street, Bond Street, St James's Street and the Strand. By 1816, there were at least sixteen other imitators in London alone. Bazaars were widely praised by customers but criticised by those whose conventional business was hampered. These sites became a pleasure ground for upper-class customers as the variety of goods was a novelty. Despite resistance from traders and small shopkeepers, by 1840 bazaars, often established in large warehouses, became a fad in the urban retail scene.[26]

Spatial concentration and articulation of economic interests in bazaars led to the emergence of collective identity and solidarity among business owners enhanced by mutual help and exchange networks. Bazaar merchants, producers and money lenders formed a peculiar and resilient social stratum. Sometimes they were victimised as culprits of economic declines and shortages leading to bazaars being plundered by angry mobs during civil unrest. The urban poor periodically looted bazaars in the Middle East and India during the nineteenth and twentieth centuries. At other times bazaars instigated instability and upheavals due to their political and economic discontent. Major bazaars exerted decisive influence on politics and economic privileges between rulers and business groups. Information and rumours, which are articulated and spread from bazaars, have long played a pivotal role in influencing public opinion. The articulation of business and political opposition in bazaars often led to conflicts with the central authority and fuelled dissent. Traders' upheavals and revolts not only inflicted instability but also, when combined with other societal alliances, toppled rulers.

In the contemporary context, the regime change in Iran illustrated the power of alliances between merchant classes and the Islamic clergy.[27] Arang Keshavarzian's study of the political role and mobilisation of merchants during the Shah regime and its aftermath provides a nuanced analysis of bazaars in relation to coercion and co-option strategies of the state. Tehrani bazaar merchants, like most of their counterparts, long craved independence from state authority. The Shah and the Islamic regime pursued different strategies towards bazaars. These shaped the institutional setting and physical location of the networks that constitute the organisation of the Tehran Bazaar and aimed to engender its commonly noted capacity to mobilise. In the case of the Pahlavi monarchy, the regime followed a strategy of high modernism that tended to downgrade the state's incorporation of the bazaar while openly promoting alternative retail modernisation projects through shopping centres and new outlets. This strategy unintentionally fostered the economic autonomy of the bazaar by insulating it from social and economic engineering. Concentrated business linkages within the physical confines of the bazaar further protected bazaar merchants but their political opposition also sharpened. The economic polices of the Shah regime was most vocally opposed by these entrepreneurs in bazaars. Along with mosques and coffee houses, bazaars played a critical role in the mobilisation and organisation of popular opposition during the Iranian revolution. An alliance emerged between the bazaar and the clergy and contributed to the forceful removal of the Shah.[28] After the revolution the popular movement became more ideologically and less economically motivated as the ideal of the Islamic state began penetrating into social and economic institutions.

Subsequently, the Islamic regime moved to curb the potential political power of bazaars through a range of coercive policies and co-option mechanisms. Old merchant families were edged out by the new men with connections to clerics in the government. State policies have not simply threatened the Tehran Bazaar or changed its composition, but also radically restructured its internal organisation and its relationship to the state and economy. This had severe consequences for the political efficacy of the bazaar. Under the Islamic Republic's populist transformative agenda, the state incorporated traders and business groups as individuals and the co-optation, regulation and reterritorialisation of commercial value chains physically dispersed beyond the bazaar. Before the revolution, relations within the bazaar constituted a series of cooperative hierarchies fostering a great sense of group solidarity despite differences in economic power, social status and political proclivities. Under the Islamic regime, however, the bazaar's coordinating and distributing authority was transformed into coercive hierarchies with a diminished sense of collective solidarity. This shift from cooperative to coercive hierarchies limited the Tehran Bazaars' capacity to mobilise against the state and explains its relative quiet stance since the revolution.[29]

In Central Asia, bazaars as new hubs of capitalist market relations have massive economic and political significance as was the case in Iran. Contemporary bazaars initially emerged spontaneously in response to economic turmoil and political vacuums. Therefore, in their current nascent stage, bazaars in Almaty, Tashkent, Bishkek and elsewhere in the region do not yet rely on a conscious collective identity or political ideology. Apart from a very small number of eviscerated craft and merchant families, divided along ethnic lines, the region retains no collective memory or material wealth linking its people to the glories of the Silk Road or generations of merchant traditions. Bazaars such as Dordoi and Baraholka are nascent markets where mere survival, as opposed to pursing group interests, delimits entrepreneurial activities. Evidence from many interviews and focus group discussions shows how weak political engagement and opposition interests are. The upper strata groups frequently apply their arbitrary coercive powers to minimise collective obstinacy. Individual and group survival, mainly defined along family and friendship ties, takes precedence over civil and collective forms of engagement, especially given the high degree of mistrust endemic to these bazaar merchants.

However, as is evident in the Tehran Bazaar as well as many others, political power is an affordance of bazaars. Historically, the entrepreneurial middle stratum has been a source of powerful political movements. Concentration of business activities and strong network links makes these sites highly sensitive to official polices and municipal practices. This sets up an uneasy power relationship that is difficult to keep in balance. Frequent clashes occur between bazaar merchants and the upper social strata that exert control over the market. The tools used to assert power are usually in the form of licenses, fees, rent regulations, planning permissions and property rights, etc. all of which are means of accumulating wealth in the hands of controlling groups. Iran's experience illustrates how bazaars resisted economic policies that aimed to eliminate the collective power and identity of middle stratum merchants. Following the fall of the Shah's regime, bazaar merchants were again seen as a political threat and the Islamic government worked to co-opt and pacify them.

In Central Asia, bazaar merchants are frequently subject to the reallocation moves in the Mikado game of power relations. They are sensitive to alternative governance mechanism and constitute an index of tensions and conflicts in the economy. The position of the entrepreneurial middle stratum is precarious precisely because it is situated between those greater powers and the marginal traders, impoverished hawkers and jostling crowds who outnumber them within the bazaars' crowded alleys. Yet these merchants do not yet have a strong collective identity and political power to obstruct upper strata interests.

Coercion and reallocation

Throughout the 1990s bazaars emerged spontaneously out of veiled and apparently chaotic ownership structures. Many kolkhozes retained their control over legacy market sites initially through semi-privatised, joint-stock companies. Later these sites were expanded and new ones established by the kolkhoz administrators and municipal officers were able to take advantage of erratic deregulation and land privatisation. Other private groups took over market sites or existing bazaars, exploiting favourable deals with municipal authorities.

A variety of political and economic methods of coercion have been applied to tame and intimidate bazaars. By the late 1990s, many bazaars were becoming noteworthy political and economic players in the Mikado game. The largest of these, such as Baraholka and Dordoi, have become internationally significant. Controlling such assets required insider knowledge and protection from upper strata interest groups. Thereby, municipal authorities became indispensable in shaping land regulation and the ownership of bazaars. As the politics of ownership evolved, early insiders faced the challenge of stronger new rivals aiming to take control.

Recognising their economic value, the upper stratum players began to take control of bazaars by altering the rules in the allocation regimes. The two most common forms of these tactics are relocating a bazaar in a new site or reconstructing it on the same site with more units in a planned and controlled space. Other tactics of coercion include various forms of red tape, rental charges, administration fees and, when needed, brute police force. Protégés and their apparatchiks (such as city officials and legal advisors) have used diverse techniques to facilitate both relocation and reconstruction attempts. As official and legal bodies, they also regulated and herded bazaar traders into new locations. These groups handled the resistance and opposition of traders with a variety of tactics.

The first round of reappropriation and reallocation began with the change of ownership status of the kolkhoz bazaars during Perestroika. Small vegetable and consumer markets were restructured in order to provide more incentives that would ameliorate urban supply problems. The cooperatives that controlled such bazaars became vehicles for engineering new ownership structures in the post-1991 period. The second round came about through privatisation. Poor management led to the disillusion of consumer cooperatives, and ownership was transferred to individuals. Throughout the 1990s these small owners clashed leaving the most powerful ones in charge.[30] However, by the mid-1990s, local governments increased their control over land use and ownership of prime sites in urban areas. Meanwhile, the property of cooperatives became subject to land speculation. This pattern was most visible in Kazakhstan and Kyrgyzstan. However, in Uzbekistan the government kept Soviet cooperative structures intact. They slowly modified them to accommodate powerful private interest groups while maintaining state and municipal controls.

A third round of reappropriation coincided with the growth of retail and wholesale businesses in the early 2000s. Private group interests further diffused into new retail and wholesale sites. In Kazakhstan a diverse set of ownership structures emerged, expanding the positions for upper strata players as well as others along with economic growth and land speculation in all major cities. In Uzbekistan, limited liability companies were used as a vehicle to redesign property ownership and profits among stakeholders. Although often opposed by the traders, old bazaars were more often repaired and expanded, and given a modern appearance so that local government and private group insiders could collect further rents. This latest round of reallocation generated a new dynamic relationship among courtiers, protégés and the ruling families.

The status of bazaars

Bazaar owners rarely get involved in day-to-day affairs and in most cases their identity remains obscure. Bazaar administrators manage these sites on behalf of owners and act as liaison between traders and city officials. They collect daily charges and rents from retail and wholesale businesses. In many cases, several groups coordinate the rule of large sites. In Kyrgyzstan and Kazakhstan, rumours abound along with trickles of information in the media about the identity of courtiers, protégés and other stakeholders. In Kyrgyzstan, intra-business disputes reveal the role of the underworld. Exposure of such business clashes reaches the public eye through local journalists and reports in web sites of Western news agencies. Although it is often hard to verify the content of such rumours and reports, killings of a few key figures in recent years unearthed some truths about the activities of several illicit groups.

In Kyrgyzstan, bazaar owners led political opposition and reform movements. When Askar Salymbekov and his close friend Kubatbek Baybolov established the Dordoi bazaar in 1992, they both utilised their high standing in the Soviet era and strong ties to the Akayev regime. Both had former KGB ties and komsomol positions. Along with their extended families, both men established a strong regional base in the north of the country and retained close ties with the Akayev government. Salymbekov was the regional governor of Naryn province and later became the mayor of Bishkek. Soon after independence, the Salymbekov family built a business conglomerate with diverse investments in construction materials production, bottled water, tourism and textiles. These two families managed to protect their business interests through their personal roles in public office.[31] Following the ousting of President Askar Akayev, large economic interests began to change hands through a new reallocation regime controlled by the new president, Kurmanbek Bakiyev and his supporters. The business fortune of the Salymbekov and Baybolov partnership came under threat due to their links to the Akayev family. While the Salymbekov family abstained from political action during the popular upraising, a Baybolov family member, who supported the anti-Bakiyev rally in 2006, was threatened and reportedly transferred abroad some of his ownership assets in Dordoi.[32]

These rounds of reappropriation under the Bakiyev regime unleashed a power struggle among self-governing syndicates and their interests in bazaars.[33] The murder of a parliamentarian, Tynychebek Akmatbayev, from the Balykchy district of Issyk-Kul province in a prison riot in October 2005 let loose tensions among several groups. The subsequent events showed the convoluted ties between the legislature and several self-governing syndicates built into the political system. Tynychebek Akmatbayev's brother, Ryspek Akmatbayev, reportedly ran the biggest syndicate in the Issyk-Kul region with a strong political and social base. Ryspek recruited ex-sportsmen and bodyguards to protect business interests, and they reportedly carried out dirty tasks on behalf of former president Akayev. He posed an arguably stronger threat to the Bakiyev regime than political opposition groups. The southern leader Bayaman Erkinbayev, who was the owner of the Karasuu Bazaar, was believed to have sponsored the popular uprising which ousted Akayev. Another leader, from the north, Jyrgalbek Surabaldiyev, supported Akayev and is thought to have been behind the looting during anti-Akayev demonstrations.

Several criminal charges were filed against Erkinbayev, Surabaldiyev and Akmatbayev before the regime changed, all of which were suspended. Erkinbayev and Surabaldiyev were members of parliament and Akmatbayev had a brother in the parliament. Surabaldiyev was shot dead on 10 June 2006. Abdalim Junusov, a businessman, who took control of the Karasuu Bazaar away from Erkinbayev, was killed three months later. A few weeks after that Erkinbayev was also killed. Ryspek was suspected of carrying out these two killings.[34] But, he was also assassinated shortly after being elected to parliament in 2006. Clashing business interests left these three big bosses dead, probably through the manipulation by Bakiyev's secret police. For the time being, major bazaar owners were crippled by infighting and were rendered impotent to mobilise anti-government actions in Kyrgyzstan.

The Baian Aul bazaar in Almaty demonstrates alternative types of coercion and appropriation regimes.[35] Baian Aul started as an automobile and spare parts bazaar in 1995, accumulating around 3,000 traders by 2005. In five years, its initiators raised enough money to buy the site. However, in 2005 their property rights were challenged by the city authorities, who followed up their coercive pressure by using municipal police to close down the bazaar on grounds of poor sanitary standards. The traders and bazaar owners appealed to the parliamentarian Dariga Nazarbayev, President Nazarbayev's daughter, who opened the bazaar for one year. In June 2006, however, the conflict reemerged and the security forces closed it down again. Violent clashes and police brutality resulted in 19 traders being injured and the following month one of the bazaar owners was beaten up by hoodlums working for private syndicates. In response to intensified efforts of intimidation, most trade ceased and traders moved to other locations by the end of 2006. According to unofficial accounts, the dispute began when owners were forced to sell the bazaar land below market prices for a new development project. Local newspapers reported that the new players were high-level officials and family members including the regional governor and the president's brother, Bolot Nazarbayev, who is thought to have control of at least six large bazaars in Almaty. Altynbek Alpiev managed these large bazaars on behalf of the hidden owner Bolot Nazarbayev. Thus, the closure of the Baian Aul appears to be directly linked to a new allocation regime dictated by the members of the ruling family and courtiers in the city administration.

The Baian Aul case is part of a larger process of growing construction and land speculation in major Kazakh cities. The oil boom and increasing prosperity in Kazakhstan led to a massive increase in the retail spaces. The modernising ambition of the young Kazakh elite and government policies aimed to change the Soviet urban landscape as a sign of social progress and the prestige of the regime. Such initiatives are used to bring new business deals for construction companies closely associated with local governments.[36] Rental incomes for new commercial spaces and urban land speculation attracted businessmen and local governors to new projects. Bulat Abylov, the opposition leader of Ak Zhol Party, argued that urban land is being accumulated in the hands of governors, mayors and their associates. With the new urban development schemes envisaging massive shopping malls and commercial expansion, the governor of Almaty is generating new wealth for his close associates and government insiders, Abylov claimed.[37]

In Uzbekistan, bazaars are fragile and potentially explosive in their own ways. While reconstruction efforts remained mostly small scale compared to Kazakhstan, entrepreneurs in the bazaars often complained about the repair and rebuilding activities as they disrupted trade and invariably increased charges. One such bazaar was converted from an old silk factory in the town of Margilan, in the Fergana Valley. The space was massive but only a small proportion of it was taken up by traders. In a cold November day they shivered over their meagre offerings beneath massive concrete ceilings. The city officials and governors along with their business associates control bazaars through complex ownership structures. It is almost impossible to perceive the precise composition of the partners, the ownership of shares and the scale of revenues as they are shielded beneath layers of distorted information. Unlike in Kyrgyzstan and Kazakhstan, apart from vague rumours, there is no alternative information source to the government-controlled media. While both central and local governments claim to have a duty to keep order, fairness and law in bazaars, their assertion is rather deceptive. It is the insiders who periodically extract money from the traders and keep them on their toes. My observations and interviews in Siyob and other bazaars in Tashkent convinced me that the worsening economic conditions and authoritarian control make traders submissive to the regime that controls their business future. I was told by many traders that along with the militia, secret service operatives patrol bazaars in civilian clothes. Traders shun all sorts of anti-government remarks and activity to avoid trouble.

However, their silence rests on a fragile truce frequently interrupted by outbursts of anger. Thousands of people living on their small income from trade survive on the economic margins. Exposure to heat in the burning summer and cold during winter days damages their health. Their anger about government decrees and regulations limiting economic freedoms occasionally erupts in spontaneous clashes with authorities and the police. In 2004, one such eruption killed dozens of people when in Tashkent's biggest bazaar, Chorsu, traders clashed with the police. These violent protests took place in response to the government's new rules for private commerce and export-import operations aiming to extract further taxes and charges. Similar spontaneous protests occurred at bazaars in Kokand, Bukhara and Samarkand where traders voiced their opposition to government restrictions. Thousands filled the main bazaar in Kokand, shouting angrily against the new laws.[38] The biggest of such eruptions came when thousands of traders and their families along with local sympathisers joined anti-government protests organised by a group of political activists and armed militia in Andijan in May 2005. These groups demanded the release of around two dozen businessmen who were arrested for their alleged ties to radical Islamic groups. Many protested the restrictions imposed by customs and tax officials on cross-border trade, in particular with the Karasuu Market across the border in Kyrgyzstan. This was brutally silenced by the security forces leading to a massacre of civilians. Another incident occurred in Samarkand's Chuqur Bazaar in August 2005, only a few months after the massive protests in Andijan. Reporters claimed that the local authority decided to relocate the bazaar to make way for a music festival, prompting another angry protest.[39]

Uncertainty and herding

The peculiarity of bazaars rests on the nature and consequences of spatial agglomeration of retail and wholesale businesses. The logic and drive behind such clustering has multiple practical reasons. The availability of urban infrastructure is one of them. Having water, electricity and accessible roads are necessary for establishing business premises and these are often limited in Central Asian cities. Spatial concentration reduces the costs of such services for individual businesses and offers a range of externalities. Another reason is the coercive power of authorities. The municipal permissions for trading locations and zoning rules determine the locations of such clusters. In some cases these forge clusters in planned areas, in other cases they might lead to the formation of illegal and informal markets as means to avoid official surveillance. However, these factors are not sufficient to explain the economic rationale of bazaars and how clustering choices benefit entrepreneurs' businesses. As I illustrated above, bazaars are subject to surveillance and value extraction of both the state and private group interests. One crucial question that comes to mind is that, given the fact that entrepreneurs are subject to the absorption and reallocation mechanisms of rents, charges and taxes, why do they still choose to operate in bazaars? Why do they choose spatial proximity and persist in clustering rather than disperse to avoid surveillance?

The answer to these questions lies in the logic of business concentration and the economic benefits of agglomeration in relation to dealing with uncertainty, information asymmetries and the need for protection from arbitrary governance regimes. Entrepreneurs are not fooled by the talk of their governments about order and virtue. They know that they are subject to value extraction and appropriation and they are aware of the uncertainty of this regime. However, they also are conscious that the concentrated location of commercial activities in bazaars provides much benefit. Thus, bazaars offer economic externalities to both traders and customers and help to reduce uncertainty in dealing with information asymmetries and insecure property rights. In the 1920s, Harold Hotelling argued that firms cluster because it provides them the best competitive positions to attract consumers who have travel costs. Hotelling showed that two ice-cream vendors on a linear market contrive to cluster together in the centre of a beach because minimum differentiation provides a simple case of agglomerative benefit. This work has been highly influential in retail location analysis among geographers and also applied to political party spectrums in political science. However, later studies on the economics of clustering pointed out other aspects of agglomeration. Stephen Brown showed that agglomeration does more than simply induce stability in competition and reduce the costs of doing business through economies of shared services and goods (such as car parking, lighting, security services, maintenance, advertising and promotion). More critically, agglomeration provides an all-important means of uncertainty reduction in dealing with imperfect information.[40]

Uncertainty is part of any market, but even more of a problem in conditions of weak law enforcement and uncertain property rights. Traders in bazaars run highly personalised businesses and they determine product range and pricing based on the signals they get in the market. Thus, they rely on fellow traders and customers to obtain information. In his extensive anthropological studies of bazaars, Clifford Geertz showed how systematic information channels were seriously lacking in bazaars

and the activities within the bazaar benefited from other people's ignorance.[41] A range of other studies pointed out why clientalisation or
personalised exchange relationships are strategies employed to reduce
search costs. These findings apply to Central Asian bazaars, too. As seen
in Table 4.2, a great majority of all entrepreneurs interviewed stressed
the significance of obtaining information from others within the same
locality in walking distance. Those who stated that they never did so
were mostly in manufacturing enterprises or other specialties. Almost
all traders I talked to emphasised the importance of communication
among friendship and business ties. Countries did not differ with
respect to the frequency of consulting peer entrepreneurs for advice.

Bazaars have a range of activities that generate and circulate information. These include money lenders, currency dealers and second hand
gold traders who signal financial changes and trends. As elsewhere,
informal credit market activities have been an integral part of the
bazaar system and they insulate traders from formal obligations, erratic
market fluctuations and the banking regime. Porters, hawkers, private
security guards and others who patrol the alleys carry the news. Others
such as cafes and mosques provide channels for information circulation, social contact and solidarity networks. Even events covered in
newspapers, Internet, cell phones or media outlets get disseminated in
bazaars through dense face-to-face personal and social interactions with
additional views and angles. These interactions shape entrepreneurs'
perceptions and help them to reduce political as well as market related
uncertainty in their dealings with day-to-day business.

Thus, clustering behaviour brings strong complementarities and
network externalities in dealing with imperfect information and uncertainty. Traders cluster because they can hedge on each others' business
style, merchandise and rumours of trends and news. They also attract
many more consumers to a specific location by offering a variety of
outlets. This reduces the search and information costs for customers as
they can compare prices and goods more easily. However, information
about competitors, products and market changes are not evenly spread
in bazaars due to different network endowments, access channels and
the capacity of entrepreneurs.

Traders imitate each other a great deal. Almost all bazaar traders
I talked to stressed the intensity of competition and imitation. As
trading is an easy entry business, many jobless people enter bazaars
to buy and sell. Since retailers have no monopoly over products,
imitating the businesses of others is easy. Therefore, there is a continuing struggle between differentiation and uniformity which breeds

Table 4.2 How often entrepreneurs consult other businessmen in the same locality

			Country			Total
		Kyrgyzstan	Uzbekistan	Kazakhstan		
Consulting fellow businessmen nearby	Never					
	Count	15	9	9		33
	% within this category	45.5%	27.3%	27.3%		100.0%
	% within country	20.5%	18.8%	15.5%		18.4%
	Rarely					
	Count	6	6	15		27
	% within this category	22.2%	22.2%	55.6%		100.0%
	% within country	8.2%	12.5%	25.9%		15.1%
	Often					
	Count	30	21	17		68
	% within this category	44.1%	30.9%	25.0%		100.0%
	% within country	41.1%	43.8%	29.3%		38.0%
	Very Often					
	Count	22	12	17		51
	% within this category	43.1%	23.5%	33.3%		100.0%
	% within country	30.1%	25.0%	29.3%		28.5%
Total	Count	73	48	58		179
	% within this category	40.8%	26.8%	32.4%		100.0%
	% within country	100.0%	100.0%	100.0%		100.0%

Note: Missing cases are not included. A locality is defined within walking distance facilitating face-to-face contacts.

herding behaviour. Through herding, traders can smooth the jagged information channels of the market. Herding potentially can expand their reach to customers and at the same time it redistributes their information risks to fellow traders. This process negatively generates many free riders.[42]

The consequences of herding in bazaars have several implications for middle stratum entrepreneurs. It creates downwards pressure as open entry modes intensify competition among imitators, reducing the chances of economies of scale and scope for business growth. Businesses remain small and entrepreneurially oriented. They require rapid adjustments through hedging on information externalities. Individualised business orientation relies on group support without formal organisational structures and interfirm specialisation to reduce transaction costs. Thus, there emerges a degree of evenness among business owners. But, sharp positions exist between casual marginal retailers and established middle stratum entrepreneurs. Upward pressure leads to differentiation and exit strategies within the first group. Differentiation requires specific information, excess capital and know-how and these are inaccessible for a great majority of traders. Demarcation does occur along horizontal and vertical specialisation. Through strategies of differentiation, bazaar traders try to capture niche markets or alternatively they exit. Those who can afford to, relocate themselves to shopping malls and new commercial centres. These are the sites within which exit and entry are controlled by the small number of available locations and high occupancy costs. Others, although small in number, innovate and move into new businesses.

Conclusion

In this chapter I argued against traditionalist views of bazaars and illustrated that Central Asian bazaars are modern institutions with critical economic and political roles. First, bazaars host thousands of businesses generating employment and income for urban populations. The entrepreneurial energy of the middle stratum is the driving force behind the flourishing retail and distribution activities. Mega bazaars such as Dordoi and Baraholka emerge not only as national hubs but also transnational centres for cross-border trade in wholesale and retail distribution. Second, large bazaars generate massive amounts of capital in the form of rent, taxation and fees. Therefore, such bazaars attract the growing attention of upper strata groups in the Mikado game for new allocation and repositioning. Consequently, bazaar owners and traders frequently clash with upper-strata courtiers and protégés as changing taxation regimes, red tape and zoning regulations impose new regimes on them in favour of changing interests. Traders and administrators often squabble about rents, charges and services. Finally, there are periodic collisions of business interests among the middle stratum entrepreneurs as they compete against one another for larger profit margins.

My survey evidence and other information emphasise how critical the economic and political role of bazaars is in the state-market relationship. To avoid collective resistance, a range of coercive methods have been used to confine traders' political ambitions and treacherous opposition. There emerge three forms of such methods in the region: direct state control exercised by private groups in conjunction with the city administration (as we have seen in Uzbekistan); divided ownership and control mechanisms through self-governing syndicates and their collusion with the state (as in Kyrgyzstan); and finally fragmented business interests represented by the city administration and a diverse group of protégés and courtiers (as in Kazakhstan).

In Uzbekistan the Karimov regime protects the positions of narrow interest groups and the old elite along with major merchant families. These groups clog up market opportunities for both the middle stratum and newcomers. The violent eruptions in bazaars can be seen as public outbursts in response to the lack of economic freedoms and suppressed upward mobility. In Kazakhstan, the rapid growth in the number of bazaars expands opportunities to new players along with state coercion. This strategy generates more locational choices and market positions for traders. Modernisation projects create new prospects for a set of business groups; they also widen the scope of benefits to others including architects, engineers and construction groups. Nevertheless, its dynamic growth and upward mobility rests on arbitrary coercion and collusion between the upper strata and local authorities. In Kyrgyzstan, the political coercion of bazaars is subject to a fractured authority. Confrontations among competing groups paralyse the market-state interface and weaken the security of property rights.

Despite its apparent control by the upper strata, being in the bazaar brings a range of agglomeration benefits to traders. The advantages include lower costs in obtaining physical infrastructure, access to a customer base and more critically, access to market information. Under conditions of deep information asymmetries working in favour of the powerful players of the Mikado game, entrepreneurs rely on each others' resources and personal networks to overcome uncertainty.

Because of this nature, bazaars facilitate easy entry which leads to excess concentration and cut-throat competition. Rivalry and reliance on hedged information leads to herding (especially in the form of business imitation), which in return diminishes profits. Consequently, free riding and herding in bazaars leads to downward pressures which hamper business growth. It is precisely this situation which generates new entrepreneurship and innovation originating from bazaars into new locations and sectors.

5
The Gendered Economy

Men are not talkative enough; they are cold to the customer. Women have the advantage of being communicative and persuasive.

A male entrepreneur, Tashkent, Uzbekistan

Women are better in business, they are more economical, more responsible, and more trustworthy.

A female entrepreneur, Bishkek, Kyrgyzstan

Women are moody and tend to be emotional.
This negatively affects their business activities.

A male entrepreneur, Almaty, Kazakhstan

Women have intuition, this is important in business and men lack this.
However, women's prime role is to look after children and carry out family duties.

A male entrepreneur, Semey, Kazakhstan

Introduction

Despite the growing influence of patriarchy and conservative religious sentiments, the number of businesses owned and managed by women has been growing all across Central Asian since 1991. This trend is most pronounced in bazaars where major consumer goods and foodstuffs are traded in large areas laid out on a simple grid pedestrian system. The high concentration of female entrepreneurship in bazaars is an important phenomenon with widespread implications that has, to date, received little scholarly attention.[1] Bazaars emerged as incubation zones for enterprises, entrepreneurial repositories for women and new communal neighbourhoods shared by many participants day and night. The new social stratification and its interest base is often contested and articulated in these immense sites.

In this chapter, I describe the nature and origin of female entrepreneurship, its labour market implications and the characteristics of female-owned businesses. Female entrepreneurs in the middle strata play a significant role in increasing business diversification. They alleviate economic and social stress in households and communities through their entrepreneurial initiatives, domestic efforts and emotional resources. These women shape their societal roles as owners and distributors of property in ways that they could have not done as salaried employees of state-owned enterprises. However, their ownership of property is socially constructed and guaranteed, and this is often a function of their social network endowments and status. Therefore, the role of enterprising women is embedded in a highly unequal market position between lower and upper echelons of society.

Here I argue that the diversity of female roles can be seen through the prism of a gendered economy in an increasingly patriarchal form of nation building. The position of women in the state and through market relationships has been shaped by two paradoxical dynamics. On the one hand, women feel the influence of traditional mundane gender roles that are reinforced by national symbols that emphasise the patriarchal order of the society. On the other hand, many women experience new economic opportunities that broaden personal freedoms by becoming entrepreneurs. Thus, the growth of female entrepreneurship has major implications for the labour market and reconfigures the structure of the gendered economy. Patriarchal values put men in a more vulnerable position because their social status is measured in relation to their ability to function as breadwinners. High unemployment and the burden of non-transferable skills of Soviet-era jobs disadvantage men in the labour market, while women can take refuge in the household. However, by becoming entrepreneurs, women disrupt the supposed balance of gender roles. By gaining access to resources and exploiting market opportunities in small-scale commerce and service sector activities, women reconfigured the patriarchal asymmetries in resource allocation.

We will first consider the rise of female business ownership and the diffusion of economic and political power of upper strata women in the market. Transition changed male and female roles but regional differences and the Soviet legacy remain powerful. From this understanding we can examine some cases that show how women responded to market competition. The shuttle trade was one strategy that women perfected to hone their entrepreneurial skills and they later diversified their business activities. We conclude this chapter with an analysis of the qualities and skills of female entrepreneurs and show how middle strata women play crucial roles and negotiate their positions in the Mikado game through their relational entrepreneurship.

Women, the state and markets

Stalin-era modernisation was advanced by brute force along with ideological indoctrination. Women became the prime targets of Soviet ideals and social transformation. Mass unveiling campaigns among Muslim women incited deep societal controversies and were met by stiff resistance especially in conservative areas such as in the Fergana Valley. Once the opposition was silenced, the modernisation efforts of the USSR penetrated quickly into society and brought profound changes to women's lives through mass education and wide participation in the workforce. However, modernising missions fell short and the mass social convergence into a monolithic Soviet society was a myth. While Central Asia remained economically underdeveloped with limited industrialisation, it was bifurcated into modern and pre-modern societies with many contradictions, paradoxes and overlaps.[2]

One approach the new states used to legitimise their artificial identities was to resurrect some idealised forms of traditional authenticity. A new synthesis was sought that would blend religious values and traditionalism into a patriarchal authoritarian state.[3] The masculine state promoted familial values and traditional women's roles. In this process, women's positions got dislocated from its Soviet characterisation. One interpretation of this is that women lost ground in terms of gender equality. However, women's business opportunities and property ownership have been expanding. These bring new liberties and personal wealth, opportunities for leisure travel and the chance to explore new life styles.

In striving to legitimise independent statehood, ruling elites mobilised society to embrace new symbols and meanings. The Soviet cult of Lenin and Stalin was replaced by ethnic heroes and so we see Timur and Chingiz Khan and other medieval warriors and dynastic rulers elevated to symbolise the continuity of the state. Cultural narratives of glory and continuity hailed in ancient epics, legends and shrines legitimated the new nations. Urban squares and roads were renamed to celebrate warriors and patriarchs.

Feminist scholars have long identified the state as the central institution of gendered power. Both in parochial language and common psyche, women emerge as symbols of procreation, continuity and the honour of the nation as mothers and cultural transmitters.[4] Women's central role can also be seen in the context of post-colonial state building and in the effort to reconnect with the pre-colonial heritage.[5] However, despite the intensified momentum of nation building, the public debate on post-colonialism and women's new social position remains muted. During my survey, many middle class entrepreneurs and government officials expressed ambivalence regarding their new nationhood.

Islam becomes a new source of social change along with an emerging consciousness of identity and lifestyle linked to faith and communal belonging. Along with the increasing influence of religious practices, there emerges a resurgence of old customs, including polygamy, bride kidnapping and the public separation of women from men. Most of these old traditions work in favour of deepening patriarchal practices, especially in small towns and rural communities. But, they also offer social safety nets through Islamic charities and self-help groups in otherwise cut off and impoverished communities. The almost entirely depleted state provisions in health and education, and the poor local economies all inhibit women's educational attainments, participation in the workforce and social liberties.[6] Middle strata women resented these shrinking freedoms and harboured some nostalgia for the Soviet era but these were distant problems to their seemingly prosperous urban lives.

Despite the deterioration of women's societal position, we have not yet seen a catastrophic reversal of women's roles in Central Asia. Emancipation during the Soviet era was neither full-heartedly pursued nor was it evenly absorbed. Great divisions remained along ethnic lines and regions, and women's roles in Soviet ideology entailed many contradictions. Soviet policies used women as agents of social transformation, yet they utilised masculine and patriarchal language and image building.[7] Male dominance found many expressions in the Communist Party leadership and its cadres in youth organisations and trade unions. Only 5.6 per cent of Soviet managers were women and very few women rose to the highest level of the Communist Party hierarchy. Soviet women were largely invisible in key decision-making institutions and managerial positions.[8] Women frequently carried out physically debilitating tasks in factories and workshops and often suffered from overwork and unhealthy job conditions.[9] Across the

USSR, socialism was only quasi-egalitarian; Central Asian women most commonly were restricted to unskilled and semi-skilled work in factories and kolkhozes.[10] Despite the provision of health and child care services, full employment policies remained an imposition for many women. Case studies and anecdotal evidence describe excessive exploitation of the female workforce in industry and agriculture. A Soviet-era rhyme sung by Uzbek women tells about this hardship in cotton farming[11]:

> Ruling over us from time immemorial
> White cotton, black days!
> Heaven beyond the grave, but for now
> All we get is work, while others grow rich!
> The white cotton grows tall,
> But our wage packet is small.
> God is in heaven, but for now
> All we get is work, while others grow rich!

Soviet urban life promoted women in professional occupations. However, Central Asian women were disproportionally marginalised in this multi-ethnic professional workforce, as it was dominated by Europeans, Slavs and others. Starting from the 1970s, indigenous women benefited from widening educational and professional opportunities. Thus, a minority of urban women started to play critical roles in education, health and academia. Despite this trend, rural areas were insular and since the collapse of the USSR, they have defended their insularity by reviving traditionalist attitudes. However, the cosmopolitan and multiethnic character of major cities in the region has so far resisted this recidivism. Urbanite women in major cities continue to play greater economic and social roles and enjoy broad freedoms.

My survey evidence shows that in addition to the rural-urban divide, women's positions in society are becoming increasingly stratified and differentiated between generations. Women of the middle and upper strata, who were educated during the Soviet period, are more likely to have greater personal freedoms and more access to wealth. There is room in the Mikado game for women and those in the upper strata to wield more power than men in the lower strata. These women tend to play several roles at once. They are indispensable members of clans and kinship relations; they are political activists taking leadership roles with executive decision making; and they also play major roles in the market as entrepreneurs.

The leading female members of the ruling elite and presidential families play active roles as politicians, business partners and strategic decision makers. In addition to offering business opportunities to others through kinship and clan ties, their wide range of social activities help to diffuse the influence and good will of ruling groups into society. Through various forms of social projects and charitable activities, upper strata women present themselves as guardians of social cohesion. Through channels provided by civil society and NGO groups, elite women also take leadership positions in government-funded initiatives and international projects; aiming to promote women's health, social inclusion and public service delivery such as building schools, hospitals and shelters for the poor. In doing so, they frequently utilise government and local authority resources. These efforts help to reduce social stress, soften tension between rich and poor and strategically provide alternative channels of welfare, filling the gap left by state institutions.

Sara Nazarbayeva, Kazakhstan's first lady, runs several social projects and non-governmental organisations including Bobek, an international children's foundation, established in 1991. Bobek has massive resources and provides a wide range of care for mothers, school children, the disabled and the needy; the organisation has extensive facilities and runs orphanages. Her elder daughter, Dariga Nazarbayeva, a member of parliament since 2004, has been a major force in business. Formerly married to the now disgraced Rakhat Aliyev, Dariga has control of several commercial banks and stakes in Kazakh media outlets. The family's tentacles also extend through Dinara Nazarbayeva whose Elite Construction Company has built many of the new skyscrapers and other developments in Astana and Almaty.[12]

This pattern of business interests is repeated in Uzbekistan where President Karimov's daughter, Gulnara, has systematically gained partial control in almost every key sector: tourism, retailing, mobile telecommunications, gold mining and even entertainment. In addition, Gulnara performs several roles with Uzbek non-governmental organisations and despite holding some official governmental positions, she is believed to keep her massive fortune in Moscow and Dubai. During President Askar Akayev's fifteen-year rule, his wife Mairam was a conduit for their family's extensive economic power and interest. Her charitable foundation, Meerim, is thought to have been the beneficiary of illegally appropriated state assets including foreign aid.[13]

Through both their charitable activities and their business interests these women project the powers of the authoritarian 'personal states'. They have also gathered an entourage consisting of the wives and daughters of other leaders in government and business. While they symbolise the soft and kind face of raw power, there is little ambiguity about the menace they represent. Everyone in the emerging entrepreneurial class, especially women, recognises the danger of clashing with the interests of these powerful women.[14]

Labour market implications

While state building is undeniably masculine in tone, there is a parallel feminisation of certain market niches in post-Soviet states. These are shaped by the characteristics of post-Soviet market distortions and economic turmoil. Severe unemployment, skill shortages and extreme market distortions have directly affected high levels of male unemployment, household poverty and consequent mass emigration. Entrepreneurial women have emerged as the most resilient group, better able to overcome economic shocks and periodic turmoil. Another factor in the restructured gendered economy is cultural differentiation, linked to different historical legacies.

Unemployment is especially severe in Kyrgyzstan and Uzbekistan where hundreds of thousands of men leave for seasonal jobs every year. Even in Kazakhstan, a net migrant receiving country, many distant regions and old Soviet industrial towns suffer from endemic unemployment and poverty.[15] This high unemployment among young men is regarded as a threat to patriarchy and the region's governments have responded by giving men priority in the job market, supporting the view that men ought to be the breadwinners of their families.

All kinds of people seek opportunities to emigrate: ambitious and clever young people seek educational opportunities; those with skills search for the best jobs; lesser-skilled men traverse a path through construction jobs widely scattered throughout Russia and other CIS states. One consequence of this emigration is that many local economies are left in the hands of women. Seasonal male emigration is so high in the countryside of Uzbekistan and Kyrgyzstan that some villages rely entirely on enterprising women. I met many such women, hardened by their conditions, resourceful in their efforts to compensate for the absence of their husbands and sons who send back their small wages from distant construction sites in Siberia.

As a consequence of declining incomes and economic hardship, there has also been a surge in human trafficking and the sex trade orchestrated by racketeering groups. Women living in poverty and isolation resort to prostitution as a last desperate effort to provide income for their families. They are often tricked and enslaved by gangs and human traffickers. A recent report by the International Organisation for Migration quantifies the massive scale of human trafficking associated with labour migration and sexual exploitation. The study also reveals the weakness of state institutions in handling this tragedy.[16] A more benign solution is available to some through marriage agencies that facilitate emigration through match making as an exit strategy. Stories of new lives established in Western Europe and America circulate among young women and lead to further speculation and interest in emigration.

There are three aspects of the gender divide in the labour market. These stem from social and psychological characteristics, historical legacies and labour force endowments. We consider them under the headings of male pride, nomadic and settled peoples, and problems with skills sets.

Male pride

The Soviet state not only shaped the workplace, it also penetrated into the family and social life in ways that challenged male authority by usurping many traditional male responsibilities. The principal of 'to each according to his needs' undermined the pride men took in being family breadwinners. By allocating jobs, homes, children's education and social care, the state weakened masculine ambitions to achieve.[17] Women's traditional roles, however, were far less threatened by these allocative regimes. Their responsibilities as homemakers and the pride they took in their family roles were preserved. Indeed, opportunities in the labour market afforded some much greater responsibilities that they could take pride in. Thus, Soviet women played a central role in family finance, consumption and livelihood.[18] Soviet men were often perceived and portrayed as weak: 'inappropriately feminine, drunk, irresponsible and shiftless'.[19]

Drinking is the most commonly apparent response to loss of responsibility and threat to pride. Vodka has long played an important social and political role in Russia and has been both a source of pleasure as well as a nemesis. Vodka politics was embedded in late Imperial Russia and controlled through a liquor monopoly. Vodka drinking was introduced to Central Asia through trade in the nineteenth century, and invading Russian soldiers were often reported to be heavy drinkers.[20] Later it became part of urban social life and family celebrations in Central Asia as it was in Russia. Although alcoholism was condemned by Bolsheviks as a tool of capitalist suppression, following the death of Lenin, vodka production increased.[21] Alcohol consumption steadily rose and even Mikhail Gorbachev's aggressive campaign against vodka had little effect. The post-Soviet transition contributed to another surge of alcoholism and new forms of addiction in the region. This weakened the image of Soviet men as role models, and, along with economic hardship, bred further disillusion among youngsters in both Russia and Central Asia.[22]

The impact of economic stress and marketisation has been devastating for men in the bottom strata. In isolated localities and poor neighbourhoods, households were left to look after themselves with no public provision. Numerous personal accounts show that in such circumstances men slipped in societal grace, lost their status and fell into depression and addiction.[23] Stereotypes of female socialisation might have had an effect on women's response; Central Asian women seemed better able to work together and switch occupations while men seemed entrenched and became increasingly isolated.[24]

Pastoral versus agrarian

The role of women is different in pastoral versus agrarian societies. Traditionally nomadic women enjoyed extensive physical freedom side by side with men as managers of seasonal movements, breeders of animal stock and leaders of rituals. Although still patriarchal in nature, the steppe society of women in Turco-Mongolian tradition was not strictly hierarchal and mobility was facilitated by a flexible tribal structure.[25] Nevertheless, in these societies men's entitlements defined their self-image and status. Such entitlements, including livestock ownership and status in tribal lineage, defined masculine roles and authority. These traditions assisted Soviet reforms for women in Kazakh and Kyrgyz societies, but less so for the agrarian Uzbeks. The Sovietisation of social structures, shaped as it was by Slav and European settlers, was much harder for nomadic men whose loss of livestock and tribal status brought severe social dislocation along with physical displacement.

Agrarian cultures are more socially conservative and rigid in their gender roles. Women are more absorbed in their family and community and in their religious roles. Their labour is subordinated to that of men in the fields but they also have traditional economic functions as market traders and producers of traditional crafts. These societies are more hierarchical and patriarchal, often re-enforced by constraining interpretations of Islam. In contrast to the Turco-Mongolian social structures prevailing in the northern steppes, the Turco-Persian societies of the Silk Road and southern urban centres have more strongly defined gender roles. These settled communities absorbed Islam earlier, retained strong connections to Islamic centres and were more resistant to Russification. Just as in pastoral societies, Soviet collectivisation destroyed masculine roles when it eliminated the property rights of merchants and landowners. Nevertheless, women were better able to continue their traditional familial and community functions. While men's domain was in the fields, barns and market places under traditional order, their authority was reduced to family quarters during the Soviet era. Surviving patriarchal relations in these communities have been woven into the thick network of social relations, obligations and reciprocity in extended family quarters and neighbourhoods.[26]

Obsolete skills for transition

Skills appropriate for Soviet enterprises were often devalued in the post-Soviet economy. Industrial meltdown resulted in closure of many old industries and in high unemployment. Many men fared worse than women in middle and lower social strata because they tended to be trained to perform specific tasks within industries that failed to survive transition. Those who were employed in low skill jobs did not have any useful expertise for new markets. Women, however, often had more transferable skills that they were able to apply to commerce and the growing service sector.[27]

Flat pay scales and similar consumption alternatives diminished individual incentives for hard work. Whether they worked hard or not, labourers and professionals all earned the same salary according to fixed pay scales based on their positions. Social differentiation through hard work, innovation and competition was not encouraged in the collective norms of work places. Instead, more frequently party links and patronage networks allowed better returns. Absenteeism, violent disruptions and work irregularities were commonly reported as a lingering consequence of Soviet-era work habits.

Women took leading positions in retail activities as street sellers, distributors and providers while men found such activities awkward and shameful. Because of their skill mismatch, different socialisation experience and status expectations, men found it hard to move in this new market regime. As they were not prepared to take such new challenges and roles, men retreated from the market place. Consequently, lower social strata men found themselves idle with no obvious job prospects. For post-Soviet generations the situation is similarly grim as unemployment and poor skills continue to be a serious problem. This is one reason why the self-governing syndicates and small racketeering groups have been able to recruit easily among the growing number of young and unskilled men in the region.

From shuttle trade to bazaars

Small traders, disproportionately women, took the initiative to travel first to markets in Istanbul to engage in small-scale business that became known as the shuttle trade.[28] Women had already been trading and bartering when the Soviet economic system collapsed and small salaries forced them to continue to extend these activities. For many, it seemed a simple extension of their household activities and such small enterprises served to accommodate shortages. Even by the mid-1970s, this constituted a household black market that was essential for survival.[29] For some this form of dealing opened channels for social differentiation and wealth accumulation.

Throughout the early 1990s, shuttle traders found ample opportunity to expand while domestic demand soared due to the inadequacy of production and distribution networks. Many professional and semi-skilled women took up trade initially to get by while retaining their state employment. They bartered household items and consumer goods on streets and in kolkhoz bazaars and later began travelling abroad to obtain foreign products. Female shuttle traders (*chelnoki*) initially developed links in a few popular destinations, mostly to Istanbul, Karachi, Urumchi and Dubai.

Women travelled in small groups and established networks with small and medium-sized business owners through the help of tour operators and intermediaries. In Turkey, Istanbul's Laleli district was the hub of shuttle trade from the early 1990s for tens of thousands of Russian, East European and Central Asian entrepreneurs. Initially at least, these small traders relied on credit and the system operated through informal contracts guaranteed through personal networks.[30] Over the longer term, personal reputations were built and after repeated transactions a considerable amount of trust emerged. By the late 1990s, further elements of trade infrastructure had solidified so that traders could rely on guarantors, ethical dealings and their personal security. Despite what appeared to be a haphazard, informal and risky system, the shuttle trade boomed throughout the 1990s and became a multimillion dollar business.

The Russian financial crisis of 1998 almost brought the trade to a halt; in Laleli the annual turnover fell from around 9 billion USD in the mid-1990s to 3 billion USD in 2001.[31] However, by this time, alternative business forms had developed; former shuttle traders started placing orders for cargo deliveries and sourced their goods more widely from the Middle East, East Asia and Russia. By the early 2000s, import businesses with effective distribution channels limited the scope of shuttle trade and importers also satisfied consumer demands for luxury goods. National governments applied stringent customs policies to control cross-border trade and unregistered economic activities and strangled the shuttle traders.

The shuttle trade helped to build women's confidence in doing business. Their skills in marketing improved and their perceptions about the world changed. Although it involved enormous time, energy and personal risks, many women spoke with excitement about the days they were first able to travel abroad and experience a degree of freedom and leisure. Travel abroad made these women confront the heroic image of Central Asia that Soviet indoctrination had created. Traders repeatedly expressed their surprise that countries like Turkey and China were not dismal third world places. They saw that in contrast to their own impoverished state, Istanbul, Shanghai and Dubai and other such places were vibrant cities full of goods and people with optimistic outlooks. A Kazakh woman spoke enthusiastically about her first trip together with her female companions to Istanbul in the mid-1990s:

> We thought it was a bad place to go first because during the Soviet time we had poor ideas about other countries ... But, in fact it was Istanbul which opened our eyes to a new world. We saw everything first there and from then on began exploring other places in Europe, China, Malaysia.

Others expressed how they gained new ideas by travelling and interacting with different cultures. These trips provided them certain privileges within their community as they gained wider experiences and had access to new goods and ideas. The material wealth and the consumption spree brought about by the shuttle trade not only alleviated some of the misery of early economic decline but also fostered the emerging consumer culture. An Uzbek woman described it this way:

> People began saying great things about their travels and I realised that we needed to explore how things worked elsewhere. I had the opportunity to travel to Istanbul, Dubai and Shanghai and saw many new things, bought nice clothes, shoes, electrical appliances, etc.

Nowadays, the clear majority of women's entrepreneurial activities are concentrated in large bazaars. As more capital has become available, some bazaar women who initially built their business with small suitcases in shuttle trade are now proprietors of gleaming retail stores in fashionable districts of Almaty, Astana, Bishkek and Tashkent. Along with this business growth and diversification, female entrepreneurs became a conduit for the new brand building and franchising activities of international companies.[32]

Khrushchev's daughters

The vast majority of this wave of women entrepreneurs was born before the late 1960s. This generation of the Khrushchev era were the beneficiaries of higher quality education, better health standards and social mobility. A clear majority of my survey women came from professional Soviet cadres with high educational attainments and were mostly in their 40s. Soviet-era school teachers, accountants, doctors and civil servants are today running commercial businesses. As seen in Table 5.1, more than half of the surveyed women had university degrees and overall had higher educational attainments than men in the sample. Interestingly, women's educational qualifications did not significantly vary between those who established their businesses in bazaars and others who were running services or other commercial businesses.

Table 5.1 Educational attainments of entrepreneurs

Graduated from	Male number of cases & (%)	Female number of cases & (%)	Total number of cases & (%)
Secondary & below	9 (10.0)	3 (3.4)	12 (6.7)
High school	32 (35.6)	30 (33.7)	62 (34.6)
University	46 (51.1)	50 (56.2)	96 (53.6)
Postgraduate & above	3 (3.3)	6 (6.7)	9 (5.0)
Total (*)	90	89	179

Note: (*) The total number of cases observed is 179. The missing cases are not included.

However, significant regional differences were also observed; both sexes had lower educational qualifications in Uzbekistan compared to their counterparts in Kazakhstan and Kyrgyzstan. The age distribution of entrepreneurs showed a bias towards those who were 41 years and older (more than 60 per cent of the total female sample). This result supports my earlier observation that Soviet-era professionals and civil servants play a prominent role in the rank and file of today's entrepreneurial middle class. The survey evidence shows that the Khrushchev generation women had managed to keep their urban advancement and translated them into business ownership over the years. This is striking in a region so overwhelmingly dominated by young people. Because of slow economic growth in Uzbekistan and Kyrgyzstan, those who seek employment in their 20s and 30s find it especially hard to secure jobs or initiate their own business.[33] This shows the increasing dependence of post-Soviet generations on the income and jobs generated by middle aged Soviet-era professionals. Khrushchev's daughters support subsequent generations while they also distort market opportunities for the youth (see Table 5.2).

Opportunities for entrepreneurship have frequently been linked to women's social standing and occupation. Some directly benefited from privatisation of the state enterprises they worked for and many utilised their Soviet employment and social networks. For example, I met many women who bought land, store equipment and merchandise from their

Table 5.2 The age distribution of entrepreneurs (*)

Age groups	Male number of cases & (%)	Female number of cases & (%)	Total number of cases & (%)
17–30	16 (17.4)	9 (10.2)	25 (13.9)
31–40	28 (30.4)	25 (28.4)	53 (29.4)
41–50	37 (40.2)	40 (45.5)	77 (42.8)
51–65	11 (12.0)	14 (15.9)	25 (13.9)
Total	92	88	180

Note: (*) The total number of cases observed is 180. The missing cases are not included. The age of respondents is calculated according to the survey years of 2004 and 2006.

former employment place during the early years of enterprise collapse when state enterprises were either dissolved or privatised. Running one of the best pastry and bakery shops in the north eastern Kazakh city of Karaganda, Anna told me that she used to be an employee of a baking and candy enterprise and bought the factory ovens in an auction when it was dissolved. A group of female dentists in Bishkek explained how their office was furnished with equipment from the state hospital that they worked for previously. In Osh, a former cashier, Aigula bought the massive space of the retail store when it was privatised and turned it into a guesthouse. In trade, many female entrepreneurs got their initial start-up capital by selling products of state enterprises. These and countless other examples indicate that access to goods and opportunities have been a function of Soviet social stratification for women.[34]

The motivations pushing women to set up their own businesses are often linked to three family circumstances. First, a sizeable number of single mothers work to support their children and sometimes their extended family. Many are the only breadwinners for their family and they are often under pressure to generate employment and income opportunities for their children and other close relatives. Secondly, women often work with their male partners, most commonly with husbands, in order to generate family income and share the multifaceted responsibilities. Women often remain in charge of trade while their partner carries out the external tasks of purchasing and arranging daily chores. Finally, women take up trade while husbands or fathers are employed in other jobs or run other business ventures. In most of these businesses, women rely on several casual workers.

In the second decade of market building, female-owned businesses matured and entrepreneurs who survived began to follow new opportunities. When we compare the trajectories of different enterprises, there emerge three patterns of business growth and diversification in bazaars: horizontal expansion, vertical specialisation and sliding and skipping through new ventures. With these diversification strategies women try to overcome competition and market distortions, protect their capital through reinvestments and grab opportunities to deliver new goods and services. Vertical expansion occurs most commonly when those women who put their earnings together with family labour begin expanding through multiple selling points. In many instances they rent or buy more than one trading location; this could be typically in the form of additional containers, small stores or stalls. By relying on family members and sales assistants, they diversify merchandise and price options to increase the sales volume and profits (see Cases 5.1 and 5.2). Thus, a certain degree of capital accumulation leads to further employment and income for families and allows for business diversification.

Case 5.1 – Çınara (Dordoi, Bishkek)

From selling small items on a street stall to her first trip to Turkey for shuttle trade, and then to Pakistan and Syria, Çınara managed to grow her business and now owns two containers in Dordoi. At the age of 32, she has been in trade for almost 10 years. Over the years she developed good contacts in Istanbul taking advantage of her Kyrgyz and Turkish parentage and regularly sources merchandise through her contacts. Most of her customers come from the neighbouring countries. Some of them are retailers, some are middlemen. They travel to Bishkek frequently to buy garments and other consumer goods to trade or sell in their home countries. Several transactions often lead to mutually rewarding relationships and Çınara aims to keep her regular customers content. This requires not only setting the right price and providing reliable services but it also means meeting changing demands and expectations. She learnt a great deal from her trips abroad and feels toughened by stiff competition in Dordoi. Large numbers of traders in ready-made garments force entrepreneurs to look for new niche markets and Çınara stresses that she always searches for new styles and goods.

Case 5.2 – Ainura (Dordoi, Bishkek)

Ainura is a 42-year old Kyrgyz gynaecologist, who, like many of her colleagues, took up trade in order to supplement her poor salary. With her civil servant husband, she managed to expand the business to four containers in Dordoi selling leather bags and purses and later established a retail store in Dordoi Plaza, a new shopping mall in central Bishkek. She sends goods to her relatives in Osh and Karakol where they market them. The business is controlled by the couple and four relatives. Ainura travelled extensively in 1997 across China as part of the shuttle trade boom and later to Korea. She now maintains regular contacts in Urumchi. Her travels shaped the current business and she also has many new business ideas, among them to set up a private health clinic where she can practice her profession more rewardingly.

Other successful entrepreneurs deepen their product control and business opportunities through vertical integration and thus also diversify their risks (see Cases 5.3 and 5.4). By increasing their management role in the production and delivery of goods, women often aim to increase reliability of quantity, quality and delivery at once. Vertical integration reduces their exposure to market fluctuations and risks while generating further income and job opportunities for their family members. In many instances, women are also forced to expand their businesses in such a way due to the paucity of business linkages and the high transaction costs for goods and services. It is costly to rely on wholesalers and producers and constant foreign travels. Many goods and services suffer from poor sources of supplies. Therefore, retailers occasionally enter into manufacturing and packaging foodstuffs, tailoring garments and producing their own consumer goods. These ventures require additional capital investments and carry business risks. Business space is expensive and limited. Such new ventures often take place in single storey family homes, depots and derelict sites. Therefore, many such ventures remain small with simple production techniques, amateurish management and poor standardisation. Despite these challenges, though, a few who manage to achieve a good product quality, affordable prices and respectable reputations gain a competitive edge. The following cases provide a snapshot of the motives and situations of such diversification.

Case 5.3 – Zulfiya (Dordoi, Bishkek)

Zulfiya is a 40-year old Uyghur woman who sells ladies garments. She employs three sale assistants and operates from two containers. Her family fled Xinjiang in the 1960s during the Cultural Revolution when Mao's revolutionaries were terrorising the countryside. Throughout the Soviet era Zulfiya's parents were involved in small-scale smuggling and black market trade while retaining their menial state jobs. With the collapse of the USSR, their venture grew quickly. Most of her goods are transported with commuter busses or airplanes and money is sent in cash through relatives or via other trusted intermediaries. Zulfiya took over the business with a well-established network of traders and relatives and international connections. Her main trade used to involve bringing in goods from Xinjiang but more recently she thought she could earn more and travel less frequently by producing her own range of garments. She decided to bring textiles from Xinjiang and tailor them in Bishkek. She set up a small workshop in a depot near her house and got her relatives involved. Although she continued to sell imported garments, her manufacturing venture was growing in 2004.

Case 5.4 – Olga (Baraholka, Almaty)

Olga, a native of Almaty, is a 43-year old Russian garments trader in Adem market, Baraholka. She was an accountant in a state enterprise until losing her job in the early 1990s. Olga had no option but to do as many others did and she began to engage in shuttle trade. With her savings she later managed to open a retail shop selling women's garments. She has long been interested in fashion design and began developing contacts with firms in Turkey, Italy and China. She wanted to design, make and sell. Recognising the need to differentiate her products along with the increasing fashion consciousness in Kazakhstan, she established a small atelier at home and began designing and sawing dresses, ball gowns and other luxury garments. She developed catalogues with drawings and used amateur fashion models. Along with her husband, Olga travelled abroad to meet textile and accessory producers and traders. Later on the couple decided to expand on the design and production of fashion items through contacts in Moscow. By employing around ten people for sewing and a new staff for marketing and design, Olga hopes to excel in this business and move to a new location in downtown Almaty.

Diversification into new trades through skipping and sliding appears as another strategy for scooping market opportunities and avoiding the business saturation that prevails in overcrowded bazaars (see Cases 5.5 and 5.6). Entrepreneurs often renew their merchandise and trading strategies but increasingly they think about changing their business models, too. The two cases below illustrate these dynamics. There was no observed gender difference in entrepreneurs' attitudes towards business change. Although women often said they liked stable jobs and routines, they also admitted the need to enter new ventures to create niche markets and/or take advantage of new opportunities. However, in many cases such switching is associated with larger family dynamics in addition to individual aspirations and market opportunities.

Case 5.5 – Bayan (Baraholka, Almaty)

Bayan is in her mid 40s and was born in a village of the southern region of Kyzyl Orda. Bayan studied history at Kazakhstan State University to become a teacher. In the early 1990s she noticed that many people were travelling to Turkey and Iran for shuttle trade. In 1993 she started selling woman's underwear and glasses and later traded garments and textiles. In 1998, she switched to the shoe trade and for several years she has been working with producers in Urumchi. She has customers coming from as far as Bishkek, Tashkent and Yekaterinburg. Most money transactions were carried out without the involvement of banks through friends and phone orders and she relied on the honesty of others for the security of her trade. Bayan diversified her business with a new venture in construction materials as the Kazakh construction sector has been booming. With a son studying in a UK university, she relies on her brother and sister to run daily business chores.

Case 5.6 – Jin (Baraholka, Almaty)

Jin runs a café and wedding banquet hall in Baraholka. Her family left China due to the religious discrimination against Han Chinese Muslims, *Dungans*. Now in her late 30s, Jin is a high school graduate and previously traded a variety of goods. In her last venture, she was selling children's toys in Baraholka along with her relatives. As the trade brought less and less income, she decided to switch to a new business. Along with two brothers they decided to open a café and a banquet hall as they noticed increasing demand for such services. Jin, as a manager and partner, decorated the massive hall using her savings and relies on family help with preparing food, arranging entertainment and providing music. Jin expresses a certain degree of frustration about the coordination of these many tasks among family members and other workers.

Women's advantages in relational entrepreneurship

The survey illustrates how female entrepreneurship is embedded in community and family relations. Across cultures, entrepreneurship has often been linked to the scope and wealth of social networks and cultural attainments. Entrepreneurs, who have access to resourceful networks, are more likely to benefit from wider opportunities. Paradoxically, local cultural traditions and community values might also critically limit business opportunities and hinder innovation and might even bring a gender bias in favour of men.[35] Many personal accounts attest that, in the Central Asian context, female entrepreneurship emerged as a survival necessity rather than in response to attractive market opportunity or innate entrepreneurial drive. In many instances, salaried women found themselves in the position of generating alternative incomes and they imitated each other in the market. This was indeed a widespread phenomenon across all post-Soviet societies.

Rather than having access to large social networks, women more typically relay on a small number of close friends and family members. While their male counterparts tend to enjoy larger networks, entrepreneurial women seem to prefer linear channels to accommodate each set of needs. Wider and looser networks that male entrepreneurs rely on have high social cost and are exposed to more of the risks of moral hazard that are widespread in the market. Female entrepreneurs weave denser networks that are smaller but built on more in-depth and complex trust and reciprocity. It seems that the lean networks that female entrepreneurs rely upon better protect them from cheating, market fluctuations and other business problems.[36]

When asked about how gender differences affected their businesses, male and female respondents did not display significantly diverging views. However, views on gender differences in doing business showed significant variations among the countries. The significance tests showed that sexist views and positive gender discrimination in favour of men were strongest in Uzbekistan. In this country, around one in every three business owner, men and women alike, believed that male-female roles are gendered due to their biological and social differences and women's ideal roles are not in the market but in motherhood. While only 13 per cent of Uzbek respondents thought there was no difference between the sexes, there was a radically different attitude in Kyrgyzstan where the majority of respondents thought there was no difference between the sexes in attaining business entrepreneurship (54.3 per cent). For Kazakhstan the corresponding result was one-third (32.6 per cent).

Uzbeks are clearly more influenced by traditional, patriarchal views and they emphasised biological differences and women's domestic responsibilities. In all three countries, but especially in Uzbekistan, weakening state provisions of schools and childcare influence women to stay at home. Respondents pointed out the limitations placed on women by men and female peers that reduce their physical mobility in smaller towns and neighbourhoods. This statement from one female entrepreneur in Uzbekistan summarises a widespread sentiment:

> Trading is easier for men. They are more mobile and they don't have family responsibilities. Women need to get the permission of their husbands to travel abroad.

The response from a male entrepreneur in Samarkand illustrates the increasing distinction between male and female socialisation patterns as well as the masculinisation of state power over female-owned businesses:

> Women could find it difficult to do this business. First of all, they cannot drink as much as I can with authorities, businessmen and the police.

Other views concentrated on biological differences between men and women arguing that women were emotionally and physically not fit for running businesses. A Kazakh entrepreneur stressed that:

> Women are moody and tend to be emotional and this negatively affects their business.

Respondents also pointed out that women had an advantage in dealing with authorities since, they claimed, officials can be more lenient to female traders and women knew better how to deal with these cases. Kazakh and Kyrgyz male entrepreneurs often emphasised this view:

> There are more advantages if the entrepreneur is a woman. The state and customs organs are softer on them and women can talk better with these people.

The majority of Kazakh and Kyrgyz respondents also thought of retailing as a good niche market that suited women's skills. These views stressed that women dealt with customers better and knew how to choose merchandise. When asked about ethnic differences, over 90 per cent of the Kyrgyz and Kazakhs, and 87 per cent of Uzbek respondents stated that it did not affect their business activities. Many insisted that despite the heterogeneous ethnic structures in urban societies and business ownership, ethnic differences were not a problem and it did not play a negative role in their business dealings. Based on these results, gender stereotyping is clearly a stronger influence than ethnic divisions in post-Soviet societies.

Despite this response, in informal settings Central Asians frequently make ethnic slurs that reflect commonly held prejudices.[37] Disparaging connotations are made about Uzbek or Uyghur businessmen in Kazakhstan and Kyrgyzstan. In such narratives, canny Uzbek and Uyghur traders are envied as opposed to the 'laidback Kyrgyz or Kazakhs'. Uzbeks consider Tajiks to be more astute but also ruthless merchants. Overall, Tajiks, Uyghurs and Uzbeks are considered to be the most entrepreneurial among Central Asian Muslims. 'Uyghur is an occupation, not a nationality' goes one such saying.[38] Russians in the region, however, are both despised and paradoxically considered more 'trustworthy' by titular groups.

These stereotypes are mainly male pejoratives and such expressions have almost no direct relevance for female entrepreneurs. Although members of ethnic diasporas are disproportionally numerous among female business owners, there is no statistically significant ethnic difference observed in entrepreneurial talent among women. Successful entrepreneurs typically come from a large pool of different ethnic groups. Indeed, most enterprising women do not necessarily come from societies that are supposedly more entrepreneurial, that is, Tajik, Uyghur and Uzbek. On the contrary, Kazakh and Kyrgyz women, having lived in nomadic cultures, show greater freedom and success in running modern businesses than their counterparts from more traditional agrarian societies.

Women as well as men consistently stated that female intuition and communication skills are better suited for commercial activities. Women see themselves as more skilled and adept for trade. As much as the highly liberal Kyrgyz, traditional Uzbeks seem to accept that women are simply better at trade by nature. Women are often considered to be more economical and good money managers for families and businesses. The advantages stressed of female entrepreneurs over men amount to three qualities that women seem to possess: canny in trade and good communicators, good money managers, and fast adaptors.

1) Canny in trade and good communicators: With no misgiving or regret, many men and women from all backgrounds stated that women were more talented in buying and selling a product. However, this emphasis also rests on the fact that female entrepreneurs often deal with female customers in the market. The following attributes were mentioned frequently during the survey:

Women know how to talk and to persuade customers;
Women can understand the desires of a customer better;
Women are more patient with an undecided customer;
Women are more stable and determined in trade;
Women make careful choices and have good intuitive skills.

2) Good money managers: Women were considered to be better managers of business finances and more responsible in dealing with money. The laid-back manner of men is often referred to as an old Soviet attitude of idleness. Thus, female entrepreneurs are central for family finances and survive through economic hardship as expressed with the following:

Women save money for their families and children;
Women don't easily give in to those who seek bribes;
Women are more economical;
Women price products more carefully and they do not give lavish discounts.

3) Fast adaptors and observers: Women appear to be better equipped to adjust to rapid change. They are also believed to observe competition carefully and shift their merchandise and business strategy accordingly.

Women respond to changes faster;
Women are creative and generate new ideas about their business;
Women are more adept in responding to business changes;
Women observe more carefully and understand trends;
Women know styles and trends better in retailing.

Conclusions

Central Asian women increasingly faced consequences of resurgent traditionalism. The deterioration in women's educational attainments, their shrinking social liberties and high male unemployment enhances the view that men ought to be the breadwinners of their families. I have shown that increasing patriarchal influences are not monolithic and they are still evolving within the context of social class, religious adherence and cultural diversity. Despite growing gender inequality in access to economic and political power, upper strata women play central roles in business and politics. Middle stratum women also found new economic and social freedoms in entrepreneurship. Female entrepreneurs, especially in Kazakhstan and Kyrgyzstan, continue to play a significant role in new social stratification and increasing business diversification.

Central Asian women are pivotal for the survival of households and communities through their entrepreneurial initiatives and social roles. The survey evidence pointed out several notable trends. First, the impact of patriarchal practices on women's economic roles differs between cosmopolitan urban centres and provincial towns as well as between upper and lower echelons of the social order. Another recent phenomenon is the growing generational difference in access to markets that favours the middle-aged over post-Soviet generations. Second, a clear majority of enterprising women came from ethically diverse urban professional cadres. Many were born and raised during the economic boom of the Khrushchev era. Third, the origin of female entrepreneurship stemmed from early shuttle trade as this form of commerce allowed both capital accumulation and business know-how to flourish. Finally, women gradually learnt to shape their ventures through vertical and horizontal diversification. In doing so, they often acted along with their family members and developed business skills and social networks to sustain their enterprises.

Despite their hard work and commonly agreed superior skills in trade, enterprising women in bazaars also face limitations brought about by stiff competition and market distortions. In many ways women act as men do in dealing with governance problems; they choose avoidance and individual rather than collective circumvention. The day-to-day management of business requires constant negotiations and women appear capable to deal with authorities and tax officials at least as well as their male counterparts. Although they had a certain degree of nostalgia for the salaried and regimented life, the Khrushchev generation women would not like to go back to their former positions. They are neither willing to give away freedoms they have experienced in physical mobility, wealth accumulation and consumption choices, nor do they pretend that they have any ideology or mission to change their society. This pragmatism is deeply embedded in the survivalist strategies that women have been following for decades in the increasingly uncertain environment of the post-Soviet states.

6
Business Interest Representation

In this country, nobody asks our view,
they dictate all these laws from the top.

An entrepreneur Tashkent, Uzbekistan

Doing business here is like collecting gold coins scattered
among landmines.
If you step on powerful interests you are finished.

A foreign entrepreneur, Astana, Kazakhstan

Introduction

Interest representation and collective action among private business owners is still nascent in Central Asia. In response to poor legal protection, unjust inspection charges and the arbitrariness of tax and customs duties, small businesses mainly rely on individual solutions. While large businesses exert great influence in shaping the underlying rules of the Mikado game through strong personal relationships with upper strata players, there is little evidence of growing solidarity among small and medium-sized businesses. Other than top-down institutions such as youth organisations and workers' unions, civil society organisations are rare and the most active ones are often supported by external donors. In addition, Central Asian entrepreneurs tend to regard civil engagement with suspicion and shy away from taking leadership roles in establishing solidarity platforms. This attitude is especially fostered by prevailing mistrust towards those who are outside of family and clan links. Powerful groups in upper strata make it difficult to form alternative groupings that threaten their vested interests. However, impersonal societal trust would be needed to forge alliances and new lateral structures appropriate for more open social and capitalist market relations.

During the Soviet era, interests were organised and monitored by professional and intellectual groups. The most powerful and vocal of these were the writers' unions, youth organisations (komsomol) and trade unions. There also existed a range of professional associations for teachers, engineers and doctors. These were top-down bureaucratic organisations within which voluntary action was not encouraged.[1] Although monolithic, some of these groups eventually acquired new roles that allowed political participation, dissent and the representation of heterodox interests. For a time, the intelligentsia played an effective role in voicing opposition, discontent and demands for change. For example, writers' unions were active and influential as voices of opposition. Although the Communist Party monopolised the media and the normally one-directional nature of communications put severe limits on freedom of expression, this did not prevent sharp confrontations. Intellectuals used public speeches and published letters to voice their criticisms. *Izvestia* and *Pravda*, the two major newspapers, along with literary magazines and specialist publications had degrees of flexibility that allowed dissent and eventually served as a social pressure valve.[2]

Post-Soviet social transformations rendered these groupings defunct. The intelligentsia was marginalised, professionals lost their status and the industrial working class was dislocated; most everybody sought refuge in small business activities. These groups brought with them a familiarity with the idea of interest groupings but lacked a clear vision for new formations. Lateral and multiple social structures, unlike monolithic top-down ones, are better suited and more effective in arbitrating between economic resources and political interests. Thus, opening new interest representation and participation channels remains imperative for stable social and economic development in the region. There is also a two-way relationship between deepening market relations and the growing sophistication of lateral organisations: they nurture each other. Diversification of associational ties and interest representation can also loosen the grip of hierarchical patronage relations that currently dominate state and market relations. Thus, one would expect to see new interest-group formations mediating between entrepreneurs' interests and political power.

Here we will see four different forms of interest representation with illustrative cases. The most common form is the state-monitored chambers of commerce and industry; which is a continuation of the Soviet organisations. All three countries have these institutions where businesses are required to take up membership. In Kyrgyzstan and Kazakhstan, the chambers neither function well nor offer much to attract members. Instead, they seem to be increasingly controlled by a small number of insiders close to the governments. In Uzbekistan, however, Soviet-style herding prevails in societal organisation; farmers, artisans and businessmen and women are required to be members of state co-opted associations. Secondly, alternative interest representation emerges through new business solidarity associations. This trend is overall weak but visibly developing in Kazakhstan where businesses have more room for manoeuvre and experience less intervention from top-down state co-option. The third form is ad-hoc groups that are usually motivated by immediate self-interest. These groups are ephemeral, lose their meaning and tend to terminate when the initial purpose or mission is fulfilled or failed. Finally, self-governing syndicates provide alternative governance and they are typically dissolved into submarkets and state structures. In Kazakhstan and Uzbekistan, most self-governing syndicates work under the state's control in a symbiotic relationship. In Kyrgyzstan, however, they openly clash with the state.

Entrepreneurs' struggle with poor governance

The most commonly identified business issues in all three countries are related to abuse by tax officials and state inspectors, illegal extortion by criminal gangs and bureaucratic hurdles. In dealing with these problems a great majority of the respondents (84 per cent) said they would prefer to sort out their business problems on their own rather than seeking judicial help. Along with personal strategies, many entrepreneurs commonly use their friendship and kinship relations to address these problems. Seeking personal connections to officialdom and bribing when necessary are the two most common strategies of 'getting by' (see Tables 6.1 and 6.2). As illustrated in Chapter 3, there are widespread abuses in governance structure for entrepreneurs. However, the most critical ones are related to the judiciary, customs authorities and the police. Central Asian entrepreneurs have little trust in their courts, state officials and parliaments. These indicators point to a deep-seated uncertainty and insecurity for businesses in relation to property rights, contract enforcement and personal security. Since political participation and opposition channels are mostly closed or strictly monitored and there exist deep information asymmetries, one would expect businesses to form common platforms to voice their concerns and remind their governments that they are the real bearers of the market and local communities. This does not seem to be happening.

Table 6.1 The effects of bureaucracy and bribery on businesses

Effects of bureaucracy and bribery			Country			Total
			Kyrgyzstan	Uzbekistan	Kazakhstan	
Don't know	Count		1	1	0	2
	% in bureaucracy and bribery		50.0%	50.0%	0%	100.0%
	% in Coded Country		1.4%	2.2%	0%	1.1%
None	Count		25	16	16	57
	% in bureaucracy and bribery		43.9%	28.1%	28.1%	100.0%
	% in Coded Country		33.8%	34.8%	27.6%	32.0%
Some	Count		9	4	12	25
	% in bureaucracy and bribery		36.0%	16.0%	48.0%	100.0%
	% in Coded Country		12.2%	8.7%	20.7%	14.0%
Quite	Count		18	8	16	42
	% in bureaucracy and bribery		42.9%	19.0%	38.1%	100.0%
	% in Coded Country		24.3%	17.4%	27.6%	23.6%
Much	Count		21	17	14	52
	% in bureaucracy and bribery		40.4%	32.7%	26.9%	100.0%
	% in Coded Country		28.4%	37.0%	24.1%	29.2%
Total	Count		74	46	58	178
	% in bureaucracy and bribery		41.6%	25.8%	32.6%	100.0%
	% in Coded Country		100.0%	100.0%	100.0%	100.0%

Table 6.2 Addressing business problems or issues through business associations (*)

			Country		Total
		Kyrgyzstan	Uzbekistan	Kazakhstan	
Use of business associations	Never				
	Count	50	33	43	126
	% in business associations (*)	39.7%	26.2%	34.1%	100.0%
	% in Coded Country	71.4%	73.3%	74.1%	72.8%
	Rarely				
	Count	10	4	9	23
	% in business associations (*)	43.5%	17.4%	39.1%	100.0%
	% in Coded Country	14.3%	8.9%	15.5%	13.3%
	Often				
	Count	5	1	5	11
	% in business associations (*)	45.5%	9.1%	45.5%	100.0%
	% in Coded Country	7.1%	2.2%	8.6%	6.4%
	Very often				
	Count	5	7	1	13
	% in business associations (*)	38.5%	53.8%	7.7%	100.0%
	% in Coded Country	7.1%	15.6%	1.7%	7.5%
Total					
	Count	70	45	58	173
	% in business associations (*)	40.5%	26.0%	33.5%	100.0%
	% in Coded Country	100.0%	100.0%	100.0%	100.0%

Note (*): The total number of observed cases is 173. The missing cases are not included.

For the time being the behavioural norms of 'getting by' seem to have entrenched business uncertainty in efforts to ensure marginal survival. However, such accommodation strategies are neither optimal nor sustainable for long-term business interests. Conformity with the arbitrariness of the rule of law brings only ephemeral gains for small businesses. Despite widespread discontent with endemic corruption and bad inspection systems, there are very few cases of collective efforts by entrepreneurs that aimed to alleviate such difficulties in day-to-day business practices. After decades of imposed, but now discredited, collectivisation and communist ideological indoctrination, there appears to be no moral base for collective action and impersonal trust. Indeed, low levels of institutional and impersonal trust are observed in all post-Soviet states. In a study dealing with Estonia, Russia and East Germany, scholars found that Russian and Estonian entrepreneurs faced governance problems similar to those in Central Asia, and they were less likely to search for outside help beyond their known network of friends and family.[3]

By the logic of collective action that Mancur Olson described, this is not so surprising. Individuals do not necessarily follow rational behaviour patterns in order to maximise their common gains through collective action.[4] Olson stresses that unless the number of individuals in a group is quite small, or unless there is coercion or some other special device to make individuals act in their common interests, rational self-interested individuals will not act to achieve their common or group interests. However, Olson also points out that when there is a possibility of making a gain that would match everybody's interests, we see collective action making a difference such as when trade unions and business lobby groups are formed. In Western democracies collective action in business and society is an important part of democratic life, playing a crucial mediating role between the state and interest groups.

However, groups need social glue to forge collective action. A vision, a sense of belonging and a common language and purpose are essential to formulate and act together for shared interests. Often competition for opportunities in the market leads to a proliferation of interest groups and business associations. Such fragmentation breeds variety and opens new entry points and alternative opportunity structures for entrepreneurs.[5] However, non-kin-based group formations require a degree of civic engagement based on agreed common interests among participants. One of the fundamental ingredients of such groups is interpersonal (among individuals) and impersonal trust (among individuals and institutions). In post-Soviet states such interpersonal trust beyond family, friends and tribal relations is rather weak. This societal deficiency, along with impositions of authoritarian presidential regimes, is a major obstacle for lateral interest formation and representation in politics as well as business.

There were hardly any statistical records or reliable company data, and no business directory at the time of my survey between 2004 and 2007. Business directories are recently being developed by local authorities and only state-sponsored chambers of commerce and industry have some listings of businesses. Most of the time information about the nature and size of businesses remains in segmented quarters of officialdom, creating further information barriers. A great majority of businesses are not part of any association and have never engaged in collective action. On the contrary, they prefer to keep a low profile so that they are not detected by tax officials and state inspection authorities. This is most pervasive in Uzbekistan where many entrepreneurial activities remain underground to hide their existence from the state. However, the countries show some differences in relation to the role of business associations. In Kyrgyzstan 71 per cent and in Kazakhstan 74 per cent of those interviewed said they never dealt with business associations. In Uzbekistan, there is a higher degree of associational involvement for small businesses and one-fourth of businesses address their issues through associations (see Table 6.2). However, as will be seen, this is mainly due to the fact that the government regulates business and craft associations and monitors them through a territorially structured vertical bureaucracy.

There are three peculiar characteristics of business interest formation in the region. First, the relationship of the entrepreneurial layers with the ruling elite determines the way in which solidarity networks are formed. This takes place often through informal links of favouritism and protection and is generally not expressed through formal associations. This character of the business environment undercuts the function of associations, making them distinctly different from their Western counterparts. It also distorts markets in favour of politically well-connected businesses. The second characteristic is apparent in the goals of ad-hoc alliances, in that they aspire to appropriate state assets, or control newly emerging market niches, or some combination of these functions. Here, we see many imaginative and practical skills put forward in solidarity groups for survival, growth and the reallocation of economic opportunities. However, this is a risky process as it relies on courtiers, oligarchs and protégés. In the event of disagreements, the cost of arbitration is high especially when upper strata participants are the major beneficiaries. Finally, there are self-governing syndicates which are groups formed around a charismatic leader that carry out the function of the state through coercion and protection. They are similar to the Sicilian Mafia but they are more diverse ethnically and far more fluid in their territorialisation, recruitment and organisational nature.

Thus, the state does not have a monopoly over the use of coercion or full control over its institutions. The weaknesses and arbitrariness of state coercion and of law enforcement create opportunities for the emergence of alternative institutions of governance as well. Different sizes and forms of self-regulating syndicates, typically consisting of civil servants, business people and racketeering groups, emerge as regulatory institutions.[6] Thus, ad-hoc groups and self-governing syndicates carry out two tasks at once as market players and alternative governments. They control important economic assets while at the same time they provide businesses with protection, alternative finance and network externalities. The number of individuals involved and the size of economic assets they hold can vary and often is difficult to verify. However, these groups, meshed with Soviet political clans, function in sectors such as cotton, bazaars and cross-border trade of all types, including human trafficking.[7]

Co-option by the state

In all three countries, the chambers of commerce and industry are the most widespread and typical form of business group. Originating from Soviet-era institutions, they are organised hierarchically in a bureaucratic fashion in all major cities and often consist of heterogeneous businesses bundled together for a variety of purposes. However, during the past two decades there has been a diverging pattern in the nature of these chambers and in business interest representation as well. In Uzbekistan, the chambers of commerce and industry have been reorganised and regimented as an arm of the state. This is consistent with similar organisations such as the ones for farmers and artisans. With a presidential decree, the Chamber of Commerce and Industry of the Republic of Uzbekistan (CCIU) was established in 2004 as a single national entity with an appointed executive board working under the cabinet of ministers. The Uzbek government's general mistrust towards its citizens is reflected in its extensive societal control mechanisms and its willingness to herd its citizens in regimented bureaucratic structures. Associations and chambers expand state surveillance of private earnings. The state's co-option of private interests is most extensive in Uzbekistan.

The Chambers of Commerce and Industry [CCI] in Kyrgyzstan and Kazakhstan are structured similarly to their Uzbek counterparts. However, their role in business and politics has been gradually weakening. The Kyrgyz Chamber of Commerce and Industry was renamed with a decree of 1994. This aimed to restructure the former state organisation presiding over industry and commerce; but in many ways the chambers retained the same Soviet principals, dependent on the political will of the government and powerful groups.[8] In 2004, the CCI in Kyrgyzstan had 350 members nationwide with a head office in Bishkek and representative offices in Osh, Jalalabad, Naryn, Tokmak and Issyk-Kul. The membership fees were not sufficient to run the organisation and the CCI relied on fees collected from its routine tasks and international aid programmes. The services of the Kyrgyz CCI included advice on foreign economic relations, organising exhibitions, issuing business certificates and co-ordinating events and trips; all mostly Bishkek orientated. Cabinet ministers were directly involved in business deals as well as related international activities. The CCI was considered to be one of the most vocal 'civil society' groups by some donor programmes and attracted financial and technical help. For example, through a seven-year engagement with a German government assistance programme, the Kyrgyz CCI furnished their offices with new computers and other supplies.

In Kazakhstan the Chamber of Commerce and Industry had 16 branches across the country and also worked as an extension of the state apparatus. However, entrepreneurs have not been keen on being part of this bureaucratic organisation and increasingly sought to form smaller and stronger solidarity networks and associations where they could resolve their business matters faster without the intermediary role played by minor bureaucrats in the CCI branches. In the second largest city and one of the main industrial centres, Karaganda, the Kazakh CCI was reduced to only 30 members.[9] This looked somewhat bizarre in contrast to the 20 staff the CCI office employed. How this high staff ratio could be justified was not obvious. Interpersonal ties of businessmen with various ministers and high-ranked civil servants determined the extent of service they obtain from the CCI, where staff appointments and salaries were also linked to government employment policies. The chairman of the Karaganda CCI took time personally to help President Nazarbayev's 4 December 2005 election campaign, an example of state co-option and the presidential system. This is not surprising as all Kazakh CCI national chairs are appointed by the president. The CCI officers claim that their organisation extends 'protection' and 'justice' to their members. This claim itself indicates the degree to which political protection matters for the day-to-day management of businesses. Nevertheless, there is a notable difference between total state co-option in Uzbekistan and partial state co-option in Kazakhstan. The following cases from Uzbekistan illustrate the nature and scope of state co-option of business interests.

Chamber of Commerce and Industry of Uzbekistan [CCIU]

Although business associations have been allowed in Uzbekistan since 1995, they remained small and often dominated by large companies. The CCIU was reorganised from different oblast units by a presidential decree of 2004 and an eloquent and visionary former ambassador was appointed to revitalise and strengthen business development and provide more useful services to its members. The CCIU is organised in 13 regions, each employing around 10–15 staff members, plus an additional 4 specialised advisory subdivisions, all located in Tashkent.[10] One of these divisions is responsible for providing legal and consulting services. Another is concerned with tax issues. In 2005, over 1000 businesses applied to the CCIU for tax advice, a major difficulty for businesses. In order to realise this, the CCIU works with tax consultants and accounting groups, as well as various departments of government. The CCIU membership can be individual and collective through associations. Individual members of the Chamber can be entrepreneurs of private, small and large businesses, or the physical persons.

The state forges collectiveness to maintain a dialogue with businesses through the Chamber. The CCIU collects membership fees but mainly relies on government funding (5 per cent of the special 'Privatisation Fund' comes to the CCIU).[11] Its governing principals and policies are mainly shaped by the government. The organisation's leaflet states the main purposes of the CCIU as to promote individual entrepreneurs, improve business conditions, encourage investment inflow and protect the rights of the members of the Chamber. Despite its supposed autonomy, the members have minimal power and play a consultation role in relation to the government. The top executives of the CCIU are elected by the national congress from among high-ranking state officials, Central Bank representatives and ministry civil servants, along with businessmen. The chairman of the executive committee of the CCIU and its deputies are appointed to their posts by the central council of the CCIU in coordination with the Cabinet of Ministers of the Republic of Uzbekistan.[12] The chairman of the CCIU expressed his view of the organisation thus:

> Many people think of us as a government institution. I came from the government but we are trying to create something different here; independent from the government we are incubating the Chamber here.... There are many misconceptions ... we are still looking at the market economy as something very dangerous. We are trying to change [personal] privilege to privilege for all.

The CCIU actively seeks the collaboration of 250 local chambers of commerce and industry scattered across the country. The cooperation of ministries and government departments is sought to launch educational, business information and advice services in all areas in what appears to be a very ambitious programme. The Chamber plans to diffuse international standards and new technologies through education and executive MBA degrees and extensive public relations through the state-controlled media. Yet I have not been able to confirm any impact of these efforts in the course of my fieldwork. I observed that most middle stratum entrepreneurs avoided the CCIU.

Oltın Miras (Golden Heritage)

Crafts are widespread across all Uzbek regions but more concentrated and varied in the Fergana Valley. These include silk and cotton weaving, woodcarving, metal working, embroidery, calligraphy, painting and other artisanal products. Tashkent, Samarkand and Bukhara are three centres where most of the craftwork is collected and traded. Uzbeks and Tajiks have deep-rooted traditions in crafts and often produce these in their homes. Traditional crafts developed concomitant with their history of sedentary culture and farming in the fertile plains of the Amu Darya and the Syr Darya, as well as along the Silk Road. Uzbek traditional values promote the preservation, repetition and re-production of old forms and techniques. These craft traditions were severely damaged during collectivisation and the associated glorification of industrial production and modernisation. Although artisans have always relied on communal ties in the production, organisation and marketing of craftwork, for the Soviets they were a class of small individual capitalists and therefore they had to be destroyed. A very few of these artistic traditions, especially in silk fabrics and pottery, were reorganised into collective enterprises. Many others survived simply because devoted families continued these traditions discreetly.

The Karimov government recognises the economic as well as social power of resurging artisans in the economy as well as society. Oltın Miras was founded by a presidential decree in 1996, uniting three separate artisans' organisations.[13] Although the association defines itself and is promoted by the government as a non-governmental organisation, it is another example of state co-option. Oltın Miras has 150 branches, many of them very small, throughout Uzbekistan. The national secretary of the association was appointed by the president and all branch representatives are appointed by the secretary with the approval of President Karimov. In order to function and stay on good terms with local authorities, artisans need to be registered with the Oltın Miras.

The headquarters of Oltın Miras in Bukhara is located in the historic buildings of the Kukeldash Madrasah, which was one of the largest theological colleges of Central Asia in medieval times. The restored site, with many learning and worshiping cells, was converted into trade shops and Oltın Miras was granted use of the site by the municipality. The organisation runs exhibitions and fairs in order to encourage both artisanal production and retailing. The appropriation of state and municipal assets on behalf of artisans extends the state's patronage and solidifies the loyalty of craftsmen. The chairwoman of Oltın Miras in Bukhara was involved in the association since 1999 as a dressmaker, and was appointed to head the local organisation in 2004. Despite her lengthy involvement, her responses to my questions about marketing and tourism were rather superficial. She also seemed to be in doubt about the organisation's purpose and activities. As I observed elsewhere in the country, she acted like civil servants and officials with deep insecurity and lack of clarity. When I asked about the organisation's mission, the chairwoman searched among papers in her drawer with a visible sense of panic.

The state demands full loyalty to the regime and an apolitical stance in exchange for favours and protection. In this case, Oltın Miras was given the prime location in the city and artisans were allowed to function and sell their work there. The chairwoman also runs her craft business but she presides over the allocation of 30 cells together with a couple of other appointees and high-ranking city officials. Moreover, she and her brother use several cells for their family trade. Thus, artisans and traders in Kukeldash Madrasah are aware of their dependence on the goodwill of the municipality and the state. While pursuing their capitalist interests, their fear of changing the status quo is evidence of the thoroughness of the state's ability to co-opt them.

The Farmers' Association (FA)

The Farmers' Association is a national body whose head is appointed by the government. Farmers are automatically members of the association, they are expected to follow government directives but they play no role in decision making. They are only nominally consulted on association matters by the FA's technocratic managers. The agricultural sector has always been the major source of income and employment in Uzbekistan and around 60 per cent of the population still lives in rural areas. There are about 4 million small farmers in the country whose lands are mostly privatised former collective farms. During the cooperative wave of the Perestroika period, a few of these farms were broken up and gained some managerial flexibility. Throughout the Soviet era, the kolkhoz (collective farms) and sovkhoz (state-owned farms) dominated the agricultural sector with complex internal structures. Although kolkhoz farms had in theory rights to sell their output to markets, they were mainly dependent on the state. The state set production targets and purchased products at fixed prices. This situation did not change much despite the increasing number of small subsistence farmers through privatisation.

The Karimov governments pursued extensive land privatisation and lease programmes for farmers, arguing that the former Soviet structures did not fit well with Uzbek traditional life. Uzbekistan today has a three-tiered rural economy with collective shirkats, privatised farms (*dekhqon*) and small subsistence holdings coordinated through a strictly controlled regime. Starting from 1997, shirkats have been divided up among small subsistence farmers. During 2003 alone, one thousand shirkats were turned into private farms. During the first three months of 2005, 24,000 new farmers emerged on 700,000 hectares of allocated land.[14] The sector remains highly dependent on the state to market produce as well for agricultural inputs.

The twin ecological disasters of decreasing soil fertility and increasing salination have created massive agricultural problems. For individual farmers they bring immense hardship because they not only diminish productivity but also require considerable extra labour. In Karakalpaskistan, Khorezm and northeast Bukhara for example, farmers have to rinse salt from their plots two or three times before seeding. Despite this obviously being the overwhelming agricultural issue, the FA does not seem to be equipped to grapple with the enormity of the problem.

The FA has two main goals: its political objective is to monitor potential social upheavals in rural areas and its economic objective is to maintain the cotton harvest and push centrally designed policies forward. Keeping farmers on the land and monitoring migration from rural areas is a major governmental goal. Through the expansion of small household farming, the Karimov leadership hopes to enhance the survival of thousands of rural families which form the backbone of his traditionalist policies. However, the non-market-driven elements of the sector not only constrain farmers but also create price distortions. Seeds and fertilisers are sold by state enterprises and the state holds the monopsony on the cotton and wheat harvests.

Most technocrats interviewed expressed their utmost loyalty to the presidents' wisdom in organising farming and defended the FA's role as the key player.[15] The association communicates with farmers through bureaucratic channels. It sends directives to all FA branches across the country. It periodically offers training and occasional farmers' bulletins provide information on new policies, seeds and opportunities. This information flow is slow. According to a senior civil servant, a new decree might typically take two months to reach a farmer. Further delays occur as local officials slowly interpret how these decrees are applied. The FA is at the centre of the system by which farmers are at the mercy of the state.

New business associations

In addition to the fully state co-opted business associations such as CCIU, other business associations have been formed in a variety of ways in Central Asia. In Kazakhstan, in particular, there has been a proliferation of new business interest formations and organised lobbying. This comes in the form of cooperation within the business elite and in sectors not controlled by large powerful players, and has developed relatively free from the state's direct control. These Kazakh business associations are less subject to the state's absorption techniques than their counterparts in Kyrgyzstan and Uzbekistan. With a moratorium declared by President Nazarbayev, all state inspectors were barred from carrying out periodic controls in work places since 2005. This substantially reduced the state's surveillance and corrupt practices by officials.

One of the reasons for this relative freedom to form associations is the preoccupation of the upper strata with larger financial opportunities in substantial oil, gas and mineral resources. Another is the generally more relaxed business atmosphere which tolerates a diverse set of players. The newly emerging associations are being shaped by the diverging needs and expectations of the second generation business elite and the growing size of small and medium-sized enterprises. In 2005, there were nine such business groups headquartered in Almaty and some branches in other towns. These included the Independent Businessmen's Association, the Association of Construction Companies, the Employers' Confederation of the Republic of Kazakhstan, the Kazakhstani Association of Logistics Companies, the Association for the Development and Support of Construction, the Kazakhstani Tourism Association, the Association of Manufacturers and Service Companies in the Oil and Gas Sectors, the Kazkahstani Entrepreneurs' Forum, the Association of Market Traders and Entrepreneurs of Kazakhstan. Two cases below illustrate the nature and scope of emerging business interest formation and representation.

The Food Retailers' Association [FRA][16]

A group of retailers formed an association to strengthen their bargaining power over wholesalers, suppliers and foreign company distributors. One activist, Cumaogul Urazov, was a former KGB officer who initiated several failed business ventures and eventually built a small chain of grocery stores in Almaty. Along with his fellow retailers, Urazov faced many hurdles from the bureaucracy and had tough competition from bazaars and large distribution companies. A group of retailers decided to form a solidarity platform. Urazov's rich social life and good communication skills helped the group to grow fast. They had the modest expectation that they could lower the wholesale prices and increase their competitive advantage over large stores and bazaars. Urazov explained, 'our association doesn't exist only on paper, it also forms an active collective bargaining group'. After consolidating some of its gains and persuading its members, the FRA joined the influential Independent Businessmen's Association but was careful to retain its organisational autonomy. The members were aware of the need for political protection and sought to establish a secure business environment for their ventures. These retailers not only perceive domestic competitors in the crowded food retailing sector as a problem, they also think that foreign companies are given undeserved advantages by the government. Preferential treatments towards different country imports cause loss of business for some while making other insiders rich overnight. Urazov explained how import privileges given to Russian and French companies as opposed to Ukrainian ones caused his refrigerator trade to go bankrupt despite his attempts to import parts from Ukraine and reassemble them in Kazakhstan.

Aligning business interests is not always easy, as many food retailers see each other as competitors. Business people often have several enterprises and a history of involvement in different types of trade. Consequently, the need to form a solidarity-based interest group is often undermined by the fluidity and ephemeral nature of their commitments. Increasingly as businesses mature and the need to increase living standards for families and relatives becomes imperative, these entrepreneurs recognise the need for collective bargaining and power. Urazov stated with some hope and pride that:

> We, as Kazakh businessmen, are learning to trust each other and seek common goals. Rather than cheating for a quick return, we are interested in long-term business deals.

Those who are active in the association are also enthusiastic about being part of a respected business group. This worked in their favour and membership increased to 600 retailers. The FRA is increasingly forming a reputation as a distinct social group and it prints a newspaper to communicate with its members. Social activities for children, discounted tickets to members for entertainment and social events make the association indeed a club where wealth and the tastes of the new entrepreneurial social stratum are collectively constructed and displayed.

Independent Businessmen's Association (IBA)[17]

Talgat Akyol is the founder and manager of the consultancy company the Independent Businessmen's Association (IBA). He is an energetic former manager of Karmet, which used to be one of the largest Soviet steel mills in Temirtau, Karaganda in northern Kazakhstan. Akyol diversified his business knowledge and links while working in the construction sector for 20 years, followed by five years of experience in banking. His 25 years of business experience in the state sector provided him with the necessary political links and a good understanding of economic matters. With the growing private business sector, he identified the lack of consultancy advice available in the market. Many of his friends sought his help in establishing a business or developing a new contact. Initially happy to offer advice to individuals and small partnerships, with time Akyol realised that his business skills and connections had value beyond one-to-one advising. He also realised that he could no longer manage these links and constant phone calls on his own. Thus, he decided to establish his own business, which is now the IBA consultancy. With only a few secretaries and accountants, the company originated in a small office space in his native Karaganda in 1999. Akyol's business grew quickly and reached 1,600 clients in 2005. In 2002 he moved the business headquarters to a large modern building in Almaty.[18]

In essence his business carries the characteristics of a consultancy company as well as a lobby group. The majority of clients are owners of SMEs from a variety of sectors, including manufacturers, wholesalers and many foodstuffs retailers and convenience store owners associated with the FRA. The early reputation of Akyol as a respectable old guard and an effective contact to address business issues and bureaucratic problems grew quickly through networks of businessmen and clan relations. The IBA became a popular address for accounting, business advice and bureaucratic handling. Growing small and medium-sized businesses increasingly sought to outsource routine accounting and paper work to those who had resources to handle the complicated and opaque state bureaucracy. This popularity allowed IBA to grow to 7 branches across Kazakhstan including Almaty, Karaganda, Petroplask, Uralsk and three smaller northern towns.

The IBA is well positioned to take advantage of establishment power structures and also has access to critical clan and friendship ties in Kazakh society. There are three key aspects of the IBA's business success. First, Akyol enjoys very important vertical connections, most importantly friendship ties with President Nazarbayev. Both men worked at Karmet as good friends and comrades during the Soviet period.[19] Akyol can leverage such connections and other strong links to the state bureaucracy. Secondly, as an experienced manager, he has good business aptitude and an understanding of the needs and expectations of the emerging entrepreneurial class. Thirdly, he is a good communicator, network builder and a charismatic person. These qualities make him a popular leader of the business community and he is liked by the political and bureaucratic elite. Moreover, the IBA's main headquarters provides good links to businesses through quick and open access to state bureaucracy and influential officials. As a display of power and respect for state authority, the main office, located in a new large building, is decorated in a stately fashion with official desk fixtures, maps and national symbols. Akyol spends hours nurturing connections with businesses and within the bureaucracy while routine services are carried out by his 80 strong staff.

The IBA has a centralised accounting department employing 40 staff who advise as many as 500 businesses on accounting standards and problems. Making sense of the accounting and tax law is a highly valued service for businesses because of the widespread irregularities and complications in the interpretation and implementation of the tax code. Those who receive these services can also get advice on new business ventures and market research any time, providing that they pay additional charges above their membership fees. There are also legal advisors working with 80 fee-paying businessmen. Mergers and acquisitions is another field where relationships are cultivated and deals are secured by Akyol through long negotiations and bureaucratic pinpointing. The IBA works closely with municipalities which are important players in business formation and survival since they issue business permits and control land and building regulations. The flexibility of the IBA allows businesses to participate when they feel necessary. There is no competition for leadership at the moment as Akyol is the business owner as well as a self-appointed popular representative and voice of the growing second generation entrepreneurs in Kazakhstan.

Ad-hoc groups

Ad-hoc groups of the form now common in Central Asia are a product of the peculiar economics of post-Soviet transformation. Privatisation schemes and some donor projects aiming to encourage enterprise development, such as many run by the European Union (TACIS) and the United States (USAID), assisted the formation of such interest groups. Many large donor projects also acted as power brokers and arbitrators. These formations tended to be exclusive and small, often with as few as a dozen participants but occasionally with more than three-dozen members. They sometimes seem broad-based, but are usually motivated by immediate self-interest.[20] Given their limited remit, these gatherings are ephemeral, lose their meaning and tend to terminate when the initial purpose or mission is fulfilled or has failed to bring rapid financial and/or business benefits. Regrouping these business interests leads to other informal associational linkages that are supposed to take advantage of emerging market opportunities. These kinds of ad-hoc groups could be seen in all countries in Central Asia and were more of a norm during the early post-Soviet years. However, since they are highly insular and exclusive, it is not easy to decipher their full story. One such case I was able to observe was a privatising scheme in Karakol. As we will see, this is a typical case of ad-hoc group formation designed to carry out a specific mission: in this case privatising a massive Soviet concrete factory and replacing it with a free trade zone.

The Karakol facility was one of the largest concrete block factories in the region and was situated on the eastern shore of Issyk-Kul in the town of Karakol. Production stopped after independence and the site became contested property. A free trade zone association was established by members of the local elite who intended to convert this massive industrial site in the late 1990s. This initiative came about as a result of a Western donor project that aimed to assist enterprise development in the region. The ad-hoc group included former Soviet party leaders, professionals and other members of the local nomenclature. In essence, this became a forum to advance business opportunities during the early years of privatisation. The project ran into difficulty soon after its establishment as members of the group began grabbing a personal share. Eventually, it was Aigula who successfully gained control of the site. She had previously worked for the state trading company and developed her skills and cultivated useful connections from then on. When I visited the site, she utilised only a small section of the plant which was separated by walls for her flour milling and packaging businesses. The rest of the huge building was divided into smaller units that were rented out to businessmen. Yet, most of the space remained un-utilised.[21]

Massive rusty pipes circled in and out of the building, the courtyard was full of monstrous lifting equipment and scrap metal, the cranes and tools looked as if they belonged to another century. Inside the complex, the sheer size of the space was frighteningly gigantic; it was only comfortable during the summer heat but was freezing cold during the rest of the year. Most of the windows were broken; whatever tools the factory once had were all gone. Every single chair, lamp shade and door handle had been grabbed by intruders. Small walls built to separate workshops made the building resemble squatters' quarters. Yet, most of the interior space remained eerily dark and empty. There were not enough manufacturers to fill such spaces while elsewhere bazaars were flooded with small traders. This gigantic size and the sheer power of the concrete voids was by no means an exception. The domination of steel and concrete continuously reminds one how Soviet industrial glory squashed the individual and diminished the meaning of self.[22] Many such Soviet ghosts remain, scattered across Central Asia. Transforming and reutilising such sites is a huge problem. But, once they were grabbed, they offered different opportunities. Utilising old machinery, renting some spaces and selling scrap metal proved to be profitable in the short term. In addition, this sort of commercial space is a business asset that has been very limited in post-Soviet cities.

A similar situation occurred in Kyzylsu village, near Karakol, where a formerly state-owned winery is now an apple juice factory. The plant is set in a big courtyard with massive tanks, pipes and old equipment dating from 1973 and 1977. The current owner, formerly a senior kolkhoz manager and social security officer, managed to purchase the factory in 1997. He explained how he joined an EU-TACIS initiated project along with other businesses to get financial and technical help.[23] His ad-hoc group was selected to form a business community by the project consultants to facilitate the transmission of project objectives. However, the promised technical support was slow to come and participants grew impatient with the bureaucracy of the TACIS programme. The group was eventually dissolved and its members pursued different interests.

Self-governing syndicates

In addition to these forms of ad-hoc groups, a common channel through which businesses seek protection and solidarity is through self-governing syndicates. These private groups emerged as alternative governance bodies in the region with diverse business interests and organisational structure. Offering mafia style protection for businesses and securing property rights through contrived market forces evolved into alternative governance forms. As Diego Gambetta illustrated in the case of the Italian Mafia, the protection of business interests is a private enterprise in itself and mafia organisations corrupt, collaborate with and incorporate the state and society in doing so.[24] Mafias are a form of organised crime but they also act as businesses as well as agencies of governance. In a region where legality and the protection of property are highly contested, private governments fill the gap between dysfunctional state institutions and the market. Such groups existed during the Soviet Union but they grew rapidly along with the criminalisation of the market in Russia and other successor states of the USSR.[25] Many believe that self-governing groups are a real barrier to the consolidation of states and the growth of capitalist markets. Nevertheless, they fill a gap in the state-market relationship. Additionally, they play a functional role in ameliorating institutional malaise while they offer business protection, facilitate transactions and extend support to communities by redistributing wealth often robbed from the state. Because of these functions they curb and sometimes challenge the power of authoritarian states and divert resources to their own beneficiaries. These groups do not yet hold strong private armies, nor is there a cohesive alliance among them, but they have armed men and use violence when needed.

In Kazakhstan and Uzbekistan, most self-governing syndicates work under the state's control in a symbiotic relationship. In Uzbekistan, these groups offer alternative governance regimes by bending and relaxing the state's coercive force while at the same time serving their own interests in the economy. Mafia-style protection, sanctioned and cushioned by the state, also helps to maintain law and order in a disorderly economy. Thus, as long as they do not openly clash with the political authorities and the presidential regime, these self-regulatory groups are, by and large, tolerated by the ruling elite. This incorporation is most evident in Uzbekistan where many large sectors are governed by the involvement of such syndicates. The state monopoly in extractive industries and major sectors such as cotton require the intermediation of these syndicates for a smoother operation and revenue generation.

These syndicates are highly fluid and vary in size. Some are localised and meshed with state officials, local gangs and racketeers, others form international syndicates. Many urban businesses, including casinos, restaurants and nightclubs are apparently linked to money laundering activities of international criminal groups such as arms of the Russian and Chechen mafias in the region.

While self-governing syndicates are relatively benign in Kazakhstan and mostly function under the state apparatus in Uzbekistan, in Kyrgyzstan they are openly on stage as overt players of businesses and political games. These groups have recently engaged in an open struggle for control. They diffused into the ministries, security services and the parliament. Former President Akayev and his family acted as power brokers among business interests and held the centre of gravity. Thus, the ruling family co-opted self-regulatory groups into state affairs and relied upon their protection. Akayev's son, who controlled major financial and business interests, allegedly negotiated his deals with the biggest self-governing group in the country run by Ryspek Akmatbayev.[26] However, during the presidency of Akayev alternative regional power bases also gained economic strength. The story of Akmatbayev's death, along with his bother and several business rivals has already been told in Chapter 4. It is a tragic, but perhaps typical, tale of syndicate activities gone wrong.

Conclusion

For almost two decades Central Asian entrepreneurs hid behind their personal ties and social networks in order to handle their day-to-day affairs and address distorted law enforcement and weak institutions. In doing so they mainly utilised their instinct for survival combined with a deep cynicism towards the rule of law. After decades of imposed collectivisation and communist ideological indoctrination, it is astonishing to note that there seems to be no societal and impersonal trust for collective action beyond tribal and family ties. Despite this generally dismal state, there is a range of situations whereby different business interests are articulated. This chapter illustrated four forms through which state and private interests overlap and function under different regimes.

First, the state's co-option of business interests through chambers and associations has become a major tool for the allocation of resources. Through these groupings the state imposes its order and extends its patronage to new market players. This form of top-down control is typical in Uzbekistan as the state spreads out its powers to all sectors of the society. This is presented as a legitimate and progressive approach by the Uzbek government; a 'just allocation of resources' as portrayed in Uzbek patriotic mottos and posters. Second, there are new business associations and groupings based on solidarity networks and collective support. These are most numerous in Kazakhstan. Their formations indicate that flexible government policies facilitate new organisational structures that help to improve overall market conditions. Third, ad-hoc groups and self-governing syndicates emerge as alternative institutions for appropriation and protection from state and non-state actors in the market. Such groups are often hidden and function within the state in Uzbekistan but are more open and politically contested in Kyrgyzstan.

In Kazakhstan, both the F R A and I B A show that business groups are increasingly interested in forging collective action to facilitate business transactions, to minimise bureaucratic hurdles and to seek state protection and preferential treatment. The emergence of such business groups is a positive development in the direction of more complex economic relations and denser markets. The IBA shows that strong political careers can serve business interests and induce impersonal trust for profit. Where vertical power and authority is still important, political connections are used to solidify horizontal business interests. Thus, a mixture of social network relations and vertical political and bureaucratic structures create new opportunities for business solidarity, especially when this form of interaction is permitted without direct state coercion or co-option.

Overall, low civic engagement with associations and extensive use of personal networks in addressing overwhelming governance problems as well as Soviet habits of using 'getting by' tactics indicate that entrepreneurs do not intend to challenge strong interests in the upper strata. Instead, they use self-governing syndicates as mediators between them and the state when they need to. In the three countries studied, entrepreneurs widen their opportunities in relation, and not in opposition to the upper strata. The prevailing business norm is to accommodate the dominant powers that control economic resources. This is mainly because, for the time being, the positive spillover effects of this symbiotic relationship are much greater for them than its alternatives of indifference or confrontation. This behavioral strategy works reasonably well in Kazakhstan but rests on fragile foundations in Kyrgyzstan and Uzbekistan.

7
International Assistance and Enterprise Development

A Kyrgyz shepherd was tending his flock when a Land Rover sped up from across the high meadow. A well-dressed young foreigner jumped out and asked: 'Tell me young man, if I guess the exact number of sheep you have here, will you give me one?' When the shepherd agreed, the foreigner pulled out his laptop computer, connected it to his satellite phone, downloaded some NASA data, scanned the hillside region with his digital video camera and said 'You have exactly 1,586 sheep over here'.

'Indeed', said the shepherd 'now take your lamb'.

The man grabbed the nearest animal and carried it to his vehicle. The shepherd then asked: 'If I guess your profession, will you give me the animal back?'

'Alright, then', said the man.

'You are an international management and development consultant', said the shepherd.

The foreigner was impressed, 'Correct, but how did you know?'

'Easy', the shepherd replied. 'First, you came all the way up here when nobody ever asked for you. Second, you demanded payment to tell me things that I already know. And third, you don't know anything about who we are and how we live. Now give me back my dog!'

Adapted from Ferguson[1]

Introduction

Immediately after the fall of the Iron Curtain, a wide range of Western aid initiatives, governmental programmes and non-governmental organisations rushed in to shape political alliances and new markets, and to support social development in the former communist bloc. With varying missions and capacities these groups sometimes left positive marks but in many cases exacerbated already existing distortions and created new problems for the region. Consultants of the International Monetary Fund (IMF), the World Bank (WB) and others who advised on economic reforms knew little of the capabilities of the general population and of their governments. They instead used analogies with Eastern Europe and Russia and often applied the same prescriptions. They also failed to appreciate that the regions' leaders understood almost nothing about how a Western-oriented market economy might operate for them. Consequently, ephemeral and disjointed policies led to confusion and a crippling lack of focus. The absence of any credible international engagements analogous to the role played by the European Union in Eastern Europe left the region without an anchored vision or concrete incentives about any transition. After almost two decades of engagement we now witness wariness on both sides. Western organisations and their experts who spent years in this vast geography express their pessimism about any 'successful transition' of, what they dismissively call, 'the Stans'. On the receiving end, a general lack of enthusiasm among the region's politicians and policymakers reveals deep scepticism towards Western prescriptions and suspicion about their ultimate intensions.

Despite their curiosity about the West, many entrepreneurs in my sample were not interested in aid organisations or donor projects. Some were strongly critical about their objectives and had experienced their apparent ineffectualness. I heard many stories of disappointment and jokes critical of Western organisations and foreign consultants in Central Asia. Rob Ferguson's joke ridicules external help and highlights local suspicions about outsiders. Diverging positions between Western organisations and their local contacts increasingly halt social projects and reform initiatives. Ferguson's book on the politics of international aid to ameliorate the Aral Sea disaster shows how a clash between local bosses and Western experts during a one-year World Bank programme ruined the well-intended aims. His narrative also illustrates how ineffectual experts and consultants were, local and international alike, in solving large problems such as the shrinkage of the Aral Sea. Despite this discouraging state of affairs, the Kyrgyz economy has become dependent on aid and donor-run projects.

In this chapter, we will see to what extent international aid has been effective in enterprise development and how externally shaped interventions and their financial, technical and advisory provisions have contributed to enterprise development. Kyrgyzstan is a good case to examine the pros and cons of international assistance and donor-supported initiatives due to its extensive exposure to all forms of international aid and assistance since the mid-1990s. To illustrate, we will consider the tourism industry, one of the few sectors with the potential for rapid growth and see why trapped regional economies and labour markets, combined with catastrophic privatisation, exacerbated sectoral transformations and hindered entrepreneurship. Despite the general pessimism about externally funded projects and aid, small but successful implementations do exist and I will show how a project of the Swiss development agency, Helvetas, has been successful in sewing the seeds of entrepreneurship through a community based tourism initiative.

International aid and Kyrgyzstan

Most reform policies and donor-funded projects aimed to alleviate poverty and bring economic and political reform to Central Asia. Aid and reform prescriptions came in different forms: from multilateral financial institutions including the WB and the IMF, international organisations such as the United Nation's Development Programme [UNDP], and other bilateral initiatives (most notably by the United States, Japan, Germany and Turkey), Western and Asian NGOs and faith-based initiatives (including many evangelical Islamic charities and Christian groups). A selection of these institutions and aid programmes that I was able to observe in Kyrgyzstan included the United States Agency for International Development [USAID], Technical Aid to the Commonwealth of Independent States of the European Union [TACIS], the European Bank for Reconstruction and Development [EBRD], the Asian Development Bank [ADB], the German Marshall Fund, the Aga Khan Fund and the Turkish Agency for Cooperation and Development [TIKA].

However, not only did the priorities and missions of these organisations differ, they have not been consistent in applying their own principals. This broadly overlaps with the much-criticised state of aid in providing tangible long-term effects in general. There is little evidence to show that international aid was determined by domestic politics. Nor is there strong evidence that the policies of recipient countries were fundamentally changed by the role of these international institutions.[2] As priorities and interests diverge among donors, they also vary among the political constituencies of donors and recipient countries.[3] Kyrgyzstan is no exception: the policy field and implementation of project objectives have been highly contested and subject to periodic modifications according to the vested interests of donors and upper strata parties.[4] Therefore, international and bilateral financial and technical support has been subject to the social dissemination mechanisms of the Mikado game as well. While the highly authoritarian and centralist Uzbek and Turkmen governments guarded their autonomy from Western influence and limited their exposure to international agencies, the liberal elite with poor domestic resources welcomed all forms of international assistance in Kyrgyzstan. These elites, taking their lead from the outward-looking rule of then President Akayev, saw international assistance as a prerequisite for their survival. This strategy allowed more resources to be brought in for the reallocation rounds of the Mikado game and helped to control poverty and to foster political stability. In essence, this strategy replaced Soviet subsidies with international aid without curing the country's long-term dependence on outsiders. However, unlike the command regime of the USSR, the state's capacity to provide public provisions was reduced dramatically. With no fair trickle-down regimes, aid benefited only a small minority: the Bishkek-centred elite.

In the early 1990s, Kyrgyzstan began embracing the philosophy of the 'Washington Consensus', which was mainly concerned with macroeconomic stability and monetary and fiscal discipline. The Akayev regime quickly became the most ardent economic reformer in post-Soviet Central Asia and a test case for the policies of the IMF and the World Bank. In return for implementing a programme inspired by the Polish economic reforms of 1990, the country received generous financial assistance and technical support. Kyrgyzstan became the first Soviet successor state, in 1998, to accede to the WTO (World Trade Organisation), long before any other CIS countries. This process was enthusiastically escorted by political leaders, but after they achieved WTO membership policymakers were not sure what the real consequences of this global engagement might be.

Through these past years the Kyrgyz government welcomed all forms of assistance. This provided a test case for many NGOs and other aid organisations to experiment with their ideas in the region. The total amount of international aid to the Kyrgyz Republic reached 1.7 billion USD for 1992 and 2000.[5] Microfinancing became a major source of income and poverty alleviation, especially in rural areas dependent on external financing. By 2002, the Kyrgyz Agricultural Finance Corporation [KAFC] had 35,000 active clients and a 22 million USD loan portfolio; making it the largest in the region.[6] However, this extensive penetration also highlighted the problems of microfinancing in the region as high interest rates, small loan sizes and high transaction costs created long-term dependency rather than building local capacity. According to World Bank indicators, Kyrgyzstan was the most aid-dependent country among the CIS in terms of the ratio of aid to total imports of goods and services. With less than 350 USD per capita income, aid constituted almost 21 per cent of total Kyrgyz receipts. This figure was 16 per cent for Tajikistan and 14 per cent for Armenia, the two other aid-dependent small nations. While there were no data available for Uzbekistan and Turkmenistan, Kazakhstan showed no significant reliance on aid (1.2 per cent).[7]

For the most part, enterprise development and small and medium-sized business growth failed to benefit from international assistance and funding despite the diversity of projects that were initiated by donors. For example, the EU's TACIS small business support programme ran from 2001 to 2004 and included 45 local projects that received almost half of the designated budget of 1.3 million Euros. It created five enterprise incubators in remote areas through which entrepreneurs were offered training in Israel, with additional funding by USAID. Throughout my fieldwork I met only a handful of entrepreneurs who were involved in these projects in Karakol, the Issyk-Kul region and in Bishkek. They were doubtful about the benefits of their engagement and complained about 'too much talk and too little substantial help'.

Another initiative, by the Turkish government's small and medium-sized business development agency [KOSGEB], established a small industry zone near Bishkek. This was modelled on seemingly successful organised industrial zones in Turkey. Built on the premise that entrepreneurship can be incubated in planned sites, the zone aimed to help the growth of new businesses. Although several Turkish and Kyrgyz entrepreneurs began operating in manufacturing activities such as furniture, plastic water pipes and others, the zone failed to achieve its objective to become an incubation zone. The poor manufacturing base and scarce know-how in the country required broader policies to incubate rather then merely an emphasis on physical and fiscal incentives. Entrepreneurs in the zone claimed that the Kyrgyz economy is too heavily oriented towards the trade and service sectors and there is a lack of entrepreneurship in manufacturing. They also emphasised that the lack of security and a workable property rights regime exposed manufacturers to large and not easily transferable risks. These and other diverse circumstances of market transition dissuaded potential investors from entering into production rather than distribution.[8]

As evidenced throughout my talks with entrepreneurs, consultants and aid specialists, international agencies and their projects make choices influenced by objectives often determined by outsiders who are not grounded in the intricacies of the subject country. Although they can be successful in co-opting national elites, their success depends on the degree of local cooperation, dissemination and overall societal improvements. This is often contingent on the time horizon of the planned projects. After years of enthusiastic involvement with foreign agencies and donor projects, several local experts interviewed expressed cynical views about the Kyrgyz dependency on foreign aid. One claimed,[9]

> Foreign consultants don't know the realities of the country and their advice cannot be relied upon ... many [international agencies] crowd into Kyrgyzstan because they can not function freely elsewhere in the region and so they compete with each other for projects here. As for the government and the bureaucracy, they have been opportunistic and casual with foreign agencies.

There are surely many devoted and highly qualified consultants working in various capacities: designing policy, connecting with recipients and supervising implementation. In some cases, well-intended legal and institutional reforms remained on paper because of the lack of political will and institutional capacity to implement them. A telling example is the ARD/Checchi project which aimed to develop a legal infrastructure for a market economy. As the director of the programme admitted, his eight years of work in Kyrgyzstan produced mixed results in the field of new legislation and legal enforcement. He emphasised that unless governments set a good example in enforcement and change people's old habits of circumventing institutions, there will not be significant improvements in the workings of institutions or in the judicial system, despite the recent legislative reforms, improvements in education and the legal profession. His argument echoes the deeper problems of transition[10]:

> During the USSR period everything was organised from the top with many vertical relations but there was not much horizontal cross

cutting structure.... The [Kyrgyz] state doesn't have moral authority and lacks resources to rule and improve things ... there is a murky legality ... no shared destiny in civil society.

Thus, while the donor agencies often fail to have deeper understanding of the problems they face, or lack the willingness to tackle them directly, they are also handicapped by the inability of the state to provide umbrella support with industrial policies, law enforcement and institutional capacity. Donor support for SMEs has especially suffered from these ills and failed to generate sustainable impact with thinly spread projects. They rarely found dedicated and competent organisations to work with and eventually handed over their projects to weak local institutions.[11] The real issue has been a profound lack of industrial policy to guide SME development. This was not a mere result of local institutional incapacity but it is intermeshed with the ideological orientation of international organisations and their short-sighted positions. A foreign advisor to the Akayev government argued,[12]

Many projects are going on here and they all have great titles; they generate donor attention and funding but in reality very little has been done. These projects are rarely concentrated on long-term issues and real problems ... The IMF's firm belief in the market and its position against any form of state-driven stimuli in industrial policy is mere hypocrisy.

Another expert with many years of experience in the region also pointed out,[13]

Kyrgyzstan, at the donors' behest, pursued a poverty reduction strategy which has focussed on the psychology of the poor and all this borrowing failed to generate sustainable enterprise development.

Collective leisure and ideological purification: tourism in the USSR

Tourism was not recognised as a significant economic component of the command economy, yet the concept of leisure developed fairly early on and led to a wide range of provisions across the USSR. As with all aspects of life, tourism was heavily regulated by the state. Various institutions and agencies dealt with coordinating and managing recreational facilities across the Soviet territories. Facilities were managed by multiple bodies and regulated under the categories of 'physical and mental health' and the 'ideological development of working people and the youth' by the Communist Party. For instance, the overall development and planning of health-oriented facilities was managed by the Central Council for the Administration of Health Resorts. The facilities themselves, however, were distributed among various state enterprises, ministries and organisations for periodic use by their employees. Sport and touring-oriented activities were coordinated by the Central Council for Tourism and Excursions, while youth recreational facilities were controlled by several organisations, including an arm of the Ministry of Education, the Central Children's Excursion and Tourism Station. The Pioneers organisations and the Young Communist League [Komsomol] also provided tours.[14]

Regions were divided according to the type of tourism characterising them: coastlines, lakes and rivers and natural beauty spots. There was also a strong correlation between population density and the distribution of tourist accommodations. Most facilities were in the European part of the Soviet Union. Zone I, for example, included highly populated regions, such as the Black Sea coast, the mountainous North Caucasus and the Caspian Sea resorts. Central Asia occupied the 5th place in the number of sanatoria and holiday resorts with medical treatment, and 2nd place after the northern and eastern Black Sea coast in the number of rest and holiday homes.[15]

The majority of tourist facilities, such as hotels and campsites, catered to large groups and organised tours. Other facilities served educational, work and recuperation purposes, and there were many summer camps for children. There were also popular mountaineering camps, some in Central Asia but most situated in the Caucasus. Although egalitarian in philosophy, resorts and spas ranged from those suitable to host high-rank party bosses and government officials to those catering for ordinary citizens and workers. Underinvestment and lack of control undermined the quality of accommodation and service in the recreational facilities for ordinary people. Over the years this resulted in a preference by two-thirds of Soviet people to spend holidays and vacations at home, with relatives and friends, enjoying unplanned, spontaneous leisure. Another phenomenon of the system of providing leisure was 'dachas', organised as garden cooperatives. Typically located near residential areas to provide inhabitants of large cities opportunities to escape the pressures of city life, these simple houses with small allotments kept urban people in touch with the virtues of agriculture and rural life. In the 1970s over three million people were members of such cooperatives.[16]

While many restrictions hindered travel outside the country, the number of foreign citizens visiting the Soviet Union, especially from socialist countries, rose every year during the post-war period. Foreign tourists began to arrive from the mid-1920s, and in 1929 the tourist agency *Intourist* was founded to serve them. Altogether in the pre-war period the country was visited by about 100,000 tourists, many of them communists, trade unionist or from workers' groups whose visits were organised for political purposes. After the war, foreign tourism remained small until the end of the Stalin period and then began to grow steadily. Towards the end of the 1960s and throughout the early 1970s, the Black Sea coast, Central Asia, the Caucasus and Siberia were officially opened for foreign tourism as places for sightseeing, cultural tourism, health travel and sports. Later, the Baltic States and the Volga region were added to this scheme. The number of visitors reached 486,000 in 1956 and 711,000 in 1960, growing to over 2 million in 1970, over 5 million in 1980 and 6 million by the mid-1980s.[17] This rise was met with an expansion of tourism facilities in Central Asia, which attracted over a million tourists by the 1980s. This growth brought attention to medieval historical and cultural sites that began to get substantial assistance with historical renovations and museum expansions. Historic cities such as Bukhara, Samarkand and Khiva attracted funds for new preservation and rehabilitation projects. Over 60 per cent of visitors were from socialist countries. Likewise, the number of Soviet citizens travelling abroad, mostly to communist countries, grew from 561,000 in 1956 to over 1.8 million in 1970 and over 4.5 million in 1985.[18]

Despite limited statistics on trends, we can discern general characteristics of the institutions that preceded tourism. First, the tourism movement across the USSR was heavily health-orientated. Soviets believed that working people had a right to leisure and good health that would stimulate high achievements, and this contributed to the growth of sanatoria and resorts with medical treatment facilities. The number of these facilities increased from 240 in 1940 to 614 in 1988. This tradition dates back to the period of Peter the Great and was continued by Lenin through the nationalisation of all spas and resorts. The free time of workers had to be monitored and utilised for collective purposes and communist purification of mind and soul. The utilisation of these facilities of the former bourgeoisie and the aristocratic classes continued across the USSR. Recreational activities were commonly provided to employees by their employers, be it a governmental organisation, factory or other enterprise.[19]

Second, public holidays and travel, as in other aspects of life, were controlled and utilised by the state to enhance collective identity and communist ideology. Tourism and travel played a significant role in solidifying territorial loyalty to Soviet power in the vast geography of the USSR. In particular, it worked to blend many different nationalities in resorts and camps from the far-flung regions of the Soviet Empire. This helped to deepen integration of different nationalities and edify the bureaucratic and intellectual elite, confirming party loyalty and the virtues of the multinational character of the USSR. With the increasing number of Eastern Europeans visiting the USSR in the 1970s, tourism took on an international dimension, promoting solidarity across the communist world. Although indoctrination through summer camps and resorts lost its edge in the 1970s and 80s, it played an important role during the early years of Soviet power consolidation. In Central Asia during the 1930s and 40s, young people were systematically recruited to attend communist training and recreation camps where they were co-opted by the Soviet regime as comrades. Later, these same youth worked to foster a sense of solidarity among Soviet people and loyalty within their communities. Many personal accounts verify the importance of youth camps and leagues in the early development of communist allegiance among indigenous people.[20]

New transformations in tourism

Tourism suffered dramatically from the economic upheavals of Soviet dissolution. The region's governments failed to recognise the need to develop policies in order to preserve their income from the Soviet leisure infrastructure. At the same time, intraregional tourism suffered drastically from the worsening economic conditions and sharp fall in household incomes. The number of tourists visiting Central Asia declined substantially from over one million to mere thousands per annum. This trend is most sharply observed in Uzbekistan, which was an important hub for intra-USSR tourism in the region, hosting one million visitors each year. They still attracted more than half a million tourists in 1990.[21] Due to the Uzbek government's stringent customs and border controls, industry representatives estimated that the number of tourist visiting the country dropped to around 50,000 in 2005, indicating a situation far worse than portrayed by official statistics.[22] Soviet tourism and Silk Road tours were initially interconnected but this is now interrupted by bureaucratic hurdles, as border crossings have became much more difficult. The Uzbek government introduced stringent customs controls on its borders since the Tashkent bombings in the late 1990s. The Fergana Valley has been under a security blockade following the Andijan protests in 2005. Regional disintegration and economic meltdown negatively affected Kyrgyz tourism as well. Thus, formerly silent autonomous state borders became symbols of a new assertiveness of the emerging independent states and neighbours casually established diverging customs rules and border controls that hampered trade and tourism. For these reasons, and because of changing regimes of taxation, currency and foreign policies, many tourism-related activities also went into a decline along with most Soviet-period industrial complexes.[23]

At the fringe of the Soviet Union, Kyrgyzstan was the least industrialised among the Autonomous Republics. As it mainly depended on animal husbandry, hydroelectric power generation and gold mining, plus the defence industry, tourism stood out for its potential. In recognition of its state of backwardness, the Kyrgyz economy was also heavily subsidised. In the immediate aftermath of its independence, most of the Soviet-period industrial establishments collapsed. This took place for a variety of reasons including the loss of subsidies but mainly due to the dissolution of systems of production distributed throughout the USSR in which Kyrgyz enterprises contributed only minor elements. Regional economies, skewed towards a single Soviet enterprise or a sectoral specialisation, impinged upon enterprise development with resultant labour market distortions. Many people who were trapped in such towns had neither transferable skills nor a feasible job alternative. One consequence of deindustrialisation and rising poverty was emigration and deurbanisation, which saw many middle class professionals move to rural areas in order to survive on subsistence farming and animal husbandry. At the same time a surge of rural migration to towns and cities took place from the most distant and poor rural areas that no longer received any public services or subsidy.

With economic recovery and the stabilisation of currencies, tourism from the CIS countries began to increase from 2000. The official statistics are not always consistent and clear about the composition of these figures, but tourism and recreation activities are apparently becoming more promising in Kyrgyzstan. Although it only constituted 3.1 per cent of gross national product in 2005, the number of establishments is currently increasing (see Tables 7.1 and 7.2). The industry statistics indicate a sharp rise in the number of tourists visiting the country from 2003 onwards, surpassing half a million in 2004 while the number of tourist enterprises reached over 4,700. Foreign tourist traffic quadrupled

Table 7.1   Tourism indicators in the Kyrgyz Republic between 2002 and 2005

Indicators	2002	2003	2004	2005
Number of registered enterprises rendering tourist services	3918	4261	4479	4771
The total added value in the sphere of tourist activity (in millions of som)	3019.7	3010.9	3592.2	2288.1
Percentage of gross national product (GNP)	4.0	3.6	3.3	3.1
Investments in tourism in fixed capital (in millions of som)	1357.1	739.5	988.8	584.9
Turnover of retail trade in tourism (in millions of som)	1691.3	1930.8	1566.9	1709.5
Turnover of restaurants, bars, cafes, others. (in millions of som)	1143.8	1469.9	1196.6	1457.7
Export of tourist services – i.e., the income received for the reception of foreign citizens – Inbound tourism (in millions of USD)	35.7	47.8	58.7	55.8
The number of foreign citizens arriving into the country (in thousands)	139.6	211.3	737.7	601.1

Source: The National Statistics Committee of Kyrgyzstan, Bishkek, 2006.
For comparison purposes: 1 USD = approximately 40 som and 1 EUR = approximately 55 som

Table 7.2   The growth of tourism in the Kyrgyz Republic

	2002	2003	2004
Total number of tourism-related establishments:	325	349	379
Sanatoria	37	46	44
Boarding houses	55	58	53
Rest houses	11	11	11
Camp sites	11	7	9
Children's activities	45	39	38
Hotels	84	79	101
Tourist agencies, tour operators and travel agencies	80	103	115

Source: The National Statistics Committee of Kyrgyzstan, Bishkek, 2006.

between 2002 and 2005, mainly from Russia and Kazakhstan, indicating a reversal of the earlier dissolution of tourism patterns from the CIS countries. However, most tourism businesses as well as international tourists tend to concentrate in Bishkek and on the northern shores of Issyk-Kul, the alpine lake that was popular during the Soviet period and is now one of the main attractions for Kazakh and Russian tourists. The accessibility of summer resorts around Cholpon-Ata on Issyk-Kul, only a few hours drive away from Almaty, make them popular for the increasingly affluent Kazakhs. New ski resorts and nature tourism are also developing around old Soviet resorts in the town of Karakol, on the eastern end of the lake.[24]

However, there are three main sources of business uncertainty in tourism.[25] The most common form is related to governance problems in defining and protecting property rights. With the collapse of the Soviet Union, many recreational facilities were privatised but rarely found competent owners or the new owners were exploited by gangs. Many old large establishments were eventually divided up floor-by-floor to be rented as business premises. I stayed in one such old hotel in Karaganda where several floors of a gigantic Soviet building were rented to other businesses, and many suspicious-looking men were roaming around among the security guards at the entrance. Since property rights are not well-defined and protected for resort owners, self-governing groups such as racketeers and gangs influence transactions and determine ownership rights. More recently, tourism became another way to hide illicit earnings, to build influence and to channel money for self-governing groups. My interviews and other anecdotal evidence point out that illegal earnings are being camouflaged by investments in new restaurants and hotels.[26] Thus, businesses face dual governance 'distortions': state absorption through bureaucratic corruption and illicit group influence and extortion.

Second, demand-related uncertainty is linked to larger-scale economic and political distortions that create unpredictable booms and busts in the demand cycle. Businesses need customers to survive, and there was neither a regular flow nor a fair spread of tourists beyond the Issyk-Kul region. Due to both the poor attention paid by mass tourist operators and the ignorance of foreign tourists about a region that has long been a distant backwater, large Soviet-era hotels initially failed to attract sufficient customers to meet their capacity. Furthermore, many of these large establishments either failed to find competent, genuine investors or simply could not survive the slow emergence of the market economy and the decline in intra-CIS tourism. In other instances, racketeering groups stripped the establishments of their assets, including décor and furniture, and left them abandoned as massive ghostly concrete blocks. Such sights are apparent throughout the region. What had previously been the most attractive elite hotel in Semey, the north-eastern Kazakh town, no longer had members of the nomenclature staying there. When my assistant and I entered the building to check in, we were surprised by its vast marble-covered empty spaces. The lounge had no chandeliers, chairs or tables left, the reception desk was a hole in the wall and there were bodyguards everywhere. The hotel was full of shady residents including drug addicts and sex traders. Hours later when a fight broke out among the distressed people in the hotel we got the full picture and quickly left.

The third form of uncertainty is linked to supply side distortions. Unexpected electricity and gas outages or restrictions, a limited range of consumption goods and poor public services all create day-to-day management problems and long-term uncertainty that businesses have to address in order to maintain their products or services. Others include the lack of credible banking services and saving schemes, poor urban infrastructure, inadequate transportation and health provisions. All these are common problems that businesses face and they have to bear additional costs in tackling them. Overall, in the hospitality business, the provision of essential public services hinders the scope of tourism and business growth.

Incubating entrepreneurialism: the case of CBT

In 2000, the Swiss Association for International Cooperation (Helvetas) initiated the Kyrgyz Community Based Tourism (CBT) project.[27] It set up a CBT association and developed a network of entrepreneurs to promote tourism and hospitality services across the country. By using a blend of urban and rural traditions and nomadic cultural elements, CBT aimed to diffuse tourism into rural areas and to small settlements [*auls*].[28] In the subsequent years it became a successful initiative and an effective incubator for innovative entrepreneurialism embedded in local traditions. Many aspects of the project were designed pragmatically with a good understanding of the economic and social circumstances of the country. The project was initiated with communities and families directly involved at the local level and aimed to use the skill and imagination of local players in building its network. This character of the project and its successful incubator role set it apart from a rather congested market of donor projects overpopulated by international consultants working with the small political elite. The CBT's main difference from other nationwide projects, such as the TACIS-initiated SME development network, lies in its commitment and focus on enhancing local capabilities along with sustainability measures. Not surprisingly, Helvetas was able to achieve much more with a relatively small budget and fewer international experts and consultants.

The Helvetas initiative identified ten town centres and villages across the country, namely, Arslanbob, Jalalabad, Karasuu, Kazarman (near Jalalabad), Karakol, Kochkor, Naryn, Osh, Talas and Tamchy, in addition to a main office in Bishkek. A related initiative, Shepherd's Life, was also introduced to support the rural economy and to attract tourism revenues to the much neglected countryside. The CBT connects shepherds and nomads with owner-run family guest homes and the ten largest Bishkek-based major tour operators. With each of the ten local offices coordinating 15–25 family enterprises, the CBT is connecting a couple of hundred enterprises. Although modest, this generates business for other enterprises and employment for locals in all CBT centre locations.

After conducting initial planning and educating the participants, each centre established a CBT office, a coordinator and a list of individual members. All these were formed into a national network connected through telephone and e-mail in most cases. The CBT centre in each locality was organised through a community tourism office. With no strict hierarchy, a team leader and a secretary took the coordination role and maintained the communication both with CBT networks and CBT enterprises. These centres typically functioned from small one- or two-room offices equipped with simple office furniture, local information and a list of guesthouses displayed on a board. These offices became a meeting point for local participants where they exchanged ideas and information. They were able to organise periodic meetings, assess community finances and develop actions to solve common problems.

CBT in southern Kyrgyzstan

Dispersing tourism from northern to southern regions has been a real challenge. Due to its limited accessibility and general lack of promotion, southern towns and their scenic countryside remained isolated from the north with increasingly fewer tourists over the years. The CBT helped to overcome this distortion with a diffused network of local operators and promotional leaflets. They offered budget tourism to those who have interests in trekking, horse riding and nomad living. Food, transport, sightseeing and accommodation are all provided by local CBT enterprises. For as little as 10 or 20 USD per night one could get accommodation and food in clean and decently furnished homes. Tourists are treated as guests staying with local families, sometimes with the added luxury of private bathrooms. This form of tourism relies on the families' own efforts with occasional casual labour and a minimum of other resources such as bedding and decorated rooms or yurts.

During my visit to Jalalabad and Osh in autumn 2004, I had the opportunity to observe the workings of CBT in this region. I spent a few nights in CBT guest houses in Osh and Jalalabad talking to mostly female entrepreneurs involved in the hospitality business and travelled to the much praised valley of Arslanbob and the majestic alpine lake Sary-Chelek, near the town of Karasuu, 210 km north of Jalalabad. The most striking experience for me was the lack of roads and absence of signs. My research assistant and I, along with our driver, travelled to Sary-Chelek, following convoluted instructions from the CBT guide in Arslanbob. Every now and then the village roads would disappear in fields and hills. Thus, we had to stop repeatedly and ask for directions from herdsmen and villagers. We quickly became overloaded with contradictory estimates of distance and direction. After searching for the lake well past midnight, a massive gate of the national park finally appeared. However, about ten miles further down a tiny road, we still saw no sign of the lake and it was too dark to travel further. After dozing in the car for several hours we woke up with the sun and found ourselves beside a creek. It took another hour of driving to climb the hill to our destination. The idyllic alpine lake shimmered in the morning sunshine surrounded by bushes and trees, a glorious sight and probably worth the effort.

Osh, Kyrgyzstan's second largest city, sprawls across the banks of the Ak-Buura (White Camel) River, flowing out of the majestic Pamir Mountains. It is the administrative centre of a fertile agricultural hinterland at the eastern end of the Fergana Valley. Locals claim that the city is older than Rome and it was a secondary commercial centre along the Silk Road for many centuries. The most famous symbol of the town is the so-called Solomon's Throne, a small cave-pocked hill in the middle of the city. Babur, the founder of the Mughal dynasty in India, is believed to have sought refuge in Solomon's Throne when he was fleeing his native Andijan. The blend of sedentary Uzbek and nomadic Kyrgyz traditions survive in the city along with the smaller influence of Tajik, Uyhgur and other cultures.[29] The region between Osh and its northern neighbouring town Jalalabad has noteworthy archaeological and natural sites for visitors and these are increasingly becoming authenticating symbols of independent Kyrgyzstan. The former capital of the Karakhanid Empire, Uzgen, with origins dating back to Alexander the Great, is widely recognised as the symbol of the region's rich cultural heritage.[30]

Mythological and historical legacies which have been whispered by the locals and recounted in travel books generate an attractive mystery about sites like Arslanbob. At an altitude of 1600 metres, this is a valley ideal for trekking with many lakes and waterfalls along with legendary wild walnut trees. Some believe these trees live up to 1000 years and give nuts of high nutritious value and purported special healing effects.[31] According to local legend, Arslanbob was a servant of the Prophet Muhammad. The Prophet appreciated his modesty and hard work and asked him to find the most beautiful place on earth. After a long search, Arslanbob found a very picturesque valley with foaming waterfalls, but the place had no trees. When the Prophet heard this he sent a bag of seeds and nuts to beautify the valley. Arslanbob climbed to the top of the highest mountain and scattered these throughout the valley. Thus, the whole area was turned into a region of lush green trees with plentiful berries and nuts. Today the valley is a living symbol of surviving pre-Islamic shamanistic traditions and Sufi Islam. Visitors make wishes in diverse forms for different purposes: they light candles in numerous caves, wrap ribbons on the branches of holy trees, make wishes at several major waterfalls and perform many unorthodox Sufi rituals and Muslim prayers.

Despite the range of these attractions in the region, tourism is growing slowly and any hope for cross-border tourism from Uzbekistan and Tajikistan looks dim. The sustainability of the CBT network is dependent on their ability to keep strong ties among members along with ensuring financial independence. A fair allocation of tourists to each entrepreneur was an essential part of solidarity and trust building. This has not been easy and participants remained highly sceptical about fellow entrepreneurs and their motives. While the local CBTs tried to control the number of business entries and tried to prevent imitators from overcrowding the market, they also feared that their imitators would undercut already modest accommodation prices. Saving and investments for individual enterprises and also for the collective CBT budget was a serious problem. When I talked to CBT members in Osh, they said they were able to save money but they did not trust local banks. These entrepreneurs could not see any alternative saving schemes. Thus, they formed a savings scheme and systematically invested in lambs and foals to be sold in the spring. This was not an uncommon practice in Kyrgyzstan: people invested in animals as an alternative to placing their savings in gold. This scheme generated further income and protected their savings from inflation and the predatory absorption of state officials and other private groups.[32] The following cases illustrate the diverse origins of the CBT-linked family oriented businesses, and of women's strategies in entrepreneurial initiatives.

Case 7.1 – A pioneering organiser, Dinara

As a successful entrepreneur and network builder, Dinara thinks there is good money in tourism. In her late 30s, she has many obligations and responsibilities with much financial debt; as a single mother and bread-winner she also has to support her relatives in Bishkek. She inherited a large house with a courtyard from her high-ranking parents. The family had seen better days as evidenced by her art deco furniture, many pictures and family memorabilia. There is also an interesting array of Soviet art, mostly from the 1970s. Dinara had been skipping and sliding among jobs for many years until she got involved in CBT. As a graduate in Russian language and literature, she could only secure administrative jobs. One day she met an English couple who rented a room from her friend. These people wanted to open bars in Bishkek and Osh, and Dinara agreed to manage the business. However, the venture was quickly abandoned in the aftermath of the September 11th, 2001 attacks in New York and Washington due to security fears of the couple, and other ambiguities that Dinara was not even sure of. Soon after, Dinara lost her last office job and began renting rooms to foreign experts and consultants who came to Osh to work for various projects. This suited her much better as she was going to spend more time with her 9-year-old daughter. She first heard about the Helvetas initiative through a friend and with her education and good communication skills she soon took a leadership role as the CBT representative in Osh coordinating 22 CBT entrepreneurs. When I stayed in Dinara's guesthouse, she was busy calculating the number of sheep she needed to purchase for that season as a from of saving. The hospitality business had many fluctuations, the future seemed uncertain and she supplemented the business with other small ventures.

Case 7.2 – A former sales manager, Aigula

After working 30 years for state-run stores and cooperatives as a sales manager, Aigula discovered the world of tourism in her 50s. With Dinara, I visited her guesthouse, situated on the ground floor of a massive five-storey building. The neighbourhood was formerly inhabited by

Soviet local elites and is now filled with newly built large houses and surrounded by gardens and allotments. There was no sign outside the building or on the road announcing the location of this six-room guest house. Later that night while walking back home we used our mobiles as torches to avoid holes and stones on the unlit roads in pitch dark. The first striking character of Aigula's apartment was the immensity of its space and high ceilings. Compared to Dinara's cheerfully cluttered house, this neatly decorated interior with Western-style furniture and heavy curtains looked serene but serious. No works of art or frivolous objects were in sight. This business was built step by step after Aigula and her husband secured the ownership of the property in 2001. The space had been the store where Aigula worked and she had to use her husband's komsomol position and other contacts to secure ownership when it was privatised. The hospitality business looked convincing and brought reasonable income. Thus, Aigula hoped to further expand the business into a hotel if Aigula could buy an additional floor in the same block. She not only managed this venture with the help of her husband but she was also an active farmer and producer of foodstuffs. With adult children working in various jobs in Bishkek and Osh, Aigula seemed more worried about them than her own future.

Case 7.3 – The manager of a dispersed family, Sultan

In the outskirts of Jalalabad among gardened houses, Sultan has two small rooms and a bathroom allocated for guests while she and her disabled son in his early 20s share the remaining two rooms, a kitchen and a bathroom. Naturally blond with green eyes, Sultan is in her late 50s but looks much older. Her husband passed away some years earlier and she is now the centre point of the family. She can't leave her son alone for long hours, so working from home suits her much better. During the summer months, her daughter joins them and helps with daily chores. The rooms have simple bedding and a few traditional textiles. In the living room there are decorative hangings and wall signs of pious Muslim living. Since being deported from their homeland in the Crimea during the Stalin era, Sultan and her family have been living between lands and all their relatives are now scattered in different parts of Russia and Central Asia. Although they are grateful to the Kyrgyz, Sultan says, they feel uprooted. She has a bizarre nomadic life: once the tourism season is over, she and her children fly to a small Russian town where they have a flat, owned by her daughter. She does casual work and her daughter teaches school children through the winter since there is hardly any income for them in Jalalabad. They have to calculate every move in order to minimise expenses and accumulate some savings. Her son-in-law works in seasonal jobs and construction sites in Siberia and elsewhere in Russia. The family is pleased with the opportunity they have with the CBT initiative and Sultan's daughter is actively involved in the coordination office. Business is slow and their income barely enough to survive. The long-term hopes are all tied to the economic and political stability of the country and rising tourism in the region. For the time being, to generate income they spread their risks between far lands and depend on strong family ties.

These cases and other entrepreneurs like them illustrate how increasingly families, often organised by their female members, take new initiatives and bear risks in establishing tourism ventures. They are willing to listen and learn from external actors and adapt to new market conditions. The successful spread of CBT illustrates this willingness to adapt and the importance of capacity-building rather than raw aid spending. However, many conversations also unveiled deep anxiety about the future of the country, the corrupt upper strata and the continuing economic struggle facing families with limited means. Although middle stratum entrepreneurs in the urban centres of Osh and Jalalabad are reasonably well off, they nevertheless feel deeply insecure about increasing poverty and unemployment in their region. In Osh, after the closure of the cotton works, the silk factory and the pump manufacturer, each of which employed five to eight thousand workers during the Soviet period, many thousands lost their only source of income. Government and international aid was slow to reach southern regions. Many unemployed workers took to small trade and casual jobs while hundreds of men left to work abroad, sending back their remittances. If these alternative sources of income stop, everyone fears that serious social breakdown will be unavoidable.

Conclusion

Kyrgyzstan is an extreme case of a former Soviet republic left without new markets or overseas connections. This, coupled with hastily established and poorly administered privatisation programmes, brought about the collapse of most large enterprises less than a decade after independence. Thousands of people moved to make a living on small trade. Regional economies that had been skewed towards a single Soviet enterprise or a sectoral specialisation further inhibited enterprise development with labour market distortions. Many people who were trapped in such towns and localities had neither transferable skills nor feasible job alternatives. In the midst of this dismal state, the Kyrgyz governments have been sluggish in drafting effective industrial and enterprise development policies that would have channelled external borrowing to sustainable capacity-building projects in the country. This lack of insight was partly linked to their poor understanding of the necessary steps to be taken towards a market economy and partly due to opportunistic accumulation of much foreign economic aid by the upper strata that was channelled to maintaining their vested interests. While Kyrgyzstan became the most heavily aid-dependent country in its region, there also emerged a trend of poverty alleviation at the expense of a concerted focus on enterprise development strategies. These objectives skewed rural and urban development projects towards small income generation and in the long-term distorted entrepreneurship, competition and market growth. Consequently, external financial assistance facilitated the reshuffling and allocation of the Mikado game in favour of Bishkek-centred groups. This in turn contributed to the growing clash of interests among groups and regions in the country.

Long-term capacity building requires sophisticated policies, a wide range of tools and committed institutions. However, in Kyrgyzstan, neither domestic players nor international aid organisations had such a vision for building new markets. With highly competitive and over populated aid and international assistance programmes, a new set of distortions emerged. Each programme had different political and economic objectives; their time horizons and scope varied substantially. The continuity and sustainability objectives of these projects were subject to policy changes and interruptions at home as well as abroad.

Some of the major conclusions include the following: first, market distortions and poor governance limited successful implementation and diffusion of project implementation to lower levels of society. Second, diverging interests and priorities led to misunderstandings and unrealistic expectations between donors and their local counterparts. Finally, there is now an ample opportunity to rethink and assess the achievements and shortfalls of international aid and assistance with a new focus on economic targets and enterprise development.

Despite these pessimistic findings, however, there have been some successful implementations in enterprise creation and in support for entrepreneurship. The case study of the CBT shows that when appropriate tools are used, donor projects can induce new entrepreneurialism even in the most unfavourable circumstances. The CBT initiative illustrates a rare project design that is set in the realities of Kyrgyzstan and has been enthusiastically implemented by skilled community leaders and local entrepreneurs. Helvetas experts communicated well with locals and did not create illusions about unrealistic gains and business benefits. The project aimed to link major centres to many distressed and isolated provincial areas. As per capita income plummeted and many people had no capital to invest, the business model had to be adjusted to target small dispersed owners and their families, using all their assets including homes, yurts and animals. While linking community tourism with a wider network of tourist agencies and tour operators, the CBT model helped to build further market capacity and development. Thus, the CBT initiative played a successful incubator role for entrepreneurship development and this sets it apart from a rather congested market of donor projects.

Nevertheless, this initiative is small, comprising only a couple of hundred families. For a country with a poor entrepreneurial and industrial base, this is a very modest contribution and cannot bring about big changes. Yet it makes a difference to these communities and helps to contribute to sectoral transformation from Soviet leisure and holiday structures to new diverse customer-oriented tourism development. The legacy of Soviet sanatoria and youth camps could not have been revived; fashions in tourism and realistic understanding of Kyrgyz capacity required a complete transformation of most of the tourism sector to small, dispersed and flexible enterprises. The alternative of modernising the Soviet leisure infrastructure would have required massive, risky investments and global marketing.

However, the long-term survival of the CBT is linked to economic and political developments in the country. Three prevailing sources of uncertainty: poor governance, demand-side distortions, and supply distortions negatively affect the potential scope of CBT and business development in general. The failure of government and regional authorities to provide adequate public goods such as efficient banking, roads, street lighting, health clinics, education and other infrastructure impinges on business development and the scope of tourism. The penetration of criminal groups and self-governing syndicates into leisure and tourism-related activities also threatens the future of industry as well as community-based initiatives and networks. Nevertheless, the CBT case is a demonstration of possibilities for gradual transformations that alleviate poverty and contribute to sustainable local economies.

8
Entrepreneurs as Moral Men

Don't break anyone's heart, even if he is an unbeliever.
To break the heart of a man is equal to hurting God.
Sufi philosopher Ahmed Yesevi, twelfth century[1]

Let the beauty you love
Be what you do.

Out beyond ideas of wrong-doing and right-doing
there is a field. I'll meet you there.
Sufi philosopher Mewlana-Jalaluddin-Rumi,
thirteenth century[2]

We repudiate all morality that is taken outside of human,
class concepts ...
We say: morality is that which serves to destroy the
old exploiting society
and to unite all the toilers around the proletariat.
Vladimir I. Lenin's speech at the Komsomol
Congress, 1921[3]

Which is better:
to be indifferent to your neighbour's fate in a moral
society
or to be concerned about it in an amoral society?
On 'Homo Sovieticus', Aleksandr Zinoviev, 1985[4]

Introduction

Moral harmony is an invisible yet formidable part of state and market building. Moral polarisation brings societal upheavals and conflicts. Modern state-building processes not only require national identity formation and power consolidation but also a societal moral harmony. In order to forge this, as the experiences of modern Western nation states illustrate, the state uses its coercive powers to eliminate opposing groups and promote agencies of moral harmony in many realms. Legal and institutional foundations safeguard society from moral disarray. Although the modern state has been subject to new pressures in the post nation-state era and top-down uniformity is no longer regarded as necessary, moral harmony remains a central problem in many postcolonial states and newly emerging ones. In the post-Soviet context, the transition to markets, dissolution of state legitimacy and ideological void dislocated individuals from their value systems. Although individuals continue to accommodate these major changes in their day-to-day lives, societal and individual moral reference points become unstable and confused.

Morality plays a role in the market, too. Philosophers and economists have dealt with morality in social and economic order. However, beyond the growing body of work on business ethics, which mainly deals with managerial enterprises in advanced economies, morality in markets and entrepreneurship has been a neglected area of academic scholarship. The moral dimension of economic transition has similarly received little attention.[5]

Here we consider the inner world of entrepreneurs and their moral dispositions. This issue emerged as a paramount concern in numerous discussions and interviews as business people talked about their frustrations, ambitions and choices. Taken together, these hundreds of reflections on common experiences reveal ideological and religious undercurrents as they also illustrate profound divergences among people and regions. Entrepreneurs frequently face moral conflicts in their day-to-day struggle to survive. These are exacerbated when they must deal with market distortions, the weak rule of law, erratic institutions and deep information asymmetries. On top of that, the social inequalities and anxieties about money and power add to their day-to-day challenge to survive. Trust-based personal relations are paramount to business transactions where the market is manipulated by powerful political elites. Since these relations are built mainly on verbal guarantees, they are often difficult to enforce and consume much effort. Under these conditions, business is deeply embedded in communal ethics, group identities and relational networks, and business owners must apply moral judgements in their dealings every day.

The quotes at the beginning of this chapter illustrate the opposing moral positions between Sufi Islam, which originated in Central Asia, and Soviet ideology, which was transplanted by outsiders to the region. Communist social engineering repudiated all moral obligations associated with individual sentiments and social norms beyond a single collectivistic morality. The aim was to nurture a singular being: *homo sovieticus*. However, during the past 60 years, Central Asian societies did not evolve into a single Soviet morality nor did they entirely resist it. Instead, a blend of multiple influences shaped the day-to-day morality as reference points. These came from a wide range of old beliefs such as shamanism, Buddhism and Islam. Today, the resurgence of Islam, as a binding force and moral compass, points to a slow but significant societal transformation.

I will first introduce the range of moral dilemmas entrepreneurs face in the post-Soviet market. These are related to social-status anxiety, daily moral dilemmas and guilt, and the moral vacuum of post-Soviet materialism. Then, I will examine entrepreneurs' responses in relation to corresponding moral realms of virtue, justice and greater good.[6] Claiming moral purity or homogeneity under a single ethical domain is unrealistic, but we still observed strong patterns which identify three domineering moral positions among businessmen. In their virtue of duty and attempts to seek justice and greater good, these entrepreneurs display three distinct moral dispositions: Soviet scientific rationality, Sufi pragmatism and conservative Islam. Based on extensive empirical observation and reading of secondary literature (including folk songs, poetry and dictums), I examine the moral world of entrepreneurs in these three positions with illustrative case studies.

Morality dilemmas

I found three fundamental patterns of discontent related to the clash between moral preferences and the activities of entrepreneurs: social-status anxiety, daily moral dilemmas and guilt and the moral vacuum of post-Soviet materialism. These stem from the divergence of personal positions from proclaimed faith.

First, most business owners born before 1975 were once state employees or had their formal education under the Soviet system. They often held professional positions and enjoyed certain social status. These men and women were forced through a personal journey from secure employment to a state of deep personal insecurity associated with societal upheaval and economic uncertainty. In order to survive and look after their families, they had to become independent income earners. Even the highest ranked professionals, judges, doctors, engineers and teachers were forced to supplement their declining salaries. As their previous positions became untenable, many moved into new sectors, and they gradually lost their skills as well as their prestige. For many, this brought about deep psychological trauma and social-status anxiety.

Second, entrepreneurs encounter moral dilemmas on a day-to-day basis and often find themselves in contradictory positions. When the gulf between inner moral disposition and real-world action grows wider, we observe what Timur Kuran calls 'preference falsification' which leads to a sense of guilt.[7] As individuals, we all face moral dilemmas in our daily encounters in deciding to act the way we think or the way we should or must according to our personal convictions and commonly agreed norms. The behavioural pattern of preference falsification was a common phenomenon under communist regimes. Informal resistance to state and single-party rule led to habits of circumvention, falsification and alternative networks that undermined state socialism.[8] These habits and norms take new shapes in market economies today. The market rules are fragile and many relations remain the hostage of corruption. The gulf between entrepreneurs' inner self-judgement about right and wrong and the publicly expressed positions grow wider with each action. For example, many vehemently defend societal fairness and the need for just governance rules, but in reality the same individuals habitually avoid paying taxes, exploit their employees and seek influence above the law. Successful entrepreneurs are the ones who can take advantage of market opportunities and information asymmetries to maximise their self-interest. Thus, especially in tough economic circumstances, being virtuous as opposed to selfish and greedy is a highly risky route for entrepreneurs.

Third, money and political power occupied the central position in social relations while societal injustices grew over the years. Post-Soviet materialism is most visible in the popularity of luxury cars, fashionable clothes and conspicuously walled villas as these have become new status symbols irrespective of how they are obtained. Such materialism leads to a blurred ethical environment in which there is a shortage of acceptable and commonly binding reference points in moral judgements about money and power. There is little difference between legal, fair earnings and illegal, unjust wealth accumulation given the weak and ambiguous judicial and law-enforcement systems. In this murky state, business and criminality gets mixed, further eroding altruistic social values.[9] Recent studies involving the youth show the growing gap between generations in value judgements and point out the lack of respect for hard work to obtain wealth. The use of violence, racketeering and other illegal ways to obtain wealth is becoming acceptable and even respectable among some.[10]

Most of the entrepreneurs in this sample were not directly involved in criminal rings. However, given the state of laws and institutions in the region, one can assume an inevitable criminality on the part of all individuals and businesses. Nevertheless, like anyone else, entrepreneurs too are naturally overwhelmed by changing value systems. However, their position is complex since they both feel the threat of these societal contradictions and the absorptive nature of market criminality and yet at the same time benefit from the growth of affluence and consumption. Market growth, even under criminal conditions, often serves their interests. While grabbing opportunities and assets in the market has become the norm, entrepreneurs need to cultivate politically stronger and wealthier connections in order to widen their opportunities. They use these links and other reciprocal relations to address uncertainty in their day-to-day operations. By aligning their interests with the stronger elements of the society, entrepreneurs often choose to abandon or ignore more general societal moral obligations beyond their immediate family circles.

In dealing with these challenges and ethical contradictions, entrepreneurs develop cognitive defence mechanisms in relation to the core morality of doing business. Their personal strategies aim to contain uncertainty, insecurity and changes in the market. For this they can call upon three moral dispositions: Soviet scientific rationalism, Sufi pragmatism and conservative Islam.

The shaman encounters Soviet man

A segment of entrepreneurs today retains the Soviet mindset in a hybrid morality composed of nomadic spiritual beliefs along with their interpretation of Marxist ideology. These middle stratum entrepreneurs, educated in Soviet schools and universities, learned to identify societal and technical advancement and personal skill development through Russian culture and language. While being Russified and Sovietised, some lost their native identity and culture completely, but the majority retained a strong spiritual link to their clan and ancestors. They rationalise the change in their lives in deterministic terms. A survivalist rationale forms the core of their moral being. A sense of realism and lax religious indoctrination bring moral flexibility in applying new rules to changing circumstances, and they emerge as rapid adapters in the market.[11] These individuals, once virtuous communists, transformed principles of *homo sovieticus* into individual opportunistic precepts.[12]

Soviet-era teaching brought about a legitimisation of human actions by appealing to rationality and collectivism as if they were historically determined natural laws. These brought about two conceptual positions. First, the belief that principles of behaviour and structure found at one scale and in one domain, in one-time frame and under a particular set of circumstances, could be extrapolated to others. Second, the same laws could have been applied across domains and situations in order to generate or accelerate cultural, social and political change. Modernist Soviet enterprise and the planned economy exemplified the scientific method.[13] The ideals of liberal morality were countered by the ideals of distributive justice, the contributing individual, freedom as freedom-to-be and collective action in economic affairs.[14]

The power of knowledge and technology that Russification brought about played a defining role in the societal fabric and in the minds of Central Asian intellectuals for a century. Russian language education and the communist propaganda of Soviet teaching diffused rapidly once the indigenous alternatives to modernisation were fully purged.[15] In the Soviet Union, Russian became the first language of the elite while titular languages faded away into domestic conversations and were considered primitive and rural.[16] Generations of Central Asians were absorbed into the dogmatic teaching of Marxist determinism and a single truth mindset. However, scientific modernity and communist ideology had an uneven spread.[17] It was more influential among the urban middle class, educated professionals and party members and penetrated more easily in the steppe lands along with the mass migration of Slavs; but remained less effective among the densely populated native towns of the Fergana Valley.

While cynicism towards communist ideals among common folk and some of the intelligentsia continued to grow throughout the 1970s and 1980s, the influence of rational scientific thinking remained strong among intellectuals and professionals because of education, socialisation and the media. The mindset of scientific determinism remains an undercurrent moral and intellectual influence among middle-stratum urban entrepreneurs today.[18] However, the propensity to follow the Soviet mindset is also blended with other influences: Islam and pastoral traditions.[19]

In their late conversion to Islam, Kazakhs and Kyrgyz incorporated centuries of naturalistic nomadic traditions and shamanistic rituals into monotheism and developed a pragmatic attitude towards the teachings of Islamic law.[20] Shamanistic rituals along with ancestral lineage held them together and provided a vehicle for societal survival.[21] The shaman improvises methods in a do-it-yourself style. As the most ancient form of spirituality for Central Asians, shamanism is a source of collective wisdom that has survived in symbolic rituals, veneration of saints and special sites. The healing of shamans and the sacred cult of ancestral spirits were partially incorporated into Islamic rituals.[22] The collective memory of land and its association with lineage and saints remained a forceful source of identity.

Atheism blended with shamanism and tribalism cohabited reasonably well in Kazakh and Kyrgyz societies. The former was public and the latter was pushed to the private sphere, often regarded as part of national traditions. For many centuries nomads, scattered in the vast steppes that stretched between Siberia and Central Asia, worshipped nature and adhered to Tengri.[23] By tradition, shamans emerged as mediums between the earthly beings and heavenly sky. Just as in some native cultures of America and Africa, shamans are commonly described at once as doctors, priests, social workers and mystics[24]. In the early history of Turco–Mongol tribes, shamans had significant political power. Being a shaman not only required a good understanding of the mystic heritage of the society, but more importantly it necessitated wisdom and skill to understand the hopes and desires of fellow nomads.

Ancestral lineage and shamanism are symbolised in a shared territorial continuity and identity among tribes. In more modern times, as tribes dislocated, individuals carried their ancestral memory through knowledge of forefathers and ritualised belonging to land. There remain many burial sites, holy shrines with commonly cited legends – mountain peaks, water sources, lakes and waterfalls – that constitute landmarks of belonging. The folkloric themes and old myths recounted by the Kyrgyz writer Chingiz Aytmatov illustrate territorial belonging. In his celebrated work, *The Day Lasts More Than a Hundred Years*, Aytmatov narrates the legend of the Ana-Beiit Cemetery in the Sarozak Desert and its importance for Kazakhs as a site of worship, belonging and spiritual cleansing. Ana-Beiit wanted to save her son from being enslaved by invading Junarians. Her enslaved son loses his memory and his identity following the form of a 'mankurt'. A 'mankurt', a soul-less person, later became a potent symbol of cultural annihilation and a metaphor for the alienation of Central Asians living under Soviet rule. In Aytmatov's story, the cemetery tragically disappears behind the vast fence that encloses the Cosmodrom, the Soviet space centre.[25]

Entrepreneurs who are most influenced by Soviet teaching and pastoral traditions and least affected by Islamic beliefs are more likely to adhere to the following principles of business (see Table 8.1 for a comparison):

I   *A core morality for conducting business*: They believe that business is a means to survive and the change of the regime is a consequence of dialectic materialism. Life is seen through the prism of determinism but sacred lineage, family and tribal relations constitute an exception. Care for others is limited to these lineages and the veneration of progenitors of their clan.

II *The virtue of duty*: An entrepreneur's duty is to survive and serve the needs of family and lineage. The law of nature applies: whoever is stronger will survive; this often takes on a predatory character. In order to achieve success and manage to survive one might occasionally be ruthless and bend the rules when necessary.

III *Justice and greater good*: There appears a bounded sense of justice for the clan and the family. However, the entrepreneur is open to new ideas and curious about the world. They suffer from moral dissonance in relation to their formative Soviet training. These entrepreneurs often have faith in and expectations of a good capitalist life-style as a form of personal advancement.

The two former professionals described below provide some reflections on the lives and thoughts of entrepreneurs. A Kazakh former KGB agent and a Kyrgyz chief hospital surgeon each discovered their own ways to survive and prosper. These are pragmatists and willing to replace the Soviet scientific teaching with market-based rationality for the sake of survival.

Case 8.1 – Juma: The ex-spy retailer

Juma was busy visiting his several retail sites in containers across Almaty and agreed to meet us in a café. There he appeared on time with a smile on his face; a massive man, with slanted eyes, broad shoulders and a Mongolian beard. He walked like a rectangular concrete block carrying a small colourful gift bag. He looked unsettled, with almost a hunter's anxiety. Our conversation revealed not just a profit-seeking entrepreneur but a man with rational ideas and dreams of a new world mixed with Soviet sentiments. Juma was clear about his options.

199

Table 8.1 A typology of entrepreneurs' moral dispositions

	Core morality of business doing	Virtue of duty	Justice and greater good	Moral dissonance
Soviet rationality *Disjointed*	–Survivalist –Consequence of rational laws –Straight forward opportunism	–Surviving and adapting –Preserving the family and sacred lineage –Continuity of family lineage	–Materialistic and flexible –Indifferent or lacks enthusiasm for greater moral goods –Predatory in character	Medium
Sufism *Normative*	–Responsibility as a human being –Accomplishing the world by labour –Pragmatism	–Serving good –Hard work, search of an harmony between divine and worldly –Respecting the master	–Seeking both material and divine return –Humanistic –Universal goodness	Low
Conservative Islam *Utopian*	–Duty of a believer in search of perfect order –Preserving family lineage –In search of blessed and fair share –Uncompromising search for autonomy	–Living as a god sees it –Establishing perfect Islam –Maintaining paternal traditions, family trade or craft	–Seeking a fair and just society for Muslims –Hard work to serve worldly and divine –Loyalty to Islamic world and fraternity	High

In his late forties, Juma, a graduate of Moscow State University, was a middle-rank KGB officer in Almaty. He was shocked to realise that his profession would bring him nothing after many years of study and work. As an ex-security professional, he had several employment options, but he lacked expertise and the necessary powerful links for some. Making money from narcotics and prostitution has been popular among some locals, he stressed, but they were out of consideration for him due to ethical and moral considerations. One popular moneymaking field, the oil industry controlled by 'criminals and mafia', he stated, was in any case closed to him since he did not enjoy powerful political connections or a benefactor. Many other fields related to manufacturing and trade, such as pharmaceuticals, require specialist knowledge that he did not have. He first tried to trade refrigerators imported from Ukraine but when the customs law changed and brought new standards in favour of Russian and French exports to appease some trading groups, the new tax and customs procedures forced him out of business. The food trade appeared to be one of the essential businesses and was easy for him to get in.

Juma stressed his admiration for the teaching of Felix Edmund Dzerzhinsky, the founder of the Bolshevik secret service, Cheka, widely recognised as the mastermind of the KGB, the Committee for State Security of the USSR. Dzerzhinsky is supposed to have said that 'a member of the Cheka should have a cool head, a hot heart and clean hands'.[26] For Juma this teaching shaped his life under communism and he says he is still applying what he learned from his readings of Dzerzhinsky. Yet he is also beginning to discover and admire American business gurus' writings and finds them useful and fascinating; this forms an interesting position for a proud former KGB employee. He thinks the new generation of Kazakh businessmen are more reliable and competent as they learn how to become capitalists.

Although Juma made the personal transition to capitalism, he believes that strong family and kin ties make Kazakhstan different from Western societies. According to him, strong presidents and their family involvement in the economy and business of the country are natural results of Kazakh social structure and for the most part, it is and should be tolerated by the society. Juma looks after his brothers and other kinsmen in need by sending them money and goods, finding them jobs and financing weddings and other family occasions. He says:

This is my duty as a Kazakh. There is no job for my relatives in rural Kazakhstan, they need everything and it is my duty to help them ... The conditions in rural areas are miserable, agriculture is not getting support from the government, many people don't have the machinery and equipment necessary for farming. They are cut off from the growing urban markets.

Since 1997, Juma managed to develop his foodstuffs trade and established four stores in Almaty. Along with his two brothers who moved to Astana to work for the expanding government bureaucracy, he is building a hotel in the new capital. Juma elaborated on his experience of corruption in building permissions at all levels in regional and local administration. Corruption was part of Soviet life but with independence it became far more pervasive, unleashed from the party control and authority. But, as much as these distortions, his societal obligations held him back.

> If I were on my own with no social responsibilities, I could have become an airplane flying high at great speed ... but what slows me down is the responsibilities that I need to carry out ... I am a Kazakh and our family bonds are important and stand above everything else.

With some pride and some guilt, he stressed he had three houses and three cars, employed 20 people, but only five were officially registered, and he avoided bureaucracy through bribery whenever necessary. Juma, a kind of Soviet-man-turned-capitalist, a Kazakh with a Russian veneer, wants to embrace the world. His son is studying for a master's degree in the US. His wife runs a small distribution and marketing business for a Turkish textile company. Juma dreams of long distance travel:

> I heard from others and saw their images; Australia and New Zealand look like heaven.

He invited us to his home for a future conversation and gave us the gift bag at the end of our conversation. Inside the bag were a note pad, a soft toy and a Kazakh flag.

Case 8.2 – Aybek: The ex-physician taxi man

We were sitting in a small rundown Suzuki minibus covered in dust with fellow passengers waiting in front of the Ak Tilek market in the town of Karakol, near the eastern end of Issyk-Kul in Kyrgyzstan. Ak Tilek was established in 1987 as part of the Perestroika programme's aim to loosen state control and encourage cooperative and entrepreneurial activities.

From 100 traders in those days the market expanded to 1000 traders in 2004 as unemployment in the town grew exponentially. Mostly poor and rural people shopped there. Unbranded items ranging from food-stuffs to second-hand clothes sold on open stalls. Many brought small items to sell to make ends meet for the day. A few jars of jam, a few cups of pickled vegetables, several kilograms of apples and other goods were on display. It was mostly women, but some men and children dressed in many layers of clothes were waiting for buyers. It was dusty, noisy and cold. Porters were pushing their carts with a singing tone 'jol ver, jol ver' (open the way).

Aybek, in his forties with hazel eyes and a black moustache dominating his round face, was wearing a dark leather waistcoat and a hat. Fond of Pushkin and Tolstoy, he preferred to talk in Russian. He was deeply nostalgic about the Soviet era; yet saw the inevitability of economic changes and their consequences, too. He was educated and lived briefly in Moscow before rising in his profession as the chief physician of a hospital in Karakol. Soon after the dissolution of the USSR, however, hospitals, like other public institutions, began having financial problems and failed to maintain basic services. There were shortages of much essential medical equipment, even electricity. Salary rises remained way below the inflation rate. In the mid-1990s, he was earning as little as 30 USD a month. This forced him to seek other income-generating jobs to survive. There was nothing to do. He felt depressed for weeks. Gradually, he came to accept the state of turmoil and decided to establish a business to help his income. After several trading jobs, he began running a shuttle taxi service with two minibuses and a car. He owned the vehicles, hired the drivers and supervised their daily routine.

While talking, the minibus began filling up with massive shopping bags and other trading items including a small lamb. Since he had no office space we had to carry on our talk in his vehicles. He took us to his second minibus, which was next in line. The driver left us alone and only a couple of old peasants with their bags and a young girl with a beautiful round face framed by ruby earrings were there. They all looked disinterested. Aybek looked unsettled and spoke in Russian about his moral stance:

> My main aim is to survive and keep the family together. This business has been doing well so far. You never know, things might change ... Everything looks calm and stable right now as if it has always been. But, since the end of the Soviet Union, we have been going downhill ... and the future remains uncertain.

Aybek looked around with some displeasure and avoided communication with his fellow customers. He praised the Soviet system and complained about the new Kyrgyz state. When we came close to finishing our conversation we left our seats to fellow passengers carrying bags. Before departing, Aybek looked out over the bustling market place. While bitterly smiling, he sighed:

> During the Soviet Union life was good for professionals like me and I miss those days. You know, when I was a chief medic, if someone told me that I would run a taxi service in front of a dirty bazaar one day, I would have only laughed ... Well here I am.

Seeking divine harmony: Sufism

Sufism has played an integral role in the formation of Muslim society as a spiritual practice, intellectual discipline, literary tradition and social institution.[27] Sufism does not rest on a monolithic body of thought and extends beyond philosophy and the requirements of Islamic law.[28] It is a system of thought that teaches universal kindness to all creatures, as the verses at the beginning of this chapter illustrate. The key philosophy of Sufism is moral refinement through the elimination of personal impurities of the heart such as greed and injustice. Sufi thought treats any self-regarding orientation as a source of both individual and communal disharmony.[29] It was Sufism that promoted flexibility within Islam for centuries against Muslim orthodoxy.[30] Because of this, it was also condemned for perpetuating schism in Islam. Sufism has recently become a popular mysticism and has been attracting followers in the West as well.[31]

Sufism first appeared in the eighth century in Arab and Persian lands and later spread across Central Asia around the time when Turkic tribes were on the move westward. Sufi dervishes, resembling in many ways shaman healers and wandering priests, played a crucial role in making Islam attractive to nomadic Turkic tribes. With the influence of Persian speaking priests and settled people, Western tribes began converting to Islam en mass during the tenth and eleventh centuries. In this process of conversion and westward movement, Sufism played a significant role in providing a new moral spirit for rulers and common folk alike. Ahmed Yesevi, the most important Turkic Sufi, settled in Yesi, known today as the town of Turkestan in Kazakhstan and played an instrumental role in the conversion of the surrounding Turkic tribes.[32] Societal acceptance of Islam among Central Asians was uneven in many ways. In a theological sense, tribes did not abandon some of their old traditions but blended them with Islam. Politically adept, Sufism endorsed a more plural acceptance of religion and promoted peace, harmony and divine love while endorsing dynastic order. Thus, dervishes who began spreading the message of god and divine love faced little resistance. In doing so they employed miracles and prophecies in a fashion similar to shaman priests.[33]

However, after the commercial glories of the Silk Road faded and a deep-seated decay set in within the formerly vibrant learning centres, Sufism became absorbed in mysticism, stagnation and idleness. In his pioneering work, first published in 1951, Sabri Ülgener explored the morals and mentality behind the economic dissolution of the Islamic world in the middle ages and compared this moral and economic descent to the rise of the West, which witnessed increased entrepreneurial activities and overseas expeditions and the emergence of dynamic capitalist enterprises. Ülgener drew his evidence from religious documents, literature and poetry and convincingly argued that the intolerant moral and ethical values and increased mysticism and fanaticisms in Islam hindered enterprise growth by condemning the pursuit of wealth, shaming risk taking, and eventually perpetuating economic laxity. This moral and ideological decay, which took place over several centuries, subsequently limited market expansion and inhibited the growth of capitalist enterprises along the Silk Road. Consequently, prolonged feudal and semi-feudal relations led to the control of traditional markets by a narrow group of artisanal and rentier classes along with political despotism and dissolution. The eventual shrinkage in capital, production and trade brought about the isolation of markets, ambiguous morals for business, and introverted communities.[34]

There is now a revival of modern Sufi groups promoting wealth generation through private business ownership and charity in many Muslim societies. Most of Sufi philosophy is not against worldly activities and moneymaking. Sufi poems, common folk tales and proverbs indicate a sense of pragmatism. However, moral responsibility and the importance of searching for divine harmony between worldly and heavenly realms remains central. One frequently cited saying of Prophet Muhammad illustrates this point:

> Work for this world as if you will never die; and work for the other world as if you will die tomorrow.

One cannot speak of Sufism as a surviving institution or a coherent belief structure in Central Asia. The Soviet Union eradicated their teaching institutions, publications and leaders. Since Sufism had only a fragmented and loose ecclesiastical hierarchy it was more susceptible to dissolution. Yet Sufi ethics survived within folk culture and were recultivated in the master-apprenticeship tradition and in collective memory. Ahmed Yesevi's shrine along with others is a standing symbol of this resilience. For many believers and non-believers in Central Asia, Yesevi's shrine represents an important cultural identity and a reference to sacred beliefs. It is a symbol of national consciousness for Kazakhs and was historically venerated by Uzbeks and other Central Asians. Thousands visit the tombs and monuments of Sufi dervishes in Uzbekistan and Kyrgyzstan. These sites often combine the characteristics of Muslim and native beliefs.

The current revival of Sufism coincides with an increasing preoccupation with faith, guilt and reward. Sufi groups often proliferate under the spiritual guidance of modern preachers and community leaders who offer moral guidance, arbitrate disputes and extend material opportunities to their followers. Businessmen benefit from joining such solidarity and support groups as followers of a leader acting as a teacher or a counsellor. Entrepreneurs who believe more in Sufism than other influences are more likely to display the following traits:

1 *A core morality for conducting business:* They see business as part of a moral responsibility that they have to accomplish in the world through labour. Hard work in this world is a preparation for death. Working is also a form of reaching god and seeking blessing.
2 *The virtue of duty:* Their virtue is based on the principal of serving god by their search for harmony and providing wealth for their family. The old Sufi master-apprentice tradition is reflected in the workplace. This requires obedience to hierarchy and seniority. Learning a business or a craft from a master or elder is preserved as a means to pass good moral attainments and work style from the elderly to younger generations and from one believer to another.
3 *Justice and greater good:* They do not have the compartmentalised morality of communism or fundamental Islam. At the very core there is humanism and universality but this is also open to interpretation and diverse influences. Therefore, it is both pragmatic and non-monolithic.

Case 8.3 – Ali: The humanist multitasker

At the age of 43, Ali was upbeat about business, family life and his achievements. He began as an apprentice at 16 years old to a Jewish master leather worker, for whom he worked 12 years in Tashkent. His master became an inspiration and role model in life for him. Over the years his business grew into a small shopping centre in a newly acquired site employing 82 people in 8 stores. He later followed some links to Jewish businessmen in the United States and sold semi-processed leather for a few years to them. Then he traded garments and foodstuff between Turkey and Uzbekistan for a couple of years and later brought construction materials from China. He was pragmatic, not doctrinal and argued that Uzbeks needed to learn how to establish and run businesses from other countries like China and Turkey.

After entering into a large courtyard surrounded by a single storey building where eight different businesses were located (a hairdresser, an internet cafe, a dry cleaner, a billiard room, a café-restaurant, a home appliances store, a watch repairer and a barber), we were met by Ali's secretary who took us into a meticulously clean and orderly room with a desk, a table and bookshelves full of files. Ali came to greet us, dressed in white well-ironed trousers and a colourful shirt. He was short, looking fit and smiling with big round dark eyes. The business life and serenity of order he built around his modest courtyard had more to it. This was a world within a world; a shelter. Ali was a man of principles, ideals, duties, and he claimed to have higher values beyond making money and enjoying a good living. It was easy to follow his Khorezm dialect.

> It is not enough that you are good. Your workers have to be good, well behaved and disciplined, too. The master-apprenticeship relations are important. They need to respect their elders, have a good social and spiritual discipline. They also should know the business well ... If you don't satisfy your customers they won't come back.

Ali stressed the importance of recreation, travel and learning, and above all a spiritual density. According to him, there are three respectable spaces in life and we should approach them with purity: God's realm (mosque and cemetery), family (home) and enterprise (work place). In the harmony of these three divine realms, there exists a humanistic and tolerant view of the world.

While obsessively organised and disciplined, Ali had many liberal and pragmatic ideas along with a Sufi style Islamic adherence. He did his deeds and adhered to Islam. Yet he did not believe in orthodoxy. He had a deep affection for the Jewish faith and praised his old Jewish master. Ali's desk had a large PC, many files and books. He had several photos of his well-groomed children and Russian wife, and he was very proud of his family. Ali first met his wife at a Japanese art exhibition in Tashkent. He was not only impressed by her looks but also by her taking notes while looking at the items on exhibit. For him marrying a woman of a different faith and race was even a blessing. He claimed that children from mixed marriages are better looking and smarter.

The more you know the less you lose.

Ali first proudly took us around and showed his large courtyard and shops, and later explained his new business ideas and plans. He was exuberant and believed that he could open more businesses and create more opportunities for others and even generate work for up to 3000 people. He was planning to develop the bakery business further by importing new machinery that would provide novelty and productivity. He joked with a confident smile on his face:

I often lose in chess but usually win in business.

Conservative religion and traditions: Artisans and peasants

The Fergana Valley, with over eight million people, is the most populous region in Central Asia. It has a distinct Islamic character, rich agricultural traditions and a long history of artisanship.[35] This large fertile area stretches across the eastern reaches of Central Asia on the skirts of the Tien Shan Mountains and is cut by several national borders. Although most of the land mass is in eastern Uzbekistan, the valley continues into Kyrgyzstan, Tajikistan and Kazakhstan. Compared to sparsely populated mountainous and steppe lands, the Valley is dotted with many small and medium-sized towns renowned for their crafts and productive small farms. The major towns include Andijan, Osh, Kokand, Namangan and Margilan.[36]

Although the valley is populated mostly by Uzbeks, there are Tajik, Meshketian, Kyrgyz and Kazakh towns and villages scattered through-out. The Fergana Valley has witnessed ethnic and religious strife for a long time.[37] In 2005, a popular anti-government uprising took place in Andijan as there has been growing dissatisfaction with the economic policies of the Uzbek government.

Collectivisation and Soviet industrial planning aimed to eradicate the independent artisanal spirit and production in the Valley. Following the failure of early cooperative experiences during the 1920s, silk and pottery factories were established and all privately held equipment and looms were confiscated in order to prevent household production. Artisanal traditions, channeled into Soviet factories, deformed the quality and style of traditional craftsmanship. However, traditional crafts survived underground in homes. Home-based craft production not only passed from one generation to another but also became a symbol of resistance to the Soviet efforts to annihilate it.

Although to a casual observer, the Fergana Valley appears as a harmonious ethnic and economic unit, many in the Valley are proud of the distinct character of each city.[38] Old city states and small dynasties still survive in sprit through diverse artisanal traditions blended in with local cultures. The three most prominent crafts, ceramic pottery, metal working and silk weaving, were initially brought from China and evolved over centuries under Islamic and Turco-Persian artistic traditions. A closer look at city economies and craft traditions illustrates a significant social and economic diversity defined by merchant and craft family dynasties that have discretely been maintained under Soviet rule. Pottery, iron works, wood carving, *atlas* (silk) and *adras* (mixed silk and cotton) ikat weaving are the most commonly observed forms. Kokand has copper and iron smiths and is renown for beautiful knifes. A Tajik town, Rishton, hosts more than 200 families involved in pottery making in close cooperation with each other for the final product. The adras and atlas designs of Margilan, and the embroidery of Namangan all have their unique colors and styles.

The diversity in artisanal family traditions is also reflected in the social nature, temperament and skill of Fergana towns. Margilan, once a centre of Soviet silk production, is known to have a more relaxed attitude to Islamic traditions. This was also noted by the British travel writer, Colin Thubron:[39]

> The women seemed more vivid than elsewhere. They went in a shimmer of violent-coloured silks … They flooded the pavements in a broken rainbow.

The town of Fergana was established near the ancient city of Sim by Russian settlers and intellectuals who had a more open modern urban outlook. Namangan, in contrast, is an introverted city with grim looking streets. There, women don't stroll as freely. Namangan has long been at the centre of Islamic politics in the region.[40] Situated in the northern part of the Fergana Valley, it is one of the biggest cities in the country with almost half a million inhabitants. The population of the city and its surrounding district is almost two million, mostly engaged in small crafts, cotton farming and food processing. Today Namangan's vernacular architecture has certain similarities to old Mesopotamian buildings with mud brick walls and houses set around snaking roads. The Soviet town planning with wide boulevards and public buildings is juxtaposed with this old fabric along with star-like main intercity axes. The result is a seemingly detached cohabitation of two forms, awkwardly out of touch with one another. The one is characterised by long cement blocks, meaningless large open spaces and wide roads and the other is comprised of small blocks of buildings hiding behind the curling traditional pattern of roads with low-rise houses protected by tall fences and garden walls veiling vivid, colourful, traditional quarters.

Namangan's engagement with Islam has been associated with militant movements since independence. Despite decades of resistance to Soviet indoctrination against Islam, Saudi-financed Wahhabism has found some followers in the Valley, and Namangan has become its leading centre.[41] The promise of solving the problems of underdevelopment, economic exploitation and spiritual decline attracted young Muslim men to Islamic groups that saw the future of Islamic societies in the restoration of an imagined perfect society reminiscent of early Islam during the period of the Prophet Muhammed. Two groups, the Islamic Movement of Uzbekistan (IMU) and Hizb at-Tahrir al-Islami (also known as Hizb ut-Tahrir) became active in the Fergana Valley and maintain international ties.

Sporadic militant activity in the early 1990s openly turned against the Tashkent government in later years. In February 1999, a series of bombs were exploded that aimed to kill President Karimov. There are competing claims about the real motive and groups behind this attack; it could have been carried out by militant Islamists intent on eliminating the president or the Uzbek secret service acting to justify political purges to further consolidate power in Karimov's hands. Other plausible culprits might have been mafia or clan-based infighting within the state by powerful interest groups against Karimov.[42] In any case, the attack was used by the government to justify a broad wave of repression against Islamic groups and opposition parties, such as Erk and Birlik. This gave way to further power consolidation in the hands of President Karimov, his family and their associates.[43]

A more recent clampdown followed the Andijan protests, and civilian protesters as well as militants were being killed by the security forces during the period this research was conducted. On 13 May 2005 a group of gunmen stormed the Andijan town jail and freed 23 local businessmen along with their supporters and scores of other inmates.

A small number of people were reportedly killed during this violence, and hostages were taken. This was followed by demonstrations by several thousand people in the town's main square in support of the 23 men and against Karimov's disastrous management and lack of economic freedoms. The government refused to negotiate and a large number of troops in a convoy of armored vehicles entered the city and opened fire on the civilian protesters. The Uzbek government claimed that 187 'Islamic militants' were killed, while human rights groups say more than 600, among them many women and children, were killed indiscriminately by Uzbek troops, and many more wounded.[44]

Despite the government's claim to radicalism, Islam continues to be a binding force in the lives of people in this region, as it has been for many centuries.[45] Islam is expressed in many shades and through diverse practices, especially in the Fergana Valley. It has an important function to play in an impoverished nation, such as Uzbekistan, that is held together by brute force. Indeed, Islam even provides the necessary moral ground for submission and patience for people who otherwise might have unleashed violence and generated social eruptions in the wake of hardship. Islamic social groups, known as 'cemaats', fill the vacuum left by the state by delivering public goods and welfare provisions. Even in the most zealous towns, the local representatives of state organs tolerate Islamic groups because they compensate a bit for the state's poor economic performance, mediate between corrupt institutions and plaintiffs and improve local service delivery.[46]

Some such groups are organised in the Sufi fashion while others pursue authentic Islamic utopian goals. They aim to carve an autonomous realm in the market for their own benefit, to avoid the state and protect their wealth. Mutually beneficial networks help to exchange capital, goods and business opportunities. They utilise Islam to foster trust and legitimise their business and group behaviour. This twin promise, worldly and spiritual, has a considerable appeal to ordinary people; many of whom try to survive on marginal incomes from agriculture and small trade. Since Uzbekistan's independence, the Soviet silk and pottery factories were mostly dissolved and crafts and agriculture became the main sources of income. Nevertheless, after the early euphoria and sense of freedom, today's artisans see no future in a backward and isolated region with strict customs controls and lack of access to new markets. The fields of product design and marketing are in dire condition.

Efforts to revitalise traditional techniques for dyeing, weaving and carving are primitive. The whole sector is dependent on selective and highly unimaginative state promotion and administrative schemes. Along with marketing problems, there are production and design issues as well. Dye material and other ingredients are extremely hard to get. Those smuggled from Kyrgyzstan, Tajikistan and Afghanistan are expensive, are subject to periodic shortages, and create quality problems. Because there is no standardisation for ingredients or final goods, product improvement, skill development and enthusiasm are dampened.

While artisans are slowly being suffocated in the Valley, there is a continuous power struggle for societal domination between Islamic business groups and the state. This struggle formed one of the core fault lines beneath the Andijan crisis. One such cemaat, Akromiya, was founded by a charismatic businessman, Akram Yuldashev; once a member of Hizb ut-Tahrir. He later established a teaching group, giving talks on Islam and spiritual self-improvement, and wrote pamphlets on Islamic ethics. He gained widespread respect and popularity as a spiritual leader. In 1993, a business zone was created with ten enterprises – including a bakery, hairdressing salons, a cafeteria and a shoe factory – by the followers of Yuldashev. By 2005, the number of firms reached 40.[47] Yuldashev's group created an Islamic 'moral economy' with good communal links and welfare provision for the needy on almost utopian principals. In 2004, the 23 businessmen arrested were from this network; they were accused of forming an illegal Islamist extremist organisation.[48]

Entrepreneurs who follow the teachings of conservative Islam wish to construct a different realm for themselves, mainly through peaceful methods. An imagined pure Islamic society, they believe, would bring material wealth, spiritual richness, and inner calm. These are more likely to have the following traits (see also Table 8.1):

1 *A core morality for conducting business*: They see business as part of the duty of a Muslim and associate it with the continuity of paternal ties and family. Performing family trade or craft is an honour as well as a responsibility. Carrying out the master craftsmen tradition and maintaining the paternal lineage of business preserves order with responsibility and obedience.

2 *The virtue of duty*: Their virtue is based on the principal of serving god and helping to re-establish the perfect order by going back to their interpretation of pure Islam during the age of the Prophet Muhammad. The duty of an entrepreneur is to maintain business as a living and a way to be a good Muslim. One has to conduct oneself as if god, the omnipotent and omnipresent, is watching.

3 *Justice and greater good*: Political tyranny leads to moral suffocation. Within conservative Islam, entrepreneurs see their future within the

fraternity of groups and paternal lineage rather than state institutions or a broader cosmopolitan society. The outside world is troubling and distressing. Entrepreneurs dream of restoring perfect Islamic order by following Islamic law and building virtuous communities enhanced by mutual business interests.

Case 8.4 – Osman: The bewildered silk weaver
Osman, tall by Uzbek standards with hazel eyes and a restless spirit disguised in an ill-fitting dark suit, accompanied us to his home in the suburbs of Namangan. A tall gate took us into an open porch surrounded by rooms and a wide open garden. My two assistants, Osman and I sat on the floor around a low table symmetrically and colourfully decorated with Fergana nuts and fruits: grapes, apples, pistachios, pomegranates, almonds, candies and others. Two young girls around 12, veiled and looking down at the ground, brought tea bowls. They shyly avoided our eyes but secretly watched from behind the curtains. We saw no adults from the family. After breaking his Ramadan fast, Osman was eager to talk and the girls brought in a delicious soup. Then came the Uzbek pilau, the master dish of Uzbek dining, rice with meat, raisins, chickpeas and grated carrot. Each colourful bowl of pilau was topped with a succulent piece of baked quince.

Osman came from a typical artisan-merchant family common in the Valley. His father was a silk weaver as his eight brothers were all involved in silk production, dying, weaving and marketing. He was an atheist until the age of 20, when doing his military service on the cold Kazakh steppe he fell ill. The Army sent him back home where he remained bedridden for a year. Recovery was slow and he claimed that during that period he had many thoughts and reflections on life and god. After his recovery, he came in contact with Muslims who preached the purity of Islam. It felt good to believe and to 'start again'.

Osman believes in Islamic salvation through the teachings of the Prophet Muhammad; reaching for purity and the fundamentals of Islam. Like most of his fellow Fergana folk, he is neither an extremist preacher nor a militant. His approach to work, life and religion had signs of Wahhabi teaching although he simply said that he was attending mosque meetings where he learned Arabic in the 1990s.

A devout man in the Muslim faith would not touch unlawful substances and would not take others' share. A man without faith can do anything and get lost in life. If you are faithful, you know what is at stake. I work with people who have this faith and I do my trade and business with such men. I get my blessed share. In this village we don't lock our doors we just close them.

During the Soviet era, the Namangan silk factory employed around 3000 people. One of his brothers served eight years in prison for weaving silk at home, a prohibited pursuit of personal wealth. During those years they used to steal materials from the factory and weave at home. Their silk patterns and the quality of weaving done at home were always better then the factory ones which lacked care, patience and attention. The brothers then used to sell these to black market traders in Samarkand and Bukhara.

Osman explained the miracles of silk and emphasised how maintaining family traditions was his duty to his father and generations of grandfathers, how silk is blessed by god and how he is a 'slave of god' pursuing a craft that has such sanctity. Osman produced a treatise on silk and in that he wrote the following:[49]

Women wore silk to look pretty but the health of skin is the essence of silk. If you wear one hundred per cent silk, bugs don't get close to you, and even if you don't wash, you don't get ill.

If there was another more significant fabric then Allah would have dressed all heavenly people with that fabric but the Koran says: ... They all will be dressed in pure silk in heaven.

I am proud of choosing my father's profession, being a national atlas weaver.

Osman, in common with many other artisans I met, has a deep resentment towards the policies of the Tashkent government. According to him, laws come from above with no prior deliberation with people concerned. The only role expected from them is to cheer, clap and bend down to whatever comes from this government. Artisans face deep problems and have a tough time surviving in the Fergana Valley. Despite several government initiatives to protect traditions and train artisans, the region is entirely cut off from the world. There is no tourism and with the decline of local merchant traditions and physical isolation, artisan families are increasingly at the mercy of large traders who often have a bad reputation for being opportunists. Many such merchants come from Samarkand and Bukhara where there is a bigger market and international tourism.

While we were chatting the girls brought in towels and Osman initiated the final course by peeling and slicing apples and dividing the watermelon. He then dismantled the sweet, glassy red seeds of pomegranate with patience. At the end of the long and slow chatty meal, our casual togetherness was ritualised and evolved into friendly bonding and Osman felt comfortable enough to show us his hidden underground workshop.

Where we dined, Osman later told us, was his sister's house. We crossed the street to another big mud brick house with a large garden on a slope. Ten to fifteen kilometres out of the city centre this suburb was new, built in the northern hills of Namangan in 1996, and it followed local architectural traditions with single houses surrounded by tall walls and spacious gardens; in contrast to Uzbek houses elsewhere. Osman's atelier was next to his house dug under several basement floors with many small rooms connected to one another. There were at least 10 large Soviet-made spinning machines, dye material and other items. Several floors beneath the entrance, this maze-like basement was protected from outside intruders. But, despite his treatise on silk, Osman was producing bright red and white nylon. Harsh economic circumstances intensified competition and low incomes fuelled the demand for cheap products. The colourful shades of adras and atlas are giving way to cheap Chinese imports and lowering the quality of local production. But, sadly and more profoundly, a centuries-old craft and artisanal tradition, together with sophisticated artistic forms and values, was slowly fading away. Silk was what god prised, craft was his ancestors' legacy, but Osman was spinning nylon thread in a disguised workshop to earn his livelihood. Osman summarised his sentiments with a sad look:

> If you don't hope and take sadness lightly in the face of the problems we have here, you cannot endure. Life becomes a pain, sour ... I often act silly and take it lightly to survive ... We have a saying: a man can get used to even his grave within three days.

Early the following morning, we departed from the Namangan guest house built for high-ranked Soviet bureaucrats out of granite and marble, yet with little charm compared to Osman's suburb. He insisted the night before that we should have breakfast in his home before leaving the town. Most of his family had just gone to sleep after finishing their Ramadan meal before the crack of the dawn. He was overjoyed by our return and watched us drink tea and eat our breakfast. For him, we were a novelty, maybe a hope, in isolated and mundane Namangan.

Case 8.5 – Ibrahim: The sad shoemaker

Visiting Ibrahim in his house was an experience similar to meeting Osman in some respects. They both expressed a desire to construct their social, spiritual and economic spheres of life according to the principals of original and true Islam. At the eastern end of the Valley within the borders of Kyrgyzstan, Osh shares many similar characteristics with other Valley towns surrounded by lush agricultural fields. However, craft traditions among its residents are sparse here due to varying methods of production and life style between the Kyrgyz and Uzbek communities. The Uzbek population is large in the city, over 50 per cent, and they maintain their close-knit neighbourhood and family structure. Craft production is often carried out in Uzbek traditional houses but is increasingly being threatened by border closures and customs difficulties between the Kyrgyz and Uzbek sides of the Valley. In this isolated southern corner of Kyrgyzstan, the depressed local economy has been pushing many adult men abroad, mostly to Russia and Kazakhstan, to seek seasonal jobs. Following the closure of Soviet industries, the Osh Bazaar, with its several thousand traders, appears to be the major income and employment generating activity in the town.

After driving 30 minutes from the centre of Osh on bad roads, we arrived at a street framed by walls and the tall gates of Uzbek houses. Some were decorated with elegant wood roofs and grand gates. These ornaments indicated the wealth of the household, as Uzbeks invested much effort and money to build their homes. A male apprentice of Ibrahim came to the gate while I saw fully covered girls and a woman quickly running into one of the rooms around the courtyard so as not to be seen by other males.

Born in 1973, Ibrahim looked older than his age. He set up his own shoe making business in 1994 and prior to that he was working with his father who taught him the craft. He also attended the local vocational high school. Ibrahim grew up as an agnostic while his family retained many rituals and traditions. He began taking Islam seriously in his twenties after the fall of the USSR. The artisanal work and Islam gradually became the core of his life. He came into contact with the Nurcu Islamic brotherhood when he travelled to Turkey to trade.

Ibrahim had big almond-shaped brown eyes, a small body and dark olive skin. He wore a long kaftan with trousers underneath and a prayer cap on his head. In the guest room, decorated with Islamic prayers and a wall carpet showing Mecca, we sat around the low Uzbek dining table. A young male brought in tea and beautifully baked round Uzbek bread followed by fresh cream, nuts and fruits. The conversation began after a ritual of greetings and had to be accompanied with offerings of food and drink as a sign of hospitality and good will. Sitting around the table, Ibrahim first prayed and then divided the warm bread with his large tired hands; we dipped our bread in delicious fresh cream and sipped tea. Then he spoke in a soft voice often mixing Uzbek with Turkish dialects.

> Education, health and public services are full of problems. All of society has many problems, too. How can one deal with this massive number of issues? It is almost impossible. There is no motivation here to work; on the contrary, the state officials try to exploit you all the time. The electricity meter man comes and says 'you have used 5,000 som worth of electricity but if you give me some money I can show this as 1,000 som'.[50] I prepared my forms and went to pay my taxes and the first thing that happened was that someone suggested I pay a bribe to the tax officer and reduce the tax rate. Everything is sold here ... All governmental positions have a price.

We went out to see Ibrahim's home and workshop ensconced in a large courtyard surrounded by rooms with a garden in the middle. Although clearly separated from the family's living quarters, the workshop was an indispensable part of the cosmos Ibrahim had built for himself. From the entrance, on the left side there was the space for family life and the feminine world and on the right there was the corresponding male world and masculine workspace. These male and female spaces were connected with a depot and at the centre was a rose and vegetable garden. On the left side, there was a dining room and a kitchen connected to Ibrahim's family space with a porch, bedrooms and a guest room. The right side had a male dining room – where I was hosted – the workshop, depots and another room where the workers ate and prayed. A group of 15 men between 20- and 40-years old were working in a large room filled with some old sewing and shoe-making machines. As in many other manufacturing workshops I had seen in Central Asia, this sight was reminiscent of images of nineteenth-century industrialisation; a clear reversal from the massive scale of Soviet industrial establishments to embryonic small manufacturing.

His wife, Diloram, although not visible throughout the interview, has been involved in the trading part of the business along with

Ibrahim's father and other male friends. Because women dominate Kyrgyz trade, he was eventually convinced that Diloram would be better at the marketing side of the business. Ibrahim looked calm but sounded deeply depressed about the present and future of his craft and family. He stressed the importance of living Islam, doing deeds and wished to live in a society 'ruled by Islam's order and justice'. He said in a sad tone:

> I like my home and working here is good and fulfilling. My life style is different and I find it hard to live with others. The moment I step out of the gate to the street the problems begin. I don't see my Kyrgyz neighbours and don't share a life with them. I have nothing in common with these people.

Cheap Chinese products are destroying all production activities, there are not many shoe makers left. Ibrahim complained that the state did not encourage production. Five or six fellow producers left the business within the past few years. His connections in Turkey offered him shoes to sell to make more money but he was reluctant:

> Selling is easy and I can make money, but this is my craft and my family tradition. Anybody can sell shoes but not many, unless trained, can make shoes. Why did I work so hard up to this age trying to learn and improve this craft if I was to sell factory shoes in the end?

Conclusion

The Soviet Union fostered a collective belief in building a future utopia; the perfect and just socialist order for a common destiny. The desired Soviet man, bounded by collective morality, never of course materialised. Instead a distorted ethics of falsification and opportunism shaped societal relations and individuals' self-interest maximisation within patronage networks. The examples provided here of different moral paths illustrate the pervasiveness of longstanding societal overtures against the forced convergence of Soviet engineering that aimed to eradicate the past by building a timeless future. As the Soviet regime collapsed, there emerged a moral void and many people searched for a new direction to compensate for their worsening conditions. They needed to be able to cope with the burdens of increasing corruption and the authoritarian regimes that presided over the ruthless process of economic reallocation.

In response, three patterns of moral disposition arose based upon naturalistic shamanism, Sufi harmony and utopian Islam. In relation to the core morality of conducting business, virtue, justice and greater good, these three patterns are associated with radically different moral dispositions: pragmatic, normative and utopian. These correspond to stances at different levels of moral satisfaction, guilt and dissonance. The highest moral dissonance is observed among entrepreneurs who yearn for Islamic purity.[51] However, the conditions presented here are not static and entrepreneurs' moral sentiments are not monolithic. The entrepreneurs' own life stories illustrate how they switched from one moral code to another, such as the ones who switched from communism to conservative Islam (see Table 8.1).

Central Asian societies aspire to imitate rich Western countries with a new upsurge in consumerism and wealth accumulation. Although they avoided total chaos, these societies appear to have too weak a moral foundation for any large-scale societal rebuilding. Tribalism and the shamanism of the steppes display considerable strength and pragmatism, but they are weakened because they lack civic consciousness beyond clan lineages. Although highly flexible on its own, steppe culture is ideologically too weak to steer new states; all they seem able to do is to provide authenticating symbols. Islam, on the other hand, has been making significant advances, in particular among artisans and peasants in the Fergana Valley and nearby regions of Kyrgyzstan, Kazakhstan and Tajikistan. However, many preachers of conservative Islam lack any broad understanding of economics beyond utopian notions of recreating a perfect and just society of pure Islam. Others take a more pragmatic Sufi route, arguing for a forward-looking economic perspective and a lawful society.

The desirability of institutions that lessen cultural or moral polarisation is important and indeed the function of the state is to converge and co-opt these positions under a web of institutions. The process of building states and markets in Central Asia requires the promotion of harmonious moral regimes, safeguarded by formal and informal institutions.[52] However, the weakness of intellectual cadres and the greediness of political leadership delay reforms for a lawful society and consequently hinders market growth. Widespread corruption damages societal trust while the Mikado game's ruthless rounds of opportunity allocation intensify the moral confusion. The upper stratum disregard the virtues of altruism and justice in market and nation building. The corresponding societal responses for survival bring moral disarray; ranging from mimicking predatory strategies to a utopian enclosure of conservative Islam. These divergent positions bring about societal polarisation and political tensions, as most dramatically observed in Uzbekistan. Neither the promotion of official Islam nor superficial nation-building attempts by the regions' governments puts forward a convincing path to the moral harmony of a common destiny.

9
Conclusion

The collapse of the Soviet economic order and its colossal bureaucratic system brought about irreversible changes to the lives of millions of people in a vast territory. On the one hand, the dissolution of its governance mechanisms had devastating effects on regional economies and people's livelihoods as Soviet enterprises and markets rapidly dissipated and became redundant. On the other hand, this collapse liberated millions from the tentacles of a Moscow-centred regime in which they played a peripheral role under a supranational administration headed by a single party and an extensive bureaucracy. For Central Asia the development of an entrepreneurial middle class along with market expansion signifies a remarkable turning point. For the first time since its merchant and artisanal classes were severely weakened by the eighteenth-century colonial Russian advances and later almost destroyed by the Soviets, this region today is experiencing the proliferation of businesses generated by the persistent efforts of indigenous entrepreneurs. Although they function under increasingly unaccountable and authoritarian regimes and operate in highly constrained markets, the growth of the entrepreneurial middle stratum is the most momentous development to have emerged out of the rubble of the Soviet regime. It is this entrepreneurial drive of the middle stratum that provides many of the essential goods and services, supports highly risky ventures, and sustains local economies. Despite poor legal provisions and market distortions, which work in favour of the upper strata, these middle stratum entrepreneurs will play an increasingly critical role for the future of market and state building in this region.

Social differentiation as well as societal inequality has been growing under new governance regimes and market forces since 1991 in all former Soviet states. This phenomenon, however, has received limited attention as most scholarly focus is concentrated on the regime transition debate, on macroeconomic stabilisation and on enterprise restructuring. Consequently, this neglect of societal change and social stratification in the process of market and state building has left a large lacuna in policy circles and in the scholarly community working on post-Soviet transition. In this study we turned the spotlight onto enterprise development and social stratification, linking their changing opportunity structures and reallocation mechanisms. However, the main emphasis here has been on the nature and power of the entrepreneurial middle stratum. When formerly state-owned enterprises were dissolved and Communist Party structures were reorganised, many Soviet workers and professionals lost their positions and sought alternative jobs through entrepreneurial activities. Survey evidence gathered from Kazakhstan, Kyrgyzstan and Uzbekistan illustrates the development of capitalist markets, the character of the entrepreneurial class and social differentiation, and shows how they have been following different trajectories. The region's former communist presidents and their governments reacted to the advice of international institutions and other actors initially with enthusiasm but later their Soviet habits and norms prevailed. The legacy institutions provided quicker solutions to their power legitimisation problems and readily available assets useful to support their economic interests. These countries diverged further under the leadership of their upper strata and the presidential families. Their trajectory of state-market development evolved into three distinct patterns: neo-Soviet consolidation (most clearly observed in Turkmenistan and Uzbekistan), authoritarian developmentalism (in Kazakhstan) and chaotic authoritarianism (in Kyrgyzstan and Tajikistan).

The former communist leaders Islam Karimov in Uzbekistan and the now-deceased and highly eccentric President Saparmurat Niyazov in Turkmenistan quickly reverted from their early euphoria and promises for reforms. In both countries, privatisation efforts allowed small close-knit oligarchic groups under the authority of the presidents and their ruling cadres to diffuse into markets. Both, albeit with some differences, retained and selectively modified Soviet state institutions for their new nation states. They reconfigured the top-down ruling ethos and opacity of Soviet governance. Niyazov went further by personalising Soviet structures to construct a personality cult and a nationalist sect while his regime insulated itself from the rest of the world and its neighbours through a virtually closed economy and through police surveillance. Uzbekistan, the region's most populous and exuberant country, initially looked very promising as a leader in market and state building.

President Karimov's promise to establish a democratic and just society in the early 1990s quickly, however, vanished.[1]

Along with his family and a group of close-knit oligarchs, President Karimov has further consolidated his regime's political and economic powers and reneged on earlier promises of privatisation and democratic reforms. Over the years the single leader and party control of the economy and governance has grown even stronger. The constitutional and parliamentary system now functions as a supporting institution for this regime. By retaining state ownership and family involvement in major economic sectors and infrastructure such as irrigation, cotton, oil and gold mining, the regime's insiders determine the scope of markets and opportunities for the rest of the society. The neo-Soviet oligarchy generated in Uzbekistan has narrowed the range of economic and social freedom in the country and the growth of opportunities for middle stratum entrepreneurs. Due to limited political participation and the lack of any opposition, the middle stratum has no voice or power beyond the superficial consultation rounds offered by the state organs which aim to address individual concerns and grievances about market constraints. This was not only a purely political strategy but also an economic one as the regime deepened its control of the markets through its coercive bureaucracy and affiliated oligarchic groups eager to eliminate their business competitors.

Nursultan Nazarbayev followed a different form of authoritarianism for Kazakhstan through single party domination. President Nazarbayev and his young elite took advantage of their vast resources and endeavoured to generate a state-led developmentalist path. While the Kazakh economy benefited from the oil bonanza, its leadership recognised the opportunities associated with economic reform policies. Nazarbayev and a changing guard of the bureaucratic elite around him carried out successful reforms in banking and finance, private business establishment, and in the oil industry. With growing oil revenues since the end of the 1990s, the Kazakh government managed to stabilise macroeconomic indicators while expanding the opportunity structures in the economy and bureaucracy. Kazakhstan invested in the education and training of the young while expanding rank and file bureaucratic positions. Thus, the Nazarbayev leadership, while suppressing opponents and narrowing every possible democratic avenue, managed to create a new, better educated and more market-oriented elite. At the same time they recognised the importance of entrepreneurs and the structural necessity of the middle stratum.

A third path of divergence was towards unconsolidated authoritarianism and it occurred in the two small states, Tajikistan and Kyrgyzstan.

They suffered from chaotic governance and intensifying inter-elite conflict over political leadership. Deepening confrontations among business groups and regional power bases brought about a form of conflictual state which led to a legitimacy crisis and resultant political instability. In both countries leaders utilising regional power structures and clan relations, which had long been appeased and controlled by the Soviet regime, aimed to have unconstrained access to resources and political institutions. The limited appetite for consensus and cooperation after independence brought about regime changes. In Tajikistan the northern elite, who had dominated the Tajik Soviet republic since the 1930s, faced opposition from Islamic parties and others who opposed the continuation of communist rule after independence. The leadership of Rakhmon Nabiyev, representing the incumbent elite, failed to find a compromise and the country plunged into a full-fledged civil war between 1992 and 1993. The violence went on for several years until a peace agreement was reached in 1997. Between 50,000 and 100,000 people lost their lives and more than half a million were displaced as a result of the war. Instability continued until President Emomali Rakhmanov managed to consolidate his power in 2004. Yet, despite the promise of reconciliation and reconstruction, increasing authoritarianism bred resentment among regional powers, further deepening instability.[2]

Kyrgyzstan began well with speedy market and democratic reforms and was hailed as one of the most liberal and open regimes in the region until the early 2000s. Deepening regional divisions brought about civil unrest in March 2005, in what quickly became known as the 'Tulip Revolution'. The mainly peaceful popular unrest succeeded in removing the old communist leader Askar Akayev who was associated with the northern clan alliances, and initiated a new government under the leadership of two politicians: Kurmanbek Bakiev from the south and Feliks Kulov from the north. This consolidation was short-lived as large-scale protests took place against President Bakiyev in April and November of 2006, with opposition leaders accusing the president of failing to live up to his election promises to reform. Despite the promises of reconciliation and political consensus, there is an increasing tendency towards more repressive and authoritarian polices under the Bakiyev leadership.

The Mikado game and oligarchic markets

In all these states former communist party leaders and the Soviet elite infiltrated markets through business and property ownership.

Presidents, their courtiers and protégés along with new businessmen, formed hierarchically structured power networks and private governments. Over the years they not only emerged as major beneficiaries of the growth of capitalist markets and private ownership, but also determined the direction of economic reforms and opportunities. The major consequence of this process has been the emergence of oligarchic markets in all major sectors of the economy whereby a small number of insiders scoop up the benefits and determined the rules of entry and exit to many sectors. In a wide range of fields, including cotton, oil, gas, electricity, telecommunications and the media, the power exercised by such groups created highly distorted conditions for labour markets, competition and pricing. These oligarchic markets also funneled capital away from the economy, constraining the growth of small and medium-sized enterprises.

The post-Soviet markets under this oligarchic structure generated a dynamic reallocation regime which extended new opportunities to a diverse set of players in a hierarchical manner. This regime functioned as the Mikado game through which parties contested in different rounds. The corresponding social structure rests on a thin layer of the upper strata dominating the large number of marginal income earners with the enterprising middle stratum sandwiched between. In the upper strata some have direct political powers and official appointments while others come from the new class of oligarchs. The presidential family provides the main source of legitimacy and the power base for the reallocation rounds while oligarchs and courtiers expand their economic control according to the favours they get from the ruling family and the special ties they enjoy with foreign actors and international financial markets. They are the leading entrepreneurs and major beneficiaries of the capitalist system. Their business aptitude and world vision plays a critical role in the degree of tolerance and benevolence they extend to others in reallocation regimes. Beneath them apparatchiks and protégés act as functionaries for the higher strata, but as opportunists they also periodically grab businesses within their reach. Infighting and conflicts of interest are inherent in the Mikado game and the regime periodically faces small and large scale purges. As we have seen in all three countries, the stability of the Mikado hierarchy and its reallocation rounds rests on three critical mechanisms: competition and compromise, coalition and cadre retention, and repression and exile. These help to eliminate deviance and tame ambitions in order to maintain the durability of the game.

State institutions, when captured by particularistic interests, emerge as integral to the Mikado game's function. The game was played slightly differently, reflecting the divergence among the countries as their post-Soviet trajectory followed different paths. The most common form was the co-option of market forces by the state and its insiders, as was the case in Uzbekistan. There the state provided endurance to the Mikado game and its corresponding social stratification. The diffusion of the state into the markets often took place through state ownership, arbitrary government intervention and by the actions of the coercive bureaucracy. This occurred as part of an intricate network of economic relations governed by a loyal elite in strategic bureaucratic positions. Middle-stratum entrepreneurs are highly dependent on the state but also constantly work to avoid its surveillance mechanisms, leading to many shadow markets. Such an extensive co-option has been possible through a modification of the former command economy's management and bureaucracy along with the security and intelligence apparatus built in Tashkent during the Soviet era.

Kyrgyzstan symbolises another phenomenon where the state is dissolved in the markets with periodic clashes among its major groups. The divided loyalties of the strategic elite coupled with weak state institutions and security apparatus have led to the growth of powerful and occasionally armed alternative governments. Market penetration became the key source of power and legitimacy for political elites. Different interests and self-governing groups penetrated the state apparatus and deepened conflictual relations. This led to a highly unstable and chaotic state-market relationship. Initially, state organs partitioned among the ruling elite dissolved into markets through privatisation and liberal economic policies that were introduced by the former President Akayev. This process continued, albeit with increased authoritarian tendencies, under his successor Kurmanbek Bakiyev. Not only does the presidential family and its regional allies control all the major assets in the economy, but the state's provision of public goods is severely handicapped by this regime. At the same time, deep regional loyalties and the growing influence of self-governing syndicates began to exert power over the state apparatus while co-opting its bureaucratic elite into their reallocation rounds. Competing patronage networks nourish alternative power centres that periodically challenge the authority of the state and the hierarchy of the Mikado game. Despite the new coercive strategies of Bakiyev, the state's dissolution in the market and its depletion seems to have continued since the 2005 uprising. Hence, the Mikado game rests on a fragile truce.

Competition between major actors of the state and the market has provided new opportunities for players in the Mikado game. This has been most pronounced in Kazakhstan where diverse players shaped new prospects in the market through multifaceted contest between state and market actors. This competition was fuelled further by the growing number of assets exposed to market forces in mineral resources, the oil and gas sector and construction. The scramble for rich natural resources by the upper strata left considerable freedom and a range of opportunities for the entrepreneurial middle class. Thus, many entrepreneurs widened their opportunities in relation, and not in opposition, to the upper strata. Along with the increasing oil prices and the consolidation of power by Nursultan Nazarbayev, the country embarked on a new trajectory in which the state promoted a controlled but steady development of market conditions, including corporate governance and banking reforms and the promotion of industrial clusters. These developments, albeit with mixed results, can be considered fruitful outcomes of competition between markets and the state. This process has also made way for more engagement with the broader world and for attracting foreign direct investment. Despite the negative implications of the global financial crises on the Kazakh economy in recent years, such a competitive arena is more likely to be beneficial in the long term.

The Mikado game is not exclusively a domestic regime, but it has significant international components and ramifications. By broadening their economic links and cooperation with other countries and international companies, the region's upper strata aim to reduce their exposure to a single source or neighbour and provide further assets and energy to the game. Uzbekistan limits this participation through rigid trade policies and personalised networks while other countries use more diverse selective incentives to bring new players. There are now entrepreneurial groups who come from outside of the borders of the former Soviet Union. These, most numerously, include Koreans, Chinese and Turks who bring additional entrepreneurial know-how and dynamism in the production of goods and services. However, the key players in major sectors remain Russian-speaking allies of the upper strata and the presidents' families. These come from diverse ethnic backgrounds and tend to have associations with the secret service (KGB) and the communist cadres of the former Soviet Union. Young oligarchs who became key finance providers and the personal bankers of Central Asian regimes also enjoy special access to the ruling groups.

Therefore, there is a degree of continuity of Soviet cadres in the international politics of the Mikado game as well. While Russia's economic and military retreat since 1991 is now reversed, its new geopolitical role has focused on the diffusion to markets through new ownership structures. This has opened novel opportunities for Russia in the region while its oligarchs have cooperated well with their Central Asian counterparts in the Mikado game, especially in gold mining, mineral industries, metallurgy, telecommunications and other profitable sectors. In strategic sectors, such as oil, gas and energy infrastructure, Russia and China are becoming key stakeholders in the Mikado game, too. Overall, the presidents and their courtiers and oligarchs have been incorporating these external actors for multiple purposes through highly selective and sometimes erratic strategies. The inclusion of foreign players, among them many Western companies, helps the upper strata to curb or eliminate opposition groups, to protect their political regime and economic gains from domestic and external threats, and to diversify their business investments further beyond their national territories.

The middle stratum entrepreneurs

Who are the middle stratum entrepreneurs? What social roles do they play and how do they operate in post-Soviet markets? Almost 60 per cent of all entrepreneurs surveyed have university education and a clear majority come from previous Soviet professional urban cadres. These high educational attainments, metropolitan backgrounds and the professional character of Central Asian entrepreneurs clearly confirm their middle-class status. Many became entrepreneurs as a necessity and sought new positions and income when the Soviet economic system began to melt down. Only a small number of Perestroika entrepreneurs, many of whom later became market insiders, existed when the capitalist market relations were unleashed and privatisation was introduced along with new ownership structures. The empirical findings illustrate clearly that today's entrepreneurial middle-class has been mainly growing out of Soviet middle-class professionals and middle- and lower-rank bureaucrats. In this new emerging class, there is a pronounced presence of the Khrushchev-era generation of middle-aged entrepreneurs, who were more at ease with the Soviet regime than their parents' generation. Another peculiar aspect is the multiethnic character of this stratum and its Russian cultural and linguistic veneer, especially in all major urban areas. This is evidence of the continuity of the Soviet middle-class character. The less numerous post-Soviet-generation entrepreneurs also come from Soviet middle-class parentage who had professional attainments and/or middle-rank Communist Party positions. A fringe group in this stratum comes from provincial and lower educational backgrounds, most pronounced in Uzbekistan. Market building in general has been a function of the Soviet hierarchy as regional and local nomenclature played a critical role in shaping market conditions and business opportunities, especially for the major economic assets. Although not all former party leaders and heads of influential organisations such as Komsomol and the KGB have been successful in transferring their Soviet positions into the new order, many secured key positions as insiders and controllers in capitalist market relations with specific knowledge of and access to market information, ownership and capital sources. Thus, what we see is an interesting phenomenon of a de-facto class relocation that took place in less than two decades. The speed of this relocation and the penetration of capitalist relations into society have been remarkable, arguably faster than the early Soviet attempts to create the revolutionary class, the mass labourers. The manor in which the Soviet middle stratum transferred itself into an entrepreneurial class deserves much sociological and anthropological analysis to understand the influence of markets on social differentiation, identity and politics.

How do these entrepreneurs align their business interests with the autocracies and how do they relate to the Mikado game? What defines the entrepreneurial middle class is its relative access to opportunities and resources and the ability of its members to utilise them. Their market opportunities are mostly determined by the three layers above them: the presidential family, oligarchs and courtiers and apparatchiks and protégés. Beneath them thousands of people survive on marginal incomes from small trade, farming and informal jobs. The survival of the Mikado game necessitates the survival of these entrepreneurs, too. They function as a cushion between the upper strata and the masses living on marginal incomes, and they also meet societal needs by compensating for weak public services. Their entrepreneurial pathways are intricately linked to market opportunities, regional dynamics and state-market relations. Their Soviet-era positions, education, friendship ties and reciprocal relations often play a critical role in their access to goods and opportunities.

This emerging entrepreneurial stratum is concentrated in sectors such as services and consumer-goods retailing, where there are low entry barriers. Compared to the oligarchs and courtiers or apparatchiks, their business structures are detached from the major sources of economic fortunes in the region. However, they suffer from information asymmetries, poor legal provisions, endemic corruption and state absorption. These entrepreneurs mistrust their governments and their justice system. One of the weakest institutions with the lowest public respect is the court system. Nonetheless, these entrepreneurs are fully aware of their precarious position in the reallocation rounds and the weak power they posses against the upper strata. In response, they try to minimise clashes by not stepping on the toes of stronger market players, and they aim to minimise their dealings with state institutions by creating increasingly autonomous realms for their business transactions. More critically, they insulate their market positions through socially embedded networks and informal relations. Under conditions of deep information asymmetries working in favour of powerful players of the Mikado game, entrepreneurs hedge on each others' resources and personal networks to reduce uncertainty.

The effects of international assistance and Western involvement through multilateral and bilateral relations on the growth of the entrepreneurial class and business development have also been subject to the Mikado game. In some instances they exacerbated market distortions, in others they remained entirely ineffectual. A small number managed to introduce durable changes for market deepening and enterprise development. While outsiders brought their own agendas to influence the hearts and minds of the people in the region, the upper strata players in each country used international aid opportunistically. When they deemed necessary, they circumvented reform efforts and assistance. When their interests clashed with international organisations and NGOs, they either diverted or curbed their activities. While Uzbekistan was the least welcoming environment for intervening outsiders, the Kyrgyz upper strata and society in general was the most hospitable and liberal about all forms of foreign assistance. Divergence between the objectives of donors and upper strata players paralysed many projects and drained resources. Thus, an engagement that lasted almost two decades consuming large investments brought about little gains in enterprise development. The failure of governments and regional authorities to provide adequate public goods such as efficient banking, roads, street lighting, health clinics, education and other infrastructure continues to impinge on donor-initiated business-development projects.

When we analyse this entrepreneurial class in relation to their demographic, regional and moral character, we come across several critical aspects that define their changing identity. Increasingly patriarchal influences and nationality cults alter the social context of Central Asian societies and gender roles. However, despite growing gender inequality in access to economic and political power, upper strata women play important roles in business and politics. Middle stratum women also found new economic and social freedoms in entrepreneurship. Female entrepreneurs, especially in Kazakhstan and Kyrgyzstan, continue to play a significant role in new social stratification and increasing business diversification. Although they had a certain degree of nostalgia for the salaried and regimented life, the Khrushchev-generation women would not like to go back to their former positions. They are neither willing to give away the freedoms they have experienced in physical mobility, wealth accumulation and consumption choices, nor do they pretend that they have any ideology or mission to change their society.

The basis of their social stratification does not rest on consciously formed cultural entities, pure wage or income levels, or ethnic homogeneity or identity. There is no binding moral or ideological glue for this entrepreneurial class either. This is also evident in their general nihilism towards collective action and lack of interpersonal trust. Instead, they hide behind their personal ties and social networks in order to handle their day-to-day issues and address distorted law enforcement and weak institutions. In doing so, they mainly utilise their instinct for survival combined with a deep cynicism towards justice and the rule of law. After decades of imposed collectivisation and ideological indoctrination, there seems to be no societal and impersonal trust for collective action beyond tribal and family ties. Widespread co-option and coercion strategies by the states severely limit their ability to manoeuvre and form solidarity platforms. However, there are early and timid signs of change, most notably in Kazakhstan and Kyrgyzstan, as new associations and ad-hoc groupings have begun to flourish. These new capitalists are on the way to define their boundaries and collective identities in an assertive way.

As they relocated themselves from their Soviet-defined lives and titles at the whims of market forces, the entrepreneurial middle stratum went through a massive ideological and moral shift. The critical issue is how they accommodate the ideological dislocation that they have experienced. The evidence presented here shows that this process has been riddled with many day-to-day moral dilemmas. These dilemmas are related to daily moral conundrums and guilt that is a by-product of the moral vacuum of post-Soviet materialism. As the Soviet regime collapsed, there emerged a moral void and many people searched for a new direction to compensate for their worsening conditions. Three patterns of moral disposition, shamanism, Sufi harmony and utopian Islam, affect the behaviour of entrepreneurs. Yet there are also diverging trends among the three countries in relation to the increasing influence of Islam and the pervasive elements of Soviet ideology. The shades of Soviet influence in the thinking and behaviour of entrepreneurs intermingle with local traditions of nomadism, shamanism and Sufism leading to highly pragmatic moral standings in Kyrgyzstan and Kazakhstan. An increasing number of Islamic brotherhoods and some self-governing groups aim to bring a moral compass and protection to society that lacks binding moral harmony and a just state. However, there are diverse interpretations of Islam in the region. Most influential brotherhoods, often organised and financed by local entrepreneurs, have broad audiences in provincial areas of Kyrgyzstan and Uzbekistan, with a strong presence in the Fergana Valley.

The spread of competing Islamic brotherhoods has long-term implications for the future of middle stratum entrepreneurs. On the one hand, the penetration of Islam, and other small faith-based initiatives, represents a break from the Soviet past for a new moral future. Entrepreneurs seek both material market benefits and spiritual guidance through these groups. On the other hand, sharply different moral teachings distinguish hard-line utopian Islamists from their more pragmatic counterparts. If this gap between pragmatic moderates and conservative Islamists continues to grow, we are likely to see an intensified fight not only between upper and lower layers in the Mikado game but also within the middle stratum itself. So far, presidents and their allies have succeeded to remain in control and such an upheaval, beyond sporadic unrest, looks distant. Class relocation of the middle stratum from the Soviet order has also been possible through the promotion of moral harmony through the authentication of their national history, religion and patriarchy; this also ties them to the Mikado game. These values continue to bind social groups together. However, ideological splits in the middle stratum and the plight of large numbers of the dispossessed will remain potential sources of instability in the region.

The future of the entrepreneurial middle stratum

The entrepreneurial middle stratum does not have a clear agenda for its own advancement and given its ideological and moral paucity it is tied to the Mikado game. The future growth of the entrepreneurial middle class will contribute further to social diversification, and this has the potential to put pressure on power concentrations and the vertical control of the market. With fragmented interests and growing alternative and multiple power bases, a diversification between the state and the market has already begun taking shape. Yet the symbiotic relationship between the layers of the Mikado game strengthens the regime's stability as entrepreneurs absorb the social costs of the allocation rounds.

The emerging entrepreneurial groups might remain dependent and ineffectual due to market inhibitors reinforced by the ruling elite, or they may emerge as a powerful pressure group against their interests in the future.

For the time being these entrepreneurs submit to the deepening authoritarian state structures which work in favour of the upper strata. The Mikado game's reallocation rounds provide a degree of dynamism, and for the most part entrepreneurs are keen to expand their business opportunities in cooperation with the upper strata. In the current state of affairs, the middle stratum is not willing to take high political risks to work against the regime's inner circle. The diverse co-option and coercion mechanisms of the upper strata discipline and punish deviance from the status quo. Many of those who tried to form opposition groups were eventually eliminated, and their punishment and exclusion dissuade many other potential contenders. There are other reasons behind this quiescent stance: they are fed up with Soviet ideological indoctrination and the loss of moral compass in post-Soviet society. Their political apathy and ideological focus, combined with a deep sense of mistrust in collective action, make these entrepreneurs suspicious of the value of political activism and idealism. The excessive indoctrination of Soviet ideology and its externally determined, that is, Moscow-based, policy significantly contributes to this cynicism towards societal cooperation and civic engagement; this is now worse for the post-Soviet generations who grew up witnessing a ruthless grab for wealth.

However, this state of calm is misleading as there is continuous tension that has occasionally surfaced as open clashes. This stratum, squeezed between wealth-controlling groups and the dispossessed, has periodically sought to change the Mikado game's order and its source of political legitimacy. These rebellious entrepreneurs want to have more market power and they stand opposed to the reallocation regime. In doing so, they occasionally align their interests with the dispossessed masses and mobilise them against the governments. They reach the poor and marginalised by activating bazaar politics, extending financial aid, and through societal networks. Seeking fair play, justice and accountable economic distribution unites these groups against their governments which they describe as deeply corrupt. In Uzbekistan, the government crushed all opposition groups in the country and brought stricter control over its defiant entrepreneurs, especially in the Fergana Valley. In Kyrgyzstan, the putsch was successful in ousting the Akayev regime, however his successors restored the Mikado game in their favour rather than toppling it.

When we consider how the middle stratum affected the structure of political power in Egypt and Turkey, we can see how a set of contrasting conditions can emerge. In Egypt the middle stratum has long contributed to economic and political stability by submitting to the powers of the upper strata. In Turkey during the 1990s, in contrast, the middle stratum became rebellious and split. Those influenced by political Islam formed business associations, and interest groups used their democratic avenues and went on to build the foundation for the ascent in 2002 of the first stable, economically liberal, political Islamic party. Central Asian entrepreneurs could similarly either continue to submit or harness their disaffection to build institutions that effectively challenge the economic and political order. So far there are no clear indications of whether one of these situations or some other manifestation of economic pressures will emerge, thus we cannot predict whether they become a source of stability or not. What is evident is that the political support base remains fragmented both regionally and institutionally. Two further necessary resources that are lacking are organisational ability and intellectual capital. Given the depletion of the Soviet-era intelligentsia, entrepreneurs seek other sources of direction and support through self-governing groups and faith-based initiatives.

Both Islamic charities and self-governing groups rely on individual charisma, entrepreneurialism and group solidarity and often have controlled entry and exit. While Islamic groups mostly work through persuasion and collective retribution, self-governing syndicates often use force and violence to recruit young sympathisers and achieve their objectives. Islamic brotherhoods with some international contact are especially influential in Kyrgyzstan, Tajikistan and Uzbekistan. Self-governing groups active in all countries also have international ties as they control cross-border smuggling and other forms of illicit trade. Over the years such big and small groups have become key players in the market. Both Islamic brotherhoods and self-governing syndicates periodically cooperate against the state and aim to advance in the reallocation rounds.

Middle stratum entrepreneurs do not greatly benefit from international assistance and are in general sceptical about the sincerity and value of Western organisations in bringing democracy and fair play to their societies. Hence, they do not see them as credible anchors or partners for any potential mobilisation for reform. Instead, many consider Western NGOs and international institutions part of a global game between Russia and the US, racing against one another to grab opportunities. Perhaps it is not surprising then that after two decades of inconclusive engagement with the West, the region's upper and middle strata remain cautious about Western democracy and a free market economy. A similar caution is shown towards their big neighbours, China and their former partner Russia, both with long-standing geopolitical ambitions in the region. The entrepreneurial middle stratum has divided loyalties. While the Khrushchev generation is more sympathetic to Russia, younger generations see both China and Russia as threats to their national interests and economic future. The growing influence of Islam and nationalism also influence their new orientation towards other Muslim countries, most significantly towards Turkey and to a lesser extent to the Middle East.

Enterprise development and entrepreneurship in the region have evolved while political and economic powers were transferred from their Moscow-based Soviet character to authenticating authoritarian presidential regimes. The trajectory of this change, however, is now moving towards a new phase with institutional modifications and legal frameworks. In many spheres of life the Soviet legacy has been fundamentally changed, in some others gradually adapted to the needs of emerging market control. If the Mikado game continues to provide opportunities for survival and growth of middle stratum entrepreneurs, it is highly likely that they will remain mostly loyal to their regimes.

Central Asian middle stratum entrepreneurs are not unique in their display of opportunism. The political behaviour of middle classes is driven by their social and ideological priorities and above all by their assessment of mobility prospects.[3] Increased social mobility might facilitate democratisation and broaden the scope of the Mikado game by bringing greater inclusivity.[4] However, social mobility also helps to keep an authoritarian regime stable by reducing incentives for mass movements or opposition against the middle and upper strata. As for the Islamic groups and self-governing syndicates, there is no evidence to suggest that if they succeed in obtaining more economic power, they will bring more accountable regimes. There is no strong correlation between the shift to alternative power bases and democratisation with economic justice. In Latin America, for example, the rise and fall of democracies have corresponded less to the whims of the voting majority than to the concrete opposition of business and military leaders.[5]

In numerous middle-income countries (including for example Argentina, Chile, Mexico and Thailand), middle classes have supported regimes based on their prospects of social mobility, their racial and/or ethnic identities and the power of ideological persuasion; they are otherwise inconsistent and unpredictable. In Central Asia, too, we cannot assume any direct link between an empowered middle class and democratisation. Nevertheless the support of the middle class is usually essential to sustain democratic governance.

New horizons and policy implications

The analysis provided here suggests that two broad conceptual frameworks, namely the sociology of class transformation and the political economy of markets, open new avenues for future scholarship and policy formation. The evidence of transition from Soviet to capitalist markets points out a societal shift that occurs along with the emergence of private enterprises and new opportunity structures. The associated social stratification of this transformation corresponds to a relocation of former social classes in new allocation regimes. This class relocation rests on fluid value systems. Its state of flux is further exacerbated by the contested legitimacy of the state-building process.

Sociological analysis of this transformation will shed light on the dynamics of stratification and the future of post-Soviet regimes. Class relocation also has broad relevance for other post-colonial and developing states where the relationship between markets and state formation should be taken further into consideration. Development economics, international relations and political science will benefit from such an understanding of markets and their relationship to politics and society.

Here we used a concept of the political economy of markets that allows for a coherent analysis of all kinds of exchange regimes. In this way we can best understand how markets changed from their pre-Perestroika forms to Perestroika and then to the post-Soviet forms. There are often multiple overlapping forms characterised by for example the different exchange regimes and transactions associated with bazaars, cross-border trade and oligarchic markets. Some have identifiable spatial and sectoral boundaries, some are entirely abstract and have permeable borders. Rather than a regime whereby market exchange is determined by price as a signal, competition among firms and information gathering between buyers and sellers, we showed how the ownership of the markets shapes entry and exit, the nature of information and coercion. One critical characteristic of this ownership is that it breeds oligarchic markets and a myriad of personalised exchanges. In all post-Soviet states and in many developing economies, especially in resources-rich countries, these oligarchic markets hamper enterprise development and limit the broad diffusion of wealth.[6]

Thus, understanding the politics of the market can sensibly be seen in a dynamic interaction among the players that determines the direction of control and ownership. A layered reallocation game of opportunity picking emerges that is critical to the future of oligarchic markets. Such allocation mechanisms are inherently volatile and open to legitimacy crises. Yet, somehow entrepreneurial activity persists and contributes to economic growth and societal survival. We have seen how this works in Central Asia and our analysis contributes to a general understanding of the political economy of markets and the conditions that might be needed for sustainable and socially justifiable development. From one perspective this account of post-Soviet markets and society is a deeply pessimistic story. However, market and state building has never been easy, and today's advanced markets too have traversed bumpy routes and incurred heavy social costs.

Oligarchic markets in Central Asia have an invidious symbiotic relationship with the state. They provide bad resource allocation, skew market relations, and create hegemonic dependency. Thus, breaking them up is necessary for sustainable economic growth.

In doing so, however, international and bilateral support needs to be convincing to the region's people and leaders. Rather than being fixated on vague notions of democratisation, such policies should concentrate on concrete good governance practices. Instead of willy-nilly privatisation, they should focus on industrial policies, accountable corporate finance and support for enterprise development. The Aral Sea disaster furthermore graphically demonstrates the need for internationally assisted policies for environmentally sustainable growth.

The advice the Central Asian states received on building a market economy was misleading and muddled. There was almost an utter neglect of industrial policies and regional planning. Neither gradual (as in Uzbekistan) nor big bang (as in Kyrgyzstan) transition models provided useful paths. Mass privatisation, enterprise restructuring and legal reform efforts were rushed in without foresight or long-term commitments to credible anchor institutions and organisations. Some international engagement only intensified the economic disorder and, in Kyrgyzstan in particular, oligarchic markets emerged along with foreign-aid dependency. Major players such as the European Union, the US, Turkey and Japan could focus on building competent and fair bureaucracies, reduce corruption, and guide the region towards good governance. Finally, the upper strata should recognise that the legitimacy of their statehood and their freedoms rests on a peace that can only come from responsible economic practices. The alternative is to see the persistence of economic disparities and infighting underpinned by an authoritarianism that relies on the constant threat of coercion.

Appendix – The Survey Data

The empirical survey was carried out in the major towns of Kazakhstan, Kyrgyzstan and Uzbekistan between 2004 and 2007. The survey questionnaire consisted of five themes: (i) the personal profile of entrepreneurs; (ii) the type of enterprise and its organisational structure; (iii) entrepreneurs' opinion on state provisions and public services; (iv) ease in obtaining market information; and (v) future business plans and intensions. The face-to-face interviews allowed useful interactions with the entrepreneurs and a better understanding of their business setting. With 183 valid cases, the survey data provided a rich source of information for comprehensive analysis.

Table A.1   Number of enterprise surveys by town

Kazakhstan		Kyrgyzstan		Uzbekistan	
Almaty	25	Bishkek	30	Tashkent	25
Astana	10	Osh	20	Samarkand	11
Karaganda	17	Jalalabad	10	Bukhara	13
Semey	6	Karabalta	7		
		Karakol	6		
		Cholpon-Ata	3		
Total	**58**		**76**		**49**
Sample	183				

The sites of surveyed businesses included urban and semi-urban locations as given below:

1. Bazaars (open stalls, containers, and shops), 46 cases
2. Suburbia/rural areas (homes and workshops a minimum of 5 km outside city centers), 25 cases
3. High street (businesses located on major streets and in apartment blocks), 92 cases
4. ZUM (the former Soviet shopping centres converted into commercial malls), 14 cases
5. Old Soviet sites converted (Soviet factories, industrial zones and warehouses), 6 cases

Table A.2   Sectoral composition of the sample

Trade/Retail (35%)	Manufacturing (17%)	Service (40%) and Others (8.0%)
Food-stuffs retailing Garment retailing Specialised retailing (e.g., pharmacies, cosmetics, furniture, etc.)	Food-stuffs production Hand-made garments, clothing, shoes, etc. Weaving and pottery Construction (e.g., tiles, ceramic, etc.)	Restaurants and cafés Tourism Entertainment (e.g., DVD rental, Internet cafés) Specialised services (e.g., medical practices, consultancy, media agencies, etc.)

Another source of empirical information came from semi-structured interviews and focus group discussions with journalists, politicians, NGO groups and others. In addition to this, I carried out over 30 semi-structured interviews with the artisans in Khiva and in the Fergana Valley (namely in Kokand, Fergana, Margilan, Namangan and Anjidan).

Notes

Preface

1. See for example the household surveys conducted by the United Nations Statistics Division and the Proma and International Business Council Survey (2003), *National Business Opinion Survey in Kyrgyzstan*, Bishkek, June.
2. See McMillan and Woodruff (2002) on transition entrepreneurship and Ageev et al. (1995) on economic freedoms and entrepreneurship in post-Soviet Russia.
3. See Knight (1921), *Risk, Uncertainty and Profit*. The risk-taking nature of entrepreneurship is more fundamental than the innovative characteristic as popularised by Schumpeter (1950) or the personal traits described by McClelland (1961).
4. See the Appendix for detailed information on the sampling and the data set.
5. For a discussion of methodological and empirical complexities of doing research in Eastern Europe and Russia see Clark and Michailova, 'Doing research in transforming contexts: Themes and challenges', in *Fieldwork in Transforming Societies: Understanding Methodology From Experience* pp. 1–19. Also see Rivera et al. (2002), 'Interviewing political elites: lessons from Russia', *Political Science and Politics*, 35/4 (2002), pp. 683–8.
6. Two industrial projects are worth mentioning. The EBRD gave 7 million Euros to build a modern welding plant in Uzbekistan and a loan of 6 million Euros to Interglass, the bank's first industrial project in the Kyrgyz Republic. See *Central Asia*, EBRD Report, 2005.
7. The amount of EBRD finance to Kyrgyzstan was similar to those of Estonia and Slovenia, each with around 11 million Euros. They all got the smallest share among the transition states bar Turkmenistan which received 2.6 million Euros, the smallest financial assistance. European Bank of Reconstruction and Development (EBRD), *EBRD Commitments'* (http://www.ebrd.com/pubs/general/ar07a.pdf accessed on 15 June 2009).
8. A World Bank study, *Microfinance and the Poor in Central Asia: Challenges and Opportunities*, listed the problems of microfinancing in the region as high interest rates, small loan sizes, high transaction costs and lack of trust in financial institutions.
9. The Kazakhstan Small Business Programme the (KSBP) was initiated in March 1998. Since the launch of the programme, a total of seven Kazakh banks have joined the KSBP. The first six banks to join the programme, ATF Bank, Tsesna Bank, Kazkommertsbank, Halyk Bank, Bank CenterCredit and Bank TuranAlem, have been involved in the KSBP since 1998. They were followed by Temir Bank, which joined in February 1999. As of October 2005 the number of outstanding loans was over 50,000 accumulating in the total of 402m USD. The total loans dispersed was 168,000 (1,114m USD). The Japan-Uzbekistan Small Business Programme (J-USBP) was set up in 2001 and received two loans totaling 5 million USD under the programme for on-lending to local micro and small

enterprises. The total number of loans and their financial volume has been much smaller in Uzbekistan. By 2008, the outstanding number and volume of loans granted in these three countries were: Kazakhstan (number of loans: 27,365 and volume of loans: 61m USD), the Kyrgyz Republic (number of loans 141, 480 and volume of loans 131m USD) and Uzbekistan (number of loans 5,630 and volume 16m USD). In Kazakhstan eight, in Kyrgyzstan ten local banks were involved while in Uzbekistan only three local banks offered loans (Ipoteka Bank, Hamkor Bank and Pakhta Bank).

1   Introduction: Building States and Markets in Central Asia

1. 'Bey' is a wealthy owner of land and livestock. 'Myrza' is a nobleman and, a philanthropist. 'Volost chief' is the head of a small district administration. 'Biy' is a judge. Abay Qunanbayuli (1995: 140–1).
2. The official name of Kyrgyzstan is now the Kyrgyz Republic. However, I will be using both terms interchangeably.
3. Acemoglu and Robinson (2006).
4. Sometimes the borders are extended to include northern regions of Iran, Pakistan and India as well as Inner Mongolia and Tibet in China. Throughout the book I will be referring only to post-Soviet Central Asia.
5. Bregel (2003); Çağatay and Kuban (2006).
6. Abazov (2008); Roy (2005); Soucek (2000: 46).
7. See Togan (1998) for a detailed analysis of the nature of this fluidity.
8. Roy (2005: 6).
9. The Fergana Valley is the most populous region, located at the heart of Central Asia. It is currently divided among the national borders of Kazakhstan, Kyrgyzstan, Tajikistan and Uzbekistan. Most of the land mass remains in eastern Uzbekistan with Namangan, Andijan, Kokand and Fergana being the major towns. In Kyrgyzstan, Osh along with Batken and Jalalabad form the eastern most end of the Valley. In the south, Khodjend is the main urban center in Tajikistan. The Valley has a small extension into Kazakhstan near Shimkent.
10. Wheeler (1957).
11. Hayit (2006); Park (1957).
12. Dave (2007); Shayakhmetov (2006).
13. The destruction of cultural and intellectual memory of people was also carried out by mass murders. In Kyrgyzstan, over 130 intellectuals charged with 'bourgeois nationalism' were executed in 1938; among them there was also the father of the renowned Kyrgyz writer Chingiz Aytmatov.
14. The second largest group were Tatars with only 3.8 per cent (5.5 million) followed by Ukrainians with 3 per cent (4.3 million) and the Turkic Chuvash tribes with 1.7 million which comprised 1.2 per cent of the total population. See Botev (2002) and Williams (2002). See also Kreindler (1986) on the Soviet deportations.
15. Matley (1994: 106).
16. Clem (1980: 141).
17. Clem (1980: 141).
18. Kulchik (1995).

19. As a result of this emigration coupled with higher birth rates, ethnic Kazakhs became the majority in their country for the first time since the 1920s.
20. State legitimacy can be defined in terms of vertical and horizontal structures. Vertical legitimacy refers to the existence of an agreement over the principle(s) upon which the right to rule is based. Horizontal legitimacy entails a consensus about the definition of the community over which rule is to be exercised. See Englebert (2000: 11).
21. Alexander (2002) provides a detailed discussion on the notions of the State. Axtmann (2004) examines the fate of the territorially consolidated sovereign nation state and challenges posed by globalisation on its sovereignty.
22. Dixit (2004: 3) argues that states often are unreliable, biased and corrupt.
23. For personalised states see Alexander (2002) and Luong (2004a and 2004b).
24. See the discussion on post-colonial states in Kandiyoti (2002), Cole and Kandiyoti (2002) and Dave (2007).
25. Murrell (1996: 34) called the state of laws in post-Soviet countries as 'a façade without a foundation'. Allina-Pisano (2008) linked the cosmetic and superficial reform attempts of the post-Soviet elite to 'Potemkin institutions' while arguing that these institutions emerged out of concrete incentives between local and international actors and they are durable (p. 42).
26. Kuran (1995). Numerous other scholars pointed out widespread corruption and institutional malfunctioning in the USSR and its ramifications for successor states. For example, for Russia, see Ledeneva (1998) and for Central Asia, see Gleason (2003); Çokgezen (2004); Çokgezen et al. (2007).
27. According to Collins (2006), a clan is an informal organisation comprising a network of individuals linked by kin and fictive identities. The kinship ties are rooted in the extensive family organisation, and fictive kinship ties go beyond blood ties and incorporate individuals into network through marriage, family alliances, school ties, localism, neighbourhood, etc. See Collins (2006: 17).
28. Kandiyoti (2002: 292) points out the long lasting impact of the 'Asian immobility' or 'failed transformation' in the Soviet ethnography and nationality policy towards Central Asia. For example, while condemning traditionalism and the pervasiveness of 'the Asiatic mode of production', these ethnographers also argued that the culture of indigenous people carried 'irrational' social patterns that were not conducive to modernisation.
29. For affirmative action empire see Martin (2001) and Dave (2007: 11–12) for a discussion on how post-colonial theory illuminates the constitutive and enduring effects of the Soviet legacy.
30. In addition to Collins, others such as Olcott (2002) and Schatz (2004), argue that clans play a defining role in the economy and politics of Kazakhstan.
31. Togan (1998).
32. For example, see Schuyler (1966).
33. Frank (1999).
34. On colonisation patterns, see Allworth (1994); on Russian education and indigenous responses, see Sabol (2003); and on the Tsarist co-option of Islam, see Crews (2006).
35. The most detailed work on Jadids is Khalid (1999), *The Politics of Muslim Cultural Reform: Jadidism in Central Asia*. See also Crews (2006) on Russian use of Islamic theology and clergy; Sabol (2003) on Kazakh intellectuals in the Jadid

movement; D'Encausse (1994) on the influence of Tatar intellectuals in establishing modern education and new schools in Central Asia; and Ortaylı (2004) on the links between Tatar and the Ottoman modernists.

36. See Khalid (1999), Mardin (1999) and Çeçen (1999).

37. Their representation among the rank and file of the proletariat and Bolshevik movement remained small and insignificant. For example see Park (1957) and Payne (2001).

38. During the first years of Bolshevik rule, Turkestani leaders, such as Faizulla Khojaev, Hamza and Abdalrauf Fitrat, sought to establish a new regime for Turkestan. Divisions emerged between those who wanted to promote an independent Turkestan and those who sought autonomy. However, all indigenous modernists and literary cadres were eventually either sidelined or silenced. Almost all Jadid leaders were murdered; only a few managed to escape to other countries (Khalid, 1999). See also Sabol (2003).

39. Luong (2002).

40. The Economist Intelligence Unit (EIU) reports that only 6 per cent of Soviet officers stationed in Uzbekistan in 1991 were ethnic Uzbeks, who during the Soviet era were generally placed in the construction battalions where they received little military training (EIU, 2006c: 12).

41. Allworth (1994); Hayit (2006); and Park (1957).

42. The Russian fortress of Pishpek was known as Frunze between 1926 and 1991 and became Bishkek after the independence of the Kyrgyz Republic.

43. Goloshchekin was also involved in assassination of Tsar Nicholas II and his family (See Murphy, 2006: 238). From 1954 till 1960 ethnic Russians ruled Communist Party in Kazakhstan (Dave, 2007: 75). The party heads frequently changed in Uzbek and Kyrgyz SSRs during Stalin's terror years as well.

44. Russians initially did not distinguish the Kyrgyz from Kazakhs. The Kara-Kyrgyz Autonomous Oblast was first created within the Russian SFSR and the term 'Kirghiz' was used for both Kazakhs and Kyrgyz until the mid-1920s. On 5 December 1936, the Kirghiz Soviet Socialist Republic was established as a full republic of the Soviet Union.

45. Similarly, in Tajikistan Jabbor Rasulov (1961–82) and in Turkmenistan Muhammadnazar Gapurov (1969–83) served long terms.

46. 'Blat' (favouritism) was the main method of distributing resources across the Soviet Union (Ledeneva, 1998).

47. The Commonwealth of Independent States (CIS) was established on 8 December 1991 by the Minsk Agreement signed by the heads of state of the Republic of Belarus, the Russian Federation and the Republic of Ukraine, sealing the end of the Soviet Union. The CIS later became the main organisation comprising the former Soviet Socialist Republics of Armenia, Azerbaijan, Belarus, Georgia, Kazakhstan, Kyrgyzstan, Moldova, Russia, Tajikistan, Turkmenistan, Ukraine and Uzbekistan.

48. The referendum question was, 'Do you consider necessary the preservation of the Union of Soviet Socialist Republics as a renewed federation of equal sovereign republics in which the rights and freedom of an individual of any nationality will be fully guaranteed?'

49. Ishiyama (2002: 43).
50. Luong (2002).
51. Collins (2006).
52. Bratton and Van de Walle (1994) in their a study of neo-patrimonial transition in Africa showed that political changes are more likely to be driven from below rather than initiated by elites; they tend to be marked by factional struggles over patronage. See also Migdal (1988) and Akçali (2003).
53. In a recent study, Marat (2009) shows how the Central Asian military was strongly integrated into the Soviet power structures and it played no significant role during the post-Soviet transition.
54. Andrey Platonov's (2003) novel on Central Asia, *Soul*, takes the reader through a land of the 1930s devoid of community and memory.
55. Pomfret (2006) offers a comprehensive macroeconomic analysis of the region. Gleason (2003) provides an extended overview of the economic reforms in Central Asia. He pointed out that the economic reforms pursued by Central Asian states not only had a limited effect on market transition and democratisation but it also exacerbated their Soviet inherited weaknesses.
56. EBRD, *Transition Report* (2007).
57. As Shelburn and Palacin (2007: 11) note, remittances primarily go in one direction, that is, a country is either a remittee (destination of financial flow) or a remitter (source of financial flow). Among the CIS countries, Russia stands out as both a major remitter (tenth in the world in 2003) and a remittee (19th in 2003). However, outflows from Russia are much larger than inflows.
58. The country is divided into 14 administrative regions: Akmola, Aktobe, Almaty, Astana, Atyrau, East Kazakhstan, Karagandy, Kostanay, Kyzylorda, Mangystau, North Kazakhstan, Pavlodar, South Kazakhstan and Zhambyl. These regional units are also known as 'oblast', a term commonly used in other Central Asian states. The country has also three special provinces: Astana (new capital city), Almaty (its Soviet capital) and Baikonur (the centre of the Soviet space programme, the Baikonur Cosmodrome). Most industrial establishments as well as the population are concentrated in the traditionally Russian northeastern cities of Semey (Semipalatinsk), Oskemen (Ust-Kamenogorsk), Pavlodar and Karaganda and around the northeast Caspian Sea region. The mainly ethnic Kazakh regions of Aralsk and Kyzylorda are the poorest while the region of Atyrau in the north Caspian Sea has been the new growth centre of the oil industry. The former capital city, Almaty, remains an important economic hub and a financial centre.
59. Khlevniuk (2004) on the widespread terror across the USSR. See also Shayakhmetov (2006).
60. EIU (2006a).
61. Pomfret (2006) offers a detailed analysis of Kazakhstan's early rocky economic performance and reform path and explains how the oil boom has been a major contributor to the macroeconomic improvements in recent years.
62. EIU (2006a).
63. In 2005, Kazakhstan and China inaugurated a 1,000 km-long (620-mile) oil pipeline from Atasu in central Kazakhstan to Alashankou on the Chinese border. This will supply Kazakh oil to energy-hungry western China and will

be linked to the Caspian region and new Kashagan field in west Kazakhstan, where the major oil production is being developed. There are several pipeline projects promoted by China in Central Asian to have more access to oil and gas resources of the region. This trend combined with the new large oil reserves discovered in Karachaganak in the Caspian Basin, contributed to growing attraction of Kazakhstan for multiple markets. The Baku-Tbilisi-Ceyhan pipeline is another important route linking the Caspian to western Europe and the growing Mediterranean region.

64. Several major state funds were brought under Kazyna Joint Stock Company. These include the Development Bank of Kazakhstan, the Investment Fund of Kazakhstan, the National Innovation Fund, the Centre of Engineering and Transfer of Technologies, State Export Credits Insurance and Investments Corporation, the Fund of Small Business Development, the Centre for Marketing and Analytical Research and Kazinvest.

65. Environmental and job safety are continuing problems. In January 2008 a blast killed 30 miners at the Abaiskaya mine, owned by ArcelorMittal Temirtau.

66. The shrinkage of Aral Sea began after the Soviet Union launched a grand irrigation scheme to cultivate the Central Asian steppe in the 1960s. Rivers in Kazakhstan, Kyrgyzstan, Tajikistan and Uzbekistan were tapped to irrigate large cotton and rice fields, substantially reducing the supplies of water from the Amu Darya and Syr Darya rivers, two major sources of the Aral Sea. Now large fields of dust and salt replace the soil of the dried section of the sea. Winds carrying salt and chemical fertiliser residues from the dry seabed pose an environmental and health hazard. See Gorst (2008). Firdevs Robinson's documentary (2006) provides a comprehensive analysis of the environmental consequences of this catastrophe.

67. *The Asian Development Bank and the Kyrgyz Republic Fact Sheet 2008*, Asian Development Bank, See http://www.adb.org/Documents/Fact_Sheets/KGZ.pdf (accessed 22 May 2008).

68. EIU (2006c).

69. See compilation of Dilip Ratha and Zhimei Xu, *Migration and Remittances Factbook 2008*, (Washington DC: The World Bank, 2008). Other related sites: http://siteresources.worldbank.org/INTPROSPECTS/Resources/334934-1199807908806/KyrgyzRepublic.pdf http://siteresources.worldbank.org/EXTDECPROSPECTS/Resources/476882-1157133580628/BriefingNote3.pdf. (accessed on 24 May 2003).

70. According to the EIU (2006c), Kazakhstan invested 28 million USD into Kyrgyzstan in the first quarter of 2006 and 163.2 million USD in 2005.

71. Rahta and Xu (2008), *Migration and Remittances Factbook*.

72. In 2004 when I interviewed Shrin Akiner, an expert on Central Asia at the School of Oriental and African Studies, she was dismissive of the Kyrgyz and Kazakh economic transition. She argued that Uzbeks had a deeper and more cautious understanding of market transition and their approach should be taken as a model for a successful transition. Pomfret's (2000) article on 'the Uzbek model of economic development' emphasised that the Uzbek case shed little light on a debate framed in terms of the virtues of gradualism versus rapid reform. As the 2008 global financial crisis began to hurt countries with more open financial regimes, the ones which resisted reform emerged once again as cautious reformers. This is

a misdealing debate hiding the fact that closed economies made almost no significant progress in economic development beyond preserving the status quo.
73. Environmental Justice Foundation Report (EJF) (2005).
74. EJF (2005: 2).
75. Cited in the EIU (2006c).
76. Abdullaev et al. (2009).
77. Ilkhamov (2004). See Spechler (2008) on economic policies and authoritarianism in Uzbekistan.
78. The EIU (2006c: 18).
79. Uzbekistan is among the ten largest producers of gold in the world.
80. EIU (2006c: 17).
81. The Newmont Mining Corporation agreed to receive 80 million USD for its 50 per cent stake in the Zarafshan-Newmont Joint Venture (ZNJV). In 2006, following the abolition of tax benefits provided to certain foreign joint ventures, the Uzbek government claimed 49 million USD and the company was later declared bankrupt (EBRD Transition Report, 2007).
82. *The Asian Development Bank and the Uzbekistan Fact Sheet 2008*, Asian Development Bank. See http://www.adb.org/Documents/Fact_Sheets/UZB.pdf (accessed 22 May 2008).
83. Russia's national monopolies began expanding their interests in the Uzbek economy as elsewhere in the region. Gazprom is developing gas fields in western Uzbekistan to meet European demand.

2 Market Building and Social Stratification

1. See Lucal (1994) and Barbalet (1980: 411).
2. Giddens (1991: 109–10) offers a useful discussion on relational class analysis. See also Goldthorpe (1980) and Drudy (1991).
3. Both Giddens (1979) and Parkin (1969) identified that closure is an important element of social class formation.
4. With a mindset framed in cold war competition, American scholars were comparing Soviet industrial organisations, management styles and professional cadres with their US counterparts. The works of David Granick, *Management of the Industrial Firm in the USSR* (1954); *The Red Executive* (1960); and *Soviet Metal-Fabricating* (1967) are among those interesting studies.
5. Goldthorpe's (1964) study of social stratification in industrial society was a significant and influential work of this kind. In another study Brzezinski and Huntington (1964) pointed out certain parallel developments between the United States and USSR. However, they ruled out that both systems would converge into one another.
6. Parkin's (1969) work points out the tension that emerged between workers and professionals as well as between party administrators and professionals.
7. Djilas (1957). See also Nee (1989: 644).
8. The pioneering studies of Almond (1958) and Skilling (1966) established the first interest-groups based analysis in communist regimes. An edited volume by Skilling and Griffiths (1971) argued the significance of interest groups

in Soviet politics and identified six influential groups: party apparatchiks, security police, industrial managers, economists, writers and jurists.

9. Numerous scholars pointed out that more attention should be paid to interest-group politics and economic development in order to understand the nature of former communist regimes and their differences from one another. Korbonski (1977) showed the insecurity of political decision makers in the 1970s and emphasised that they were 'eager to reassure both the elites and masses about the maintenance and survival of the system faced with the unforeseen and unpredictable consequences of reaching the post-industrial stage' (p. 23).

10. Johnson (1977) and Johnson (1970); Korbonski (1977); and Huntington (1968). See also Herbert and link (1989); Martinelli (1994); Thornton (1999).

11. These groups are often identified as clans but, as Brown (1977) pointed out, it has been difficult to identify exact shapes of prevailing informal groups and their coalition patterns in relation to formal positions and politics in Eastern Europe and the Soviet Union.

12. While pointing out the cadre closure in the USSR, Eyal et al. (1998) also argued that in most state-socialist countries of Central and Eastern Europe, ruling elites were recruited from the lower ranks of the society (p. 28).

13. Another consequence of this process was rising unemployment (Parkin, 1969: 362).

14. Mickiewicz (1977) elaborated on cadre saturation in the Soviet Union. Membership of the Communist Party had a marked increase in middle-class representation in Eastern Europe. In Yugoslavia, figures published in 1967 showed a steady decline in the proportion of peasants and workers. A similar situation was also observed in Hungary, Poland and Czechoslovakia (Parkin, 1969: 362–3).

15. See Granick (1967) for class reproduction strategies among Russian professionals.

16. Cited in Vaughan (1986: 159).

17. Vaughan (1986) argued that both theoretical constraints of functionalism and the ideological prerequisites of Marxism led to the dilemmas of indoctrinated sociology in understanding and explaining emerging stratification.

18. Peck (2004) illustrated the domination of Slavs in professional skilled positions in Kazakhstan's mining and metallurgical industries.

19. This did not prevent growing discontent as ethnic clashes grew throughout the 1980s across the region. Luong's (2002) analysis of regionalism and Collins' (2006) study of clans provide illuminating points and thoughts on the way in which regionalism and of clans politics were nurtured in generating competing power bases and state co-option during the USSR as well as after independence in Central Asia.

20. Kuran (1995) offers a stimulating analysis of patterns of behaviour under communism in his book, *Private Truths, Public Lies: The Social Consequences of Preference Falsification.*

21. The edited volume by Duncan and Holman (1994) illustrates different dimensions of ethnic nationalism in the former Soviet Union and Yugoslavia. Kaiser's (1994) study is another example of territorial and ethnic self-interest-based politics in the USSR.

22. Parkin's analysis showed that Soviet social stratification changed from a levelled process during the early years of Bolshevik power consolidation and later, new cadres acted to protect their interests. The class differentiation first levelled under the purges but once the party cadres were filled by lower classes and mobilised into white-collar positions, they held on to this by securing middle rank positions for their children.
23. Here I follow Mayer's (2002) argument about the bifurcation of dominant classes as the main social reason behind the collapse of the regime.
24. Some scholars rejected a comparative transitology perspective due to the peculiar characteristics of post-socialist states vis-à-vis other developing and emerging countries. See in particular Bunce (1995); Karl and Schmitter (1995); Bunce (2000).
25. Carothers (2002) offers a detailed critique of the transition debate.
26. Szelényi (1978).
27. Nee's (1989) study mainly rested on data from agricultural reforms in China in the late 1970s.
28. This work relied on the 1985 data on China's economic transition. See Nee and Matthews (1996) and Nee and Cao (1999).
29. Increased urban inequality was also noted in China's market transition as opposed to earlier surveys indicating improvements in rural China. See Bian and Logan (1996).
30. Kornai (2000) argued that the late reforms in the Soviet Union were implemented arbitrarily and failed to improve enterprise productivity and efficiency.
31. Nee and Cao (1999) argued that path dependency played a determining role in institutional change and social stratification showing the underlying continuity in the structure of property rights and governance regimes.
32. Stark (1992), Böröcz and Rona-Tas (1995) and Nee and Cao (1999).
33. See, Nee and Kastello (1996: 1088) and Lanczi (2006). With a data set combining different regions of China, Nee and Cao (1999) observed the power persistence and cadre advantages in all regions of China.
34. Szelenyi and Kostello (1996: 1087).
35. Eyal et al. (1998) suggested that capitalist transformation benefited mainly those with high educational attainments and experience rather than those with party positions in Eastern and Central Europe.
36. Highley and Pakulski (2000) pointed out the importance of studying elite configuration; inter-elite conflict as well as unity. See also Best and Becker (1997) and Highley and Lengyel (2000).
37. Wasilewski (1997) argued that elites in Poland contributed greatly to the transformation from communist rule and they were politicised during the two phases of the transformation from the socialist market and centralised redistributive economy to democracy and a free market.
38. A range of studies point out this precarious position of elites. See Collier (1999) on elites and democratic consolidation in Western Europe and South America; Highley and Gunther (1992) on elites and democratic consolidation in Latin America and Southern Europe.
39. Elites, according to Janowitz (1956), can be defined as those members of a functional group, a social organisation or a society who exercise most power. They are the individuals who actually and potentially have access to the dominant group values and in turn control the access of the non-elites to

these values (p. 82). The power elite, in political and sociological theory, is a small group of people who control a disproportionate amount of wealth, privilege, and access to decision-making of global consequence. The term was coined by Charles Wright Mills in his 1956 book, *The Power Elite*.

40. With the deepening banking crisis we are likely to see new sources of turbulence in economic and political stability of Eastern Europe and the Balkans. See Wasilewski (1997: 28–9) and also the collection of essays in *The Political Economy of Transition in Eurasia* edited by Graham and Lindahl (2006).

41. Bruszt, (2002); Ledeneva and Kurkchiyan (2000).

42. Olcott (2002); Collins (2004); Schatz (2004); Collins (2006).

43. Kubicek (1997); Luong (2002).

44. Luong (2002: 277–8).

45. Cummings (2005: 140).

46. The study of Cummings (2005) on power elites in Kazakhstan offers a perspective on this change. Satpaev (2007) describes Kazakhstan's ruling elite and its inner circle.

47. This stratification is top heavy, skewed towards a small number of oligarchs, courtiers and protégés. It is difficult to estimate the number of people involved in each stratum. However, perhaps in Kazakhstan there are around one hundred top players along with a handful of major oligarchs. Rumer (2005) argued that the material well-being of the population remains low in Central Asia. About 5 per cent make up the most prosperous stratum, 15 per cent are relatively well off, and 80 per cent are dispossessed. The economically and politically effective groups in the top 20 per cent aim to ensure their own prosperity and preserve the status quo.

48. The present charges against Aliyev also include the abduction of three managers from the headquarters of Nurbank, a mid-level bank under his control. The Interfax Kazakh news agency presenting the official view provides a detailed chronology on 'Rakhatgate' or failed coup. (http://www.interfax.kz/?lang=eng&int_id=13&function=view&news_id=1798) accessed on 3 July 2008. See also *The Caspian Information Centre*, issue 42, 17 February 2009, www.caspianinfo.org. Anne Penketh, 'The president, his former son-in-law, and an accusation of state murder', *The Independent*, Thursday, 1 November 2007.

49. Cummings' (2005) study in Kazakhstan found that one third of the surveyed 244 members of the elite between 1995 and 1996 served either an executive or party post in the Soviet era. They came from two main occupational categories: senior administrative officials and senior managers of economic enterprises. Luong (2002) had similar observations for Kazakhstan, Kyrgyzstan and Uzbekistan.

50. For instance, a penniless young university graduate, Oleg Deripaska, became the aluminium tycoon and Russia's richest man (with a wealth of roughly 28 billion USD). Roman Abramovich, with a wealth of 24 billion USD, started out as a black market trader, acquired the controlling interest in the large oil company Sibneft. The sale was dramatically below the stock market value of 150 million USD at the time, but the company was worth billions of dollars. See Franchetti (2009); Midgley and Hutchins (2005).

51. Russia boasted some 110-dollar billionaires, with more in Moscow than in any other city in the world. The recent financial crisis hit hard these men, too. According to one calculation, collectively Russia's tycoons have lost an astounding £150 billion. See Franchetti (2009).
52. Reported by BBC Central Asia Correspondent, Ian MacWilliam, 'Kazakhstan: a cautionary tale', *Economist Intelligence Unit*, 30 June 2005.
53. ENRC is one of the largest electricity providers in Kazakhstan, accounting for approximately 16 per cent of the country's recorded electricity production in 2006. For further details see the link below: http://www.marketwatch.com/news/story/kazakhstans-eurasian-natural-resources-list/story.aspx?guid=%7B07AF9E25-9B96-45E4-9694-DD5965BCF94C%7D (accessed on 9 April 2009)
54. Franchetti (2009).
55. See reporting by Rebecca Bream (2007), 'Kazakh group with global ambitions', *The Financial Times*, 21 December 2007.
56. A recent Reuters report about the ENRC includes the following information: The Eurasian Natural Resources Corporation PLC is the holding company of a diversified natural resources group with integrated mining, processing, energy, logistical and marketing operations. It has five operating divisions: the Ferroalloy Division, the Iron Ore Division, the Alumina and Aluminium Division, the Energy Division, which is an electricity provider in Kazakhstan, and the Logistics Division, which provides transportation and logistical services. On April 3, 2008, ENRC completed the acquisition of a controlling interest in the OAO Serov Ferrochrome Factory, the OAO Saranovskaya Mine Rudnava, the OAO Serov Metalconcentrate Works and related entities. In May 2008, it announced the acquisition of a 50 per cent stake in Xinjiang Tuoli Taihang Ferro-Alloy Co. LTD. As of 11 August 2008, Kazakhmys PLC held a 25 per cent interest in the company. http://www.reuters.com/finance/stocks/companyProfile?symbol=ENRC.L (accessed on 9 April 2009).
57. Gubin and Kostiouchenko (1997) argued that the new class of Soviet managers – economic and administrative nomenclature that emerged in 1953–89 as the 'invisible class' went through essential transformations in 1989–93 and converted itself into a class-for-itself.
58. This case material was gathered in Karaganda through interviews with several local professionals and a lawyer in March 2006.
59. Cummings (2005) pointed out that the Soviet legacy had ensured that, while Kazakhs had tended to occupy politico-administrative posts, Slavs had technocratic training. She observed the prevailing Slav dominance in regional administration in key economic and administrative positions in 1995–6.
60. Uzbekistan inherited a large military infrastructure on independence. A scheme to increase troop numbers to 100,000 was dropped in 1999 because of budgetary problems. There are no official figures on defence spending. By 2003, 90 per cent of officers were Uzbek. The most important forces are the National Security Services (SNB), the Interior Ministry troops and the National Guard. These forces are oriented towards domestic repression (the Army has 40,000 personnel, the Air Force 10–15,000 personnel, Interior

Ministry troops up to 19,000 personnel, and there are 1,000 National Guard troops (EIU, 2006c: 12).

61. Marat (2006).

62. Gubin and Kostiouchenko categorise Russian social stratification into (1) the nomenclature who control big capital, (2) entrepreneurs with a criminal past who work in the shadow economy, (3) young, well-educated entrepreneurs and (4) agricultural workers, teachers, technicians, pensioners and others who constitute the bottom 65 per cent. In their formulation, the Russian intelligentsia who occupied a middle stratum is disintegrating while the gap between the super rich and others is widening. This classification resembles the emerging form of social stratification in Central Asia. See Gerber (2002) on the labour market implications of post-Soviet transition and Gerber and Hout (2004) on declining class mobility.

63. Mikado is a pick-up sticks game originating in Europe. In 1936 it was brought from Hungary to the USA and was called 'pick-up sticks'. The game later got its name from the highest scoring (blue) stick 'Mikado' (possibly used for the emperor, as in the Japanese Emperor, Mikado). Five different categories of sticks symbolise the status and power: Mikado, mandarin, bonzen, samurai and workers. See the link (http://en.wikipedia.org/wiki/Mikado_(game)#Monster_Mikado) (accessed on 3 July 2008).

64. Findings of Cummings (2005: 142–3) on inter-elite shuffling and institution hopping support this point.

65. Temir Sariyev, now the Leader of the Akshumkar Party in Kyrgyzstan, criticised the corrupt family practices and business involvement of Akayev. He has recently voiced his opposition to Bakiyev's similar tactics. Personal interview with Mr Sariyev, November 2004.

66. Out of a total 207 USD million spent by the US on fuel contracts, Manas International Services received 87 million USD and Aalam Services 32 million USD. An FBI investigation uncovered that millions of dollars were taken from 'base-related' revenues and hidden away through a network of offshore accounts.

67. Cooley (2008: 227–8).

68. Patronage relations are based on informal partnerships and reciprocal relations among kinsmen, neighbours, co-workers, and classmates. Trust emerges as a commodity in these exchanges. See, Dasgupta (1988) and Gambetta (1988) on trust.

69. Muhammed Salih stressed that his party does not support violence and they wanted 'a secular and democratic regime like in Turkey' (personal interview, London, January 2006).

70. Umarov was a founder of Uzdunrobita, a US-Uzbek joint telecommunications venture. It reportedly was controlled by Karimov's oldest daughter, Gulnara Karimov, until she sold it in 2004 to a Russian company. See Radio Free Europe Radio Liberty reporting by Gulnoza Saidazimova. http://www.rferl.org/content/article/1059094.html (accessed 30 June 2008).

71. The interviews with Dr Nadira Khidoyatova and a female party activist of the coalition (November, 2006). Khidoyatova did her doctorate on the Basmachi uprisings and Jadid movement and later had to leave her academic position. The female activist studied psychology and worked in both public and

private sectors. She later set up her own agro-business. The both feared for the future of their children and relatives, refused to leave their country, and were thus forced to remain silent.

72. Personal interviews with Bulat Abylov (March 2006), Alikhan Baimenov (July 2005), now deceased, Nurbulat Massanov (July 2005) in Almaty.

73. The former husband of Gulnara Karimov was disgraced after their disastrous marriage and his business interests were subsequently damaged. Uzbek operations of Coca Cola, for whom her ex-husband was a representative in Uzbekistan, were effectively halted and its export and import licenses were removed and most of the assets of the company were prevented from leaving the country.

3 Entrepreneurs and their Perceptions

1. Leff (1979) explored the arguments about the assumed link between entrepreneurship and economic development.

2. The new right policies of Ronald Reagan, the President of the USA (1981–9), and his close ally Margret Thatcher, the British Prime Minister (1979–90), promoted neoliberal ideals through dismantling labour unions, privatisation and an overall reduction of the state's role became neoliberal totems, central to the policy rhetoric of economic restructuring in the 1980s.

3. Myles and Turegun (1994).

4. Poulantzas (1975), Wright (1978).

5. Bechhofer and Elliott (1981); Gerry and Birckbeck (1981); Lewin (1985).

6. Scase and Goffee (1982).

7. Once the symbols of industrial might, coal mining, shipbuilding, steel production and car manufacturing declined in all major industrial economies in the 1970s. In their highly influential study, *The Second Industrial Divide*, Piore and Sabel, argued that the crisis of mass production required a new shift in industrial organisation. Industrial districts and SMEs with flexible specialisation would be the new mode of production. They praised Italian small and medium-sized enterprises for their flexibility and innovation; pointing out the significance of networking in competition and cooperation. *Post-Fordism: A Reader* edited by Amin (1995) provides a good overview. For a critique of flexible specialisation for late industrialising countries, see Özcan (1995).

8. In Turkey, for example, the diffused industrialisation and indigenous SMEs led to the emergence of alternative middle classes in conflict with the old establishment. See Özcan (2006) and Özcan and Turunç (2008).

9. In a cross-country analysis Banerjee and Duflo (2007) argued that the average middle class person is not an entrepreneur in waiting.

10. Theoretical and methodological aspects of entrepreneurship research have been shaped by three founding disciplines: psychology, economics and sociology, each asking different questions and offering different meta-theories. See Schumpeter (1950); McClelland (1961); Thornton (1999: 34). See also Herbert and Link (1989); Thornton (1999).

11. Ageev et al. (1995), Smallborne and Welter (2001), Aidis and Sauka (2005).

12. Slider (1991) and Liuhto (1996).

13. Katsenelinboigen and Levine (1977: 62) colour-coded Soviet markets: (i) Legal markets: Red (prices established centrally), Pink (participants in transactions have some freedom to alter prices), White (participants set the prices); (ii) Semi-legal markets: Gray (transactions illegal, but tolerated by the authorities); (iii) Illegal markets: Brown (transactions illegal, but penalty less severe than criminal prosecution), Black (transactions illegal, penalty is criminal prosecution).
14. Katsenelinboigen and Levine (1977).
15. See Granick (1954 and 1960) for a detailed analysis of Soviet industrial management.
16. Rama and Scott (1999) offer an economic analysis of single-company towns.
17. Several such complexes exist in Central Asia. The satellite towns of Karaganda and Temirtau in Kazakhstan and Navoi in Uzbekistan are a few examples where ordinary lives evolve around massive industrial complexes. In *Black Earth*, Andrew Meier, describes the most unusual nature of the relationship between labour and massive factory life in Norilsk, a Russian metal complex. http://www.theatlantic.com/doc/200312u/int2003-12-17 (accessed on 25 June 2008). Recently, Norilsk was in the news. Two Russian oligarchs, Potanin and Deripaska, waged a battle to take control of the complex. See 'Russian pair battle it out over Norilsk Nickel merger' the Catherine Belton and Rebecca Bream, *The Financial Times*, (23 June 2008, p. 26).
18. This observation is similar to the findings of other studies. For example, see Welter et al. (2006).
19. Interview with Dan Balk, former chairman of LFS, microlending office (Tashkent, 12 March 2005).
20. See http://www.doingbusiness.org/economyrankings/?regionid=0 (accessed on 12 October 2007). This index averages the country's percentile rankings on 10 topics, made up of a variety of indicators including ease of starting and closing a business, employment, taxation, permits, etc.

4   The Political Economy of Bazaars

1. For a concise analysis of markets see McMillan (2003).
2. See Logue et al. (1995) on transforming Russian enterprises and the type of alternative ownership generated during Perestroika.
3. See Smith (1993) for an extensive discussion of how the Gorbachev-era reforms failed to eliminate the economic mafia built into the Soviet markets and instead resorted to a cautious administrative shake-up. Despite the fact that these reforms gave much greater autonomy to enterprises in the allocation of resources and self-financing, market distortions stemming from asymmetric information, pricing problems and shortages inhibited their flexibility. Jenkins and O'Brian (1988) analysed the nature of the Gorbachev-era reforms as a technical alternation rather than a structural change. The most visible element of such alteration was a major shake-up in cadre positions; approximately one third of men heading fifty branch ministries were replaced. Similarly, Hewett (1988) argued that all

leading institutions in the economic hierarchy and the ministries were replaced by the new appointees.

4. There are numerous studies of how early oligarchs emerged in late Soviet economic reforms and how market transition deepened their control over economic assets. See for example, Dubravcic (1995); Hellman (1998); Ledeneva and Kurkchiyan (2000); and Buiter (2000).

5. *UNDP Central Asia Human Development Report*, see http://europeandcis.undp.org/poverty/trade/show/301A44C5-F203-1EE9-B2E001AFF98B054B (accessed on 7 July 2009).

6. The area measure is based on the layout of Dordoi and its surroundings in Google Earth. These containers were used in long haul rail transportation and their sizes varied between small ones of 15–20 cubic metres and larger sizes up to tree times that volume. Traders often piled two containers on top of each other to gain additional storage.

7. This is in line with Bal's estimate (2004). Based on the city official's data, Spector (2008a) reported that it was 200 million USD per month in 2006.

8. Assuming 1,000 USD monthly rental receipts per container, the whole of the Dordoi Bazaar generated around 60 million USD annually in rental income for container site owners. Tax authorities collected around 1.2 million USD annually.

9. These are highly inflated prices. A Florida-based distributor of used steel and aluminium shipping containers charged between 1,250 and 3,000 USD. (http://www.containersnow.com/containers/jacksonville/2.htm) (accessed on 21 January 2009).

10. I interviewed traders during March–April 2004 and Ulugbek Salymbekov, Chairman of Dordoi Plaza, on 15 April 2004.

11. Baraholka is a conglomeration of many markets, called Al Farabi, Adem, Ashkat, Aral, Bolashak, Rakhat, Ayan, Olzha, Nurly, Alatau and Zhetysu.

12. Spector (2008b).

13. Nearly 200,000 Uyghurs resided in the Almaty region by 1991 (Roberts, 1998).

14. Yessenova (2006) examines Zarya Vostoka, a large section of Baraholka bazaar, divided into five major administrative units: Bolashak, Rakhat, Nurly, Alatau and Zhetysu. She counted 7,000 self-employed entrepreneurs, 3,000 casual workers and 1,000 itinerant traders, and hundreds of others.

15. These measures are based on the lay out of Baraholka in Google Earth. Yessenova (2006: 41) cites an exaggerated size of this area as 50 square kilometres, probably taking it together with its entire rural setting and states that 100,000 people work in the area.

16. This estimate is based on my interviews with marketing experts and bazaar administrators in 2006.

17. Kazakh leadership has been promoting Almaty to become a new financial centre between the Middle East and South East Asia. In an economic and financial forum held in London in 2008, the mayor of Almaty, Imangali Tasmagambetov, promoted the city as the new financial centre of Asia. He also announced major urban projects to enhance the city's outlook and make it a showcase during the 7th Asian Winter Games held in Almay in 2011.

18. Tashkent has many small and medium-sized bazaars scattered across the city. A former Procter and Gamble marketing expert identified 28 market places

and provided the bazaar names and estimated number of traders in March 2005. These are Yunusabad (300), Kara-Kamysh (100), Shirin (200), Navruz (100), Kukcha (150), Eski Juva (700), Alayskiy (unidentified), Beshagach (100), Mirabad (450), Parkentskiy (unidentified), Kadyshev (500), Urikzar (unidentified), Farkhadskiy (1300), Askiya (250), Yangiobod-Krestik (150), Risoviy (150), Yangiobod Optoviy (1200), Ippodrom (1500), Kuylik (2300), Mashinabazaar selling new and used cars (400), Sergeli (100), Akhmad Donish (500), Ibn Sino (100), Kamarniso (100), Tansykbaev (150), Sampi (400), Katartal (350) and Sergeli Yarmarka (350).

19. These are based on my observations and interviews with the administrators on 27 March 2005 in Samarkand.

20. The microfinance lending programme had around 300 business customers, roughly corresponding to the number of store owners.

21. These individual shares varied in size but were not disclosed.

22. In the 1870s, Eugine Schuyler described how unhygienic and crowded the Tashkent Bazaar looked: 'Each shop is merely a small square room with perhaps a still smaller one behind it, quite open to the street ... The customers either stand in the street or sit on their horses, or take their positions on the threshold of the shop. The whole bazaar is old and primitive.' Schuyler also pointed out a Russian Sunday market in Tashkent, known as 'Drunken Bazaar', a name given to it due to it being often full of drunken Russian soldiers. See Schuyler (1966: 98–9).

23. In the developing country context, bazaars are depicted as a function of cultural norms, poor distribution systems and as a response to low incomes. An edited collection by Findlay et al. (1990) provided several case studies from this perspective. Within a similar framework, Dana (2000) emphasised the importance of social and cultural characteristic of an underdeveloped market economy and described the market transition in Kyrgyzstan as a 'bazaar economy'. Some post-Soviet intellectuals also despised the growth of chaotic bazaars in their cities, pointing out that the market transition gave them an inferior substitution, 'bazaar economy', instead of a market economy. For example, see Yessenova (2006) and Dana et al. (2007).

24. Traditionalism emphasises stagnation rather than change, the endurance of the past permeating the present. Similarly, emphasis on social cultural characteristics relegates bazaars to a secondary economic role. In contrast, there are also those who regard the bazaar as an authentic cultural form. Keshavarzian's book, *Bazaar and State in Iran*, pointed out the shortcomings of such narrow interpretations of bazaars. This work illustrated the complex role played by bazaar merchants in Iranian society and the Islamic revolution.

25. In the Ottoman Empire, the bazaars occupied a central position in urban commercial and social fabric. Women were also allowed to trade in designated bazaars. One such bazaar was Avrat Pazari (the Women's Market). Such bazaars expanded the spatial mobility of women and allowed them to negotiate their role in society and urban commercial spaces. See Özgüven (2001).

26. Entrepreneurs who initiated bazaars utilised the newest visual and mechanical innovations along with the most fashionable methods of entertainment and live music to draw shoppers. In 1831 another large bazaar called the Pantechnicon opened on the northwest corner of Belgravia Square in London. This impressive building was 500 feet long and had 4 floors. It specialised in

selling carriages, also furniture and miscellaneous items and served as a place for public resort for gentlemen to conduct business. Whitlock (2005: 47).

27. The political power of bazaars is well-articulated in the case of Iranian revolution in 1989 by scholars such as Bashiriyeh (1984) and Keshavarzian (2007). Several other historical examples are also interesting to note. For example, Denoeux (1993) pointed out the tie between bazaars and Islamic institutions and their role in popular opposition to lack of economic protection from European imports in the early twentieth century. This opposition often turned against the government, fuelling popular urban uprisings in the Middle East. In the aftermath of the revolutions of the 1950s and 1960s, the traditional bazaars were marginalised by the creation of large state enterprises and bureaucracies along with industrialisation. Subsequently, bazaars lost their political cohesion and economic force to mobilise strong opposition. Others like Bayly (1988) pointed out how bazaars and merchant families were subject to periodic looting during civil unrests and how they negotiated their economic and social roles in colonial India.

28. Bashiriyeh (1984: 113). See also Gahaddasi (2009).

29. Keshavarzian (2007).

30. For example, the brother-in-law of President Akayev, Askar Shambetov, the regulator appointed by the president, captured 51 per cent control of the privatised large fruit and vegetable pavilion of Osh market in 1999. Shambetov was charged and removed by the Bakiyev government as one of the deputy directors and also lost his 24 per cent share. It is claimed that the new directors of the bazaar have close ties with President Bakiyev (Spector, 2008b).

31. As reported by Spector (2008b: 163) Kubatbek Baybolov has been in the national legislature since 2007 and his wife was a speaker of the Bishkek city legislature. Askar Salymbekov first became governor of Naryn province, later mayor of Bishkek, and was also previously a national deputy. Salymbekov's relatives were also in the Bishkek city legislature.

32. Spector (2008b).

33. Erica Marat had written extensively on the state-crime relations in Kyrgyzstan and Tajikistan. See, for example, 'Criminal State of Play: An Examination of State-Crime Relations in Post-Soviet Union Kyrgyzstan and Tajikistan', *Jane's Intelligence Review*, 1 March, 2007 http://www.silkroadstudies.org/new/docs/publications/2007/0702JIR.htm (accessed on 16 October 2008). 'Erkinbayev's Assassination Provokes Controversy in Kazakhstan', *Eurasia Daily Monitor*, vol. 2/179, 27 September 2005. See http://www.jamestown.org/publications_details.php?volume_id=427&issue_id=4500&article_id=2373084 (accessed on 16 October 2008). 'The Changing Dynamics of State-Crime Relations in Kyrgyzstan', *Central Asia-Caucasus Institute Analyst*, 20/02/2008). See http://www.cacianalyst.org/?q=node/4796 (accessed on 16 October 2008). 'Police Faced with New Kyrgyz 'Thief-in-Law' After a Two-Year Break', *Eurasia Daily Monitor*, vol. 5/98 (22 May 2008). See http://www.jamestown.org/publications_details.php?volume_id=407&issue_id=3473&article_id=2370267 (accessed on 16 October 2008).

34. These views emerged in interviews and can be found in various news reports: http://kyrgyzstan.neweurasia.net/2006/03/13/kulov-vs-ryspek-akmatbayev-round-3/; http://www.regnum.ru/english/638222.html; http://www.eurasianet.org/departments/insight/articles/eav052606.shtml; and

http://www.eurasianet.org/resource/kyrgyzstan/hypermail/200510/0008.
shtml (All accessed on 3 October 2008).
35. The details of this case are based on Spector (2007) and Spector (2008b).
36. For example, Astana has several large shopping malls in addition to old
    bazaars; two new shopping malls opened in Karaganda in early 2000. The
    Samal Wholesalers market with 2,000 sqm trade centre hosting 50 foodstuffs
    wholesalers opened in 2005. All wholesale business in Karaganda will even-
    tually move to this district which is still expanding.
37. Abylov specifically referred to new urban development projects on municipal
    land along the popular Al Farabi Street in Almaty. Personal interview, 26 March
    2007, Almaty.
38. Nordonov (2004).
39. The protest came only days after local residents held a demonstration
    in connection with plans to relocate them to make room for a road-
    construction project. See reporting in Eurasianet http://www.eurasianet.org/
    resource/uzbekistan/hypermail/200508/0036.shtml (accessed on 17 October
    2008). Many other such small and clandestine protests have taken place
    sporadically across the country.
40. Hotelling (1929) was actually trying to show that price stability was possible in
    the case of two-firm competition (duopoly) without collusion. Stephen Brown
    (1989) illustrated that Hotelling's principal of minimum differentiation and its
    derivatives were insufficient in explaining fully the much-observed phenom-
    enon of clustering of similar retail firms.
41. Geertz (1978).
42. Ridley (2008) showed how market entry and cost of information are
    linked. According to the econometric analysis of Banerjee (1992), free
    riding hurts the leader and can lead to socially excessive or insufficient
    market entry.

5   The Gendered Economy

1. Some recent studies include Özcan (2006) and Werner (2004).
2. Kandiyoti (2002) has an extensive analysis of the colonial and post-colonial
   discourses, pointing out paradoxes of Soviet modernisation in Central Asia.
   Her work also provides a detailed summary of Soviet ethnography and national
   policy vis-à-vis Central Asia.
3. Traditionally, patriarchy has been associated with institutions of the state,
   family and household. See Ertürk (2004) for an analysis of patriarchy and
   state.
4. See Graney (2004: p. 48) and Zhurzhenko (2001). Women's bodies have also
   been objects of acts of humiliation of ethnic or religious identity. A recent
   example is during the disintegration of Yugoslavia when Bosnian Muslim
   women were systematically sexually abused and raped by Serb nationalists.
   See Ertürk (2004) for a further discussion.
5. Lata Mani in *Contentious Traditions* shows the contradictions of nationalist
   as well as colonial modernisation projects on the social reform of women's
   status in colonial India. Kandiyoti (2002) sees complex interplay between
   Soviet modernisation in designated statehoods and continuing traditionalism

in Central Asia. The nature of Soviet modernity and the survival of their indigenous ethnic character sets the region apart from other colonial states.
6. See Akiner, (1997); Herczynski (2003); and Corcoran-Nantes (2005).
7. Ashwin (2000).
8. Cummings (2002); Kuehnast and Nechemias (2004); Cummings (2005).
9. Tokhtakhodjaeva (1995) provided many case studies and anecdotal evidence of the exploitation of the female work force in Uzbekistan.
10. Zhurzhenko (1999) and (2001) pointed out this quasi-egalitarianism and its functional approach towards women's role in the Soviet machine.
11. An anonymous folk song from Uzbakistan (taken from Tokhtakhodjaeva, 1995: 115).
12. Martha Brill Olcott's book, *Kazakhstan: Unfulfilled Promise* (2002), provides a detailed account of extensive family involvement in the economy and the powerful role played by female members and relatives of the ruling groups.
13. Marat (2006).
14. There are numerous allegations and reports on how merciless these women can be if they are challenged and confronted. I heard two personal stories of entrepreneurs who clashed with the business interests of Gulnara Karimov and Dariga Nazarbayeva in Uzbekistan and Kazakhstan respectively. These entrepreneurs not only lost their business fortunes but were also physically threatened by shady secret service agents.
15. As illustrated by Najman et al. (2008: 114), both unemployment and poverty in oil producing regions, except Aktöbe, remain above national average in Kazakhstan. The growing rural poverty beyond major city centres across the country is especially striking; often reaching over 30 and 40 per cent.
16. Kelly (2005).
17. The collectivisation, subsequent material deprivation and famine further destroyed male pride. See Shayakhmetov (2006).
18. There are numerous studies pointing out this gender gap in the Soviet Union, including several edited collections such as Buckley (1997); Ashwin (2000); and Meshcherikina (2000).
19. Ashwin (2000: 17).
20. Herlihy (2002) and Schuyler (1966).
21. According to Patricia Herlihy's analysis, alcoholism appeared in the USSR on a larger scale than under Tsarist rule. In 1914 the Tsar banned spirituous liquor. Lenin embraced the official socialist doctrine that capitalism produced alcoholism and vodka was used by the rich to suppress the poor. In 1917 he forbade the production of all alcoholic beverages, including wine. However, for fiscal reasons, in less than a decade he ended prohibition and created a new state vodka monopoly. Russia went back to old drinking habits. By the 1920s a doctor estimated that 56–80 per cent of all children drank vodka in earnest on holidays (Herhily, 2002: 152). Along with urbanisation, alcohol dependency steadily rose in Eastern Europe and the USSR during the 1960s and 1970s: see Kerr (1978). See also McKee (1999).
22. The 2005 UN World Youth Report on drug abuse stated that 'In some Central Asian countries, the proportion of the population who inject drugs is estimated to be up to 10 times higher than that in many Western European countries. In Central Asia and Eastern Europe, up to 25 per cent of those who inject drugs are estimated to be less than 20 years of age, and the use of all types of drugs has

increased significantly among young people across the region since the early 1990s'. See http://www.un.org/esa/socdev/unyin/wpaydrug.htm#footnote25 (accessed 2 October 2008). The picture for Russian youth is even gloomier. Teenage Russians have less of a chance of living to the age of 60 than they had a 100 years ago. It was estimated that there were 80 million alcoholics in Russia in 2000. Alcohol-related death rates in Russia has approached 500 per 100,000 in contrast to a US rate in 1995 of 77 (Herhily, 2002: 160).

23. Nazpary (2002) and Berg (2004).

24. Berg (2004) observed that women are less worried about social prestige in crisis and are better at getting help from outside groups.

25. Togan (1998).

26. Akiner (1997).

27. Kiblitskaya (2000b), analysing the loss of Soviet status among Russian men, points out their disillusionment and desperation vis-à-vis their enterprising female partners. See also Kiblitskaya (2000a).

28. The commonly used Russian term *chelnok* refers to a shuttle, the part of the loom that makes rapid, regularly repeated motions to and fro.

29. As addressed by Katsenelinboigen and Levine (1977), the household-to-household black market formed a second economy and was quite widespread in the USSR.

30. In her study of female shuttle traders from the post-Soviet states, Yükseker (2003; 2004) illustrates many intricacies of transnational trade, pointing out its predominantly female character and the nature of gender relations between female traders and their male counterparts. Many female traders bought merchandise on credit and paid back when they returned to obtain new merchandise. These commercial exchanges relied on informal and verbal contracts built on personal networks over a period of several years.

31. In Turkey, shuttle trade is commonly referred as luggage trade, *bavul ticareti*. The Laleli Industrialists and Businessmen's Association (LASIAD) reported a record number of business closures since the late 1990s due to loss of demand from shuttle trade from Russia and Central Asia. This was mainly related to new stringent customs rules enforced in Eastern Europe and Russia limiting the weight allocation with new duties and the emergence of local wholesale and distribution markets in former communist countries (see, reporting by Murat Öğütçen, 'The Old Days of Laleli are Long Gone' (Laleli'deki eski günler geride kaldı), *Milliyet Daily*, 26 Feb 2006, and also Yükseker (2004).

32. Interviews with female business owners in Karaganda, Astana and Almaty during March and April 2007 pointed out this trend in Kazakhstan. This is much less felt in the major cities of Uzbekistan and Kyrgyzstan. Some of the early entrants such as Procter & Gamble, who chose Uzbekistan as a stable future market and reliable entry point to Central Asia in the 1990s, relocated their operations in Kazakhstan since the early 2000s.

33. The sex distribution in Central Asia is not as distorted as in Russia. According to the figures given in 2005, women had significantly higher life expectancy rates in Kazakhstan and Kyrgyzstan. Uzbekistan had the highest ratio of the young under 15 years old (33.5 per cent). This was 31.6 per cent in Kyrgyzstan and 23.7 per cent in Kazakhstan. In all three countries the age

group between 15 and 34 years old dominated more than one third of the population in the demographic structure, outnumbering those between 40 and 54. See the link for more information on the population pyramid of each country (http://www.nationmaster.com/country/kz-kazakhstan/People. accessed on 26 December 2008).

34. Özcan (2008b).
35. Although mainstream theory and research on entrepreneurship has long been on the generic concept of entrepreneurship, in recent years there has been more research on women's entrepreneurial activities. My survey evidence pointed out the significance of the relational character, communication and intuitive skills of female business owners. A recent special issue of *Entrepreneurship, Theory and Practice* provides an extensive discussion on women's entrepreneurship. See De Bruin et al. (2007). See also Aldrich and Zimmer (1986) and Aldrich and Waldinger (1990) on social networks and ethnicity.
36. As I have shown in another case study, women utilise both exchange and patronage networks to address their day-to-day business issues (Özcan, 2008b). See also Inoyatova (2006).
37. Nazpary (2002) provides a detailed account of these cross-cultural stereotypes and prejudices.
38. Roberts (1998: 519).

6   Business Interest Representation

1. Brown (1966).
2. According to Skilling (1971: 43), this was neither a perfect monopoly of the party nor was it entirely free competition.
3. Welter et al. (2004).
4. Olson (1971, 1–2).
5. A good example is the recent proliferation of business interest groups in Turkey. Çokgezen (2000) examined social and economic rationale behind fragmentations and co-operations in the Turkish bourgeoisie and business groups.
6. Dixit (2004) shows how self-regulation and lawlessness can shape economic relations when an effective monopolistic and coercive state is very costly to achieve.
7. Marat (2006); Madi (2004).
8. Interview with Mrs. Rimma Apasova, Chief Officer of the Chamber of Commerce and Industry, Bishkek, April 2004.
9. Interviews with the former marketing manager Mr. Nikolai Pakosh of Karaganda CCI, and the chief officer, Karaganda, October 2005.
10. These regions are the Autonomous Republic of Karakalpakstan, Adijan, Bukhara, Jizzakh, Kashkadarya, Navoi, Namangan, Samarkand, Surkhandarya, Sirdarya, Tashment, Ferghana and Khorezm.
11. Interview with the Chairman of CCIU, Alisher Shaykhov, Tashkent, 13 April 2005.
12. The website of CCIU has detailed information about the organisation and its functions. See the link http://www.chamber.uz/(accessed on 20 April 2008).
13. Interview with the Chairwoman of Oltın Miras, located in the Kokildash Madrasah, Bukhara, April 2005.

14. A typical privatised family farm is 2 or 3 hectares and they pay a rent to the government. But, there are also many small farms of 600–700 sq metres which are not sustainable. Ilkhamov (1998) offers a detailed analysis of the farming sector in Uzbekistan.

15. Interviews with the Uzbekistan Farmers' Association, Tashkent, 10 April 2005 and an anonymous senior civil servant at the Economic Reform Unit, Tashkent 14 April 2005.

16. Interview with Mr. Cumaogul A. Urazov, the Chairman of the Food Retailers' Association, Almaty, July 2005.

17. Interview with Mr. Talgat C. Akyol, the Chairman of The Independent Businessmen's Association (7 October 2005), Almaty.

18. For an extensive analysis of the IBA and business interest representation see Özcan (2008a).

19. Olcott (2002) notes that Nazarbayev worked in Karmet (Karaganda Metallurgical Combine) for five years from 1965 to 1969. Karmet was the 67th largest steel mill in the world when it was privatised and sold to Ispat, the Indian Steel giant in mid-1995 (Olcott, 2002: 140). Ispat-Karmet eventually became the present Mittal Steel Temirtau.

20. Mancur Olson argued that collective action emerges when there is a possibility of making a gain that would match everybody's interests (Olson, 1971: pp. 1–2).

21. Interview with Ms. Aygul, the owner of Golden Wool Ltd., and a bank consultant, Karakol, April 2004.

22. This was a concise policy of the Soviet Union. Khrushchev, comparing the might of the USSR with the USA, frequently referred to the size of farms, plants and industrial and military complexes of his country. His 'Virgin Lands' policy transformed the Kazakh steppes into massive farming lands with detrimental environmental and social consequences (Taubman, 2003).

23. Matveeva (2006) elaborates on the EU's financial commitment and strategic involvement in Central Asia. Between 1991 and 2004, the EU, together with its member states, provided over one billion Euro assistance under the mandate of different assistance programmes. Almost half of this amount (516 million Euro) had been utilised by the Technical Assistance to the Commonwealth of Independent States Programme [TACIS]. While Uzbekistan and Turkmenistan received relatively small support, Kyrgyzstan had the highest per capita aid from the Commission (Matveeva, 2006: 88). The EU's future commitment to the region is linked to its member states' priorities regarding security and energy politics.

24. Gambetta (1993).

25. See Volkov (1999) on the nature of violent entrepreneurship in post-communist Russia. In a monograph Volkov (2002) showed how mafia groups and entrepreneurs incorporate violence in Russia's market capitalism. See also Marat (2006).

26. The inner workings of these family circles maintain a certain degree of aloofness, anarchy and rivalry that even the powerful presidents sometimes fail to control. For example, it is plausible that in their business and money deals, President Akayev's wife and son often acted without his knowledge and permission, frequently undermining his authority. Similar arguments

are put forward to explain the behaviour of the sons-in-laws of the otherwise apparently strong President Nazerbayev.

7 International Assistance and Enterprise Development

1. Ferguson (2005: 195–6).
2. Due to a campaign by the American Armenian lobby, no assistance was provided to relatively democratic Azerbaijan in early transition period of 1992–3. Limited aid to Turkmenistan and Uzbekistan was mainly due to these countries' failure to embrace the 'Washington Consensus' economic policies rather than their undemocratic regimes. Indeed, increased aid to Azerbaijan from 1995 onwards followed unilateral adoption of economic stabilisation by an undemocratic successor regime in this country (Pomfret, 2004).
3. Literature on international aid is highly critical of its role. For example, Reusse (2002) identifies selectivity, inconsistency and dependence as a general problem of international aid. Martens (2005) points out that priorities and interests diverge among donors and recipient countries and this makes the policy field highly contested and convoluted.
4. This view is supported by Luong's (2002) observation that the Central Asian political elites followed reform policies as long as these improved their ability to retain or expand influence.
5. During the second half of the 1990s, annual aid averaged an internationally high rate of around $50–60 per head of the population (Promfret, 2006: 82).
6. A World Bank study, *Microfinance and the Poor in Central Asia: Challenges and Opportunities*, highlighted the problems of microfinancing in the region. These included high interest rates, small loan sizes, high transaction costs, and lack of trust in financial institutions. The same study showed to what extent the largest NGO microfinance institutions penetrated in Central Asia. In 2002, the Kyrgyz Agricultural Finance Corporation (KAFC), had 35,000 active clients and a 22m USD loan portfolio; making it the largest in the region. It was followed by the Kazakhstan Community Loan Fund (KCLF), with 5,000 active clients and a 1,5m USD loan portfolio. Despite its larger population, these figures were only 3,000 and 0.3m USD respectively for Uzbekistan (p.22).
7. Özcan (2008b).
8. A focus group discussion with two Kyrgyz and two ethnic Turkish Bulgarian entrepreneurs in the small industry zone of Bishkek, April 2004.
9. Interviews carried out in Bishkek, April 2004.
10. This project includes judicial reforms in land legislation, business law, training of judges and diffusing awareness of legal changes. Interview with Brian Kemple, the Programme Director, was carried out in Bishkek on 14 April 2004.
11. Various Soviet agencies changed their names under new market economy and new ones were created, such as the Export Promotion Agency and the Association for Businesses in Bishkek.
12. Personal interview with Edward Edgaro, the Head of the Secretariat of the Special Representative of the President of the Kyrgyz Republic on Foreign Investment, Bishkek, April 2004.

13. David Hardy, an international expert on distance learning education.
14. Shaw (1991).
15. The USSR was divided into 20 recreational regions and four zones. The division into zones corresponded to the economic value of each region and the quantity of tourist provisions. See Bagrov et al. (1982).
16. Shaw (1991).
17. Dolzhenko (1988: 150).
18. Shaw (1991: 137).
19. See Shaw (1991) and Almakuchukov and Turdumambetov (2001).
20. In his memoire, Shayakhmetov (2006) showed how he and other Kazakhs went through a brain washing campaign in these youth camps. While becoming loyal communists, they were convinced about the goodness of the Soviet regime, despite the fact that it was the Soviet-made famine which exterminated their relatives and communities in Kazakhstan.
21. Airey and Schackley (1997).
22. Interviews with several major tour operators in Samarkand and Bukhara in April 2005.
23. For example, Pomfret (2006) showed how a sugar refinery, the largest single enterprise in Kyrgyzstan, could not function profitably once it lost subsidies and its link to Cuban sugarcane producers.
24. MacWilliam (2006).
25. In a recent paper I illustrated how entrepreneurs deal with these three forms of uncertainty through exchange and patronage networks. See Özcan (2008b).
26. Madi (2004).
27. Helvetas was founded in 1955 as the first private organisation for development co-operation in Switzerland. It has been actively supporting rural development in Kyrgyzstan (since 1995) and Tajikistan (since 2007). In addition to community-based tourism, it has been offering technical help in product development, processing and marketing in the agricultural sector. In 2008, Helevetas spent a total of 51.82 million Swiss Franc (roughly 50 million USD) on its international programmes, almost half (44 per cent) spent in Asia (with projects in Kyrgyzstan, Afghanistan, Nepal, Laos, Philippines and others). See the home page of the organisation for more information: http://www.helvetas.ch
28. An *aul* is a unit comprised of aggregated nomad tents, identifying a family and/or a tribe. Its size can vary from a few to a couple of dozen yurts. In modern times the word is commonly used for hamlets and villages.
29. But with some tension: clashes between the two ethnic groups took place in Uzgen and Osh in 1990. Other mass upheavals and violent demonstrations occurred during the time of USSR, such as the one which took place against the appointment of a non-Kazakh president in Almaty in 1986, the anti-Jewish protests in Andijan in 1989 and ethnic clashes between Meskhetian Turks and Uzbeks in the same year in the Fergana Valley of Uzbekistan. There is a lack of credible information and public awareness about these incidents.
30. Uzgen's remaining historical monuments date back to the Karakhanid period, a powerful dynasty that ruled most of today's Kyrgyzstan and Uzbekistan during the tenth and eleventh centuries. Their capitals, Balasagun in Kyrgyzstan and Kashgar in western China, were important centres of learning and science during which Central Asia was in close contact with Baghdad, then the most

important centre of learning and science in Eurasia. Two masterpieces of Turkic language scholarship, '*Kutadgu Bilig*' by Yusuf Has Hacib and *Diwan Lugat at-Turk* (Turkic Lexicon) by Mahmud al-Kashgari, were written during this dynasty.
31. The CBT handouts provide useful information.
32. In autumn 2004, a good horse was valued as high as 2,000 USD and a small sheep was valued at 30 USD in the animal markets of Osh. With the Helvetas credit of 800 USD the local CBT bought approximately 100 sheep. After the spring breeding, the CBT would get around 200 sheep in return; selling them at a price of 30 USD per head would bring a substantial income.

8 Entrepreneurs as Moral Men

1. A popular verse of Ahmed Yesevi, one of the most widely respected Turkic Sufi philosophers of Central Asia.
2. http://oldpoetry.com/opoem/38168-Mewlana-Jalaluddin-Rumi-Out-Beyond-Ideas, Old Poetry, (accessed on 28 August 2007).
3. Cited in Leites (1953: 103).
4. The term *homo sovieticus* was coined by the Soviet writer and sociologist Alexander Zinoviev. Zinoviev contended that the Soviet man was concerned much more about the destiny of their fellow beings than Westerners and this was not because of moral principals but because their higher level of collectivism. See Zinoviev (1985: 56).
5. In a recent study, Sanghera and Satybaldieva (2007) examined the moral dimension of market capitalism in the transition context and emphasised the importance of moral sentiments and social control in market capitalism in Kyrgyzstan. In another study, Sanghera and Iliasov (2008) shed light on the moral dilemmas of professionals, addressing the complexity of corruption and institutional impasse in Kyrgyzstan. What Sarah Amsler (2007) observed for social elites and scholars in Kyrgyzstan and Central Asia can be extended to entrepreneurs: national independence and market relations have brought professional dislocation and loss of privileges, social power and prestige for the middle stratum and deep insecurity for the masses.
6. As defined by *The Columbia Encyclopaedia* (2000: 933), ethics, in philosophy, is the study and evaluation of human conduct in the light of moral principals. Moral principals may be viewed either as the standard conduct that individuals have constructed for themselves or as the body of obligations and duties that a particular society requires of its members. As we illustrate on moral dissonance, such 'standardisation of conduct' is not at all easy to claim or define.
7. See Kuran's *Private Truths, Public Lies: The Social Consequences of Preference Falsification* for a stimulating discussion on the subject.
8. Nee and Matthews (1996).
9. This is identified as a common phenomenon in Russia and other post-Soviet states. See Volkov (1999) and (2002).
10. Rigi (2003).
11. See Morawska (1999) for an interesting discussion on the malleable *homo sovieticus* as opportunistic entrepreneurs of post-Communist East and Central Europe.
12. See Zinoviev (1985).

13. Scientific communism was officially defined only in the 1977 Soviet Constitution as a guiding principal for Soviet people (Alexander, 2007: 178).
14. Gallie (1949: 329).
15. The ideologies of enlightenment and modernity were embraced and adapted by Central Asian intellectuals, both as part of their colonial experience and as a from of their resistance to it (Amsler, 2007: 38).
16. Dave (2007) examines the complexities of language and identity in Kazakhstan, emphasising the role of language as a tool for constructing post-colonial identities.
17. See Payne (2001) for an interesting analysis on constructing indigenous proletariat and railroad construction in Central Asia.
18. Alexander (2007) provides interesting examples from Kazakh planners showing how their mindset adapted itself to liberal economy by a new deterministic understanding of the market. See Alexander (2007: 178).
19. After decades of underground and frail existence, Islam and Orthodox Christianity are both slowly reverting back to their earlier positions in the ordinary lives of people. There are also many proselytising groups, including Islamic charities, evangelical Protestants, Catholics and others who offer various forms of material incentives to gain a new spiritual territory in Central Asia.
20. Among many travel accounts of pastoral and shamanistic traditions in the region, Eugene Schuyler's is striking. When visiting the Kyrgyz and Kazakh nomads in the late nineteenth century, he observed, 'In religion ... [*sic*] few have any fixed religious principles, as they have no settled priests ... [*sic*] Owing to the simplicity of their life, they are far more children of nature ... [*sic*]' (Schuyler, 1966: 22). Abazov (2007) suggested that Central Asian societies followed a subtle trajectory in observing their alternative cultural and religious modes built in social institutions, communal loyalties and identities.
21. Shamanism is neither a religion, nor a body of a belief structure. In her study on Mongols, Caroline Humphrey asserted that there was no shamanism but 'shamanship' and it always coexisted with other religious practices. See Humphrey (1996). See also Krader (1963) on pastoral traditions.
22. Based on his empirical work on Kazakh religion in the town of Turkestan, Privratsky (2001) argued that Islam has been the religion of Kazakhs, not shamanism. But, his evidence also pointed out that Kazakhs had a lax and selective attitude towards following Islamic rituals and often incorporated them with shamanistic traditions. See DeWesse (1999) on the survival of lineages.
23. Saunders (1971: 13).
24. According to Vitebsky (1995), the word 'shaman' comes from the language of the Evenk, a small Tungus-speaking group of hunters and reindeer herders in Siberia. By the beginning of the twentieth century the term was commonly used in North America for a wide range of Indian medicine-men and medicine-women.
25. Aytmatov (2003) and (2005).
26. The KGB drew most of its inspiration from the secret service associated with the Bolshevik Party. The first of the forerunners of the KGB, the Cheka, was established in 1917 and was endorsed by Vladimir Lenin as a weapon against conspiracies and enemies aiming to damage Soviet power.
27. According to Heck (2006: 264), Sufism rescues Islam from being a cult, permitting a dialogue to take place between revealed and non-revealed

knowledge, between wisdom found in legal precedent and that attained by philosophical reflection.
28. Morewedge (1972).
29. Heck (2006: 262).
30. I am grateful to the suggestions of Selçuk Uygur, a Ph.D. candidate at Brunel Business School, on Sufism.
31. Howell (2001).
32. His use of Turkic language, tolerant not doctrinal teaching, and incorporation of elements of shamanism and Buddhism made Islam attractive to the nomads. See Mélinkoff (2003).
33. Mélinkoff (2003), Privratsky (2001).
34. Ülgener (2001). See also Kuran (2003) on the Islamic commercial crisis.
35. The region, as recorded by Eugene Schuyler during his travels in Central Asia in 1873, was wealthy and had diverse agricultural products such as varied and delicious fruits, wheat, rice, millet and barley and the best tobacco along with silk and cotton (Schuyler, 1966: 151).
36. Kokand was the capital of the last khanate before the Russian colonial expansion and later became the centre of an independent Turkestan movement in the nineteenth century.
37. In 1989 an ethnically motivated clash took place between Meshketian Turks and Uzbeks. A series of violent clashes also took place between Kyrgyz and Uzbeks in Osh in the early 1990s. These incidents were related to social tension over the division of limited economic resources between ethnic groups and were often inflamed by small fights among youth and families.
38. Babur in his memoir named seven towns in Fergana: Andizan (Andijan), Margilan, Osh, Isfara, Khodzent, Akshi and Kassan. Today these are divided among three countries; Uzbekistan, Kyrgyzstan and Tajikistan (*The Baburnama*, 2002: 5–8).
39. Thubron (2006: 189).
40. Visiting the region soon after the collapse of the Soviet Union, Colin Thubron noted these local nuances and pointed out an increased Islamic militancy in Namangan (Thubron, 1994: 235).
41. Wahhabism is a Sunni sect that emerged in the eighteenth centry in the Arabian Peninsula. This sect accepts the Qur'an and Hadith as fundamental texts, interpreted upon the understanding of the first three generations of Islam. Ibn Abd al-Wahhab's, *Kitab al-Tawhid* (Book of Monotheism), and the works of an earlier scholar Ibn Taymiyya (1263–1328) are texts fundamental to Wahhabism. The Wahhabi sect differs from the orthodox Sunnis as they claim to follow and interpret the words of the Prophet Muhammad in full adherence and aim to create a perfect Islamic order in line with these scriptures. Their interpretation is rigid and uncompromising.
42. Naumkin (2005: 77–9) provided these alternative reasons behind the attack and went on to claim that the real culprits were likely to be Islamist extremists.
43. My observations as well as media reports indicate that radicalism in this region should not be exaggerated.
44. For a fair and concise coverage along with the chronology of these events see the BBC reporting by Ian Macwilliam (http://news.bbc.co.uk/1/hi/world/asia-pacific/4531848.stm (accessed on 17 November 2008)). The death toll

still remains unclear since the Uzbek government did not allow observers to enter the region. The Karimov government claimed that radical Islamists and their armed insurgency were behind these events. A defensive argument was put forward by Shirin Akiner, a British academic, who was able to visit the region while human rights observers and journalists were denied access. In her special report, Akiner (2005) claimed that events in Andijan were initiated by militarily trained and armed groups in an attempt to topple the government and some insurgents came from outside of Uzbekistan. Akiner's report failed to explain why the government militia killed hundreds of unarmed civilians and why it denied access to journalists and human rights groups if the events were acts solely of armed insurgents. When I visited Andijan one year later, I went through double passport check points in and out of the Fergana Valley and saw no evidence of radical Islam that could be associated with terrorism or violence other than a deep fear and patient hatred of Karimov's leadership. Many artisans and businessmen I talked to in several towns pointed out the negative consequences of the regional blockage, lack of economic freedoms and injustice.

45. Khalid's (2007) work on Islam in Central Asia sheds light on many aspects of religion in the ordinary lives of Central Asians and it elaborates on how Islam has been part of Central Asian identity even during the years of the Soviet Union. He also shows the diversity and flexibility of Islamic interpretations in everyday routines, norms and belief structures.

46. Alisher Khamidov, a Ph.D. candidate at Johns Hopkins University, observes that despite the suppressive policies carried out against Islamic groups by the central government, the local government functionaries tolerate and even benefit from the welfare provisions of Islamic business groups.

47. Ilkahmov (2006).

48. The Akromiya, Ilkhamov (2006) argues, was influenced by the teaching of Said-i Nursi, a Turkish spiritual leader and the founder of the Nurcu brotherhood. In Turkey, business entrepreneurship under the banner of Islamic charities also led to abuse and mismanagement of savings, most notably in the case of mutual funds and collective ownership initiatives. See Özcan and Çokgezen (2003) and (2006).

49. Osman wrote this for a national festival of artisans and won an award. His pamphlet on silk contains the following information on how local silk cloth, atlas, is produced:

1. 1500–2000 units of silk caterpillar eggs, which amount to 1 gram, are placed into an incubator to turn them into caterpillars.
2. The silk caterpillar is looked after for 28–30 days and nights with mulberry leaves. During this time the caterpillar matures and towards the end of this period it begins to spin a cocoon.
3. Cocoons are sent to warehouses where they are sorted and stored.
4. Cocoons are processed into silk in special workshops.
5. The raw silk is milled and reeled.
6. The raw silk is boiled in soda and the sericin is washed out.
7. The silk is processed.
8. The dye maker prepares the warp. The silk is dipped into the dye according to the design of the fabric.

9. The artisan weaves the atlas fabric in an eight-pedaled loom.
10. The fabric is decorated and presented to the buyer.

50. In 2004, an average state employee earned around 19 USD (800 som) per month while a parliamentarian was paid 350 USD per month.
51. Kuran (1998) pointed out that conflicting interpretations of the world may breed cognitive dissonance.
52. Emile Durkheim suggested that nation building requires a convergence of values. Scholars have also argued that the homogenisation of individual values contributes to social stability and economic cooperation by reducing violence and conflict. See Kuran (1998).

9 Conclusion

1. In his essay, 'Uzbekistan: The Road to Independence and Progress', Karimov toyed with Islam as well as Uzbek nationalism and concluded with a grand promise (Karimov, 1992: 68–9):

> The reliable legal guarantees of the new society will be created and consolidated in the first Constitution of Independent Uzbekistan. This fundamental law will be adopted by democratic means following comprehensive and thoughtful nation-wide discussions ... [*sic*] The constitution will outline the building of a just, democratic, law-based state committed to protecting human rights, respecting freedom, securing stability and ensuring prosperity.

2. Pomfret (2006).
3. See Acemoglu and Robinson (2006) and Leventoğlu (2005).
4. In her cross-country analysis, Leventoğlu (2005) showed that social mobility facilitates democratisation by reducing the conflict over redistribution between rich and the poor.
5. Leventoğlu (2005).
6. In a forthcoming book on the political economy of Central Asia, Özcan (2012) analyses the scope and nature of oligarchic markets in the region.

References

Abazov, R., *The Cultures and Customs of the Central Asian Republics* (Westport, CT: Greenwood Press, 2007).

Abazov, R. *Palgrave Concise Historical Atlas of Central Asia* (Basingstoke: Palgrave Macmillan, 2008).

Abdullaev, I., Kazbekov, J., Jumaboev, K. and Herath, M., 'Adoption of Integrated Water Resources Management Principles and its Impacts: Lessons from Ferghana Valley', *Water International*, vol. 34/2 (2009), pp. 230–41.

Acemoglu, D. and Robinson, J. A., *Economic Origins of Dictatorship and Democracy*, (New York: Cambridge University Press, 2006).

Ageev, A. I., Gratchev, M. V. and Hisrich, R. D., 'Entrepreneurship in the Soviet Union and Post-Socialist Russia', *Small Business Economics*, 7/5 (1995), pp. 365–76.

Aidis, R. and Sauka, A., 'Assessing Moving Targets: The Impact of Transition Stages on Entrepreneurship Development', *Ekonomika*, 69 (2005), pp. 1–23.

Airey, D. and Shackley, M., 'Tourism development in Uzbekistan', *Tourism Management*, vol. 18/4 (1997), pp. 199–208.

Akçalı, P., 'Nation-State Building in Central Asia: A Lost Case?' *Perspectives on Global Development and Technology*, 2/3–4 (2003), pp. 409–29.

Akiner, S., 'Between Tradition and Modernity: The Dilemmas Facing Contemporary Central Asian Women', in Mary E. A. Buckley (ed.), *Post-Soviet Women* (Cambridge University Press, 1997).

Akiner, S., 'Violence in Andijan, 13 May 2003: An Independent Assessment', Silk Road Paper, July 2005, Central Asia-Caucuses Institute Silk Road Studies Programme. Link: http://www.silkroadstudies.org/new/inside/publications/0507Akiner.pdf (accessed on 17 November 2008).

Akiner, S., *Central Asia: Conflict or Stability and Development?* (London: Minority Rights Group, 1997).

Aldrich, H. E. and Waldinger, R., 'Ethnicity and Entrepreneurship', *Annual Review of Sociology*, Vol. 16 (1990), pp. 111–35.

Aldrich, H. E. and Zimmer, C., 'Entrepreneurship through Social Networks', in Donald L. Sexton and Raymond W. Smilor (eds), *The Art and Science of Entrepreneurship* (Cambridge, MA: Balinger, 1986), pp. 3–24.

Alexander, C., *Personal States: Making Connections Between People and Bureaucracy in Turkey* (Oxford: Oxford University Press, 2002).

Alexander, C., 'Soviet and Post-Soviet Planning in Almaty, Kazakhstan', *Critique of Anthropology*, 27/2 (2007), pp. 165–81.

Allina-Pisano, J., 'Klychkov i pustota: Post-Soviet Bureaucrats and the Production of Institutional Facades', in T. Lahusen and P. H. Solomon Jr. (eds), *What is Soviet Now: Identities, Legacies, Memories* (Berlin: Lit Verlag, 2008), pp. 40–56.

Almakuchukov, O. M. and Turdumambetov, B. U., 'Tourism Kirgizstana v zifrah', *Rinok Kapitov*, Vol. 7–8 (2001), pp. 33–4.

Almond, G. A., 'A Comparative Study of Interest Groups and the Political Process', *The American Political Science Review*, 52/1 (1958), pp. 270–82.

Allworth, E. (ed.), *Central Asia: 130 Years of Russian Dominance, A Historical Overview*, 3rd edn (Durham: Duke University Press, 1994).

Amin, A. (ed.), *Post-Fordism: A Reader* (Oxford: Blackwell Publishers, 1995).

Amsler, S., *The Politics of Knowledge in Central Asia: Science between Marx and the Market* (London: Routledge, 2007).

Ashwin, S., 'Introduction', in S. Ashwin (ed.), *Gender, State and Society in Soviet and Post-Soviet Russia* (London: Routledge, 2000).

Axtmann, R., 'State of the State: The Model of the Modern State and Its Contemporary Transformation', *International Political Review* 25/3 (2004), pp. 259–79.

Aytmatov, C., *Cemile* [Jamilya] (Ankara: Elips Kitap, 2003).

Aytmatov, C., *Gün Olur Asra Bedel* [The Day Lasts More than a Hundred Years], 13th edn (Ankara: Ötüken, 2005).

Bagrov, L. A., Bagrov, N. V., and Danilova, N. A., *Geographiya rekreazionnih system SSSR* [Geography of Recreational Systems in USSR], (Union of Soviet Socialist Republics: Progress Publishers 1982).

Bal, H., 'Corruption and Unregistered Economy in Transition Countries: The Case of Shuttle Trade in Kyrgyzstan', *Proceedings of the First International Conference on the Fiscal Policies in Transition Economies*, April, (Bishkek), 2004, pp. 169–95.

Banerjee, A. V., 'A Simple Model of Herd Behaviour', *Quarterly Journal of Economics*, vol. 107/3 (1992), pp. 797–817.

Banerjee, A. V. and Duflo, E., 'What is Middle Class about the Middle Classes around the World', Working Paper, Massachusetts Institute of Technology, Department of Economics, 2007. Link: http://econ-www.mit.edu/files/2081 (accessed on 31 January 2008).

Barbalet, J. M., 'Principals of Stratification in Max Weber: An Interpretation and Critique', *The British Journal of Sociology*, vol. 31/3, (1980), pp. 401–18.

Bashiriyeh, H., *The State and Revolution in Iran 1962–1982* (Kent: Croom Helm, 1984).

Bayly, C. A., *Rulers, Townsmen and Bazaars: North Indian Society in the Age of British Expansion, 1770–1870* (Cambridge South Asian Studies, No. 28, 1988).

Bechhofer, F. and Elliott, B. (eds), *The Petite Bourgeoisie: Comparative Studies of the Uneasy Stratum* (New York: St. Martin's Press, 1981).

Belton, C. and Bream, R., 'Russian Pair Battle It Out over Norilsk Nickel Merger', *Financial Times* (23 June 2008, p. 26).

Berg, A., 'Two Worlds Apart: The Lack of Integration Between Women's Informal Networks and Non-Governmental Organisations in Uzbekistan', in K. Kuehnast and C. Nechemias (eds), *Post-Soviet Women Encountering Transition: National Building, Economic Survival, and Civic Activism* (Washington DC: Woodrow Wilson Centre Press, 2004), pp. 195–216.

Best, H. and Becker, U. (eds), *Elites in Transition: Elite Research in Central and Eastern Europe* (Opladen: Leske & Budrich, 1997).

Bian, Y. and Logan, J. R., 'Market Transition and the Persistence of Power: The Changing Stratification System in Urban China', *American Sociological Review*, vol. 61/5 (1996), pp. 739–58.

Botev, N., 'The Ethnic Composition of Families in Russia in 1989: Insights into the Soviet "Nationalities Policy"', *Population and Development Review*, vol. 28/4 (2002), pp. 681–706.

Böröcz, J. and Rona-Tas, A., 'Small Leap Forward: Emergence of New Economic Elites', *Theory and Society*, vol. 24/5 (1995), pp. 751–81.

Bratton, M. and Van de Walle, N., 'Neopatrimonial Regimes and Political Transitions in Africa', *World Politics*, vol. 46/4 (1994), pp. 453–89.

Bream, R., 'Kazakh Group with Global Ambitions', *The Financial Times*, 21 December 2007.

Bregel, Y., *An Historical Atlas of Central Asia* (Leiden: Brill, 2003).

Brown, E. C., *Soviet Trade Unions and Labour Relations* (Cambridge, MA: Harvard University Press, 1966).

Brown, K. N., 'Coalition Politics and Soviet Influence in Eastern Europe', in J. F. Triska and P. M. Cocks (eds), *Political Development in Eastern Europe* (New York: Praeger Publishers, 1977), pp. 241–55.

Brown, S., 'Retail Location Theory – The Legacy of Harold Hotelling', *Journal of Retailing*, vol. 65/4 (1989), pp. 450–70.

Bruszt, L., 'Market Making as State Making: Constitutions and Economic Development in Post-Communist Eastern Europe', *Constitutional Political Economy*, vol. 13 (2002), pp. 53–72.

Brzezinski, Z. and Huntington, S., *Political Power: USA/USSR* (New York: Viking Press, 1964).

Buckley, M., *Post-Soviet Women from the Baltic to Central Asia* (Cambridge: Cambridge University Press, 1997).

Buiter, W. H., 'From Predation to Accumulation? The Second Transition Decade in Russia', *Economics of Transition*, vol. 8/3 (2000), pp. 603–22.

Bunce, V., 'Should Transitology be Grounded', *Slavic Review*, vol. 54/1 (1995), pp. 111–27.

Bunce, V., 'Comparative Democratisation: Big and Bounded Generalisations', *Comparative Political Studies*, vol. 33 (2000), pp. 703–34.

Carothers, T., 'The End of the Transition Paradigm', *Journal of Democracy*, vol. 13/1 (2002), pp. 5–21.

Clark, E. and Michailova, S., 'Doing Research in Transforming Contexts: Themes and Challenges', in Clark and Michailova (eds), *Fieldwork in Transforming Societies: Understanding Methodology From Experience* (Basingstoke: Palgrave Macmillan, 2004), pp. 1–19.

Clem, R. S., 'Regional Patterns of Population Change in the Soviet Union 1980', *Geographical Review*, vol. 70/2 (1980), pp. 137–56.

Cole, J. and Kandiyoti, D., 'Nationalism and the Colonial Legacy in the Middle East and Central Asia: Introduction', *International Journal of Middle East Studies*, vol. 34/2 (2002), pp. 189–203.

Collier, R. B., *Paths Towards Democracy: The Working Class and Elites in Western Europe and South America* (Cambridge: Cambridge University Press, 1999).

Collins, K., 'The Logic of Clan Politics: Evidence from the Central Asian Trajectories', *World Politics*, vol. 56/2 (2004), pp. 224–61.

Collins, K., *Clan Politics and Regime Transition* (Cambridge: Cambridge University Press, 2006).

Corcoran-Nantes, Y., *Lost Voices: Central Asian Women Confronting Transition* (London: Zed Books, 2005).

Cooley, A., *Base Politics: Democratic Change and the US Military Overseas* (Ithaca: Cornell University Press, 2008).

Crews, R. D., *For Prophet and Tsar: Islam and Empire in Russia and Central Asia* (Cambridge, MA: Harvard University Press, 2006).

Cummings, S. N., 'Kazakhstan: An Uneasy Relationship – Power and Authority in the Nazarbayev Regime', in S. N. Cummings (ed.), *Power and Change in Central Asia* (London: Routledge, 2002), pp. 59–73.

Cummings, S. N., *Kazakhstan: Power and the Elite* (London: I. B. Tauris, 2005).

Çağatay, E. and Kuban, D., *The Turkic Speaking Peoples: 1,500 Years of Art and Culture from Inner Asia to the Balkans* (London: Prestel Publishing, 2006).

Çeçen, A. A., 'Uzbekistan between Central Asia and the Middle East: Another Perspective', in Korkut A. Ertürk (ed.), *Rethinking Central Asia: Non-Eurocentric Studies in History, Social Structure and Identity* (Reading: Garnet Publishing, 1999), pp. 129–62.

Çokgezen, M., 'New Fragmentations and New Cooperations on the Turkish Bourgeoisie', *Environment and Planning C: Government and Policy*, vol. 18 (2000), pp. 525–44.

Çokgezen, M., 'Corruption in Kyrgyzstan: The Facts, Causes and Consequences', *Central Asian Survey*, vol. 23/1 (2004), pp. 79–94.

Çokgezen, M., Özcan, G. B. and Çokgezen, J., 'Sources of Uncertainty in Kyrgyzstan' (in Russian and Turkish), *Proceedings of the First International Conference on the Fiscal Policies in Transition Economies*, April (Bishkek, 2004), pp. 189–95.

Dana, L. P. 'Change and Circumstance in Kygyz Markets', *Qualitative Market Research: An International Journal*, vol. 3/2 (2000), 62–73.

Dana, L. P., Etemad, H. and Wright, R., 'Traditional and Emergent Forms of Global Trading', in L. Lloyd-Reason and L. Sear (eds), *Trading Places-SMEs in the Global Economy* (London: Edward Elgar, 2007), pp. 39–54.

Dasgupta, P., 'Trust as a Commodity', in G. Diego (ed.), *Trust: Making and Breaking Co-operative Relations* (Oxford: Basil Blackwell, 1988), pp. 49–72.

Dave, B., *Kazakhstan: Ethnicity, Language and Power* (London: Routledge, 2007).

D'Encausse, H. C., 'The String National Feeling', in E. Allworth (ed), *Central Asia: 130 Years of Russian Dominance, A Historical Overview* 3rd edn (Durham: Duke University Press, 1994), pp. 172–88.

Denoeux, G., *Urban Unrest in the Middle East: A Comparative Study of Informal Networks in Egypt, Iran and Lebanon* (SUNY series in the Social and Economic History of the Middle East, 1993).

DeWesse, D., 'The Politics of Sacred Lineages in 19th-Century Central Asia: Descent Groups Linked to Khwaja Yasavi in Shrine Documents and Genealogical Charters', *International Journal of Middle East Studies*, vol. 31/4 (1999), pp. 507– 30.

De Bruin, A., Brush, G. and Welter, F., 'Advancing a Framework for Coherent Research on Women's Entrepreneurship', *Entrepreneurship, Theory and Practice*, vol. 31/3 (2007), pp. 323–39.

Dixit, A. K., *Lawlessness and Economics: Alternative Models of Governance* (Princeton: Princeton University Press, 2004).

Djilas, M., *The New Class: An Analysis of the Communist System* (San Diego: Harcourt Brace Jovanovich, 1957).

Dolzhenko, G. P., *Istoriya Turizma v Dorevolyutsionnoy Rossii i SSSR* (History of Tourism in Pre-Revolutionary Russia and the USSR). (Rostov-na-Donu: Izd-vo Rostovskogo Universitata, 1988).

Dubravcic, D., 'Entrepreneurial Aspects of Privatization in Transition Economies', *Europe-Asia Studies*, vol. 47/2 (1995), pp. 305–16.

Duncan, R. and Holman, G. P. (eds), *Ethnic Nationalism and Regional Conflict: The Former Soviet Union and Yugoslavia* (Boulder, CO; Oxford: Westview, 1994).

Drudy, S., 'The Classification of Social Class in Sociological Research', *The British Journal of Sociology*, vol. 42/1 (1991), pp. 21–41.

EBRD, *Commitments*, European Bank of Re-construction and Development (EBRD), Link: http://www.ebrd.com/pubs/general/ar07a.pdf (accessed on 15 June 2009).

EBRD, *Transition Report 2007*, European Bank of Re-construction and Development (EBRD), London.

EBRD, *Transition Report 2005: Business in Transition*, European Bank of Re-construction and Development (EBRD), London.

Environmental Justice Foundation Report (EJF), 'White gold: The true cost of cotton' (London: Emmerson Press, 2005).

The Economist Intelligence Unit (EIU), *Country Profile: Kazakhstan*, (London: The Economist Intelligence Unit, 2006a).

The Economist Intelligence Unit (EIU), *Country Profile: The Kyrgyz Republic*, (London: The Economist Intelligence Unit, 2006b).

The Economist Intelligence Unit (EIU), *Country Profile: Uzbekistan*, (London: The Economist Intelligence Unit, 2006c).

Englebert, P., 'Pre-Colonial Institutions, Post-Colonial States and Economic Development in Tropical Africa', *Political Research Quarterly*, vol. 53/1 (2000), pp. 7–36.

Ertürk, Y., 'Considering the Role of Men in Gender Agenda Setting: Conceptual and Policy Issues', *Feminist Review*, no. 78 (2004), pp. 3–21.

Eyal, G., Szelenyi, I. and Townsley, E., *Making Capitalism Without Capitalists* (London: Verso, 1998).

Ferguson, R., *The Devil and the Disappearing Sea: A True Story About the Aral Sea Catastrophe* (Vancouver: Raincoast Books, 2005).

Findlay, A., Paddison, R. and Dawson, J. A., *Retailing Environments in Developing Countries* (Routledge, 1990).

Franchetti, M., 'How the Oligarchs Lost Billions', *The Sunday Times*, 22 February 2009.

Frank, A. G., 'ReOrient: From the Centrality of Central Asia to China's Middle Kingdom', in Korkut A. Ertürk (ed.), *Rethinking Central Asia: Non-Eurocentric Studies in History, Social Structure and Identity* (Reading: Garnet Publishing, 1999), pp. 11–38.

Gahadassi, M., 'Informal Financial Institutions in Bazaar', *Cemoti*, no. 26, L'individu en Turquie et an Iran, 31 March 2005. Link: http://cemoti.revues.org/document634.html#tocto2 (accessed on 18 January 2009).

Gallie, W. B., 'Liberal Morality and Socialist Morality', *Philosophy*, vol. 24/91 (1949), pp. 318–34.

Gambetta, D. (ed.), 'Can We Trust Trust?', in G. Diego (ed.) *Trust: Making and Breaking Co-operative Relations* (Oxford: Basil Blackwell, 1988), pp. 213–37.

Gambetta, D., *The Sicilian Mafia: The Business of Private Protection* (Cambridge, MA: Harvard University Press, 1993).

Geertz, C., 'The Bazaar Economy: Information and Search in Peasant Marketing' *American Economic Review*, vol. 68 (1978), pp. 28–32.

Gerber, T. P., 'Structural Change and Post-Socialist Stratification: Labour Market Transitions in Contemporary Russia', *American Sociological Review*, 67(2002), pp. 629–59.

Gerber, T. P. and Hout, M., 'Tightening Up: Declining Class Mobility During Russia's Market Transition', *American Sociological Review*, vol. 65/5 (2004), pp. 677–703.

Gerry, C. and Birkbeck, C., 'The Petty Commodity Producer in Third World Cities: Petite Bourgeois or Disguised Proletarian', in F. Bechhofer and B. Elliott (eds), *The Petite Bourgeoisie: Comparative Studies of the Uneasy Stratum* (New York: St. Martin's Press, 1981).

Giddens, A., *Central Problems in Social Theory* (London: Macmillan Education, 1979).

Giddens, A., *Introduction to Sociology* (New York: Norton, 1991).

Gleason, G., *Markets and Politics in Central Asia: Structural Reform and Political Change* (London: Routledge, 2003).

Goldthorpe, J. H., 'Social Stratification in Industrial Societies', in P. Halmos, ed., *The Development of Industrial Societies*, Sociological Review Monograph, no. 8, (1964).

Goldthorpe, J. H., *Social Mobility and Class Structure* (Oxford: Clarendon Press, 1980).

Gorst. I., 'Shrinking Sea Leaves Wasteland of Heat and Dust', *The Financial Times*, May 2008, p. 7.

Graham, N. A. and Lindahl, F., *The Political Economy of Transition in Eurasia* (East Lansing, MI: Michigan State University Press, 2006).

Graney, K. E., 'The Gender of Sovereignty: Constructing Statehood, Nation, and Gender Regimes in Post-Soviet Tatarstan', in K. Kuehnast and C. Nechemias (eds), *Post-Soviet Women Encountering Transition: National Building, Economic Survival, and Civic Activism* (Washington DC: Woodrow Wilson Centre Press, 2004), pp. 44–64.

Granick, D., *Management of the Industrial Firm in the USSR: A Study of Soviet Economic Planning* (New York: Columbia University Press, 1954).

Granick, D., *The Red Executive: A Study of the Organisation Man in Russian Industry* (New York: Doubley & Company, Inc., 1960).

Granick, D., *Soviet Metal-Fabricating and Economic Development: Practice versus Policy* (Madison: University of Wisconsin Press, 1967).

Gubin, O. and Kostiouchenko, O., 'Review: Sociology in Russia: Studies in Social Stratification', *Sociological Forum*, vol. 12/1 (1997), pp. 135–42.

Hayit, B., *Basmacılar* [Basmachis], translated from German by Elif Kıral (Istanbul: Babıali Kültür Yayıncılığı, 2006).

Hebert, R. and Link, A., 'In Search of the Meaning of Entrepreneurship', *Small Business Economics*, vol. 1 (1989), pp. 39–49.

Heck, P. L., 'Mysticism as Morality: The Case of Sufism', *Journal of Religious Studies*, vol. 34/2 (2006), 253–86.

Hellman, J. 'Winner Take All: The Politics of Partial Reforms in Post-Communist Transitions', *World Politics*, vol. 50 (1998), pp. 203–34.

Herczynski, J., 'Key Issues of Governance and Finance of Kyrgyz Education', *Problems of Economic Transition*, vol. 45/10 (2003), pp. 58–103.

Herlihy, P., *The Alcoholic Empire: Vodka Politics in Late Imperial Russia* (Oxford: Oxford University Press, 2002).

Hewett, E. A., *Reforming the Soviet Economy: Equality vs. Efficiency* (Washington DC: The Brookings Institution, 1988)

Highley, J. and Gunther, R. (eds), *Elites and Democratic Consolidation in Latin America and Southern Europe* (Baltimore, MD: The Johns Hopkins University Press, 1992).

Highley, J. and Pakulski, J., 'Elite Theory versus Marxism: The Twentieth Century's Verdict', in *Elites After State Socialism: Theories and Analysis* (New York: Rowman & Littlefield Publishers, 2000), pp. 229–41.

Highley, J. and Lengyel, G., *Elites After State Socialism: Theories and Analysis* (New York: Rowman & Littlefield Publishers, 2000).

Hotelling, H., 'Stability in Competition', *The Economic Journal*, vol. 39/153 (1929), pp. 41–57.

Howell, J. D., 'Sufism and the Indonesian Islamic Revival', *The Journal of Asian Studies*, vol. 60/3 (Aug., 2001), pp. 701–29.

Humphrey, C., *Shamans and Elders: Experience, Knowledge and Power among the Daur Mongols* (Oxford: Clarendon Press, 1996).

Huntington, S., *Political Order in Changing Societies* (New Haven: Yale University Press, 1968).

Ilkhamov, A., 'Shirkats, Dekhqon Farmers and Others: Farm Restructuring in Uzbeksitan', *Central Asian Survey*, vol. 17/4 (1998), pp. 539–60.

Ilkhamov, A., 'The Limits of Centralisation: Regional Challenges in Uzbekistan', in P. J. Luong (ed.), *The Transformation of Central Asia: States and Societies from Soviet Rule to Independence* (Ithaca: Cornell University Press, 2004), pp. 159–81.

Ilkhamov, A., 'The Phenomenology of "Akromiya": Separating Facts from Fiction', *China and Eurasia Quarterly*, vol. 4 (2006), pp. 39–48.

Inoyatova, N., *Exploring the Obstacles for Development in Central Asia through the Prism of Social Capital. Case Studies: Kyrgyz Republic and Uzbekistan*, Unpublished dissertation, Institute for Peace Research and Security Policy at the University of Hamburg, Hamburg, 2006.

Ishiyama, J., 'Neopatrimonialism and the Prospects for Democratization in Central Asian Republics', in S. N. Cummings (ed.), *Power and Change in Central Asia* (London: Routledge, 2002), pp. 42–58.

Janowitz, M., 'Social Stratification and the Comparative Analysis of Elites', *Social Forces*, vol. 35/1 (1956), pp. 81–5.

Jenkins, H. W. and O'Brien, J. C., 'Gorbachev's Economic Reforms: A Structural or a Technical Alteration?: Perestroika and Glasnost', *International Journal of Social Economics*, vol. 15/1 (1988), pp. 3–32.

Johnson, C. (ed.), *Change in Communist Systems* (Stanford: Stanford University Press, 1970).

Johnson, P. M., 'Modernisation as an Explanation of Political Change in East European States', in J. F. Triska and P. M. Cocks (eds.), *Political Development in Eastern Europe* (New York: Praeger Publishers, 1977), 30–50.

Kaiser, R. J., *The Geography of Nationalism in Russia and the USSR* (Princeton, NJ: Princeton University Press, 1994).

Kandiyoti, D., 'Post-Colonialism Compared: Potentials and Limitations in the Middle East and Central Asia', *International Journal of Middle East Studies*, vol. 34/2 (2002), pp. 279–97.

Karimov, I. A., *Uzbekistan: The Road to Independence and Progress* (Tashkent: Izdatelstvo, Uzbekiston, 1992).

Karl, T. L. and Schmitter, P. C., 'From Iron Curtain to a Paper Curtain: Grounding Trasitologists or Students of Postcomminism?', *Slavic Review*, vol. 54/4 (1995), pp. 965–78.

Katsenelinboigen, A. and Levine, H. S., 'The Soviet Case', *The American Economic Review*, vol. 67/1, The Papers and Proceedings of the Eighty-Ninth Annual Meeting of the American Economic Association (1977), pp. 61–6.

Kelly, L., *Fertile Fields: Trafficking in Persons in Central Asia*, International Organization for Migration (Vienna: International Organization for Migration, 2005).

Kerr, J. L., 'Social Deviance in Eastern Europe: The Case of Alcoholism', in I. Volgyes (ed.), *Social Deviance in Eastern Europe* (Boulder, Colorado: Westview Press, 1978), pp. 181–98.

Keshavarzian, A., *Bazaar and State in Iran* (New York, NY: Cambridge University Press, 2007).

Khalid, A., *The Politics of Muslim Cultural Reform: Jadidism in Central Asia*, Comparative Studies on Muslim Societies, no. 27 (Berkeley: University of California Press, 1999).

Khalid, A., *Islam After Communism: Religion and Politics in Central Asia* (Berkeley: University of California Press, 2007).

Kiblitskaya, M., 'Russia's Female Breadwinners: The Changing Subjective Experience', in S. Ashwin (ed.), *Gender, State and Society in Soviet and Post-Soviet Russia* (London: Routledge, 2000a), pp. 55–70.

Kiblitskaya, M., 'Once We Were Kings: Male Experiences of Loss of Status at Work in Post-Communist Russia', in S. Ashwin (ed.), *Gender, State and Society in Soviet and Post-Soviet Russia* (London: Routledge, 2000b), pp. 90–117.

Khlevniuk, O., *The History of the Gulag: From Collectivisation to the Great Terror*, translated by Vadim Staklo (New Haven, CT: Yale University Press, 2004).

Knight, F., *Risk, Uncertainty and Profit* (New York: Houghton Miffling, 1921).

Korbonski, A., 'The "Change to Change" in Eastern Europe', in J. F. Triska and P. M. Cocks (eds), *Political Development in Eastern Europe*, (New York: Praeger Publishers, 1977), pp. 3–29.

Kornai, J., 'What the Change of System from Socialism to Capitalism Does and Does Not Mean', *Journal of Economic Perspective*, vol. 14/1(Winter 2000), pp. 27–42.

Krader, L., *Social Organisation of the Mongol-Turkic Pastoral Nomads* (The Hague: Indiana University Publications, Uralic and Altaic Series Vol. 20, 1963).

Kreindler, I., 'The Soviet Deported Nationalities: A Summary and an Update', *Soviet Studies*, vol. 38 (1986). Link: http://links.jstor.org/sici?sici=0038-585 9%28198607%2938%3A3%3C387%3ATSDNAS%3E2.0.CO%3B2-I (accessed 12 February 2006).

Kubicek, P., 'Regionalism, Nationalism and Realpolitik in Central Asia', *Europe-Asia Studies*, vol. 49/4 (1997), pp. 637–55.

Kuehnast, K. and Nechemias, C., 'Introduction: Women Navigating Change in Post-Soviet Currents', in K. Kuehnast and C. Nechemias (eds), *Post-Soviet Women Encountering Transition: National Building, Economic Survival, and Civic Activism* (Washington DC: Woodrow Wilson Centre Press, 2004), pp. 1–20.

Kuehnast, K. and Nechemias, C., *Post-Soviet Women Encountering Transition: Nation Building, Economic Survival, and Civic Activism* (Washington DC: Woodrow Wilson Center Press, 2004).

Kulchik, Y., 'Central Asia after the Empire: Ethnic groups, communities and problems', in Roald Z. Sagdeev and S. Eisenhower (eds), *Central Asia: Conflict, Resolution, and Change* (Washington, DC: Center for Political and Strategic Studies, 1995).

Kuran, T., *Private Truths, Public Lies: The Social Consequences of Preference Falsification* (Cambridge MA: Harvard University Press, 1995).

Kuran, T., 'Moral Overload and Its Alleviation', in A. Ben-Ner and L. Putterman (eds), *Economics, Values and Organisation* (Cambridge: Cambridge University Press, 1998), pp. 231–66.

Kuran, T., 'The Islamic Commercial Crisis: Institutional Roots of Economic Underdevelopment in the Middle East', *Journal of Economic History*, 63 (June 2003), pp. 414–46.

Lanczi, A., 'A Post-Communist Landscape: Social and Moral Costs of the Regime Change in Post-Communist Hungary', in Norman Graham (ed.), *The Political Economy of Transition in Eurasia: Democratisation and Economic Liberalisation in a Global Economy* (East Lansing: Michigan State University Press, 2006), pp. 217–37.

Ledeneva, A., *Russia's Economy of Favours: Blat, Networking and Informal Exchange* (Cambridge and New York: Cambridge University Press, 1998).

Ledeneva, A. V. and Kurkchiyan, M. (eds), *Economic Crime in Russia* (Hague: Kluwer, 2000).

Leff, N., 'Entrepreneurship and Economic Development: The Problem Revisited', *Journal of Economic Literature*, 17 (1979), pp. 46–64.

Leites, N., *A Study of Bolshevism* (Glencoe: Free Press, 1953).

Lewin, A. C., 'The Dialectic Dominance: Petty Production and Peripheral Capitalism', in R. Bromley (ed.), *Planning for Small Enterprises in Third World Cities* (Oxford: Pergamon Press, 1985).

Leventoğlu, B., 'Social Mobility and Political Transitions', *Journal of Theoretical Politics*, vol. 17 (2005), pp. 465–96.

Liuhto, K., 'Entrepreneurial Transition in Post-Soviet Republics: The Estonian Path', *Europe-Asia Studies*, vol. 48/1 (1996), pp. 121–40.

Logue, J., Plekhanov, S. and Simmons, J. (eds), *Transforming Russian Enterprises: From State Control to Employee Ownership* (Westport, CT: Greenwood Press, 1995).

Lucal, B., 'Class Stratification in Introductory Textbooks: Relational or Distributional Models?', *Teaching Sociology*, vol. 22/2 (1994), pp. 139–50.

Luong, P. J., *Institutional Change and Political Continuity in Post-Soviet Central Asia* (Cambridge: Cambridge University Press, 2002).

Luong, P. J., 'Economic Decentralisation in Kazakhstan: Causes and Consequences', in P. J. Luong (ed.), *The Transformation of Central Asia: States and Societies from Soviet Rule to Independence* (Ithaca: Cornell University Press, 2004a), pp. 182–210.

Luong, P. J., 'Central Aisa's Contribution to the Theories of State', in P. J. Luong (ed.), *The Transformationuh of Central Asia: States and Societies from Soviet Rule to Independence* (Ithaca: Cornell University Press, 2004b), pp. 271–81.

MacWilliam, I., 'Kazakhstan: A Cautionary Tale', *The Economist Intelligence Unit*, 30 June 2005. Unpublished Report.

MacWilliam, I. 'Central Asia's Islamic militancy', BBC News, Link: http://news.bbc. co.uk/1/hi/world/asia-pacific/4531848.stm (accessed on 17 December 2008).

MacWilliam, I., 'Karakol: A Russian Town in Remotest Central Asia', *Steppe*, vol. 1/1 (2006), pp. 90–7.

Madi, M., 'Drug Trade in Kyrgyzstan: Structure, Implications and Countermeasures', *Central Asian Survey*, vol. 23/3–4 (2004), pp. 249–73.

Mani, L., *Contentious Traditions: The Debate on Sati in Colonial India* (Berkeley: University of California Press, 1998).

Marat, E., 'Erkinbayev's Assassination Provokes Controversy in Kazakhstan', *Eurasia Daily Monitor*, vol. 2/179 (27 September 2005). See: http://www.jamestown. org/publications_details.php?volume_id=427&issue_id=4500&article_id= 2373084 (accessed on 16 October 2008).

Marat, E., 'The State-Crime Nexus in Central Asia: State Weakness, Organized Crime, and Corruption in Kyrgyzstan and Tajikistan', *Silk Road Papers*, *CACI&SRSP*, Johns Hopkins University, SAIS, & Uppsala University (October 2006). http://www.silkroadstudies.org/new/docs/publications/2007/0702JIR. htm (accessed on 16 October 2008).

Marat, E., 'Criminal State of Play: An Examination of State-crime Relations in Post-Soviet Union Kyrgyzstan and Tajikistan', *Jane's Intelligence Review*, 1 March 2007. Link: http://www.silkroadstudies.org/new/docs/publications/ 2007/0702JIR.htm (accessed on 16 October 2008).

Marat, E., 'The Changing Dynamics of State-Crime Relations in Kyrgyzstan', *Central Asia-Caucasus Institute Analyst*, 20/02/2008a). See: http://www.cacianalyst. org/?q=node/4796 (accessed on 16 October 2008).

Marat, E., 'Police Faced with New Kyrgyz "Thief-in-Law" After a Two-Year Break', *Eurasia Daily Monitor*, vol. 5/98 (22 May 2008b). See http://www.jamestown.org/ publications_details.php?volume_id=407&issue_id=3473&article_id=2370267 (accessed on 16 October 2008).

Marat, E., *The Military and the State in Central Asia: From Red Army to Independence* (London: Routledge, 2009).

Mardin, Ş., 'Abdurreshid Ibrahim and Zeki Velidi Togan in the History of the Muslim Russia', in Korkut A. Ertürk (ed.) *Rethinking Central Asia: Non-Eurocentric Studies in History, Social Structure and Identity* (Reading: Garnet Publishing, 1999), pp. 111–28.

Martens, B., 'Why Do Aid Agencies Exist?', *Development Policy Review*, vol. 23/6 (2005), pp. 643–63.

Martin, T., *The Affirmative Action Empire* (Ithaca, NY: Cornell University Press, 2001).

Martin, V., *Law and Custom in the Steppe: The Kazakhs of the Middle Horde and Russian Colonialism in the Nineteenth Century* (Richmond, Surrey: Curzon, 2001).

Matley, I. M., 'The Population and the Land', in E. Allworth (ed.), *Central Asia: 130 Years of Russian Dominance, A Historical Overview*, 3rd edn (Durham: Duke University Press, 1994), pp. 92–130.

Matveeva, A., *EU Stakes in Central Asia*, Chaillot Paper 91, (Paris: Institute for Security Studies, European Union, 2006).

Mayer, T., 'The Collapse of Soviet Communism: A Class Dynamics Interpretation', *Social Forces*, vol. 80/3 (2002), pp. 759–811.

McClelland, D., *The Achieving Society* (Princeton NJ: Van Nostrand, 1961).

McKee, M., 'Alcohol in Russia', *Alcohol and Alcoholism*, vol. 34/6 (1999), pp. 824–29.

McMillan, J., *Reinventing the Bazaar: A Natural History of Markets* (New York, NY: W & W. Norton & Company, 2003).

McMillan, J. and Woodruff, C., 'The Central Role of Entrepreneurs in Transition Economies', *Journal of Economic Perspective*, vol. 16 /3 (2002), pp. 153–70.

Mélinkoff, I., 'Ahmad Yesevi and Turkic Popular Islam', *Electronic Journal of Oriental Studies*, vol. 6/8 (2003), pp. 1–9.

Meshcherikina, E., 'New Russian Men: Masculinity Regained?', in S. Ashwin (ed.), *Gender, State and Society in Soviet and Post-Soviet Russia* (London: Routledge, 2000), pp. 105–17.

Mickiewicz, E., 'Regional Variation in Female Recruitment and Advancement in the Communist Party of the Soviet Union', *Slavic Review*, vol. 36/3 (1977), pp. 441–54.

Midgley, D. and Hutchins, C., *Abramovich: The Billionaire from Nowhere* (London: Harper-Collins, 2005).

Migdal, J. S., *Strong States and Weak Societies: State-Society Relations and State Capabilities in the Third World* (Princeton, NJ: Princeton University Press, 1988).

Milliken, J. and Krause, K., 'State Failure, State Collapse, and State Reconstruction: Concepts, Lessons and Strategies', *Development and Change*, vol. 33/5 (2002), pp. 753–74.

Mills, C. W., *The Power Elite* (Oxford: Oxford University Press, 1956).

Mohanty, S., 'Colonialism and the Post-Colonial Condition', *PMLA*, vol. 110/1 (1995), pp. 108–18.

Morawska, E., 'The Malleable *homo sovieticus*: Transnational Entrepreneurs in Post-Communist East and Central Europe', *Communist and Post-Communist Studies*, vol. 32 (1999), pp. 359–78.

Morewedge, P., 'The Logic of Emanationism and Sufism in the Philosophy of Ibn Sina (Avicenna) Part II', *Journal of the American Oriental Society*, vol. 92/1 (1972), pp. 1–18.

Murphy, D. E., *What Stalin Knew: The Enigma of Barbarossa* (New Haven, CT: Yale University Press, 2006).

Murrell, P., 'How Far has the Transition Progressed?', *Journal of Economic Perspectives*, vol. 10/2 (1996), pp. 25–44.

Myles, J. and Turegun, A., 'Comparative Studies in Class Structure', *Annual Review of Sociology*, vol. 20 (1994), pp. 103–24.

Najman, B., Pomfret, R. and Sourdin, P., 'How Oil Revenues Redistributed in an Oil Economy? The Case of Kazakhstan', in *Politics and Economics of Oil in the Caspian Basin* (London: Routledge, 2007), pp. 111–32.

Naumkin, V. V., *Radical Islam in Central Asia: Between Pen and Rifle* (Oxford: Rowman & Littlefield Publishers, 2005).

Nazpary, J., *Post-Soviet Chaos: Violence and Dispossession in Kazakhstan* (London: Pluto Press, 2002).

Nee, V., 'Theory of Market Transition: From Redistribution to Markets in State Socialism', *American Sociological Review*, vol. 54/5 (1989), pp. 663–81.

Nee, V. and Matthews, R., 'Market Transition and Societal Transformation in Reforming State Socialism', *Annual Review of Sociology*, vol. 22 (1996), pp. 401–35.

Nee, V. and Cao, Y., 'Path Dependent Societal Transformation: Stratification in Hybrid Mixed Economies', *Theory and Society*, vol. 28/9 (1999), pp. 799–834.

Nordonov, K., 'Uzbek Bazaars as the Focal Point of Social Activities and a Source of Exciting Rumours', Ferghana.ru Information Agency, 14 December 2004. See: http://enews.ferghana.ru/article.php?id=721 (accessed 16 January 2009).

OECD *Harmonising Donor Practices for Effective Aid Delivery*, Paris, 2003.

Olcott, M. B., *Kazakhstan: Unfulfilled Promise* (Washington DC: Carnegie Endowment for International Peace, 2002).

Olson, M., *The Logic of Collective Action, Public Goods and the Theory of Groups* (Cambridge: Harvard University Press, 1971).

Olson. M., *Rise and Decline of Nations: Economic Growth, Stagflation and Social Rigidities* (New Haven, CT: Yale University Press, 1982).

Olson. M., *Power and Prosperity: Outgrowing Communist and Capitalist Dictatorships* (Basic Books: New York, 2000).

Ortaylı., I., *Ottoman Studies* (Istanbul: Istanbul Bilgi University, 2004).

Öğütçen, M., 'The Old Days of Laleli are Long Gone' (Laleli'deki eski gunler geride kaldi), *Milliyet*, Daily Turkish Newspaper, 26 February 2006.

Özcan, G. B., *Small Firms and Local Economic Development: Entrepreneurship in Southern Europe and Turkey* (Avebury: Ashgate, 1995).

Özcan, G. B., 'Djamila's Journey from Kolkhoz to Bazaar: Female Entrepreneurs in Kyrgyzstan', in Welter, F., Smallbone, D. and Isakova, N. (eds), *Enterprising Women in Transition Economies* (Aldershot: Ashgate, 2006), pp. 93–115.

Özcan, G. B., 'Overcoming Barriers: Business Consulting and Lobbying in Kazakhstan', in F. Welter and R. Aidis (eds), *Innovation and Entrepreneurship: Successful Start-ups and Businesses in Emerging Economies* (Cheltenham, UK: Edward Elgar, 2008a), pp. 48–68.

Özcan, G. B., 'Surviving Uncertainty through Exchange and Patronage Networks: A Business Case from Kyrgyzstan', in Welter, F. and Aidis, R. (eds), *Innovation and Entrepreneurship: Successful Start-Ups and Businesses in Emerging Economies* (Cheltenham, UK: Edward Elgar, 2008b), pp. 69–88.

Özcan, G. B. and Çokgezen, M. 'Limits to Alternative Forms of Capitalisation: The Case of Anatolian Holding Companies', *World Development*, Vol. 31/12 (2003), pp. 2061–2084.

Özcan, G. B. and Çokgezen, M., 'Trusted Markets: The Exchanges of Islamic Companies', *Comparative Economic Studies*, vol. 48/1 (2006), pp. 132–155.

Özcan, G. B. and Turunç, H., 'The Politics of Administrative Decentralisation in Turkey since 1980', in J. Killian and N. Eklund (eds), *Handbook of Administrative Reform: An International Perspective* (Boca Raton, FL: Taylor & Francis Group, 2008), pp. 177–192.

Özcan, G. B., *The Political Economy of Central Asia* (London: Routledge, forthcoming 2012).

Özgüven, B., 'A Market Place in the Ottoman Empire: Avrat Pazarı and Its Surroundings', *Kadın/Woman*, 1 December 2001. Link: http://www.articlearchives.com/society-social/sex-gender-issues-women/952663-1.html (accessed 16 January 2009).

Park, A. G., *Bolshevism in Turkestan 1917–1927* (New York: Columbia University Press, 1957).

Parkin, F., 'Class Stratification in Socialist Societies', *The British Journal of Sociology*, vol. 20/4 (1969), pp. 355–74.

Payne, M. J., *Stalin's Railroad: Turksib and the Building of Socialism* (Pittsburgh: University of Pittsburgh Press, 2001).

Peck, A. E., *Economic Development in Kazakhstan: The Role of Large Enterprises and Foreign Investment* (London: RoutledgeCurzon, 2004).

Penketh, A., 'The President, His Former Son-in-Law, and an Accusation of State Murder', *The Independent*, 1 November 2007.

Pfleiderer, O., 'Is Morality without Religion Possible and Desirable?', *The Philosophical Review*, vol. 5/5 (1896), pp. 449–72.

Piore, M. J. and Sabel, C. F., *The Second Industrial Divide: Possibilities for Prosperity*, (New York, NY: Basic Books, 1984).

Platonov, A. *Soul*, translated by R. and E. Chandler and O. Meerson (London: The Harvil Press, 2003).

Pomfret, R., *The Central Asian Economies Since Independence* (New Jersey: Princeton University Press, 2006).

Pomfret, R., 'Aid and Ideas: The Impact of Western Economic Support for the Muslim Successor States', in Y. Ro'i (ed.), *Democracy and Pluralism in Muslim Eurasia* (London: Frank Cass, 2004), pp. 77–99.

Pomfret, R., 'The Uzbek Model of Economic Development 1991–9', *Economics of Transition*, vol. 8/3 (2000), pp. 733–48.

Popov, V., 'Why Shock Therapy may Lead to Worse Performance than Gradual Transition', *Beyond Transition Newsletter*, vol. 17/1, January–March (2006).

Poulantzas, N., *Classes in Contemporary Capitalism* (London: New Left Books, 1975).

Privratsky, B. G., *Muslim Turkestan: Kazak Religion and Collective Memory* (Surrey: Curzon Press, 2001).

Proma and International Business Council Survey, *National Business Opinion Survey in Kyrgyzstan*, Bishkek, June, 2003.

Qunanbayuli, A., *Book of Words*, translated by David Aitkyn and Richard McKane (Almaty: El Bureau, 1995).

Rama, M. and Scott, K., 'Labor Earnings in One-Company Towns: Theory and Evidence From Kazakhstan', *World Bank Economic Review*, vol. 13/1 (1999), pp. 185–209.

Ratha, D. and Xu, Z., *Migration and Remittances Factbook 2008*, (Washington DC: The World Bank, 2008).

Rettig, S. and Pasamanick, B., 'Moral Value Structure and Social Class', *Sociometry*, vol. 24/1 (1961), pp. 21–35.

Reusse, E., *The Ills of Aid: An Analysis of Third World Development Policy* (Chicago, IL: University of Chicago Press, 2002).

Rhodes M. and van Apeldoorn, B., 'Capital Unbound? The Transformation of European Corporate Governance', *Journal of European Public Policy*, vol. 5/3 (1998), pp. 406–27.

Ridley, D., 'Herding versus Hotelling: Market Entry with Costly Information', *Quarterly Journal of Economics*, vol. 17/3 (2008), p. 607.

Rigi, J., 'The Conditions of Post-Soviet Dispossessed Youth and Work in Almaty, Kazakhstan', *Critique of Anthropology*, vol. 23/1 (2003), pp. 35–49.

Rivera, S. W., Kozyreva, P. M. and Sarovskii, G., 'Interviewing Political Elites: Lessons from Russia', *Political Science and Politics*, vol. 35/4 (2002), pp. 683–88.

Roberts, S. R., 'Negotiating Locality, Islam, and National Culture in Changing Borderlands: The revival of the Mashrap Ritual Among Young Uighur Men in the Ili Valley', *Central Asian Survey*, vol. 17/4 (1998), pp. 673–99.

Robinson, F. 'A Witch's Brew', BBC News. See: http://news.bbc.co.uk/1/hi/programmes/documentary_archive/5218248.stm (accessed on 12 June 2006).

Rona-Tas, A. and Guseva, A., 'The First Shall be Last? Entrepreneurship and Communist Cadres in the Transition from Socialism', *American Journal of Sociology*, vol. 100 (1994), pp. 40–69.

Rorty, A. O., 'Review: Moral Complexity, Conflicted Resonance and Virtue', *Philosophy and Phenomenological Research*, vol. 55/4 (1995), pp. 949–56.

Ross, D., 'Coalition of Maintenance in the Soviet Union', *World Politics*, vol. 32/2 (1980), pp. 258–80.

Roy, O., *The New Central Asia* (New York: New York University Press, 2005).

Rumer, B., *Soviet Central Asia: A Tragic Experiment* (Boston: Unwin Hyman, 1989).

Rumer, B., 'Central Asia at the End of the Transition', in Boris Rumer (ed.), *Central Asia at the End of Transition* (London: M. E. Sharpe, 2005), pp. 3–67.

Sabol, S., *Russian Colonisation and the Genesis of Kazak National Consciousness* (New York: Palgrave Macmillan, 2003).

Sanghera, B. and Iliasov, A., 'Moral Sentiments and Professionalism in Post-Soviet Kyrgyzstan: Understanding Professional Practices and Ethics', *International Sociology*, vol. 23 (2008), pp. 447–67.

Sanghera, B. and Satybaldieva, E., 'Moral Sentiments and Economic Practices in Kyrgyzstan: The Internal Embeddedness of a Moral Economy', *Cambridge Journal of Economics* (Published online on 17 September 2007).

Satpaev, D., 'An Analysis of the Internal Structure of Kazakhstan's Political Elite and an Assessment of Political Risk Levels', in U. Tomohiko (ed.), *Empire, Islam, and Politics in Central Eurasia*, Slavic Eurasian Studies No. 14, Slavic Research Centre (Sapporo: Hokkaido University, 2007).

Saunders, J. J., *The History of the Mongol Conquest* (Philadelphia: University of Pennsylvania Press, 1971).

Scase, R. and Goffee, R., *The Entrepreneurial Middle Class* (London: Croom Helm, 1982).

Schatz, E., *Modern Clan Politics: The Power of Blood in Kazakhstan and Beyond* (Seattle: University of Washington Press, 2004).

Scheffler, S., 'Morality's Demands and Their Limits', *The Journal of Philosophy*, vol. 83/10 (1986), pp. 531–7.

Schumpeter, J., *Capitalism, Socialism, and Democracy* (New York: Harper and Row, 1950).

Schuyler, S., *Notes of a Journey in Russian Turkestan, Kokand, Bukhara, Kulja*, edited by Geoffrey Wheeler (New York: Fredrick A. Preager, 1966).

Sen, A., 'East and West: The Reach of Reason', *The New York Review of Books*, July 20 (2000), pp. 33–8.

Shaw, J. B. D., 'The Soviet Union', in R. Derek Hall (ed.), *Tourism and Economic Development in Eastern Europe and the Soviet Union* (London: Belhaven Press, 1991), pp. 124–5.

Shayakhmetov, M., *The Silent Steppe* (London: Stacy International, 2006).

Shelburn, R. and Palacin, J., *Remittances in the CIS: Their Economic Implications and a New Estimation Procedure*, Discussion Paper Series, no. 2007.5, (Switzerland: United Nations Economic Commission for Europe [UNECE], November 2007).

Skilling, G. and Griffiths, F. (eds.), *Interest Groups in Soviet Politics* (Princeton: Princeton University Press, 1971).

Skilling, H. G., 'Interest Groups and Communist Politics', *World Politics*, vol. 18/3 (1966), pp. 435–51.

Skilling, H. G., 'Groups in Soviet politics: Some Hypotheses', in H. Gordon Skilling and Franklyn Griffiths (eds), *Interest Groups in Soviet Politics* (Princeton, NJ: Princeton University Press, 1971), pp. 19–45.

Slider, D., 'A Note on the Class Structure of Soviet Nationalities', *Soviet Studies*, vol. 37/4 (1985), pp. 535–40.

Slider, D., 'Embattled Entrepreneurs: Soviet cooperatives in an unreformed economy' *Soviet Studies*, 43/5 (1991), pp. 797–821.

Smallbone, D. and Welter, F. 'The Distinctiveness of Entrepreneurship in Transition Economies', *Small Business Economics*, vol. 16 (2001), pp. 249–62.

Smith, A., *Russia and the World Economy: Problems of Integration* (London: Routledge, 1993).

Solomon, R. C. 'Free Enterprise, Sympathy, and Virtue', in *Moral Markets: The Critical Role Values in the Economy* (New Jersey: Princeton University Press), pp. 16–41.

Soucek, S., *A History of Inner Asia* (Cambridge: Cambridge University Press, 2000).

Spechler, M. C., *The Political Economy of Reform in Central Asia: Uzbekistan under Authoritarianism* (London: Routledge, 2008).

Spector, R. A., 'Who Owns the Marketplace? Conflict over Property in Kazakhstan', Unpublished paper, Eurasian Studies Society Annual Conference (Seattle Washington, 2007) 37 pages.

Spector, R. A., 'Securing Property in Contemporary Kyrgyzstan', *Post-Soviet Affairs*, vol. 24/2 (2008a), pp. 149–76.

Spector, R. A., 'Bazaar Politics: The Fate of Marketplaces in Kazakhstan', *Problems of Post-Communism*, vol. 55/6 (2008b), pp. 42–53.

Stark, D., 'Path Dependence and Privatisation Strategies in East Central Europe', *East European Politics and Societies*, vol. 6/1 (1992), pp. 17–53.

Steiner, H., 'Elite Research in Russia', in H. Beck and U. Becker (eds), *Elites in Transition* (Opladen: Leske & Budrich, 1997), pp. 107–32.

Szelényi, I., 'Social Inequalities in State Socialist Redistributive Economies – Dilemma for Social Policy in Contemporary Socialist Societies of Eastern Europe', *International Journal of Comparative Sociology*, no. 1–2 (1978), pp. 63–87.

Szelényi, I. and Kostello, E., 'The Market Transition Debate: Towards a Synthesis', *The American Journal of Sociology*, vol. 101/4 (1996), pp. 1082–96.

Tartakovskaya, I. and Ashwin, A. 'Who Benefits from Networks?', in S. Ashwin (ed.), *Adapting to Russia's New Labour Market: Gender and Employment Behaviour* (London: Routledge, 2006), pp. 164–92.

Taubman, W., *Khrushchev: The Man and his Era* (New York: W. W. Norton and Company, 2003).

The Asian Development Bank and the Kyrgyz Republic Fact Sheet 2008, Asian Development Bank (ADB). Link: http://www.adb.org/Documents/Fact_Sheets/KGZ.pdf (accessed 22 May 2008).

The Asian Development Bank (ADB), and Uzbekistan Fact Sheet 2008, Asian Development Bank. See http://www.adb.org/Documents/Fact_Sheets/UZB.pdf (accessed 22 May 2008).

The Baburnama: Memoirs of Babur, Prince and Emperor, Translated, edited and annotated by Wheeler M Thackston (New York: The Modern Library, 2002).

The Center for Study of Public Opinion 2003 Survey, conducted in Kazakhstan, Kyrgyzstan, Tajikistan, Turkmenistan and Uzbekistan, USAID.

The Columbia Encyclopaedia, 6th edn, ed. Paul Lagassé (New York: Columbia University Press, 2000).

The Kazakhstan Monitor, Politician's Murder Rocks Kyrgyzstan, 30 September 2005, pp6.

The World Bank, Kyrgyz Republic: Update on Mining Sector, Report no: 2409-KY, (Washington DC, 2002).

The World Bank, *Microfinance and the Poor in Central Asia: Challenges and Opportunities*, Agriculture and Rural Development Discussion Paper 6 (Washington DC, 2004).

Thornton, P. H., 'The Sociology of Entrepreneurship', *Annual Review of Sociology*, vol. 25 (1999), pp. 19–46.

Thubron, C., *The Lost Heart of Central Asia* (London: Penguin Books, 1994).

Thubron, C., *Shadow of the Silk Road* (London: Chatto and Windus, 2006).

Togan, I., *Flexibility and Limitation in Steppe Formations* (Leiden: Brill, 1998).

Tokhtakhodjaeva, M., Aslam, S. and Balchin, C., *Between the Slogans of Communism and the Laws of Islam: The Women of Uzbekistan* (Tashkent: Shirkat Gah Women's Resource Centre, 1995).

Turdumambetov, B., *Problemi i Perspektivi Razvitiya Turizma v Gornih Usloviyah Kirgizskoy Respubliki* [Problems and Prospective of Tourism Development Under Mountainous Conditions of Kyrgyz Republic], (Bishkek, 2005) p. 175.

UNECE (The United Nations Economic Commission for Europe), *Environmental Monitoring in Central Asia*, Committee on Environmental Policy, January 2002. Link: http://www.unece.org/env/documents/2002/cep/ac.10/cep.ac.10.2002. 11.e.pdf (accessed 22 May 2008).

UNDP, *Central Asia Human Development Report*, Bratislava, Slovakia, 2005. Link: http://europeandcis.undp.org/poverty/trade/show/301A44C5-F203-1EE9-B2E001AFF98B054B (accessed on 7 July 2009).

Ülgener, F. S., *The World of Ethics and Mentality of Economic Dissolution* [Iktisadi Çözülmenin Ahlak ve Zihniyet Dünyası] (Istanbul: Der Yayınları, 1991).

Ülgener, F. S., *Mentality and Religion – Islam, Sufism and Economic Ethics of Disintegration Period* [Zihniyet ve Din – Islam, Tasavvuf ve Çözülme Devri Iktisat Ahlakı] (Istanbul: Der Yayınları, 2006).

Walder, A. G., 'Markets and Inequality in Transition Economies: Towards Testable Theories', *American Journal of Sociology*, vol. 101/4 (1996), pp. 1060–73.

Walder, A. G., 'Elite Opportunity in Transition', *American Sociological Review*, vol. 68/6 (2003), pp. 899–916.

Wasilewski, J., 'Elite Research in Poland', in H. Best and U. Becker (eds), *Elites in Transition: Elite Research in Central and Eastern Europe* (Opladen: Leske & Budrich, 1997), pp. 13–39.

Weinthal, E., 'Transnational Actors, NGOs, and Environmental Protection in Central Asia', in *The Transformation of Central Asia: States and Societies from Soviet Rule to Independence* (Ithaca: Cornell University Press, 2004),pp. 246–70.

Welter, F., Kautonen, T., Maileva, E. and Venesaar, U., 'Trust Environments and Entrepreneurial Behaviour-Explanatory Evidence from Estonia, Germany and Russia', *Journal of Enterprising Culture*, vol. 12/4 (2004), pp. 327–49.

Welter, F., Smallbone, D., Mirzakhalikova, D., Schakirova, N. J., and Maksudova, C., 'Women Entrepreneurs between Tradition and Modernity – The Case of Uzbekistan', in F. Welter, D. Smallbone, and N. Isakova, (eds), *Enterprising Women in Transition Economies* (Aldershot: Ashgate, 2006), pp. 45–66.

Welter, F. and Smallbone, D., 'Exploring the Role of Trust in Entrepreneurial Activity', *Entrepreneurship Theory and Practice*, July (2006), pp. 465–75.

Werner, C., 'Feminising the New Silk Road: Women Traders in Rural Kazakhstan', in K. Kuehnast and C. Nechemias (eds), *Post-Soviet Women Encountering Transition: National Building, Economic Survival, and Civic Activism* (Washington DC: Woodrow Wilson Centre Press, 2004), pp. 105–26.

Wheeler, G., 'Recent Developments in Soviet Central Asia: Dickson Asia Lecture, 1957', *The Geographical Journal*, vol. 123/2 (1957), pp. 137–46.

White, H. C., 'Where Do the Markets Come From?', *American Journal of Sociology*, vol. 87 (1981), pp. 517–47.

White, S., 'Communist Systems and the "Iron Law of Pluralism"', *British Journal of Political Science* (1978), pp. 101–17.

Whitlock, M., 'After Andijan', *Refugees*, UNHCR-The UN Refugee Agency, no. 143/2 (2006), pp. 4–12.

Whitlock, T. C., *Crime, Gender, and Consumer Culture in Nineteen-century England* (Ashgate: Avebury, 2005).

Wicks, A. C. and Freeman, R. E., 'Organization Studies and the New Pragmatism: Positivism, Anti-Positivism, and the Search for Ethics', *Organization Science*, vol. 9/2 (1998), pp. 123–40.

Williams, B., 'The Hidden Ethnic Cleansing of Muslims in the Soviet Union: The Exile and Repatriation of the Crimean Tatars', *Journal of Contemporary History*, vol. 37 (2002).

Wright, E. O., *Class, Crisis and the State* (New York: Schocken Books, 1978).

Vaughan, V., 'Socialist Stratification and Sociological Survival', *The British Journal of Sociology*, vol. 37/2 (1986), pp. 157–79.

Vitebsky, P., *The Shaman* (London: Macmillan, Duncan Baird Publishers, 1995).

Volkov, V., 'Violent entrepreneurs in post-communist Russia', *Europe-Asia Studies*, 51/5 (1999), pp. 741, 754.

Volkov, V., *Entrepreneurs: The Use of Force in the Making of Russian Capitalism* (Ithaca, NY: Cornell University Press, 2002).

Yessenova, S., 'Hawkers and Containers in Zarya Vostoka: How Bizarre is the Post-Soviet Bazaar?', in N. Dannhaeuser and C. Werner (eds.), *Markets and Market Liberalisation: Ethnographic Reflections*, Research in Economic Anthropology, vol. 24, (London: Elsevier, 2006), pp. 37–59.

Yükseker, D., *Laleli-Moskova Mekigi: Kayıt dışı ticaret ve cinsiyet ilişkileri*, [The Laleli-Moscow Shuttle: Unregistered Trade and Gender Relations] (Istanbul: Iletişim Yayınları, 2003).

Yükseker, D., 'Trust and Gender in a Transnational Market: The Public Culture of Laleli, Istanbul', *Public Culture*, vol. 16/1 (2004), pp. 47–65.

Zhurzhenko, T., 'Gender and Identity Formation in Post-Socialist Ukraine: The Case of Women in the Shuttle Business', in R. Bridgman, S. Cole and H. Howard-Bobiwash (eds), *Feminist Fields: Ethnographic Insights* (Ontario: Broadview Press, 1999), pp. 243–63.

Zhurzhenko, T., 'Free Market Ideology and New Women's Identities in Post-Socialist Ukraine', *The European Journal of Women's Studies*, vol. 8 (2001), pp. 29–49.

Zinoviev, A., *Homo Sovieticus*, translated by Charles Janson (New York: Atlantic Monthly Press, 1985).

Index

Abay 1–2, 20
Abylov, Bulat 56, 114
Acemoglu, Daron 4
Ad-hoc groups 148, 152, 163–5,
    167
Ak-Tilek bazaar, Karakol 201
Akayev, Askar 53, 112–13, 127, 166,
    172, 175, 223, 260 footnote 26
Akmatbayev, Ryspek 112–13, 166
Aliyev, Rakhat 44–5, 248 footnote 48
Almaty 56, 97, 101, 104, 113
    see also 253 footnote 17,
        256 footnote 37, and
        262 footnote 29
    Verniy 16
Andijan 90, 115, 179, 209, 211
    see also 262 footnote 29,
        265–6 footnote 44
apparatchiks 25, 32–3, 48, 110,
    224, 228
    see also protégés and courtiers
Astana 87, 127, 201, 256
    footnote 36
ARD/Checchi 174
Asian Development Bank [ADB] 25,
    29, 171
Aytmatov, Chingiz 197
Azerbaijan 40
    see also 261 footnote 2

Babylov, Kutatbek 112
Baimenov, Alikhan 56
Bakiyev, Kurmanbek 25, 54, 112–13,
    223, 225
Baraholka bazaar, Almaty 99, 101,
    103–4, 109–10
Bazaars 96–8, 107, 119–21
    and opposition 107, 109, 112,
        114–15
    clustering and herding 115–19
    economic rationale 78, 80,
        106–10, 116
    in Iran 108

London bazaars 107
    ownership struggles 48, 99, 110
    see also self-governing syndicates
Birlik opposition movement 55, 209
Bishkek 97, 137, 173, 181
    bazaars 97, 100–1
    Frunze 16
    Manas airbase 26, 53, 250
        footnote 66
Bobek 127
Brezhnev, Leonid 17, 34
    cotton scandal 28
    slow upward mobility 34
Bukhara 8, 16, 117, 157, 177
    and trade 106, 115, 156, 213
    Bukhara Khanate 9
    difficulties in farming 158
business associations 78, 150–2, 155,
    159, 167, 233
    and clan ties 162
    and Independent Businessmen's
        Association
    see also Chamber of Commerce and
        Industry of Uzbekistan
    see also Food Retaliates' Association
Byelkamit 46–7

Cadre saturation in Soviet Union
    246 footnote 14
Cheka 200, 264 footnote 26
Chamber of Commerce and Industry
    in Kyrgyzstan [CCI] 154
Chamber of Commerce and Industry
    of Uzbekistan [CCIU] 155–6
China 6, 8, 102, 103, 234
    market transition 37–9
    oil pipeline 243 footnote 63
Clans 24, 54
    clan-based autocracies 40
    identification 44, 146, 198, 246
        footnote 11
    in Mikado game 14, 40, 54,
        126, 209

in social stratification 23, 48, 51, 127
Soviet political clans 153, 223
see also Collins
Coercion and reallocation in bazaars 110–5
Collins, Kathleen 13, 19, 40
see also 241 footnote 27, 246 footnote 19
Commonwealth of Independent States [CIS] 179, 181
see also 242 footnote 47
communism in Central Asia 15, 62, 196, 200, 205
The Communist Party 16, 17–18, 33, 35, 38, 125
Community Based Tourism [CBT] 182–3
CBT enterprises 182, 186–8
in southern Kyrgyzstan 183–6
sustainability 188–90
cotton 15, 65, 159
female labour 126
irrigation and environmental degradation 28, 244 footnote 66
mono-culture 16, 28
ruling elite interests 55, 59
see also Farmers' Association
courtiers 32, 42–5, 224
and bazaars 101, 111, 113
and privatisation 46 *see also* Byelkamit
in competition 54, 57
market positioning 48, 53, 120
Cummings, Sally 41
see also 248 footnotes 46 and 49, 249 footnote 59

Dixit, Avinash 12, 259 footnote 6
Djilas, Milovan 33
Dordoi bazaar, Bishkek 100–3, 112
Dubai 43, 100, 102, 127, 132, 133
Dungans 10, 68, 103, 140
Dzerzhinsky, Felix Edmund 200

Eastern Europe 34, 37–9, 62, 91, 170, 178

Hungary 39
Poland 39, 247 footnote 37
see also 257 footnote 22, 258 footnote 31
economic indicators 21, 82
Elite Construction Company 127
entrepreneurial middle stratum 3, 43, 49, 60–3, 94, 135, 220
class re-location 230
future 231–5
identity 31, 125, 196
Mikado game 32, 52–4, 226, 228
political movements 5, 109, 234
entrepreneurship 62, 171, 234 *see also* 251 footnotes 2 and 10
and aid 171, 173, 189
and morality 192, 194, 211, 230–31
and violence 71, 165
and women 71, 123, 135, 229–30, 140–2
in Soviet markets 63–6, 67, 76–7
see also 260 footnote 25
environmental degradation 24, 158
see also 244 footnote 66
the Aral Sea 24, 28, 170
Erk Democratic Party 55, 209
Erkinbayev, Bayaman 112, 113
Eurasian National Resources Corporation [ENRC] 47
European Bank for Reconstruction and Development [EBRD] xv–xxiii, 22, 171
financial commitment 239 footnote 7
European Union [EU] 39, 170
enterprise development 39, 183
reform guidance 171, 236
TACIS 163, 164–5, 173, 260 footnote 23

Farmers' Association [FA] 157–9
Fergana Valley
artisans and business 61, 114, 156, 213
geography 184, 207–8
history and culture 71, 124
Islam 209–10, 218, 231
tension 179, 207

Ferguson, Rob　169–70
Food Retailer's Association
　　[FRA]　160–1

Gambetta, Diego　165
Geertz, Clifford　116
German Marshall Fund　171
gender divisions　69, 71, 125, 131
　in markets　126, 128, 140–2
　in state-building　123–5
　patriarchy　71, 130, 229, 231
Giddens, Antony　32
gold mining
　in Uzbekistan　28, *see also* 245
　　footnote 4
　Newmont Mining Corporation　29
　Oxus gold　44
　the Kumtor mine　25
Gorbachev-era reforms　57, 130, 252
　footnote 3
Granick, David　245 footnote 4,
　246 footnote 15

homo sovieticus　191, 193
Hotelling, Harold　116

Independent Businessmen's
　Association [IBA]　161–2
Islam　8, 14, 18–19, 55, 68, 125,
　130–1
　conservatism　193, 195, 199, 204
　during the USSR　16
　solidarity networks　125, 210–12
　see also Sufism and Fergana Valley
　Tsarist Empire　15
incassatsiya　77, 93
Ispat-Karmet　23, 47, 260 footnote 19
Issyk-Kul province　24, 112, 154, 173,
　181
　lake　26, 163, 181
Istanbul　93, 102, 132–3
　see also shuttle trade

Jadidism　15–6
　see also 242 footnote 38
Jalalabad　99, 184, 187–8
Japan　171, 207, 236, 239 footnote 9

Kara-Balta　25
Karakol　97, 137, 163–4, 173, 181, 201

Karasuu bazaar　26, 100, 102,
　112–3, 115
　town of Karasuu　80, 184
Karaganda　48, 154, 162, 181
　Temirtau　161, 252 footnote 17
Karimov, Gulnara　44, 127, 250
　footnote 70, 251 footnote 73
Karimov, Islam　18, 29, 44, 49,
　52–6, 209–10, 221, 226
　see also 267 footnote 1
Kazakhmys　23, 47, 249 footnote 56
KazMunaiGas　23
Keshavarzian, Arang　108
　see also 254 footnote 24
KGB, the Committee for State
　Security　40, 50, 112, 160, 200,
　228, 266
Khidoyatova, Nadira　55–6
Khrushchev
　de-colonisation and
　　decentralisation　17, 19, 34
　generation　144–5, 227, 230, 234
　Khrushchev's daughters　134–6
　Virgin Lands　11
Kokand　9, 115, 208
kolkhoz　42, 64–7, 97, 110, 158
kombinat　20, 64–5
Komsomol, the Young Communist
　League　48, 112, 147, 176
Koreans　10, 68, 103, 226
Kuran, Timur　13, 194
Kyrgyz Agricultural Finance
　Corporation [KAFC]　173

Lenin, Vladimir Ilyich　35, 130, 177
Luong, Pauline Jones　41
　see also 246 footnote 19

Mankurt　197
Margilan　114, 207, 208
Market transition and social
　change　36–9
Meerim　127
Meshketian Turks　10, 24, 68, 207
migration　22, 26, 29, 158
　emigration　11, 128–9
　Slavs　24, 196
Mikado game
　and female entrepreneurs　124, 126

and oligarchic markets 223–7
bazaars 97, 110
critical mechanisms 54–7, 226
re-shuffling assets 53, 67, 172,
    218
rules and features 5, 18–19, 52
Moscow 16–18, 28–9, 43–4, 102, 127

Namangan
architecture 209, 214
artisans 212–13
radicalism 208–9
Naryn 7, 24, 112, 154, 183
Nazarbayev, Nursultan 18, 45, 47,
    52, 56, 159, 162, 222, 226
Nazarbayev, Bolot 113
Nee, Victor 38
Niyazov, Saparmurat 221

oligarchs
and Russia 46, 227, 252
and stratification 42–6
in Kazakh mining 47
in Mikado game 223–7
see also upper strata
oligarchic markets 120, 222,
and their constraints 224
Oltın Miras 156–7
Osh 184–8, 207, 215
Osh bazaar 26, 215

patrimonial state 12, 18
neo-patrimonialism 18
see also 243 footnote 52
Persian 7, 203
Persian-speaking 6, 10
Turco-Persian 130, 208
Potemkin institutions 12
poverty
and emigration 128, 179
and women 128–9
in Kazakhstan 257 footnote 15
in Kyrgyzstan 25–6, 173, 188
in Uzbekistan 27, 29
protégés 48, 53, 111
and apparatchiks 48, 110, 224
and their methods 56–7
in bazaars 101, 120
Putin, Vladimir 40, 46

Rakhmanov, Emomali 223
Rashidov, Sharof 17, 28
Rishton, Uzbekistan 208
Robinson, James 4
ruling elite 4–6, 41, 166, 225
enterprise development 31, 57
identity 18, 19, 39, 247 footnote
    39
in stratification 37, 51, 232, 246
women 44–5, 127, 257 footnote 14
Russia 21, 40, 64, 165
and alcohol 129–30
emigration 11, 22
geo-politics 42, 46, 233–4
in Mikado game 44, 226–7
the Tsarist Empire 8–9, 15
Russians 10, 15, 17, 68, 142

Salih, Muhammed 55
Salymbekov, Askar 112
Samarkand 8, 71, 115, 141, 177, 213
Samarkand bread 104–5
Siyob bazaar 96–7, 101, 105
Sarsenbaev, Altynbek 56
Schuyler, Eugine
on bazaars 254 footnote 22
on religion 264 footnote 20
self-governing syndicates 50, 131,
    153, 165–6, 234
illicit trade 153, 166
in bazaars 102, 112–13, 120
in Mikado game 97, 148, 233
political influence 51, 88, 225
tourism 181–2, 190
violence 112, 233
Semey [Semiplatinsk] 76, 182
shamanism 195–7, 203–4, 218, 264
    footnote 24
and Islam 185, 193, 197, 203–4
and moral standing 204, 218,
    230–1
in nomadic traditions 197, 264
    footnotes 20, 21 and 22
Melinkoff 265 footnote 31
Shayakhmetov, Mukhamed 23
shuttle trade 66–7, 99, 102, 144
and bazaars 132–4
chelnoki 132, 258 footnotes 30
    and 31

Siyob bazaar, Samarkand 101, 104–6
Small and Medium-Sized Enterprises
    [SME]
  associations 159, 162
  cross-border trade 100
  international assistance 173, 183
  scope 60, 62, 146, 207 *see also* 251
    footnote 7
social stratification 3–4, 13, 31,
    42–52, 230
  in the USSR 32–6, 245 footnote 5,
    247 footnote 22
  market transition 37–9, 58, 247
    footnote 31
  middle class 49, 60–3
  Mikado game 54, 235, 250
    footnote 62
  women 136, 144
Soviet markets 62–6, 98, 224, 252
    footnote 13
state's co-option
  and markets 56, 153–9, 167, 255,
    230, 232
  during USSR 246
  in Iranian 108
  in Tsarist Russia 241 footnote 34
state's coercion 12, 108, 153, 235–6
  business associations 167, 230
  in bazaars 110–11, 113, 120
  in USSR 34
state-market relations 4–5, 13, 40,
    94, 120, 165, 221, 225
Sufism 199, 203–5, 218
  and business 204, 206, 210, 218
  in Islamic theology 203
  in Central Asia 193, 203
  see also Ahmed Yesevi
Surabaldiyev, Jyrgalbek 113
Stalin-era
  collectivisation and famine 9, 23
  demographic engineering 10–11
  political purges 16, 34, 65, 75,
    124
Swiss Association for International
    Cooperation, Helvetas 171,
    182–3, 190
  see also 262 footnote 27, 263
    footnote 32
Szelényi, Iván 37

Tajiks 10–11, 14, 24, 27, 61, 142, 156
Tashkent 9, 16, 27, 102, 225
  bazaars 93, 115, 253 footnote 18,
    254 footnote 22
  Tashkent bombings 179
Tatars 8, 10, 24, 27, 68, 75, 240
    footnote 14
Tengri 197
  see also shamanism
Thubron, Colin 208
tourism 179, 181–2
  during USSR 175–8, 180
  in Kyrgyzstan 26, 178–9, 180–1
  in Uzbekistan 127
  see also Community Based Tourism
Transoxania 7
Turkestan 87, 203
  in Iranian folklore 7
  Privratsky 264 footnote 22
  Soviet administration 9
  see also Jadidism
Turkey 9, 26, 132, 139, 171, 173,
    233–4, 236
Turkmenistan 6, 21–2, 27, 40, 173, 221
  see also 239 footnote 7, 261
    footnote 2
Turkish Agency for Cooperation and
    Development [TIKA] 171

Ukraine 16–17, 20–2, 25, 64, 160
Umarov, Sancar 55
underprivileged 32, 50–1
United Nations Development
    Programme [UNDP] 100, 171
United States Agency for International
    Development [USAID] 163,
    171, 173
United States of America [US] 26, 46,
    201, 233, 236
upper strata 51, 224, 226
  coercion and cooption 54–7,
    109–12, 113
  collusion and re-appropriation in
    bazaars 111–15
  democratisation 233
  in Kazakhstan 52
  in Uzbekistan and Kyrgyzstan 53
  international assistance 172,
    189, 229

Urumchi 132, 137, 139
UzDaewoo Auto 29
UzMetKombinat 29
Uyghurs 10, 24, 103, 142, 143, 253
   footnote 13
  Xinjiang 6, 68, 138
Ülgener, Sabri 204

Vahidov, Erkin 55

World Bank [WB] 26, 28, 37, 170, 172
  aid 170, 173, 261 footnote 6
  Doing Business ranking 91

Yesevi, Ahmed 191, 203, 205
Yuldashev, Akram 211